D0465943

Ethernet
The Definitive Guide

Ethernet
The Definitive Guide

Charles E. Spurgeon

O'REILLY®

Beijing · Cambridge · Farnham · Köln · Paris · Sebastopol · Taipei · Tokyo

Ethernet: The Definitive Guide

by Charles E. Spurgeon

Copyright © 2000 O'Reilly & Associates, Inc. All rights reserved.
Printed in the United States of America.

Published by O'Reilly & Associates, Inc., 101 Morris Street, Sebastopol, CA 95472.

Editors: Mark Stone and Chuck Toporek

Production Editor: David Futato

Cover Designer: Hanna Dyer

Printing History:

February 2000:   First Edition.

Library of Congress Cataloging-in-Publication Data

Spurgeon, Charles (Charles E.)
 Ethernet: the definitive guide / Charles E. Spurgeon
    p. cm.
  ISBN 1-56592-660-9 (alk. paper)
    1. Ethernet (Local area network system) I. Title.

 TK5105.8.E83 S67 2000
 004.6'8--dc21

                                                                 99-086932

[M]

Table of Contents

Preface

This is a book about Ethernet, a local area network (LAN) technology that allows you to connect a variety of computers together with a low-cost and extremely flexible network system. Virtually every computer manufacturer today supports Ethernet, and this broad support, coupled with its low cost and high flexibility, are major reasons for Ethernet's popularity.

This book provides a comprehensive and practical source of information on the entire Ethernet system in a single volume. The goal of this book is to be definitive: to describe the entire range of Ethernet technology specified in the IEEE standard for Ethernet. This includes 10 Mbps Ethernet, 100 Mbps Fast Ethernet, 1000 Mbps Gigabit Ethernet, full-duplex Ethernet, descriptions of all Ethernet media systems, and repeaters and repeater configuration guidelines. Also described in this book are switching hubs, structured cabling systems, network management, troubleshooting and more.

This book shows how Ethernet components can be combined to create Ethernet LANs. While some basic network designs are shown in this book, there are an infinity of network designs that can be built using Ethernet, ranging from the smallest workgroup on up to very large enterprise networks that support tens of thousands of computers.

The design of complete network systems that use Ethernet to carry data between computers is a major subject, and a number of books are needed to describe all of the issues that can be encountered. Since this book is about how Ethernet technology works, we stay focused on that topic. As anyone who reads the entire book would agree, this topic alone has more than enough detail for any single book to cover.

The Ethernet system has grown over the years, becoming ever larger and more complex. It now includes a wide variety of media systems, each based on its own particular set of hardware and each with its own configuration guidelines. This book covers all Ethernet systems that have ever been widely implemented, from the latest Gigabit Ethernet systems all the way back to the original coaxial cable systems. With this book you can support the entire range of Ethernet technology you may encounter.

As the Ethernet system has grown more complex, a number of misconceptions and misunderstandings have arisen about how Ethernet functions and how the system should be configured. To provide the most accurate information possible and to help combat incorrect "Ethernet folklore," I kept a complete set of official Ethernet standards at my elbow while writing this book and referred to them frequently. I have been working with Ethernet technology since the early 1980s, and that experience has included many hard-won lessons in network design and operation that have also made their way into this book.

Ethernet Is Everywhere

There are a number of factors that have helped Ethernet to become so popular. Among these factors are cost, scalability, reliability, and widely available management tools.

Cost

The rapid evolution of new capabilities in Ethernet has also been accompanied by a rapid decrease in the cost of Ethernet equipment. The widespread adoption of Ethernet technology created a large and fiercely competitive Ethernet marketplace, which drives down the cost of networking components. As a result, the consumer wins out in the process, with the marketplace providing a wide range of competitively priced Ethernet components to choose from.

Scalability

The first industry-wide Ethernet standard was published in 1980. This standard defined a 10 Mbps system, which was very fast for the times, and which remained fast enough for most uses until the mid-1990s. The development of the 100 Mbps Fast Ethernet system in 1995 provided a tenfold increase in speed. Fast Ethernet has been a major success, and network interfaces that can automatically support both 10 and 100 Mbps operation are widely available, making the transition from 10 Mbps to 100 Mbps systems very easy to accomplish.

Applications tend to grow to fill all available bandwidth. To anticipate the rising demand, Gigabit Ethernet was developed in 1998, providing yet another tenfold increase in performance. All of this makes it possible for a network manager to provide high-speed backbone systems and connections to high-performance servers. Desktop machines can be connected to the original 10 Mbps Ethernet, 100 Mbps Fast Ethernet, or Gigabit Ethernet as required.

Reliability

Ethernet uses a simple and robust transmission mechanism that reliably delivers data day in and day out at sites all over the world. Ethernet based on twisted-pair media was introduced in 1987, making it possible to provide Ethernet signals over a structured cabling system. Structured cabling provides a data delivery system for a building that is modeled on high-reliability cabling practices originally developed for the telephone system. This makes it possible to install a standards-based cabling system for Ethernet that is very reliable, as well as being simple, stable, and easy to manage.

Widely Available Management Tools

The widespread acceptance of Ethernet brings another advantage, which is the wide availability of Ethernet management and troubleshooting tools. Management tools based on standards, such as the Simple Network Management Protocol (SNMP), make it possible for network administrators to keep track of an entire campus full of Ethernet equipment from a central location. Management capabilities embedded in Ethernet repeaters, switching hubs, and computer interfaces provide powerful network monitoring and troubleshooting capabilities.

Design for Reliability

A major goal of this book is to help you design and implement reliable networks. Network reliability is of paramount importance to any networked organization. Information sharing between networked computers is an essential feature of today's workplace, and if the network fails, everything comes to a halt. This book shows you how to design reliable networks, how to monitor them and keep them working reliably, and how to fix them should something fail.

The wide range of Ethernet components and cabling systems that are available today provides enormous flexibility, making it possible to build an Ethernet to fit just about any circumstance. However, all this flexibility does have a price. The many varieties of Ethernet each have their own components and their own configuration rules, which can make the life of a network designer complex. Designing and implementing a reliable Ethernet system requires that you understand how all the bits and pieces fit together, and that you follow the official guidelines for the configuration of the media systems.

This book provides the complete set of official configuration guidelines for every commercially available media system, as well as the official guidelines for combining media systems. You'll also find a great deal of information on how to build media systems that meet the standards and that will function reliably.

Downtime Is Expensive

Avoiding network downtime is important for a number of reasons, not least of which is the amount of money that downtime can cost. Some quick "back of the envelope" calculations can show how expensive network downtime can be. Let's assume that there are 1,000 users of the network at the Amalgamated Widget Company, and that their average annual salary including all overhead (benefits, pension, etc.) is $75,000. That comes to $75 million a year in employee costs.

Let's further assume that everyone in the company depends on the network to get their work done, and that the network is used 40 hours a week, for about 50 weeks of the year (excluding holidays). That's 2,000 hours of network operation. Dividing the annual employee cost by the hours of network operation shows that the network is supporting $37,500 per hour of employee cost during the year.

When we total up all of the network outages over the period of a year in our hypothetical corporation, we find that the network was down 2.5 percent of the time. That's an annual total of 50 hours, or one hour a week, or a mere 12 minutes each day. Fifty hours of network downtime at $37,500/hour is $1.8 million in lost productivity due to network outage. Obviously, our calculations are very "quick and dirty." We didn't bother to calculate the impact of network outages during times when no one is around, but during which times the network is still supporting critically important servers. Also, we're assuming that a network failure brings all operations to a halt, instead of trying to factor in the varying effects of localized failures that cause outages on only a portion of the network system. Nor do we try to estimate how much other work people could get done while the network is down, which would tend to lessen the impact.

However, the main point is clear: even small amounts of network downtime can cost a company quite a lot in lost productivity. That's why it's worth investing extra time, effort and money to create the most reliable network system you can afford.

Organization of This Book

The purpose of this book is to provide a comprehensive and practical guide to the entire Ethernet system. The emphasis is on practical issues, with minimal theory and jargon. Chapters are kept as self-contained as possible, and many examples and illustrations are provided. The book is organized in five parts to make it easier to find the specific information you need.

These five parts provide:

- An introduction to the Ethernet standard which describes Ethernet operation in detail. This part of the book covers those portions of Ethernet operation that are common to all Ethernet media systems.

- A description of each of the Ethernet media systems, including 10-, 100-, and 1000 Mbps systems operating over twisted-pair and fiber optic cables. The older coaxial media systems are described in Appendix B, *Thick and Thin Coaxial Media Systems.*

- A description of structured cabling systems and the components and cables used in building your Ethernet system. These include twisted-pair and fiber optic cables, and repeater and switching hubs.

- A description of Ethernet performance and Ethernet troubleshooting.

- Appendixes and glossary.

Part I, Introduction to Ethernet

Chapters 1–5 provide a tour of basic Ethernet theory and operation. This section includes the portions of Ethernet operation that are common to all of the Ethernet media systems, including the structure of the Ethernet frame and the operation of the media access control (MAC) system.

Chapter 1, *The Evolution of Ethernet*
  Gives a brief guide to the history of Ethernet and the development of the IEEE 802.3 standard for Ethernet.

Chapter 2, *The Ethernet System*
  Presents an overview of how the Ethernet system operates, introducing the major concepts.

Chapter 3, *The Media Access Control Protocol*
  Provides an in-depth look at how the original half-duplex Ethernet channel operates.

Chapter 4, *Full-Duplex Ethernet*
  Describes the full-duplex mode of Ethernet operation.

Chapter 5, *Auto-Negotiation*
>   Describes the auto-negotiation mechanisms used to automatically configure
>   Ethernet equipment.

Part II, Ethernet Media Systems

Chapter 6, *Ethernet Media Fundamentals,* provides an introduction to the basic
media system components used in all Ethernet media systems. This chapter is
essential reading before going on to the individual media systems, described in
Chapters 7–12. Chapter 13, *Multi-Segment Configuration Guidelines,* completes
this part of the book with a description of the configuration guidelines that apply
when linking media systems together with repeaters.

Each of the media system chapters are based on an identical format, which helps
to organize and clearly present the information needed to cover all of the Ethernet media varieties. While every effort was made to avoid needless duplication of
text, the identical format leads to some unavoidable repetition in these chapters.
This is especially noticeable if you read several media chapters in a row.

Chapter 6, *Ethernet Media Fundamentals*
>   Describes the Ethernet media components and the basic concepts that are
>   common to each of the media systems.

Chapter 7, *Twisted-Pair Media System (10BASE-T)*
Chapter 8, *Fiber Optic Media System (10BASE-F)*
Chapter 9, *Fast Ethernet Twisted-Pair Media System (100BASE-TX)*
Chapter 10, *Fast Ethernet Fiber Optic Media System (100BASE-FX)*
Chapter 11, *Gigabit Ethernet Twisted-Pair Media System (1000BASE-T)*
Chapter 12, *Gigabit Ethernet Fiber Optic Media System (1000BASE-X)*
>   Describe the hardware components and official configuration guidelines for
>   each media variety.

Chapter 13, *Multi-Segment Configuration Guidelines*
>   Describes the official guidelines for combining media varieties using repeaters.

Part III, Building Your Ethernet System

Chapter 14 describes the structured cabling standards. Chapters 15 and 16 provide
information on the configuration and construction of twisted-pair and fiber optic
cable segments; Chapters 17 and 18 describe how to design and build Ethernet
systems using repeaters and switches.

Chapter 14, *Structured Cabling*
>   Describes structured cabling systems and the structured cabling standards that
>   specify how these systems are built.

Chapter 15, *Twisted-Pair Cables and Connectors*
> Describes the twisted-pair cables and components used in twisted-pair network segments.

Chapter 16, *Fiber Optic Cables and Connectors*
> Describes the fiber optic cables and components used in fiber optic network segments.

Chapter 17, *Ethernet Repeater Hubs*
> Describes the operation and management of Ethernet repeater hubs and how to design networks using them.

Chapter 18, *Ethernet Switching Hubs*
> Describes the operation and management of Ethernet switching hubs and how to design networks using them.

Part IV, Performance and Troubleshooting

Chapters 19 and 20 cover network performance and network troubleshooting.

Chapter 19, *Ethernet Performance*
> Describes Ethernet system performance and how to measure overall network performance.

Chapter 20, *Troubleshooting*
> Describes how to go about troubleshooting problems when they occur.

Part V, Appendixes

Appendix A, *Resources*
> Describes additional sources of information on Ethernet, including books, periodicals, and web sites.

Appendix B, *Thick and Thin Coaxial Media Systems*
> Describes the thick and thin coaxial media systems and hardware components.

Appendix C, *AUI Equipment: Installation and Configuration*
> Describes equipment and configuration issues based on the original 15-pin Ethernet AUI.

Glossary
> Provides concise definitions of the acronyms and technical terms relevant to Ethernet.

Online References

A number of online references are provided in this book, based on the Universal Resource Locators (URLs) used on the World Wide Web. Web references are live in the sense that the Web is constantly evolving and changing, which may render a reference obsolete. Sometimes a replacement link will be left, pointing to the new location for the information. If that happens, all you have to do is click on the new link to find what you're looking for.

Other times a site may be reorganized in a manner that leaves no forwarding link to the new location. If an online reference no longer works, you can try several approaches to finding the material.

One method is to access the top-level web page by using the first part of the URL, which specifies the domain name of the site. For example, if the URL *http://www.bellereti.com/ethernet/ethernet.html* should fail to work, you could try just the domain name portion of the URL, located inside the first set of slashes, *http://www.bellereti.com/*, and see what you find there.

Some web sites may also be equipped with a search feature that allows you to type in the name of the material you are looking for at that site. If all else fails, you can try one of the many web search sites that will search the entire Web for the subjects you're looking for.

How to Use This Book

The goal of this book is to provide the information needed for you to understand and operate any Ethernet system. For example, if you are a newcomer to Ethernet and you need to know how twisted-pair Ethernet systems work, then you can start with the chapters in Part I. After reading those chapters, you can go to the twisted-pair media chapters in Part II, as well as the twisted-pair cabling information in Part III. Twisted-pair segments can be connected together with both repeater hubs and switching hubs, and these are also described in Part III. Experts in Ethernet can use the book as a reference guide and jump directly to those chapters that contain the reference information they need.

Conventions Used in This Book

- `Constant Willison` is used for program examples, attribute value literals, start- and end-tags, and source code example text.

- `Constant Willison Oblique` is used for "replaceable" text or variables. Replacement text is text that describes something you're supposed to type, like a `filename`, in which the word "filename" acts as a placeholder for the actual filename.

- *Garamond Italic* is used for filenames and URLs.
- URLs (*http://www.oreilly.com/*) are presented in parenthesis after the name of the resource they describe in the book.

 The owl icon designates a note, which is an important aside to its nearby text.

 The turkey icon designates a warning relating to the nearby text.

How to Contact Us

We have tested and verified the information in this book to the best of our ability, but you may find that features have changed (or even that we have made mistakes!). Please let us know about any errors you find, as well as your suggestions for future editions, by writing to:

O'Reilly & Associates, Inc.
101 Morris Street
Sebastopol, CA 95472
1-800-998-9938 (in the U.S. or Canada)
1-707-829-0515 (international/local)
1-707-829-0104 (fax)

You can also send us messages electronically. To be put on the mailing list or request a catalog, send email to:

info@oreilly.com

To ask technical questions or comment on the book, send email to:

bookquestions@oreilly.com

The web site for *Ethernet: The Definitive Guide* lists errata and plans for future editions. You can access this page at:

http://www.oreilly.com/catalog/ethernet/

For more information about this book and others, see the main O'Reilly web site:

http://www.oreilly.com/

Acknowledgments

This book would not have been possible without the help of many people. First and foremost, I would like to thank the inventor of Ethernet, Bob Metcalfe, and his fellow researchers at Xerox PARC. Their work revolutionized the way computers are used, unleashing a powerful new communications technology based on information sharing applications running on computers linked with networks. I also thank the many engineers who have voluntarily given their time in countless IEEE standards meetings to help develop the Ethernet system and to write the Ethernet specifications.

I would like to thank Mark Stone, executive editor for O'Reilly's Open Source editorial group, for his interest in this project and for all the work that he and his colleagues at O'Reilly & Associates have put into making this book possible. Chuck Toporek at O'Reilly has spent many hours applying his copyediting skills to excellent effect, for which I thank him. Thank you to Hanna Dyer for the cover design, and David Futato, the production editor for this book. Chris North, Eric Pearce, Jesse Robbins, and Rich Seifert provided reviews of the manuscript that helped improve the final work. It's difficult for busy people to find time to provide a detailed review and to compile useful responses for a large manuscript such as this one, and I am especially grateful to the reviewers who were able to do so. Of course, I alone am responsible for any remaining errors.

Finally, I wish to thank my wife, Joann Zimmerman, for enduring yet another book project, and for her patience, her unstinting support, and her editing skills. Without her very able assistance, this book would not have been possible.

I

Introduction to Ethernet

The first part of this book provides a tour of basic Ethernet theory and operation. These chapters cover those portions of Ethernet operation that are common to all Ethernet media systems. Common portions include the Ethernet frame, the operation of the media access control system, full-duplex mode, and the Auto-Negotiation protocol.

Part I contains these chapters:

- Chapter 1, *The Evolution of Ethernet*
- Chapter 2, *The Ethernet System*
- Chapter 3, *The Media Access Control Protocol*
- Chapter 4, *Full-Duplex Ethernet*
- Chapter 5, *Auto-Negotiation*

1

The Evolution of Ethernet

Ethernet is by far the most widely used local area networking (LAN) technology in the world today. Market surveys indicate that hundreds of millions of Ethernet network interface cards (NICs), repeater ports, and switching hub ports have been sold to date, and the market continues to grow. In total, Ethernet outsells all other LAN technologies by a very large margin.

Ethernet reached its 25th birthday in 1998, and has seen many changes as computer technology evolved over the years. Ethernet has been constantly reinvented, evolving new capabilities and in the process growing to become the most popular network technology in the world.

This chapter describes the invention of Ethernet, and the development and organization of the Ethernet standard. Along the way we provide a brief tour of the entire set of Ethernet media systems.

History of Ethernet

On May 22, 1973, Bob Metcalfe (then at the Xerox Palo Alto Research Center, PARC, in California) wrote a memo describing the Ethernet network system he had invented for interconnecting advanced computer workstations, making it possible to send data to one another and to high-speed laser printers. Probably the best-known invention at Xerox PARC was the first personal computer workstation with graphical user interfaces and mouse pointing device, called the Xerox Alto. The PARC inventions also included the first laser printers for personal computers, and, with the creation of Ethernet, the first high-speed LAN technology to link everything together.

This was a remarkable computing environment for the time, since the early 1970s were an era in which computing was dominated by large and very expensive mainframe computers. Few places could afford to buy and support mainframes, and few people knew how to use them. The inventions at Xerox PARC helped bring about a revolutionary change in the world of computing.

A major part of this revolutionary change in the use of computers has been the use of Ethernet LANs to enable communication among computers. Combined with an explosive increase in the use of information sharing applications such as the World Wide Web, this new model of computing has brought an entire new world of communications technology into existence. These days, sharing information is most often done over an Ethernet; from the smallest office to the largest corporation, from the single schoolroom to the largest university campus, Ethernet is clearly the networking technology of choice.

The Aloha Network

Bob Metcalfe's 1973 Ethernet memo describes a networking system based on an earlier experiment in networking called the Aloha network. The Aloha network began at the University of Hawaii in the late 1960s when Norman Abramson and his colleagues developed a radio network for communication among the Hawaiian Islands. This system was an early experiment in the development of mechanisms for sharing a common communications channel—in this case, a common radio channel.

The Aloha protocol was very simple: an Aloha station could send whenever it liked, and then waited for an acknowledgment. If an acknowledgment wasn't received within a short amount of time, the station assumed that another station had also transmitted simultaneously, causing a *collision* in which the combined transmissions were garbled so that the receiving station did not hear them and did not return an acknowledgment. Upon detecting a collision, both transmitting stations would choose a random backoff time and then retransmit their packets with a good probability of success. However, as traffic increased on the Aloha channel, the collision rate would rapidly increase as well.

Abramson calculated that this system, known as *pure Aloha,* could achieve a maximum channel utilization of about 18 percent due to the rapidly increasing rate of collisions under increasing load. Another system, called *slotted Aloha,* was developed that assigned transmission slots and used a master clock to synchronize transmissions, which increased the maximum utilization of the channel to about 37 percent. In 1995, Abramson received the IEEE's Koji Kobayashi Computers and Communications Award "for development of the concept of the Aloha System, which led to modern local area networks."

Invention of Ethernet

Metcalfe realized that he could improve on the Aloha system of arbitrating access to a shared communications channel. He developed a new system that included a mechanism that detected when a collision occurred (*collision detect*). The system also included "listen before talk," in which stations listened for activity (*carrier sense*) before transmitting, and supported access to a shared channel by multiple stations (*multiple access*). Put all these components together, and you can see why the Ethernet channel access protocol is called Carrier Sense Multiple Access with Collision Detect (CSMA/CD). Metcalfe also developed a more sophisticated back-off algorithm, which, in combination with the CSMA/CD protocol, allowed the Ethernet system to function at up to 100 percent load.

In late 1972, Metcalfe and his Xerox PARC colleagues developed the first experimental Ethernet system to interconnect the Xerox Alto. The experimental Ethernet was used to link Altos to one another, and to servers and laser printers. The signal clock for the experimental Ethernet interface was derived from the Alto's system clock, which resulted in a data transmission rate on the experimental Ethernet of 2.94 Mbps.

Metcalfe's first experimental network was called the *Alto Aloha Network.* In 1973, Metcalfe changed the name to "Ethernet," to make it clear that the system could support any computer—not just Altos—and to point out that his new network mechanisms had evolved well beyond the Aloha system. He chose to base the name on the word "ether" as a way of describing an essential feature of the system: the physical medium (i.e., a cable) carries bits to all stations, much the same way that the old "luminiferous ether" was once thought to propagate electromagnetic waves through space.* Thus, *Ethernet* was born.

In 1976, Metcalfe drew the following diagram (Figure 1-1) "...to present Ethernet for the first time. It was used in his presentation to the National Computer Conference in June of that year. On the drawing are the original terms for describing Ethernet. Since then, other terms have come into usage among Ethernet enthusiasts."†

In July 1976, Bob Metcalfe and David Boggs published their landmark paper "Ethernet: Distributed Packet Switching for Local Computer Networks," in the *Communications of the Association for Computing Machinery* (CACM). In late 1977, Robert M. Metcalfe, David R. Boggs, Charles P. Thacker, and Butler W.

---

* Physicists Michelson and Morley disproved the existence of the ether in 1887, but Metcalfe decided that it was a good name for his new network system that carried signals to all computers.

† From *The Ethernet Sourcebook,* ed. Robyn E. Shotwell (New York: North-Holland, 1985), title page. Diagram reproduced with permission.

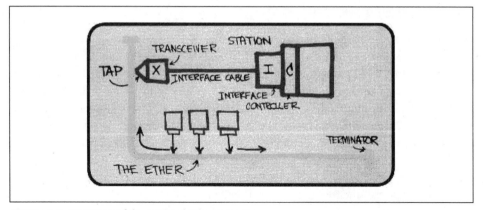

Figure 1-1. Drawing of the original Ethernet system

Lampson received U.S. patent number 4,063,220 on Ethernet for a "Multipoint Data Communication System With Collision Detection." A patent for the Ethernet repeater was issued in mid-1978. At this point, Xerox wholly owned the Ethernet system. The next stage in the evolution of the world's most popular computer network was to liberate Ethernet from the confines of a single corporation and make it a worldwide standard.

Evolution of the Ethernet Standard

The original 10 Mbps Ethernet standard was first published in 1980 by the DEC-Intel-Xerox vendor consortium. Using the first initial of each company, this became known as the DIX Ethernet standard. This standard, entitled *The Ethernet, A Local Area Network: Data Link Layer and Physical Layer Specifications,* contained the specifications for the operation of Ethernet as well as the specs for a single media system based on thick coaxial cable. As is true for most standards, the DIX standard was revised to add some technical changes, corrections, and minor improvements. The last revision of this standard was DIX V2.0.

When the DIX standard was published, a new effort led by the Institute of Electrical and Electronics Engineers (IEEE) to develop open network standards was also getting underway.* Consequently, the thick coaxial variety of Ethernet ended up being standardized twice—first by the DIX consortium and a second time by the IEEE. The IEEE standard was created under the direction of the IEEE Local and Metropolitan Networks (LAN/MAN) Standards Committee, which identifies all the standards it develops with the number 802. There have been a number of net-

---

* The IEEE is the world's largest technical professional society, with members in 150 countries. The IEEE provides technical publishing, holds conferences, and develops a range of technical standards, including computer and communications standards. The standards developed by the IEEE may also become national and international standards.

working standards published in the 802 branch of the IEEE, including the 802.3* Ethernet and 802.5 Token Ring standards.

The IEEE 802.3 committee took up the network system described in the original DIX standard and used it as the basis for an IEEE standard. The IEEE standard was first published in 1985 with the title *IEEE 802.3 Carrier Sense Multiple Access with Collision Detection (CSMA/CD) Access Method and Physical Layer Specifications.* The IEEE standard does not use "Ethernet" in the title, even though Xerox relinquished their trademark on the Ethernet name. That's because open standards committees are quite sensitive about using commercial names that might imply endorsement of a particular company. As a result, the IEEE calls this technology *802.3 CSMA/CD* or just *802.3*. However, most people still use the Ethernet name when referring to the network system described in the 802.3 standard.

The IEEE 802.3 standard is the official Ethernet standard. From time to time you may hear of other Ethernet technology "standards" developed by various groups or vendor consortiums. However, if the technology isn't specified within the IEEE 802.3 standard, it isn't an official Ethernet technology. Periodically, the latest IEEE 802.3 standards are presented to the American National Standards Institute (ANSI), which forwards them on, where they are adopted by the International Organization for Standardization (ISO). This organization is described in more detail later in this chapter. Adoption by the ISO means that the IEEE 802.3 Ethernet standard is also a worldwide standard, and that vendors from around the globe can build equipment that will work together on Ethernet systems.

Ethernet Family Tree

The title of the latest version of the IEEE standard as of this writing is *802.3, 1998 Edition Information Technology—Telecommunications and information exchange between systems—Local and metropolitan area networks—Specific requirements—Part 3: Carrier sense multiple access with collision detection (CSMA/CD) access method and physical layer specifications.*

This edition contains 1,268 pages and "includes all contents of the 8802-3:1996 Edition, plus IEEE Std 802.3aa-1998, IEEE Std 802.3r-1996, IEEE Std 802.3u-1995, IEEE Std 802.3x&y-1997, and IEEE802.3z-1998." These latter documents were developed as supplements to the standard. This edition of the standard can be purchased from the IEEE through their web site at: *http://standards.ieee. org/catalog/IEEE802.3.html.*

---

* Pronounced "eight oh two dot three."

The Latest Ethernet Standard

After the publication of the original IEEE 802.3 standard for thick Ethernet, the next development in Ethernet media was the thin coaxial Ethernet variety, inspired by technology first marketed by the 3Com Corporation. When the IEEE 802.3 committee standardized the thin Ethernet technology, they gave it the shorthand identifier of 10BASE2, which is explained later in this chapter.

Following the development of thin coaxial Ethernet came several new media varieties, including the twisted-pair and fiber optic varieties for the 10 Mbps system. Next, the 100 Mbps Fast Ethernet system was developed, which also included several varieties of twisted-pair and fiber optic media systems. Most recently, the Gigabit Ethernet system was developed using both fiber optic and twisted-pair cabling. These systems were all developed as supplements to the IEEE Ethernet standard.

IEEE Supplements

When the Ethernet standard needs to be changed to add a new media system or capability, the IEEE issues a supplement which contains one or more sections, or "clauses" in IEEE-speak. The supplement may consist of one or more entirely new clauses, and may also contain changes to existing clauses in the standard. New supplements to the standard are evaluated by the engineering experts at various IEEE meetings and the supplements must pass a balloting procedure before being voted into the full standard.

New supplements are given a letter designation when they are created. Once the supplement has completed the standardization process, it becomes part of the base standard and is no longer published as a separate supplementary document. On the other hand, you will sometimes see trade literature that refers to Ethernet equipment with the letter of the supplement in which the variety was first developed (e.g., IEEE 802.3u may be used as a reference for Fast Ethernet). Table 1-1 lists several supplements and what they refer to. The dates indicate when formal acceptance of the supplement into the standard occurred. Access to the complete set of supplements is provided in Appendix A, *Resources*.

Table 1-1. IEEE 802.3 Supplements

Supplement	Description
802.3a-1985	10BASE2 thin Ethernet
802.3c-1985	10 Mbps repeater specifications, clause 9
802.3d-1987	FOIRL fiber link
802.3i-1990	10BASE-T twisted-pair

plements (continued)

on
fiber optic
T Fast Ethernet and Auto-Negotiation
x standard
X Gigabit Ethernet
T Gigabit Ethernet over twisted-pair
extension to 1522 bytes for VLAN tag
ation for parallel links

net for a while, you may recall times when a new vari-
was being sold before the supplement that described
entirely completed or voted on. This illustrates a com-
the computer field, and especially in computer net-
always outpaces the more deliberate and slow-paced process of
developing and publishing standards. Vendors are eager to develop and market
new products, and it's up to you, the customer, to make sure that the product will
work properly in your network system. One way you can do that is to insist on
complete information from the vendor as to what standard the product complies
with.

It may not be a bad thing if the product is built to a draft version of a new supplement. Draft versions of the supplements can be substantially complete yet still take
months to be voted on by the various IEEE committees. When buying pre-standard
equipment built to a draft of the specification, you need to ensure that the draft in
question is sufficiently well along in the standards process that no major changes
will be made. Otherwise, you could be left out in the cold with network equipment that won't interoperate with newer devices that are built according to the
final published standard. One solution to this is to get a written guarantee from the
vendor that the equipment you purchase will be upgraded to meet the final published form of the standard. Note that the IEEE forbids vendors to claim or advertise that a product is compliant with an unapproved draft.

Differences in the Standard

When the IEEE adopted the original DIX standard it made a few changes in the
specifications. The major reason for the changes made between the DIX and IEEE
standards is that the two groups had different goals. The specifications for the
original DIX Ethernet standard were developed by the three companies involved
and were intended to describe the Ethernet system—and only the Ethernet system.
At the time the multi-vendor DIX consortium was developing the first Ethernet
standard, there was no open LAN market, nor was there any other multi-vendor

LAN standard in existence. The efforts aimed at creating a worldwide system of open standards had only just begun.

On the other hand, the IEEE was developing standards for integration into the world of international LAN standards. Consequently, the IEEE made several technical changes required for inclusion in the worldwide standardization effort. The IEEE specifications permit backward compatibility with early Ethernet systems built according to the original DIX specifications.* The goal is to standardize network technologies under one umbrella, coordinated with the International Organization for Standardization.

Organization of IEEE Standards

The IEEE standards are organized according to the Open Systems Interconnection (OSI) Reference Model. This model was developed in 1978 by the International Organization for Standardization, whose initials (derived from its French name) are ISO. Headquartered in Geneva, Switzerland, the ISO is responsible for setting open, vendor-neutral standards and specifications for items of technical importance. For example, if you're a photographer you've no doubt noticed the ISO standard speeds for camera film.

The ISO developed the OSI reference model to provide a common organizational scheme for network standardization efforts (with perhaps an additional goal of keeping us all confused with reversible acronyms). What follows is a quick, and necessarily incomplete, introduction to the subject of network models and international standardization efforts.

The Seven Layers of OSI

The OSI reference model is a method of describing how the interlocking sets of networking hardware and software can be organized to work together in the networking world. In effect, the OSI model provides a way to arbitrarily divide the task of networking into separate chunks, which are then subjected to the formal process of standardization.

To do this, the OSI reference model describes seven layers of networking functions, as illustrated in Figure 1-2. The lower layers cover the standards that describe how a LAN system moves bits around. The higher layers deal with more abstract notions, such as the reliability of data transmission and how data is represented to the user. The layers of interest for Ethernet are the lower two layers of the OSI model.

---

* All Ethernet equipment built since 1985 is based on the IEEE 802.3 standard.

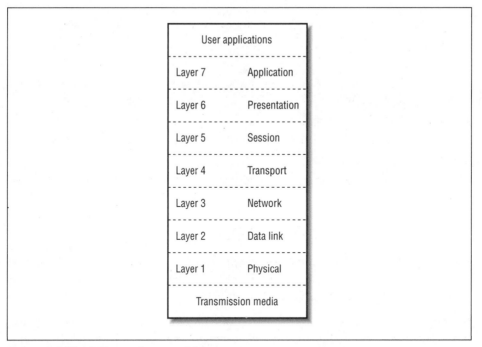

Figure 1-2. The OSI seven layer model

In brief, the OSI reference model includes the following seven layers, starting at the bottom and working our way to the topmost layer:

Physical layer
    Standardizes the electrical, mechanical, and functional control of data circuits that connect to physical media.

Data link layer
    Establishes communication from station to station across a single link. This is the layer that transmits and receives frames, recognizes link addresses, etc. The part of the standard that describes the Ethernet frame format and MAC protocol belongs to this layer.

Network layer
    Establishes communication from station to station across an internetwork, which is composed of a number of data links. This layer provides a level of independence from the lower two layers by establishing higher level functions and procedures for exchanging data between computers across multiple links. Standards at this layer of the model describe portions of the high-level network protocols that are carried over an Ethernet in the data field of the Ethernet frame. Protocols at this layer of the OSI model and above are independent of the Ethernet standard.

Transport layer

> Provides reliable end-to-end error recovery mechanisms and flow control in the higher level networking software.

Session layer

> Provides mechanisms for establishing reliable communications between cooperating applications.

Presentation layer

> Provides mechanisms for dealing with data representation in applications.

Application layer

> Provides mechanisms to support end-user applications such as mail, file transfer, etc.

IEEE Layers Within the OSI Model

The Ethernet standard concerns itself with elements described in Layer 2 and Layer 1, which include the data link layer of the OSI model and below. For that reason, you'll sometimes hear Ethernet referred to as a *link layer standard.*

The Ethernet standards describe a number of entities that all fit within the data link and physical layers of the OSI model. To help organize the details, the IEEE defines extra sublayers that fit into the lower two layers of the OSI model, which simply means that the IEEE standard includes some more finely grained layering than the OSI model.

While at first glance these extra layers might seem to be outside the OSI reference model, the OSI model is not meant to rigidly dictate the structure of network standards. Instead, the OSI model is an organizational and explanatory tool; sublayers can be added to deal with the complexity of a given standard.

Figure 1-3 depicts the lower two layers of the OSI reference model, and shows how the major IEEE-specific sublayers are organized. Within these major sublayers there are even further sublayers defined for additional MAC functions, new physical signaling standards, and so on. At the data link level, there are the Logical Link Control (LLC) and the MAC sublayers, which are the same for all varieties and speeds of Ethernet. The LLC layer is an IEEE mechanism for identifying the data carried in an Ethernet frame. The MAC layer defines the protocol used to arbitrate access to the Ethernet system. Both of these systems are described in detail in Chapter 3, *The Media Access Control Protocol.*

At the physical layer, the IEEE sublayers vary depending on whether 10-, 100-, or 1000 Mbps Ethernet is being standardized. Each of the sublayers is used to help organize the Ethernet specifications around specific functions that must be achieved to make the Ethernet system work.

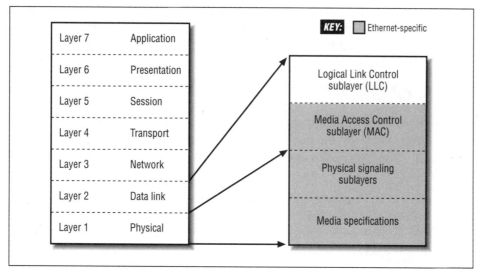

Figure 1-3. The major IEEE sublayers

Understanding these sublayers can also help us understand the scope of the various standards involved. For example, the MAC portion of the IEEE standard is "above" the lower layer physical specifications. As such, it is functionally independent of the various physical layer media specifications and does not change, no matter which physical media variety may be in use.

The IEEE LLC standard is independent of the 802.3 Ethernet LAN standard and will not vary—no matter which LAN system is used. The LLC control fields are intended for use in all LAN systems and not just Ethernet, which is why the LLC sublayer is not formally part of the IEEE 802.3 system specifications.

All of the sublayers below the LLC sublayer are specific to the individual LAN technology in question, which in this case is Ethernet. To help make this clearer, the Ethernet-specific portions of the standard in Figure 1-3 are all shown in gray.

Below the MAC sublayer, we get into the portions of the standard that are organized in the Physical Layer of the OSI reference model. The physical layer standards are different depending on the Ethernet media variety in use and whether or not we're describing the original 10 Mbps Ethernet system, 100 Mbps Fast Ethernet, or 1000 Mbps Gigabit Ethernet system.

Levels of Compliance

In developing a technical standard, the IEEE is careful to include only those items whose behavior must be carefully specified to make the system work. Therefore, all Ethernet interfaces that operate in the original half-duplex mode (described in

Chapter 3) must comply fully with the MAC protocol specifications in the standard to perform the functions identically. Otherwise, the network would not function correctly.

At the same time, the IEEE makes an effort not to constrain the market by standardizing such things as the appearance of an Ethernet interface, or how many connectors it should have on it. The intent is to provide just enough engineering specifications to make the system work reliably, without inhibiting competition and the inventiveness of the marketplace. In general, the IEEE has been quite successful. Most equipment designed for use in an Ethernet system fully complies with the standard.

Vendor innovation can sometimes lead to the development of devices that are not described in the IEEE standard, and that are not included in the half-duplex mode timing specs or the media specs in the standard. Some of these devices may work well for a small network, but might cause problems with signal timing in a larger network operating in half-duplex mode. Further, a network system using equipment not described in the standard or included in the official guidelines cannot be evaluated using the IEEE half-duplex mode configuration guidelines.

The Effect of Standards Compliance

How much you should be concerned about all this is largely up to you and your particular circumstances. Another way of saying this is: "Optimality differs according to context."* It's up to you to decide how important these issues are, given your particular circumstances (or *context*). For one thing, not all innovations are a bad idea.

After all, the thin coaxial and twisted-pair Ethernet media systems started life as vendor innovations that later became carefully specified media systems in the IEEE standard. However, if your goal is maximum predictability and stability for your network given a variety of vendor equipment and traffic loads, then one way to help achieve that goal is by using only equipment that is described in the standard.

One way to decide how important these issues are is to look at the scope and type of network system in question. For an Ethernet that just connects a couple of computers in your house, you may feel that any equipment you can find that helps make this happen at the least cost is a good deal. If the equipment isn't described in the official half-duplex configuration guidelines, you may not care all that much. In this instance, you are building a small network system, and you

---

* I am indebted to Mike Padlipsky for this useful advice, which was published in his book, *The Elements of Networking Style*, M. A. Padlipsky (Englewood Cliffs, New Jersey: Prentice Hall, 1985), p. 229.

probably don't intend for the network to grow very large. The limited scope of your network makes it easier to decide that you are not all that worried about multi-vendor interoperability, or about your ability to evaluate the network using the IEEE configuration guidelines.

On the other hand, if you are a network manager of a departmental or campus network system, then the people using your network will be depending on the network to get their work done. The expanded scope changes your context quite a bit. Departmental and workgroup nets always seem to be growing, which makes extending networks to accommodate growth a major priority for you. In addition, network stability under all sorts of traffic loads becomes another important issue. In this very different context, the issues of multi-vendor interoperability and compliance with the standard become much more important.

Equipment Included in the Standard

All Ethernet equipment sold is compliant in some way with the standard; otherwise, it wouldn't be able to interoperate with other Ethernet equipment. Therefore, mere compliance with the standard doesn't tell you much. Unfortunately, there's no LAN industry organization that will certify and stamp equipment, "This device is described in the standard and included in the official IEEE configuration guidelines." That's why you need to be wary about believing everything you read in equipment catalogs.

Sometimes vendors may not tell you whether the component they are selling is included in the IEEE system configuration guidelines, and whether it is a piece of standard and interoperable equipment that is widely available from other vendors. Some components that are not included in the official standard or media system configuration guidelines include the 10 Mbps AUI port concentrator, media converters, and special media segments. These components are described in later chapters and Appendix C, *AUI Equipment: Installation and Configuration.*

IEEE Identifiers

The IEEE has assigned shorthand identifiers to the various Ethernet media systems as they have been developed. The three-part identifiers include the speed, the type of signaling used, and information about the physical medium.

In the early media systems, the physical medium part of the identifier was based on the cable distance in meters, rounded to the nearest 100 meters. In the more recent media systems, the IEEE engineers dropped the distance convention and the third part of the identifier simply identifies the media type used (twisted-pair or fiber optic). In roughly chronological order, the identifiers include the following set:

10BASE5

This identifies the original Ethernet system, based on thick coaxial cable. The identifier means *10* megabits per second transmission speed, *base*band transmission, and the *5* refers to the 500 meter maximum segment length. The word *baseband* simply means that the transmission medium, thick coaxial cable in this instance, is dedicated to carrying one service: Ethernet signals. The 500 meter limit refers to the maximum length a given cable segment may be. Longer networks are built by connecting multiple segments with repeaters or switching hubs.

10BASE2

Also known as the *thin Ethernet* system, this media variety operates at 10 Mbps, in baseband mode, with cable segment lengths that can be a maximum of 185 meters in length. If the segments can be at most 185 meters long, then why does the identifier say "2," thus implying a maximum of 200 meters? The answer is that the identifier is merely a bit of shorthand and not intended to be an official specification. The IEEE committee found it convenient to round things up to 2, to keep the identifier short and easier to pronounce. This less expensive version of coax Ethernet was nicknamed "Cheapernet."

FOIRL

This stands for *Fiber Optic Inter-Repeater Link*. The original DIX Ethernet standard mentioned a point-to-point link segment that could be used between repeaters, but did not provide any media specifications. Later, the IEEE committee developed the FOIRL standard, and published it in 1989. FOIRL segments were originally designed to link remote Ethernet segments together. Fiber optic media's immunity to lightning strikes and electrical interference, as well as its ability to carry signals for long distances, makes it an ideal system for transmitting signals between buildings.

The specifications in the original FOIRL segment only provide for linking two repeaters together, one at each end of the link. While waiting for a larger set of fiber optic specifications to appear, vendors extended the set of devices that are connected via fiber, allowing an FOIRL segment to be attached to a station as well. These changes were taken up and added to the newer fiber optic link specifications found in the 10BASE-F standard (described later in this section).

10BROAD36

This system was designed to send 10 Mbps signals over a broadband cable system. Broadband cable systems support multiple services on a single cable by dividing the bandwidth of the cable into separate frequencies, each assigned to a given service. Cable television is an example of a broadband cable system, designed to deliver multiple television channels over a single cable. 10BROAD36 systems are intended to cover a large area; the 36 refers to the 3,600 meter distance allowed between any two stations on the system. These days, the vast majority of sites use fiber optic media for covering large distances, and broadband Ethernet equipment is not widely available.

1BASE5

This standard describes a 1 Mbps system based on twisted-pair wiring, which did not prove to be a very popular system. 1BASE5 was superseded in the marketplace by 10BASE-T, which provided all the advantages of twisted-pair wiring as well as the higher 10 Mbps speed.

10BASE-T

The "T" stands for "twisted," as in twisted-pair wires. This variety of the Ethernet system operates at 10 Mbps, in baseband mode, over two pairs of Category 3 (or better) twisted-pair wires. The category system for classifying cable quality is described in Chapter 14, *Structured Cabling*. The hyphen was added to the "10BASE-T" identifier to help ensure the correct pronunciation of "ten base tee." It was felt that without the hyphen people might mistakenly call it "10 basset," which is too close to the dog, "basset hound." Use of the hyphen is found in this and all newer media identifiers.

10BASE-F

The "F" stands for *fiber*, as in *fiber optic media*. This is the most recent 10 Mbps fiber optic Ethernet standard, adopted as an official part of the IEEE 802.3 standard in November 1993. The 10BASE-F standard defines three sets of specifications:

10BASE-FB

This is for active fiber hubs based on synchronous repeaters for extending a backbone system.

10BASE-FP

This is for passive hub equipment intended to link workstations with a fiber optic hub.

10BASE-FL

This includes a set of fiber optic link segment specifications that updates and extends the older FOIRL standard.

Two of these specifications have not been widely deployed. Equipment based on 10BASE-FB is scarce, and equipment based on 10BASE-FP is non-existent. The vast majority of Ethernet vendors sell 10BASE-FL fiber link equipment.

100 Mbps Media Systems

100BASE-T

This is the IEEE shorthand identifier for the entire 100 Mbps system, including all twisted-pair and fiber optic Fast Ethernet media systems.

100BASE-X

This is the IEEE shorthand identifier for the 100BASE-TX and 100BASE-FX media systems. These two systems are both based on the same 4B/5B block encoding system, adapted from a 100 Mbps networking standard called Fiber Distributed Data Interface (FDDI). FDDI was originally developed and standardized by ANSI.

100BASE-TX

This variety of the Fast Ethernet system operates at 100 Mbps, in baseband mode, over two pairs of high-quality, Category 5 twisted-pair cable. The TX identifier indicates that this is the twisted-pair version of the 100BASE-X media systems. This is the most widely used variety of Fast Ethernet.

100BASE-FX

This variety of the Fast Ethernet system operates at 100 Mbps, in baseband mode, over multi-mode fiber optic cable.

100BASE-T4

This variety of the Fast Ethernet system operates at 100 Mbps, in baseband mode, over four pairs of Category 3 or better twisted-pair cable. This variety has not been widely deployed, and 100BASE-T4 equipment is scarce.

100BASE-T2

This variety of the Fast Ethernet system operates at 100 Mbps, in baseband mode, on two pairs of Category 3 or better twisted-pair cable. This variety was never developed by any vendor, and equipment based on the T2 standard is non-existent.

1000 Mbps Media Systems

1000BASE-X

This is the IEEE shorthand identifier for the Gigabit Ethernet media systems based on the 8B/10B block encoding scheme adapted from the Fibre Channel networking standard. Fibre Channel is a high speed networking system developed and standardized by ANSI.

The 1000BASE-X media systems include 1000BASE-SX, 1000BASE-LX, and 1000BASE-CX.

1000BASE-SX

> The "S" stands for "short," as in short wavelength. The "X" indicates that this media segment is one of three based on the same block encoding scheme. This is the short wavelength fiber optic media segment for Gigabit Ethernet.

1000BASE-LX

> This is the long wavelength fiber optic media segment for Gigabit Ethernet.

1000BASE-CX

> This is a short copper cable media segment for Gigabit Ethernet, based on the original Fibre Channel standard.

1000BASE-T

> This is the IEEE shorthand identifier for 1000 Mbps Gigabit Ethernet over Category 5 or better twisted-pair cable. This system is based on a different signal encoding scheme required to transmit gigabit signals over twisted-pair cabling.

Reinventing Ethernet

No matter how well designed a LAN system is, it won't help you much if you can only use it with a single vendor's equipment. A LAN has to be able to work with the widest variety of equipment possible to provide you with the greatest flexibility. For maximum utility, your LAN must be vendor-neutral: that is, capable of interworking with all types of computers without being vendor-specific. This was not the way things worked in the 1970s when computers were expensive and networking technology was exotic and proprietary.

Metcalfe understood that a revolution in computer communications required a networking technology that everyone could use. In 1979 he set out to make Ethernet an open standard, and convinced Xerox to join a multi-vendor consortium for the purposes of standardizing an Ethernet system that any company could use. The era of open computer communications based on Ethernet technology formally began in 1980 when the Digital Equipment Corporation (DEC), Intel, and Xerox consortium announced the DIX standard for 10 Mbps Ethernet.

This DIX standard made the technology available to anyone who wanted to use it, producing an open system. As part of this effort, Xerox agreed to license its patented technology for a low fee to anyone who wanted it. In 1982 Xerox also gave up its trademark on the Ethernet name. As a result, the Ethernet standard became the world's first open, multi-vendor LAN standard. The idea of sharing proprietary computer technology in order to arrive at a common standard to benefit everyone was a radical notion for the computer industry in the late 1970s. It's a tribute to

Bob Metcalfe's vision that he realized the importance of making Ethernet an open standard. As Metcalfe put it:

> The invention of Ethernet as an open, non-proprietary, industry-standard local network was perhaps even more significant than the invention of Ethernet technology itself.*

In 1979 Metcalfe started a company to help commercialize Ethernet. He believed that computers from multiple vendors ought to be able to communicate compatibly over a common networking technology, making them more useful and, in turn, opening up a vast new set of capabilities for the users. *Com*puter *com*munication *com*patibility was the goal, which led Metcalfe to name his new company 3Com.

Reinventing Ethernet for Twisted-Pair Media

Ethernet prospered during the 1980s, but as the number of computers being networked continued to grow, the problems inherent in the original coaxial cable media system became more acute. Installing a thick coax cable in a building was a difficult task, and connecting the computers to the cable was also a challenge. A thin coax cable system was introduced in the mid-1980s that made it easier to build a media system and connect computers to it, but it was still difficult to manage Ethernet systems based on coaxial cable. Coaxial Ethernet systems are typically based on a bus topology, in which every computer sends Ethernet signals over a single bus cable; a failure of the cable brings the entire network system to a halt, and troubleshooting a cable problem can take a long time.

The invention of *twisted-pair* Ethernet in the late 1980s by a company called SynOptics Communications made it possible to build Ethernet systems based on the much more reliable star-wired cabling topology, in which the computers are networked to a central hub. These systems are much easier to install and manage, and troubleshooting is much easier and quicker as well. The use of twisted-pair cabling was a major change, or reinvention, of Ethernet. Twisted-pair Ethernet led to a vast expansion in the use of Ethernet; the Ethernet market took off and has never looked back.

In the early 1990s, a structured cabling system standard for twisted-pair cabling systems was developed that made it possible to provide building-wide twisted-pair systems based on high-reliability cabling practices adopted from the telephone industry. Ethernet based on twisted-pair media installed according to the structured cabling standard has become the most widely used network technology.

---

* Shotwell, *The Ethernet Sourcebook*, p. xi.

These Ethernet systems are reliable, easy to install and manage, and support rapid troubleshooting for problem resolution.

Reinventing Ethernet for 100 Mbps

The original Ethernet standard of 1980 described a system that operated at 10 Mbps. This was quite fast for the time, and Ethernet interfaces in the early 1980s were expensive due to the buffer memory and high-speed components required to support such rapid speeds. Throughout the 1980s, Ethernet was considerably faster than the computers connected to it, which provided a good match between the network and the computers it supported. However, as computer technology continued to evolve, ordinary computers were fast enough to provide a major traffic load to a 10 Mbps Ethernet channel by the early 1990s.

Much to the surprise of those who thought Ethernet was limited to 10 Mbps, Ethernet was reinvented to increase its speed by a factor of ten. The new standard created the 100 Mbps Fast Ethernet system, which was formally adopted in 1995. Fast Ethernet is based on twisted-pair and fiber optic media systems, and provides high-speed network channels for use in backbone systems, as well as connections to fast server computers and to desktop computers.

With the invention of Fast Ethernet, multi-speed twisted-pair Ethernet interfaces can be built which operate at either 10 or 100 Mbps. These interfaces are able, through an Auto-Negotiation protocol, to automatically set their speed in interaction with Ethernet repeater hubs and switching hubs. This makes the migration from 10 Mbps to 100 Mbps Ethernet systems easy to accomplish.

Reinventing Ethernet for 1000 Mbps

In 1998, Ethernet was reinvented yet again, this time to increase its speed by another factor of ten. The new Gigabit Ethernet standard describes a system that operates at the speed of 1 billion bits per second over fiber optic and twisted-pair media. The invention of Gigabit Ethernet makes it possible to provide very fast backbone networks as well as connections to high-performance servers.

The twisted-pair standard for Gigabit Ethernet makes it possible to provide very high-speed connections to the desktop when needed. Multi-speed twisted-pair Ethernet interfaces can now be built which operate at 10-, 100-, or 1000 Mbps, using the Auto-Negotiation protocol (see Chapter 5, *Auto-Negotiation*) to automatically configure their speed.

Reinventing Ethernet for New Capabilities

Ethernet innovations include new speeds and new media systems. They also include new Ethernet capabilities. For example, the full-duplex Ethernet standard makes it possible for two devices connected to a full-duplex Ethernet media system to simultaneously send and receive data. A port on a Fast Ethernet switching hub can simultaneously send and receive data at 100 Mbps with a server when using full-duplex mode, resulting in a total link bandwidth of 200 Mbps. The Auto-Negotiation standard provides the ability for switching hub ports and computers linked to those ports to discover whether or not they both support full-duplex mode, and if they do, to automatically select that mode of operation.

As you can see, the Ethernet system has been reinvented again and again to provide more flexible and reliable cabling, to accommodate the rapid increase in network traffic with higher speeds, and to provide more capabilities for today's more complex network systems. The remarkable success of Ethernet in the marketplace has been based on the equally remarkable ability of the system to adapt and change to meet the rapidly evolving needs of the computer industry.

Multi-Gigabit Ethernet

In March 1999, the IEEE 802.3 standards group held a "Call for Interest" meeting on the topic of Ethernet speeds beyond the current 1 Gbps standard. A number of presentations were made on the general topic, after which the group voted to create a High Speed Study Group. At the time of this writing, the High Speed Study Group is meeting on a regular basis to review presentations on a variety of technical issues. It is expected that this work will lead to the development of a new higher speed Ethernet standard, probably operating at 10 Gbps, within the next few years.

2

The Ethernet System

An Ethernet Local Area Network (LAN) is made up of hardware and software working together to deliver digital data between computers. To accomplish this task, four basic elements are combined to make an Ethernet system. This chapter provides a tutorial describing these elements, since a familiarity with these basic elements provides a good background for working with Ethernet. We will also take a look at some network media and simple topologies. Finally, we will see how the Ethernet system is used by high-level network protocols to send data between computers.

This chapter describes the original half-duplex mode of operation. *Half-duplex* simply means that only one computer can send data over the Ethernet channel at any given time. In half-duplex mode, multiple computers share a single Ethernet channel by using the Carrier Sense Multiple Access with Collision Detection (CSMA/CD) media access control (MAC) protocol. Until the introduction of switching hubs, the half-duplex system was the typical mode of operation for the vast majority of Ethernet LANs—tens of millions of Ethernet connections have been installed based on this system.

However, these days many computers are connected directly to their own port on an Ethernet switching hub and do not share the Ethernet channel with other systems. This type of connection is described in Chapter 18, *Ethernet Switching Hubs*. Many computers and switching hub connections now use full-duplex mode, in which the CSMA/CD protocol is shut off and the two devices on the link can send data whenever they like. The full-duplex mode of operation is described in Chapter 4, *Full-Duplex Ethernet*.

Four Basic Elements of Ethernet

The Ethernet system includes four building blocks that, when combined, make a working Ethernet:

- The *frame*, which is a standardized set of bits used to carry data over the system.

- The *media access control protocol*, which consists of a set of rules embedded in each Ethernet interface that allow multiple computers to access the shared Ethernet channel in a fair manner.

- The *signaling components*, which consists of standardized electronic devices that send and receive signals over an Ethernet channel.

- The *physical medium*, which consists of the cables and other hardware used to carry the digital Ethernet signals between computers attached to the network.

The Ethernet Frame

The heart of the Ethernet system is the frame. The network hardware—which is comprised of the Ethernet interfaces, media cables, etc.—exists simply to move Ethernet frames between computers, or stations.* The bits in the Ethernet frame are formed up in specified fields. Figure 2-1 shows the basic frame fields. These fields are described in more detail in Chapter 3, *The Media Access Control Protocol.*

64 bits	48 bits	48 bits	16 bits	46 to 1500 bytes	32 bits
Preamble	Destination Address	Source Address	Type/ Length	Data	Frame Check Sequence (CRC)

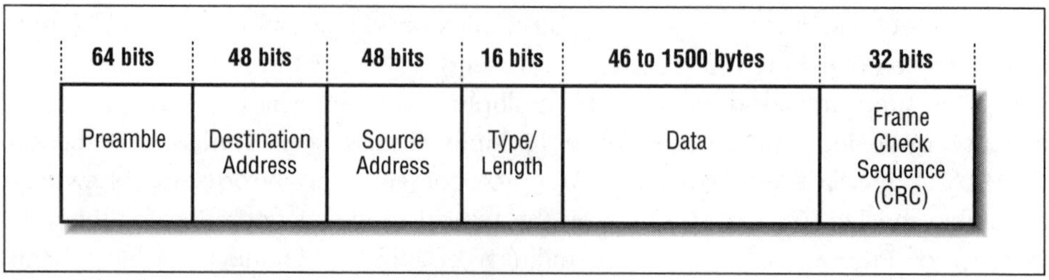

Figure 2-1. An Ethernet frame

Figure 2-1 shows the basic Ethernet frame, which begins with a set of 64 bits called the *preamble*. The preamble gives all of the hardware and electronics in a 10 Mbps Ethernet system some signal start-up time to recognize that a frame is being transmitted, alerting it to start receiving the data. This is what a 10 Mbps network uses to clear its throat, so to speak. Newer Ethernet systems running at 100 and 1000 Mbps use constant signaling, which avoids the need for a preamble.

---

* A computer connected to the network may be a standard desktop workstation, a printer, or anything else with an Ethernet interface in it. For that reason, the Ethernet standard uses the more general term "station" to describe the networked device, and so will we.

However, the preamble is still transmitted in these systems to avoid making any changes in the structure of the frame.

Following the preamble are the destination and source addresses. Assignment of addresses is controlled by the IEEE Standards Association (IEEE-SA), which administers a portion of the address field. When assigning blocks of addresses for use by network vendors, the IEEE-SA provides a 24-bit Organizationally Unique Identifier (OUI).* The OUI is a unique 24-bit identifier assigned to each organization that builds network interfaces. This allows a vendor of Ethernet equipment to provide a unique address for each interface they build. Providing unique addresses during manufacturing avoids the problem of two or more Ethernet interfaces in a network having the same address. This also eliminates any need to locally administer and manage Ethernet addresses.

A manufacturer of Ethernet interfaces creates a unique 48-bit Ethernet address for each interface by using their assigned OUI for the first 24 bits of the address. The vendor then assigns the next 24 bits, being careful to ensure that each address is unique. The resulting 48-bit address is often called the hardware, or physical, address to make the point that the address has been assigned to the Ethernet interface. It is also called a Media Access Control (MAC) address, since the Ethernet media access control system includes the frame and its addressing.

Following the addresses in an Ethernet frame is a 16-bit type or length field. Most often this field is used to identify what type of high-level network protocol is being carried in the data field, e.g., TCP/IP. This field may also be used to carry length information, as described in Chapter 3.

After the type field can come anywhere from 46 bytes to 1500 bytes of data. The data field *must* be at least 46 bytes long. This length assures that the frame signals stay on the network long enough for every Ethernet station on the network system to hear the frame within the correct time limits. Every station must hear the frame within the maximum round-trip signal propagation time of an Ethernet system, as described later in this chapter. If the high-level protocol data carried in the data field is shorter than 46 bytes, then padding data is used to fill out the data field.

Finally, at the end of the frame there's a 32-bit Frame Check Sequence (FCS) field. The FCS contains a Cyclic Redundancy Checksum (CRC) which provides a check of the integrity of the data in the entire frame. The CRC is a unique number that is generated by applying a polynomial to the pattern of bits that make up the frame. The same polynomial is used to generate another checksum at the receiving station. The receiving station checksum is then compared to the checksum generated

---

* The IEEE-SA web page for OUI assignment is listed in Appendix A, *Resources*.

at the sending station. This allows the receiving Ethernet interface to verify that the bits in the frame survived their trip over the network system intact.

That's basically all there is to an Ethernet frame. Now that you know what an Ethernet frame looks like, you need to know how the frames are transmitted. This is where the set of rules used to govern when a station gets to transmit a frame comes into play. We'll take a look at those rules next.

The Media Access Control Protocol

The half-duplex mode of operation described in the original Ethernet standard uses the MAC protocol, which is a set of rules used to arbitrate access to the shared channel among a set of stations connected to that channel. The way the access protocol works is fairly simple: each Ethernet-equipped computer operates independently of all other stations on the network; there is no central controller. All stations attached to an Ethernet operating in half-duplex mode are connected to a shared signaling channel, also known as a signal bus.

Ethernet uses a *broadcast delivery* mechanism, in which each frame that is transmitted is heard by every station. While this may seem inefficient, the advantage is that putting the address-matching intelligence in the interface of each station allows the physical medium to be kept as simple as possible. On an Ethernet LAN, all that the physical signaling and media system has to do is see that the bits are accurately transmitted to every station; the Ethernet interface in the station does the rest of the work.

Ethernet signals are transmitted from the interface and sent over the shared signal channel to every attached station. To send data, a station first listens to the channel, and if the channel is idle the station transmits its data in the form of an Ethernet frame or packet.[*]

As each Ethernet frame is sent over the shared signal channel, or medium, all Ethernet interfaces connected to the channel read in the bits of the signal and look at the second field of the frame shown in Figure 2-1, which contains the destination address. The interfaces compare the destination address of the frame with their own 48-bit unicast address or a multicast address they have been enabled to recognize. The Ethernet interface whose address matches the destination address in the frame will continue to read the entire frame and deliver it to the networking software running on that computer. All other network interfaces will stop reading the frame when they discover that the destination address does not match their own unicast address or an enabled multicast address.

---

[*] The precise term as defined in the Ethernet standard is "frame," but the term "packet" is sometimes used as well.

Multicast and Broadcast Addresses

A *multicast* address allows a single Ethernet frame to be received by a group of stations. An application providing streaming audio and video services, for example, can set a station's Ethernet interface to listen for specific multicast addresses. This makes it possible for a set of stations to be assigned to a multicast group, which has been given a specific multicast address. A single stream of audio packets sent to the multicast address assigned to that group will be received by all stations in that group.

There is also the special case of the multicast address known as the *broadcast* address, which is the 48-bit address of all ones. All Ethernet interfaces that see a frame with this destination address will read the frame in and deliver it to the networking software on the computer.

After each frame transmission, all stations on the network with traffic to send must contend equally for the next frame transmission opportunity. This ensures that access to the network channel is fair and that no single station can lock out the others. Fair access of the shared channel is made possible through the use of the MAC system embedded in the Ethernet interface located in each station. The media access control mechanism for Ethernet uses the CSMA/CD protocol.

The CSMA/CD protocol

The CSMA/CD protocol functions somewhat like a dinner party in a dark room where the participants can only hear one another. Everyone around the table must listen for a period of quiet before speaking (*Carrier Sense*). Once a space occurs everyone has an equal chance to say something (*Multiple Access*). If two people start talking at the same instant they detect that fact, and quit speaking (*Collision Detection*).

To translate this into Ethernet terms, the Carrier Sense portion of the protocol means that before transmitting, each interface must wait until there is no signal on the channel. If there is no signal, it can begin transmitting. If another interface is transmitting, there will be a signal on the channel; this condition is called *carrier.** All other interfaces must wait until carrier ceases and the signal channel is idle before trying to transmit; this process is called *deferral.*

---

* Historically, a carrier signal is defined as a continuous constant-frequency signal, such as the one used to carry the modulated signal in an AM or FM radio system. There is no such continuous carrier signal in Ethernet; instead, "carrier" in Ethernet simply means the presence of traffic on the network.

With Multiple Access, all Ethernet interfaces have the same priority when it comes to sending frames on the network, and all interfaces can attempt to access the channel at any time.

The next portion of the access protocol is called Collision Detect. Given that every Ethernet interface has equal opportunity to access the Ethernet, it's possible for multiple interfaces to sense that the network is idle and start transmitting their frames simultaneously. When this happens, the Ethernet signaling devices connected to the shared channel sense the *collision* of signals, which tells the Ethernet interfaces to stop transmitting. Each of the interfaces will then choose a random retransmission time and resend their frames in a process called *backoff.*

The CSMA/CD protocol is designed to provide fair access to the shared channel so that all stations get a chance to use the network and no station gets locked out due to some other station hogging the channel. After every packet transmission, all stations use the CSMA/CD protocol to determine which station gets to use the Ethernet channel next.

Collisions

If more than one station happens to transmit on the Ethernet channel at the same moment, then the signals are said to *collide.* The stations are notified of this event and reschedule their transmission using a random time interval chosen by a specially designed backoff algorithm. Choosing random times to retransmit helps the stations to avoid colliding again on the next transmission.

It's unfortunate that the original Ethernet design used the word *collision* for this aspect of the Ethernet media access control mechanism. If it had been called something else, such as Distributed Bus Arbitration (DBA) events, then no one would worry about the occurrence of DBAs on an Ethernet. To most ears the word "collision" sounds like something bad has happened, leading many people to incorrectly conclude that collisions are an indication of network failure and that lots of collisions must mean the network is broken.

Instead, the truth of the matter is that collisions are absolutely normal events on an Ethernet and are simply an indication that the CSMA/CD protocol is functioning as designed. As more computers are added to a given Ethernet, there will be more traffic, resulting in more collisions as part of the normal operation of an Ethernet. Collisions resolve quickly. For example, the design of the CSMA/CD protocol ensures that the majority of collisions on a 10 Mbps Ethernet will be resolved in microseconds, or millionths of a second. Nor does a normal collision result in lost data. In the event of a collision, the Ethernet interface backs off (waits) for some number of microseconds, and then automatically retransmits the frame.

Networks with very heavy traffic loads may experience multiple collisions for each frame transmission attempt. This is also expected behavior. Repeated collisions for a given packet transmission attempt indicate a very busy network. If repeated collisions occur, the stations involved will expand the set of potential backoff times in order to retransmit the data. The expanding backoff process, formally known as *truncated binary exponential backoff*, is a clever feature of the Ethernet MAC protocol that provides an automatic method for stations to adjust to changing traffic conditions on the network. Only after 16 consecutive collisions for a given transmission attempt will the interface finally discard the Ethernet frame. This can happen only if the Ethernet channel is overloaded for a fairly long period of time or if it is broken.

So far, we've seen what an Ethernet frame looks like and how the CSMA/CD protocol is used to ensure fair access for multiple stations sending their frames over the shared Ethernet channel. The frame and the CSMA/CD protocol are the same for all varieties of Ethernet. Whether the Ethernet signals are carried over coaxial, twisted-pair, or fiber optic cable, the same frame is used to carry the data and the same CSMA/CD protocol is used to provide the half-duplex shared channel mode of operation. In full-duplex mode, the same frame format is used, but the CSMA/CD protocol is shut off, as described in Chapter 4.

Ethernet Hardware

The next two building blocks of an Ethernet system include the hardware components used in the system. There are two basic groups of hardware components: the signaling components, used to send and receive signals over the physical medium; and the media components, used to build the physical medium that carries the Ethernet signals. Not surprisingly, these hardware components differ depending on the speed of the Ethernet system and the type of cabling used. To show the hardware building blocks, we'll look at an example based on the widely used 10 Mbps twisted-pair Ethernet media system, called 10BASE-T.

Signaling Components

The signaling components for a twisted-pair system include the Ethernet interface located in the computer, as well as a transceiver and its cable. An Ethernet may consist of a pair of stations linked with a single twisted-pair segment, or multiple stations connected to twisted-pair segments that are linked together with an Ethernet repeater. A repeater is a device used to repeat network signals onto multiple segments. Connecting cable segments with a repeater makes it possible for the segments to all work together as a single shared Ethernet channel.

Figure 2-2 shows two computers (*stations*) connected to a 10BASE-T media system. Both computers have an Ethernet interface card installed, which makes the Ethernet system operate. The interface contains the electronics needed to form up and send Ethernet frames, as well as to receive frames and extract the data from them. The Ethernet interface comes in two basic types. The first is a board that plugs into a computer's bus slot, and the other relies on chips that allow Ethernet interfaces to be built into the computer's main logic board. In the second form, all you'll see of the interface is an Ethernet connector mounted on the back of the computer.

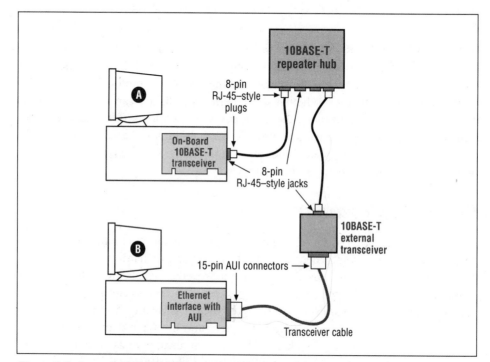

Figure 2-2. A sample 10BASE-T Ethernet connection

The Ethernet interface connects to the media system using a transceiver, which can be built into the interface or provided as an external device. Of the two stations shown in Figure 2-2, one is provided with a built-in transceiver and one uses an external transceiver. The word "transceiver" is a combination of *trans*mitter and re*ceiver*. A transceiver contains the electronics needed to take signals from the station interface and transmit them to the twisted-pair cable segment, and to receive signals from the cable segment and send them to the interface.

The Ethernet interface in Station A is connected directly to the twisted-pair cable segment since it is equipped with an internal 10BASE-T transceiver. The twisted-pair cable uses an 8-pin connector that is also known as an RJ-45 plug. The Ethernet interface in Station B is connected to an outboard transceiver, which is a small box that contains the transceiver electronics. The outboard transceiver connects to the twisted-pair segment using an 8-pin connector. The outboard transceiver connects to the Ethernet interface in the station with a transceiver cable. The transceiver cable in the 10 Mbps Ethernet system uses a 15-pin connector which is called the Attachment Unit Interface (AUI).

The final signaling component shown in Figure 2-2 is an Ethernet repeater hub which links multiple twisted-pair segments. This device is called a hub because it sits at the center, or hub, of a set of cable segments. The repeater connects to the cable segments using the same built-in 10BASE-T transceivers used by an ordinary station interface. The repeater operates by moving Ethernet signals from one segment to another one bit at a time; it does not operate at the level of Ethernet frames, but simply repeats the signals it sees on each segment. Repeaters make it possible to build larger Ethernet systems composed of multiple cable segments by making the segments function together as a single channel.

Media Components

The cables and other components used to build the signal-carrying portion of the shared Ethernet channel are called the *physical* media. The physical cabling components vary depending on which kind of media system is in use. For instance, a twisted-pair cabling system uses different components than a fiber optic cabling system. Just to make things more interesting, a given Ethernet system may include several different kinds of media systems all connected together with repeaters to make a single network channel.

By using repeaters, an Ethernet system of multiple segments can grow as a *branching tree*. This means that each media segment is an individual branch of the complete signal system. The 10 Mbps system allows multiple repeaters in the path between stations, making it possible to build repeated networks with multiple branches. Only one or two repeaters can be used in the path of higher speed Ethernet systems, limiting the size of the resulting network. A typical network design actually ends up looking less like a tree and more like a complex set of network segments that may be strung along hallways or throughout wiring closets in your building. The resulting system of connected segments may grow in any direction and does not have a specific root segment. However, it is essential not to connect Ethernet segments in a loop, as each frame would circulate endlessly until the system was saturated with traffic.

Round-Trip Timing

In order for the MAC system to work properly, all Ethernet interfaces must be capable of responding to one another's signals within a strictly controlled amount of time. The signal timing for Ethernet is based on the amount of time it takes for a signal to get from one end of the complete media system to the other and back. This is known as the *round-trip time*. The maximum round-trip time of signals on an Ethernet system operating in half-duplex mode is strictly limited. Limiting the round-trip time ensures that every interface can hear all network signals within the specified amount of time provided for in the Ethernet MAC system.

The longer a given network segment is, the more time it takes for a signal to travel over it. The intent of the configuration guidelines in the standard is to make sure that the round-trip timing restrictions are met, no matter what combination of media segments are used in your network. The configuration guidelines provide specifications for the maximum length of segments and rules for combining various kinds of cabling segments with repeaters. These specifications and rules ensure that the correct signal timing is maintained for the entire LAN. The specifications for individual media segment lengths and the rules for combining segments must be carefully followed. If these specifications and rules are violated, the computers may not hear one another's signals within the required time limit, and could end up interfering with one another.

That's why the correct operation of an Ethernet LAN depends upon media segments that are built according to the rules published for each media type. More complex LANs built with multiple media types must be designed according to the multi-segment configuration guidelines provided in the Ethernet standard. These rules include limits on the total length of segments and the total number of segments and repeaters that may be in a given system. This is to ensure that the correct round-trip timing is maintained.

Ethernet Hubs

Ethernet was designed to be easily expandable to meet the networking needs of a given site. As we've just seen, the total set of segments and repeaters in the Ethernet LAN must meet round-trip timing specifications. To help extend half-duplex Ethernet systems, networking vendors sell repeater hubs that are equipped with multiple Ethernet ports. Each port of a repeater hub links individual Ethernet media segments together to create a larger network that operates as a single Ethernet LAN.

There is another kind of hub called a switching hub. Switching hubs use the 48-bit Ethernet destination addresses to make a frame forwarding decision from one port of the switch to another. As shown in Figure 2-3, each port of a switching hub provides a connection to an Ethernet media system that functions as an entirely separate Ethernet LAN.

In a repeater hub the individual ports combine segments together to create a single LAN channel. However, a switching hub makes it possible to divide a set of Ethernet media systems into multiple separate LANs. The separate LANs are linked together by way of the switching electronics in the hub. The round-trip timing rules for each LAN stop at the switching hub port, allowing you to link a large number of individual Ethernet LANs together.

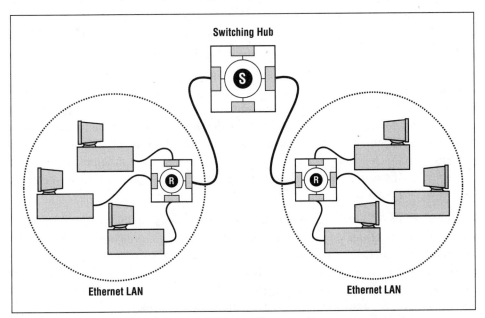

Figure 2-3. Switching hub creates separate Ethernet LANs

A given Ethernet LAN may consist of a repeater hub linking several media segments together. Whole Ethernet LANs can themselves be linked together to form extended network systems using switching hubs. Larger networks based on repeater hubs can be segmented into smaller LANs with switching hubs in a process called *network segmentation.* In this instance, the switching hub is used to segment a single LAN composed of network segments linked by repeater hubs into multiple LANs, to improve bandwidth and reliability.

Network segmentation can be extended all the way to connecting individual stations to single ports on the switching hub, in a process called *micro-segmentation.* As switching hub costs have dropped and computer performance has increased, more and more stations are being connected directly to their own port on the switching hub. That way, the station does not have to share the Ethernet channel bandwidth with another computer. Instead, it has its own dedicated Ethernet link to the switching hub. Switching hub operation and network segmentation are detailed in Chapter 18.

Network Protocols and Ethernet

Now that we've seen how frames are sent over Ethernet systems, let's look at the data being carried by the frame. Data that is being sent between computers is carried in the data field of the Ethernet frame and structured as high-level network protocols. The high-level network protocol information carried inside the data field of each Ethernet frame is what actually establishes communications between applications running on computers attached to the network. The most widely used system of high-level network protocols is called the Transmission Control Protocol/ Internet Protocol (TCP/IP) suite.

The important thing to understand is that the high-level protocols are *independent* of the Ethernet system. There are several network protocols in use today, any of which may send data between computers in the data field of an Ethernet frame. In essence, an Ethernet LAN with its hardware and Ethernet frame is simply a trucking service for data being sent by applications. The Ethernet LAN itself doesn't know or care about the high-level protocol data being carried in the data field of the Ethernet frame.

Since the Ethernet system is unaffected by the contents of the data field in the frame, different sets of computers running different high-level network protocols can share the same Ethernet. For example, you can have a single Ethernet that supports four computers, two of which communicate using TCP/IP, and two that use some other system of high-level protocols. All four computers can send Ethernet frames over the same Ethernet system without any problem.

The details of how network protocols function are an entirely separate subject from how the Ethernet system works and are outside the scope of this book. However, Ethernets are installed to make it possible for applications to communicate between computers using high-level network protocols to facilitate the communication. Let's take a quick look at one example of high-level network protocols to see how the Ethernet system and network protocols work together.

Design of Network Protocols

Network protocols are easy to understand since we all use some form of protocol in daily life. For instance, there's a certain protocol to writing a letter. We can compare the act of composing and delivering a letter to what a network protocol does to see how each works. The letter has a well-known form that has been "standardized" through custom. The letter includes a basic message with a greeting to the recipient and the name of the sender. After you're through writing the letter, you stuff it into an envelope, write the name and address of both the recipient and sender on the envelope, and give it to a delivery system, such as the post office, which handles the details of getting the message to the recipient's address.

A network protocol acts much like the letter protocol described above. To carry data between applications, the network software on your computer creates and sends a network protocol packet with its own private data field that corresponds to the message of the letter. The sender's and recipient's names (or protocol addresses) are added to complete the packet. After the network software has created the packet, the entire network protocol packet is stuffed into the data field of an Ethernet frame. Next, the 48-bit destination and source addresses are provided, and the frame is handed to the Ethernet interface and the Ethernet signal and cabling system for delivery to the right computer.

Figure 2-4 shows network protocol data traveling from Station A to Station B. The data is depicted as a letter that is placed in an envelope (i.e., a high-level protocol packet) that has network protocol addresses on it. This letter is stuffed into an Ethernet frame, shown here as a mailbag. The analogy is not exact, in that each Ethernet frame only carries one high-level protocol "letter" at a time and not a whole bag full, but you get the idea. The Ethernet frame is then placed on the Ethernet media system for delivery to Station B.

Protocol encapsulation

The independent system of the high-level protocol packet has its own addresses and data. The Ethernet frame has its own data field that is used for carrying the high-level protocol packet. This kind of organization is called encapsulation, and it's a common theme in the networking world. Encapsulation is the mechanism that allows independent systems to work together, such as network protocols and Ethernet LANs. With encapsulation the Ethernet frame carries the network protocol packet by treating the entire packet as just so much unknown data stuffed into the data field of the Ethernet frame. Upon delivery of the Ethernet frame to the station, it's up to the network software running on the station to deal with the protocol packet extracted from the Ethernet frame's data field.

Just like a trucking system carrying packages, the Ethernet system is fundamentally unaware of what is packed inside the high-level protocol packets that it carries between computers. This allows the Ethernet system to carry all manner of network protocols without worrying about how each high-level protocol works. In order to get the network protocol packet to its destination, however, the protocol software and the Ethernet system must interact to provide the correct destination address for the Ethernet frame. When using TCP/IP, the destination address of the IP packet is used to discover the Ethernet destination address of the station for which the packet is intended. Let's look briefly at how this works.

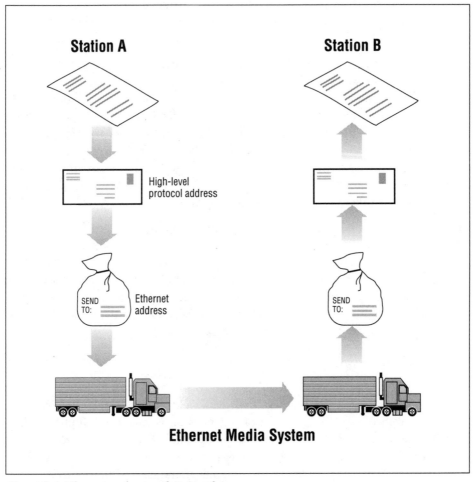

Figure 2-4. Ethernet and network protocols

Internet Protocol and Ethernet Addresses

High-level network protocols have their own system of addresses, such as the 32-bit address used by the current version of the Internet Protocol (IPv4) used on the Internet. The IP-based networking software in a given computer is aware of the 32-bit IP address assigned to that computer and can also read the 48-bit Ethernet address of its network interface. However, it doesn't know what the Ethernet addresses of the other stations on the network are when first trying to send a packet over the Ethernet.

To make things work, there needs to be a way to discover the Ethernet addresses of other IP-based computers on the network. The TCP/IP network protocol system accomplishes this task by using the Address Resolution Protocol (ARP).

Operation of the ARP protocol

The ARP protocol is fairly straightforward. Figure 2-5 shows two stations—Station A and Station B—sending and receiving an ARP packet over an Ethernet.

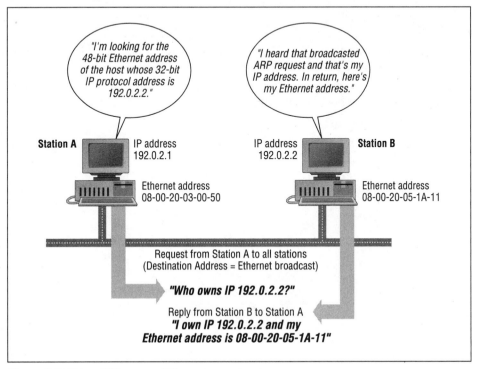

Figure 2-5. Using ARP over an Ethernet

Station A has been assigned the 32-bit IP address of 192.0.2.1, and wishes to send data over the Ethernet channel to Station B, which has been assigned IP address 192.0.2.2. Station A sends a packet to the broadcast address containing an ARP request. The ARP request basically says, "Will the station on this Ethernet that has the IP address of 192.0.2.2 please tell me what the 48-bit hardware address of their Ethernet interface is?"

Since the ARP request is sent in a broadcast frame, every Ethernet interface on the network reads it and hands the ARP request to the networking software running on the station.* Only Station B with IP address 192.0.2.2 will respond, sending a

---

* It would be a better idea to use a specified multicast address for this purpose; so that only IP-speaking computers would receive IP ARPs, and computers running other protocols would not be bothered. The address resolution system in the new version of IP (IPv6) uses multicast addressing for this reason. As of this writing IPv4 is the most widely used network protocol, although it is expected that a conversion to IPv6 will occur eventually.

packet containing the Ethernet address of Station B back to the requesting station. Now Station A has an Ethernet address to which it can send frames containing data destined for Station B, and the protocol communication can proceed.

That's all there is to it! The ARP protocol provides the "glue" between the 32-bit addresses used by the IP network protocols and the 48-bit addresses used by the Ethernet interfaces. The computers involved build a table in memory called the ARP cache to hold the IP addresses and their associated Ethernet addresses. Once this table is created by the ARP protocol, the network software can then look up the IP addresses in the table and find which Ethernet address to use when sending data to a given IP-based machine on the network.

3

The Media Access Control Protocol

The tutorial in Chapter 2, *The Ethernet System*, introduced the Ethernet system and provided a brief look at how it works. In this chapter we take a much more detailed look at the original mode of operation used for Ethernet, which is based on the CSMA/CD media access control (MAC) protocol. This is also called half-duplex mode, to distinguish it from the full-duplex mode of operation. Full-duplex mode, which has no need for a MAC protocol, is described in Chapter 4, *Full-Duplex Ethernet*.

In the original half-duplex mode, the MAC protocol allows a set of stations to compete for access to a shared Ethernet channel in a fair and equitable manner. The protocol's rules determine the behavior of Ethernet stations, including when they are allowed to transmit a frame onto a shared Ethernet channel and what to do when a collision occurs.

Since there is no central controller in an Ethernet system, each Ethernet interface operates independently while using the same MAC protocol. By equipping all interfaces with the same set of rules, all stations connected to a shared Ethernet channel operate the same way. Therefore, the MAC protocol functions as a kind of "Robert's Rules for Robots."

You don't need to know all the details of the MAC protocol in order to build and use Ethernet LANs. However, an understanding of the MAC protocol can certainly help when designing networks or troubleshooting problems. The media guidelines and MAC protocol are not some arbitrary laws dreamed up by a standards committee, but instead arise from the basic design and operation of the Ethernet system.

To simplify the description of the MAC protocol, this chapter has been broken down into three parts. The first part looks at the structure of the frame and the media access control rules used for transmitting frames, as well as how those rules affect the design of an Ethernet LAN. The next section takes a closer look at the operation of the important collision detect mechanism. Collision detection in Ethernet is frequently misunderstood, and we'll explain how it works, and how to design networks so that the collision detect system can do its job correctly. The last portion of the chapter describes how the high-level network software on your computer uses Ethernet frames to send data.

The Ethernet Frame

The Ethernet specifications determine both the structure of a frame and when a station is allowed to send a frame. Ethernet media access control is based on Carrier Sense with Multiple Access and Collision Detect, which gives rise to the CSMA/CD acronym described in Chapter 2. The Ethernet system exists to move frames carrying application data between computers; the organization of the frame is central to the operation of the system.

The frame was first defined in the original Ethernet DEC-Intel-Xerox (DIX) standard, and was later redefined in the IEEE 802.3 standard, which is now the official Ethernet standard. The changes between the two standards were mostly cosmetic, except for the type field.

The DIX standard defined a type field in the frame. The first 802.3 standard (published in 1985) specified this field as a length field, with a mechanism that allowed both versions of frames to coexist on the same Ethernet. As it happens, most networking software kept using the type field version of the frame, and the IEEE 802.3 standard was recently changed to define this field as being either length or type, depending on usage.

Figure 3-1 shows the DIX and IEEE versions of the Ethernet frame. Since DIX and IEEE frames are identical in terms of the number and length of fields, Ethernet interfaces can be used to send either kind of frame. The only difference in the frames is in the contents of the fields and the subsequent interpretation of those contents by the stations that send and receive the frames. Next, we'll take a detailed tour of the frame fields. This tour will describe what each frame field does and what the differences are between the two versions of the frame.

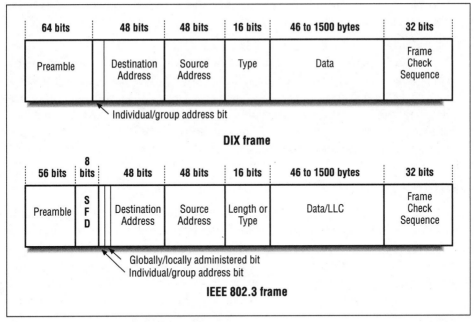

Figure 3-1. DIX Ethernet and IEEE 802.3 frames

Preamble

The frame begins with the 64-bit preamble field, which allows 10 Mbps Ethernet interfaces on the network to synchronize themselves with the incoming data stream before the important data fields arrive. The preamble exists in order to allow the beginning of the frame to lose a few bits due to signal start-up delays as it travels through a 10 Mbps system. This protects the rest of the frame from these effects. Like the heat shield of a spacecraft, which protects the spacecraft from burning up during re-entry, the preamble is the shield that protects the bits in the rest of the frame.

The preamble is maintained in the Fast Ethernet and Gigabit Ethernet systems to provide compatibility with the original Ethernet frame. However, both Fast Ethernet and Gigabit Ethernet systems use more complex mechanisms for encoding the signals that avoid any signal start-up losses. These two systems don't need the preamble to protect the frame signals, and it is preserved only for backward compatibility. The following discusses how the different standards implement the preamble:

DIX standard

In the DIX standard the preamble consists of eight "octets," or 8-bit bytes, of alternating ones and zeroes. The eighth byte of the preamble contains 6 bits of alternating ones and zeroes, but ends with the special pattern of "1, 1." These two bits signal the receiving interface that the end of the preamble has been reached, and that the bits that follow are actual fields of the frame.

IEEE standard

In the 802.3 specification, the preamble field is formally divided into two parts consisting of seven bytes of preamble and one byte, called the *start frame delimiter* (SFD). The last two bits of the SFD are 1, 1—as with the DIX Standard. Although the IEEE standard chooses to define an SFD field that includes the last eight bits of the preamble, there is no practical difference between the DIX and IEEE preambles. The pattern of bits being sent is identical.

Destination Address

The destination address field follows the preamble. Each Ethernet interface is assigned a unique 48-bit address, called the interface's physical or hardware address. The destination address field contains the 48-bit Ethernet address that corresponds to the address of the interface in the station that is the destination of the frame. The destination address field may instead contain a 48-bit multicast address that one or more interfaces on the network have been enabled to receive, or the standard broadcast address.

Every Ethernet interface attached to the network reads in every transmitted frame up to at least the destination address field. If the destination address does not match the interface's own Ethernet address or one of the multicast or broadcast addresses that the interface is programmed to receive, then the interface is free to ignore the rest of the frame. The following discusses how the different standards implement destination addresses:

DIX standard

The first bit of the address, as sent onto the network medium, is used to distinguish physical addresses from multicast addresses. If the first bit is zero, then the address is the *physical address* of an interface, which is also known as a *unicast address* since a frame sent to this address only goes to one destination. If the first bit of the address is a one, then the frame is being sent to a *multicast address.*

IEEE standard

The IEEE 802.3 version of the frame adds significance to the second bit of the destination address, which is used to distinguish between *locally* and *globally* administered addresses. A globally administered address is a physical address assigned to the interface by the manufacturer, which is indicated by setting the second bit to zero. (DIX Ethernet addresses are always globally administered.) If the address of the Ethernet interface is administered locally for some reason, then the second bit is supposed to be set to a value of one.* In the case of a broadcast address, the second bit is also a one in both the DIX and IEEE standard.

Understanding Physical Addresses

In Ethernet, the 48-bit physical address is written as 12 hexadecimal digits with the digits paired in groups of two, representing an octet (8 bits) of information. The octet order of transmission on the Ethernet is from the leftmost octet (as written or displayed) to the rightmost octet. The actual transmission order within the octet, however, is starting from the least significant bit of the octet through to the most significant bit. This means that an Ethernet address that is written as the hexadecimal string F0-2E-15-6C-77-9B is equivalent to the following sequence of bits, sent over the Ethernet channel from left to right:

```
0000 1111 0111 0100 1010 1000 0011 0110 1110 1110 1101 1001
```

Therefore, the 48-bit destination address that begins with the hexadecimal value 0xF0 is not a multicast address, since the first bit sent on the channel is a zero.

Source Address

The next field in the frame is the *source address*. This is the physical address of the interface that sent the frame. The source address is not interpreted in any way by the Ethernet MAC protocol. Instead, it is provided for the use of high-level protocols. An Ethernet station uses its physical address as the source address in any frame it transmits.

The DIX standard notes that a station can change the Ethernet source address, while the IEEE standard does not specifically state that an interface may have the ability to override the 48-bit physical address assigned by the manufacturer. However, all Ethernet interfaces in use these days appear to allow the physical address to be changed, which makes it possible for the network administrator or the high-level network software to modify the Ethernet interface address if necessary.

---

* Locally administered addresses are very rarely used on Ethernet systems, since the vast majority of Ethernet interfaces are assigned their own unique 48-bit address. Locally administered addresses, however, have been commonly used on some Token Ring systems.

To provide the physical address used in the source address field, a vendor of Ethernet equipment acquires an Organizationally Unique Identifier (OUI) from the IEEE. This unique 24-bit identifier is assigned by the IEEE. The OUI forms the first half of the physical address of any Ethernet interface that the vendor manufactures. As each interface is manufactured, the vendor also assigns a unique address to the interface using the lower 24 bits of the 48-bit address space. This results in a 48-bit physical address for each interface that contains an OUI in the first half of the address. The OUI can often be used to identify the vendor, which can be helpful when troubleshooting network problems.

VLAN Tag Header

Figure 3-1 shows what the typical Ethernet frame used by the vast majority of Ethernet devices looks like. However, a four-byte-long virtual LAN (VLAN) *tag header* may optionally be inserted in an Ethernet frame between the source address and the Length/Type field to identify the VLAN to which the frame belongs. VLANs are used in switching hubs as a way to direct Ethernet traffic to those ports of the hub which are defined to be members of a given VLAN. VLAN traffic may be sent between switching hubs and other devices by using the tag header to tag the Ethernet frames with a VLAN identifier. Until recently, VLAN tagging had been accomplished using a variety of proprietary approaches. Development of the IEEE 802.1Q standard for virtual bridged LANs provides the VLAN tag header as a vendor-neutral mechanism for identifying which VLAN a frame belongs to.

The addition of the four-byte VLAN tag header causes the maximum size of an Ethernet frame to be extended from the old maximum of 1518 bytes (not including the preamble) to a new maximum of 1522 bytes. Since VLAN tag headers are only added to Ethernet frames by switching hubs and other devices that have been programmed to send and receive VLAN-tagged frames, this does not affect traditional Ethernet operation.* VLANs and the contents and organization of VLAN tag headers are described in Chapter 18, *Ethernet Switching Hubs*.

---

* The first two bytes of the VLAN tag header contain a valid Ethernet type identifier. Therefore, if an Ethernet station that is not programmed to send or receive a VLAN tagged frame happens to receive a tagged frame, it will see what looks like a type identifier for an unknown protocol type and discard the frame. Even though a VLAN-tagged frame exceeds the original Ethernet maximum frame size of 1518 by four bytes, this is also not a problem. While developing the VLAN tag header specification, the IEEE engineers checked every Ethernet interface chip they could find and ascertained that they all could receive a 1522-byte frame without difficulty.

Type Field or Length Field

The next field in the Ethernet frame is either a type field or a length field. The following discusses how the different standards implement the type and/or length fields:

DIX standard

In the DIX Ethernet standard, this 16-bit field is called a *type field*, and always contains an identifier that refers to the type of high-level protocol data being carried in the data field of the Ethernet frame. For example, the hexadecimal value 0x0800 has been assigned as the identifier for the Internet Protocol (IP). A DIX frame being used to carry an IP packet is sent with the value of 0x0800 in the type field of the frame.

IEEE standard

When the IEEE 802.3 standard was first published in 1985, the type field was not included and instead the IEEE specifications called this field a *length field*. Type fields were added to the IEEE 802.3 standard in 1997, so the use of a type field in the frame is now officially recognized in 802.3. The identifiers used in the type field were originally assigned and maintained by Xerox, but now that the type field is part of the IEEE standard the responsibility for assigning type numbers has been transferred to the IEEE. In the most recent IEEE 802.3 standard this field is now called a Length/Type field, and the hexadecimal value in the field indicates the manner in which the field is being used.

If the value in this field is numerically equal to or less than the maximum untagged frame size in octets of 1518 (decimal), then the field is being used as a length field. In that case, the value in the field indicates the number of logical link control (LLC) data octets that follow in the data field of the frame. If the number of LLC octets is less than the minimum required for the data field of the frame, then octets of pad data will automatically be added to make the data field large enough. The content of pad data is unspecified by the standard. Upon reception of the frame, the length field is used to determine the length of valid data in the data field, and the pad data is discarded.

If the value in this field of the frame is numerically greater than or equal to 1536 decimal (0x600 hex), then the field is being used as a type field as specified in the original DIX standard. In that case, the hexadecimal identifier in the field is used to indicate the type of protocol data being carried in the data field of the frame. In the DIX standard the network software on the station is responsible for providing any pad data required to ensure that the data field is 46 bytes in length.

Data Field

Next comes the data field of the frame. The following discusses how the different standards implement the data field:

DIX standard

> In a DIX frame this field must contain a minimum of 46 bytes of data, and may range up to a maximum of 1500 bytes of data. The network protocol software is expected to provide at least 46 bytes of data.

IEEE standard

> The total data field of the IEEE 802.3 frame is the same length as the DIX frame: a minimum of 46 bytes and a maximum of 1500. However, a logical link control (LLC) protocol defined in the IEEE 802.2 LLC standard may ride in the data field of the 802.3 frame to provide control information. The LLC protocol is also used as a way to identify the type of protocol data being carried by the frame if the type/length field is used for length information. The LLC PDU is carried in the first set of bytes in the data field of the IEEE frame. The structure of the LLC PDU is defined in the IEEE 802.2 LLC standard.

The process of figuring out which protocol software stack gets the data in an incoming frame is known as *demultiplexing*. An Ethernet frame may use the type field to identify the high-level protocol data being carried by the frame. In the LLC specification, the receiving station demultiplexes the frame by deciphering the contents of the logical link control protocol data unit (PDU). These issues are described in more detail later in this chapter, in the section entitled "Multiplexing Data in Frames."

FCS Field

The last field in both the DIX and IEEE frame is the frame check sequence (FCS) field, which is also called the cyclic redundancy check, or CRC. This 32-bit field contains a value that is used to check the integrity of the various bits in the frame fields (not including preamble/SFD). This value is computed using the CRC, which is a polynomial that is calculated using the contents of the destination, source, type (or length), and data fields. As the frame is generated by the transmitting station, the CRC value is simultaneously being calculated. The 32 bits of the CRC value that are the result of this calculation are placed in the FCS field as the frame is sent. The x^{31} coefficient of the CRC polynomial is sent as the first bit of the field and the x^0 coefficient as the last bit.

The CRC is calculated again by the interface in the receiving station as the frame is read in. The result of this second calculation is compared with the value sent in the FCS field by the originating station. If the two values are identical, then the receiving station is provided with a high level of assurance that no errors have occurred during transmission over the Ethernet channel.

End of Frame Detection

The presence of a signal on the Ethernet channel is known as *carrier*. The transmitting interface stops sending data after the last bit of a frame is transmitted, which causes the Ethernet channel to become idle. In the 10 Mbps system, the loss of carrier when the channel goes idle signals the receiving interface that the frame has ended. When the interface detects loss of carrier, it knows that the frame transmission has come to an end.

The carrier sense signal may continue to be asserted by the transceiver for a short period beyond the end of the frame due to some delay in the electronics of the transceiver. If that happens, it's possible for the interface to read in some random noise as being one or more phantom bits past the actual end of the frame. These extra bits are called *dribble bits*.

The standard notes that the interface should truncate the received frame to the nearest octet boundary after the end of carrier sense, which discards the dribble bits (as long as there are fewer than eight dribble bits). If the CRC value in the received frame is correct, then the frame is accepted as valid. This mechanism allows the interface to throw away up to seven dribble bits that may appear at the end of a frame.

The Fast Ethernet and Gigabit Ethernet systems use more complex signal encoding schemes, which have special symbols available for signaling the start and end of a frame. In these systems, the interface detects the beginning and end of a frame by way of the special symbols that precede and follow a frame transmission. These signal encoding schemes are described in greater detail in Chapter 6, *Ethernet Media Fundamentals*.

Media Access Control Rules

Now that we've seen what the structure of a frame is, let's look at the rules used for transmitting a frame on a half-duplex shared Ethernet channel. When transmitting a frame the station goes through the following steps:

- When a signal is being transmitted on the channel, that condition is called *carrier*.

- When a station attached to an Ethernet wants to transmit a frame, it waits until the channel goes idle, as indicated by an *absence of carrier*.

- When the channel becomes idle, the station waits for a brief period called the *interframe gap* (IFG), and then transmits its frame.

- If two stations happen to transmit simultaneously, they detect the collision of signals and reschedule their frame transmission. This occurrence is referred to as *collision-detect.*

There are two major things an interface connected to a half-duplex channel must do when it wants to send a frame. It must figure out when it can transmit, and it must be able to detect and respond to a collision. We'll first look at how the interface figures out when to transmit, and then we'll describe the collision detect mechanism.

The rules governing when an interface may transmit a frame are simple:

1. If there is no carrier (i.e., the medium is idle) and the period of no carrier has continued for an amount of time that equals or exceeds the IFG, then transmit the frame immediately. If a station wishes to transmit multiple frames, it must wait for a period equal to the IFG between each frame.

   The IFG is provided to allow a very brief recovery time between frame reception for the Ethernet interfaces. IFG timing is set to 96 bit times. That is 9.6 microseconds (millionths of a second) for the 10 Mbps varieties of Ethernet, 960 nanoseconds (billionths of a second) for the 100 Mbps varieties of Ethernet, and 96 nanoseconds for Gigabit Ethernet.

2. If there is carrier (i.e., the channel is busy), then the station continues to listen until the carrier ceases (i.e., the channel is idle). This is known as *deferring* to the passing traffic. As soon as the channel becomes idle, the station may begin the process of transmitting a frame, which includes waiting for the interframe gap interval.

3. If a collision is detected during the transmission, the station will continue to transmit 32 bits of data (called the *collision enforcement jam signal*). If the collision is detected very early in the frame transmission, then the station will continue sending until it has completed the preamble of the frame, after which it will send the 32 bits of jam.

   Completely sending the preamble and transmitting a jam sequence guarantees that the signal stays on the media system long enough for all transmitting stations involved in a collision to recognize the collision and react accordingly.

   a. After sending the jam signal, the station waits a period of time chosen with the help of a random number generator and then proceeds to transmit again, starting over at step 1. This process is called *backoff.* The randomly chosen time makes it possible for colliding stations to choose different delay times, so they will not be likely to collide with one another again.

b. If the next attempt to transmit the frame results in another collision, then the station goes through the backoff procedure again, but this time the range of backoff times that are used in the random choice process will increase. This reduces the likelihood of another collision and provides an automatic adjustment mechanism for heavy traffic loads.

4. Once a 10 Mbps or 100 Mbps station has transmitted 512 bits of a frame (not including the preamble) without a collision, then the station is said to have acquired the channel. On a properly functioning Ethernet, there should not be a collision after channel acquisition. The 512-bit time value is known as the *slot time* of the Ethernet channel. Gigabit Ethernet extended the slot time for half-duplex Gigabit Ethernet channels. The Gigabit Ethernet extensions and half-duplex mode timing issues are described later in this chapter.

Once a station acquires the channel and transmits its frame, it also clears its collision counter, which was used to generate the backoff time. If it encounters a collision on the next frame transmission, it will start the backoff calculations anew.

Note that stations transmit their data one frame at a time, and that every station must use this same set of rules to access the shared Ethernet channel for each frame transmitted. This process ensures fair access to the channel for all stations, since all stations must contend equally for the next frame transmission opportunity after every frame transmission. The MAC protocol ensures that every station on the network gets a fair chance to use the network.

A half-duplex Ethernet operates as a logical signal bus in which all stations share a common signal channel. Any station can use the MAC rules to attempt to transmit whenever it wants to, since there is no central controller. However, for this process to work correctly, each station must be able to accurately monitor the condition of the shared channel. Most importantly, all stations must be able to hear the carrier caused by each frame transmission. In addition, the media system of an Ethernet must be configured to allow a station to receive news of a collision within a carefully specified amount of time, known as the slot time.

The slot time is based on the *maximum* round-trip signal propagation time of an Ethernet system. The actual round-trip propagation time for a given network system will vary, depending on the length and type of cabling in use, the number of devices in the signal path, and so on. The standard provides specifications for the maximum cable lengths and the maximum number of repeaters that can be used for each media variety. This ensures that the total round-trip time for any given

Ethernet built according to the standard will not exceed the maximum round-trip time incorporated in the slot time.

Essential Media System Timing

While signals travel very fast on an Ethernet, they still take a finite amount of time to propagate over the entire media system. The longer the cables used in the media system, the more time it takes for signals to travel from one end of the system to the other. The total round-trip time used in the slot time includes the time it takes for frame signals to go through all of the cable segments. It also includes the time it takes to go through all other devices, such as transceiver cables, transceivers and repeaters.

The maximum length for cable segments are carefully designed so that the essential signal timing of the system is preserved, even if you use maximum-length segments everywhere and the system is the largest allowed. The guidelines for each media variety incorporate the essential timing and round-trip signal delay requirements needed to make any half-duplex Ethernet up to the maximum-size system work properly. The cable segment guidelines are described in the media system chapters located in Part II, *Ethernet Media Systems*. The correct signal timing is essential to the operation of the MAC protocol, so let's look at the slot time in more detail.

Ethernet Slot Time

The total set of round-trip signal delays are summed up in the Ethernet slot time, which is defined as a combination of two elements:

- The time it takes for a signal to travel from one end of a maximum-sized system to the other end and return. This is called the *physical-layer round-trip propagation time.*

- The maximum time required by collision enforcement, which is the time required to detect a collision and to send the collision enforcement jam sequence.

Both elements are calculated in terms of the number of bit times required. Adding the two elements together plus a few extra bits for a fudge factor gives us a slot time that is 512 bit times for 10 and 100 Mbps systems. The Gigabit Ethernet slot time is described later in this chapter.

The time it takes to transmit a frame that is 512 bits long is slightly longer than the actual amount of time it takes for the signals to get to one end of a maximum size Ethernet and back. This includes the time required to transmit the jam sequence. Therefore, when transmitting the smallest legal frame, a transmitting station will always have enough time to get the news if a collision occurs, even if the colliding station is at the other end of a maximum-sized Ethernet.

The slot time includes the signal propagation time through the maximum set of components that can be used to build a maximum length network. If you use media segments longer than those specified in the standard, the result will be an increase in the round-trip time, and this could end up adversely affecting the operation of the entire system.

Any components or devices that add too much signal delay to the system can have the same negative effect. Smaller networks, on the other hand, will have smaller round-trip times, which means collision detection will occur faster and collision fragments will be smaller.

Slot Time and Network Diameter

The maximum network cable length and the slot time are tightly coupled. The 512 bit times were chosen as a trade-off between maximum cable distance and a minimum frame size. The total cable length allowed in a network system determines the maximum diameter of that system. The following discusses slot time and network diameter for the three types of Ethernet systems:

Original 10 Mbps slot time

In the original 10 Mbps system, signals could travel roughly 2800 meters (9,186 feet) of coaxial cable and back in 512 bit times, which provided a nice long network diameter.*

Fast Ethernet slot time

When the Fast Ethernet standard was developed in 1995, the slot time was kept at 512 bits, since changing the minimum frame length would have required changes in network protocol software, network interface drivers, and Ethernet switches.

However, signals operate ten times faster in Fast Ethernet, which means that a Fast Ethernet bit time is ten times smaller than a bit time in the 10 Mbps original Ethernet system. Since each bit time is ten times smaller, that means it is "on the wire" for only one-tenth of the time. As a result, 512 bits will travel over approximately one-tenth of the cable distance with a Fast Ethernet system, compared to original Ethernet. This results in a maximum network diameter of roughly 205 meters (672.5 feet) in Fast Ethernet.

This was considered acceptable, since by 1995 most sites were using twisted-pair cabling. The twisted-pair structured cabling standards limit segments to a

---

* The much shorter 100 m (328 feet) target length for 10BASE-T twisted-pair segments is based on signal quality limitations, and not round-trip timing.

maximum of 100 meters (328 feet), which meant that the smaller maximum diameter of a half-duplex Fast Ethernet system was not a major hardship. In Chapter 18 we'll show how twisted-pair segments can be connected to switching hubs, and you'll see how multiple LANs can be combined without exceeding a 205 meter network diameter per LAN.

Gigabit Ethernet slot time

When Gigabit Ethernet was developed, keeping the slot time at 512 bits would result in a maximum network diameter of roughly 20 meters (65.6 feet) for half-duplex operation. That's too short, since 20 meters won't reach very far in a typical building. However, all the good reasons for keeping the minimum frame size at 512 bits still existed.

In response to this dilemma, the Gigabit Ethernet standard came up with a mechanism that maintains the minimum frame size at 512 bits, while extending the slot time to 4096 bits (512 bytes). This is done with a system called *carrier extension*, which is described later in this chapter.

Use of the Slot Time

By using the slot time as a basic parameter in the media access calculations, the designers can guarantee that an Ethernet system will work properly under all possible legal combinations of standard network components and cable segments.

The slot time is used in several ways:

- The slot time establishes the maximum upper bound for a station to acquire the shared network channel. Once a station has transmitted a frame for 512 bit times (that is long enough for every station on a maximum-sized Ethernet to have heard it, and long enough for any news of a collision to have returned from the farthest end of the network back to the transmitting station), it is assured it has acquired the channel. Assuming that there has not been a collision, after 512 bit times all other stations will have sensed carrier and will defer to the carrier signal. The transmitting station can now expect to transmit the rest of the frame without a collision. The slot time sets the upper bound on 10 Mbps and Fast Ethernet channel acquisition to 512 bit times.

- The 512 bits of the slot time also serve as the basic unit of time used by the backoff algorithm to generate a waiting period after a collision has occurred. This algorithm is described later in this chapter.

- A valid collision can only occur within the 512-bit slot time, because once all stations on a network have seen the signal on the medium (*carrier*), they will defer to carrier and won't transmit. Since a valid collision can only happen within the first 512 bits of frame transmission, this also establishes an upper bound on the length of the frame fragment that may result from a collision.

Based on this, the Ethernet interface can detect and discard frame fragments generated by collisions as the fragments are smaller than 512 bits and are too short to be valid frames.

Slot Time and Minimum Frame Length

Setting the minimum frame length at 512 bits (not including preamble) meant requiring that the data field must always carry at least 46 bytes. A frame that is carrying 46 bytes of data will be 512 bits long, and therefore will not be regarded as a collision fragment. The 512 bits include 12 bytes of addresses, plus 2 bytes used in the type/length field, plus 46 bytes of data, plus 4 bytes of FCS. The preamble is not considered part of the actual frame in these calculations.

The requirement that each frame carry 46 bytes of data does not impose much overhead when you consider how the data field of a typical frame is used. For example, the minimum length for a typical set of IPv4 headers and TCP headers in a TCP/IP packet is 40 bytes, leaving 6 bytes to be provided by the application sending the TCP/IP packet. If the application only sends a single byte of data in the TCP/IP packet, then the data field needs to be "padded out" with 5 bytes of pad data to provide the minimum of 46 bytes. That's not a severe amount of overhead, and most applications will send enough data so that there is no pad data needed at all.

Collision Detection and Backoff

Collision detection and backoff is an important feature of the Ethernet MAC protocol. It's also a widely misunderstood and misrepresented feature. Let's clear up a couple of points right away:

- *Collisions are not errors.* Instead, collisions are a normal part of the operation of an Ethernet LAN. They are expected to happen, and collisions are handled quickly and automatically.

- *Collisions do not cause data corruption.* As we've just seen, when a collision occurs on a properly designed and implemented Ethernet, it will happen sometime in the first 512 bit times of transmission. Any frame transmission that encounters a collision is automatically resent by the transmitting station. Any frame less than 512 bits long is considered a collision fragment, and is automatically and silently discarded by all interfaces.

As noted in the last chapter, it's unfortunate that the original Ethernet design used the word "collision" for this aspect of the Ethernet MAC protocol. Despite the name, collisions are not a problem on an Ethernet. Instead, the collision detect and backoff feature is a normal part of the operation of Ethernet, and results in fast and automatic rescheduling of transmissions.

The collisions counted by a typical Ethernet interface are the ones that occur while that interface is trying to transmit a frame. Collision rates can vary widely, depending on the traffic rate on the Ethernet channel and on the number of transmitting stations. Even on very lightly loaded networks, collisions will occur occasionally. Collision rates may range anywhere from fractions of a percent of the number of frame transmissions on up to a larger percentage on heavily loaded networks. Collision rates can be significantly higher for very heavily loaded networks, such as a network supporting high-speed computers.

In any case, the thing to worry about is the total traffic load on the network. Since the collision rate is simply a reflection of the normal functioning of an Ethernet, the rate of collisions seen by a given interface is not significant. Chapter 19, *Ethernet Performance*, provides more information about measuring the performance of an Ethernet channel.

The Ethernet MAC mechanism, with its collision detect and backoff system, was designed to make it possible for independent stations to compete for access to the LAN in a fair manner. It also provides a way for stations to automatically adjust their behavior in response to the load on the network.

Operation of Collision Detect

Although the stations must listen to the network and defer to traffic (*carrier sense*), it is possible for two or more stations to detect an idle channel at the same instant and transmit simultaneously. A collision may occur during the initial part of a station's transmission, which is the 512-bit slot time, also called the *collision window*. The collision window lasts for the amount of time it takes for the signal from a station to propagate to all parts of the shared channel and back. Once the collision window has passed, the station is said to have acquired the channel. No further opportunity for collision should exist, since all other stations can be assumed to have noticed the signal (via carrier sense) and to be deferring to its presence.

Collision detection on media systems

The actual method used to detect a collision is medium-dependent. A link segment medium, such as twisted-pair or fiber optic Ethernet, has independent transmit and receive data paths. A collision is detected in a link segment transceiver by the simultaneous occurrence of activity on both transmit and receive data paths.

On a coaxial cable medium, the transceivers detect a collision by monitoring the average DC signal level on the coax. When two or more stations are transmitting simultaneously, the average DC voltage on the coax reaches a level that triggers

---

Collision Propaganda

The Ethernet collision algorithm is one of the least understood and most widely misrepresented parts of the entire system. You will sometimes see articles in networking magazines or trade journals that imply that Ethernets are littered with collided frames, or that the collision detection and resolution mechanism sets severe limits on the throughput of the system. Instead, the Ethernet collision detect mechanism is a normal part of the operation of an Ethernet.

If you find yourself reading such an article in which the word *collision* is presented as some sort of problem, try substituting the phrase *channel arbitration sensing* for each occurrence of the word "collision" in what you're reading. This might help clear up any misunderstandings, and may also reveal the cases in which a writer does not understand what collision detect really does in Ethernet. The collision detect and backoff mechanism is simply a fast and low-overhead way to resolve any simultaneous transmissions that occur on a network system that allows multiple access to the channel.

Those who claim collisions are a problem on Ethernet are usually unaware of how the system really works, or may have read reports that misrepresent the workings of the Ethernet system. Some of these reports have led to persistent myths about Ethernet performance that have no basis in fact. These myths are dealt with in more detail in Chapter 19. In reality, the collision backoff algorithm was designed to allow stations to respond automatically to varying traffic levels, allowing the stations to avoid one another's transmissions. The collision rate on a properly functioning Ethernet is simply a reflection of how busy the network is, and of how many stations are trying to access the channel.

---

the collision detect circuit in the coax transceiver. A coaxial transceiver continually monitors the average voltage level on the coaxial cable, and sends a collision detect signal to the Ethernet interface when the average voltage level indicates that multiple stations are simultaneously transmitting. This process takes slightly longer than collision detection on link segments; the increased time is included in the calculations used for total signal delay on a 10 Mbps Ethernet.

Late Collisions

Normal collisions occur during the first 512 bits of frame transmission. If a collision occurs after 512 bit times, then it is considered an error and called a *late collision*. A late collision is a serious error, since it indicates a problem with the network system, and since it causes the frame being transmitted to be discarded.

The Ethernet interface will not automatically retransmit a frame lost due to a late collision. This means that the application software must detect the lack of response due to the lost frame, and retransmit the information. This can take a significant amount of time, caused by waiting for the acknowledgment timers in the application software to time out and resend the information. Therefore, even a small number of late collisions can result in slow network performance. Any report of late collisions by devices on your network should be taken seriously, and the problem should be resolved as soon as possible.

Common causes of late collision

The most common cause of late collisions is a mismatch between the duplex configuration at each end of a link segment. For example, late collisions will occur if a station at one end of a link is configured for half-duplex operation, and a switch port on the other end of the link is configured for full-duplex. Full-duplex shuts off the CSMA/CD protocol and a full-duplex port sends data whenever it wants to. If the full-duplex end of the link happens to transmit while the half-duplex end is sending a frame and has acquired the channel, then the half-duplex end sees a late collision.

Late collisions can also be caused by problems with the media, such as a twisted-pair segment with excessive signal crosstalk. A twisted-pair transceiver detects collision by the simultaneous occurrence of traffic on the transmit and receive signal paths. Therefore, the occurrence of excessive signal crosstalk between the transmit and receive wire pairs can cause the transceiver to detect "phantom collisions." If the crosstalk takes long enough to build up to levels that will trigger the collision detection circuit, a late collision can be generated.

The Collision Backoff Algorithm

After a collision is detected, the transmitting stations reschedule their transmissions using the backoff algorithm to minimize the chances of another collision. This algorithm also allows a set of stations on a shared Ethernet channel to automatically modify their behavior in response to the activity level on the network. The more stations you have on a network, and the busier they are, the more collisions there will be. In the event of multiple collisions for a given frame transmission attempt, the backoff algorithm provides a way for a given station to estimate how many other stations are trying to access the network at the same time. This allows the station to adjust its rate of retransmission accordingly.

When the transceiver attached to the Ethernet senses a collision on the medium, it sends a collision presence signal back to the station interface. If the collision is sensed very early in the frame transmission, the transmitting station interface does not respond to a collision presence signal until the preamble has been sent completely. At this point, it sends out 32 bits of jam signal and stops transmitting. As a result, the collision signal will stay long enough for all other transmitting stations to see it. The stations involved in transmitting frames at the time of the collision must then reschedule their frames for retransmission. The transmitting stations do this by generating a period of time to wait before retransmission, which is based on a random number chosen by each station and used in that station's backoff calculations.

On busy Ethernet channels, another collision may occur when retransmission is attempted. If another collision is encountered, the backoff algorithm provides a mechanism for adjusting the timing of retransmissions to help avoid congestion. The scheduling process is designed to exponentially increase the range of backoff times in response to the number of collisions encountered during a given frame transmission.

The more collisions per frame, the larger the range of backoff times that will be generated for use by the station interface in rescheduling its next transmission attempt. This means that the more collisions that occur for a given frame transmission, the likelier it is that a station will wait longer before retrying. The name for this scheduling process is *truncated binary exponential backoff*. *Binary exponential* refers to the power of two used in the delay time selection process, while *truncated* refers to the limit set on the maximum size of the exponential.

Operation of the Backoff Algorithm

After a collision occurs, the basic delay time for a station to wait before retransmitting is set at a multiple of the 512 bit Ethernet slot time used in 10 and 100 Mbps Ethernet. Note that a bit time is different for each speed of Ethernet, occupying 100 nanoseconds on 10 Mbps Ethernet and 10 nanoseconds on Fast Ethernet.

The amount of total backoff delay is calculated by multiplying the slot time by a randomly chosen integer. The range of integers used in the choice is generated according to the rules of the backoff algorithm, which create a range of integers that increases in size after each collision that occurs for a given frame transmission attempt. The interface then randomly chooses an integer from this range, and the product of this integer and the slot time creates a new backoff time.

The backoff algorithm uses the following formula for determining the integer r, which is used to multiply the slot time and generate a backoff delay:

$$0 \leq r < 2^k$$

where $k = \min(n, 10)$.

To translate into something closer to English:

- r is an integer randomly selected from a range of integers. The value of r may range from zero to one less than the value of two to the exponent, k.

- k is assigned a value that is equal to either the number of transmission attempts or the number 10, whichever is less.

Let's walk through the algorithm and see what happens. Imagine that an interface tries to send a frame and a collision occurs. On the first retry of this frame transmission, the value for 2^k is two since the number of tries is one. (Two to the exponent one—2^1—gives us a result of two.) The range of possible integers to choose from for the first retry is set by the equation to anything from zero or greater, but less than two.

Therefore, on the first retry after a collision, the interface is allowed to randomly choose a value of r from the range of integers of zero to one. The practical effect is that after the first collision on a given frame transmission, the interface may wait zero slot times (i.e., zero microseconds [μs]), and reschedule the next transmission immediately. Alternatively, the station may wait one slot time, for a backoff time of 51.2 μs on a 10 Mbps channel.

If the network is busy due to a number of other stations trying to transmit, and the frame retransmission attempt happens to result in another collision, we're then on try number two. Now the random number r is selected from a set of values that range from zero to one less than the value of two to the exponent of two. As a result, this time around the interface may randomly choose the slot time multiplier from the set of numbers 0, 1, 2, 3. The integer that is chosen is used to multiply the slot time and develop a backoff time before retransmitting.

Therefore, if the interface sees a collision on the second attempt to transmit the same frame, it will randomly choose to wait zero, one, two, or three times the slot time before retransmitting again. This expansion in the range of integers is the part of the algorithm that provides an automatic adjustment for heavy network traffic loads and the repeated collisions that they cause.

Choosing a Backoff Time

Notice that the interface is *not* required always to pick a larger integer and develop a larger backoff time after each collision on a given frame transmission. Instead, what happens is that the *range* of integers to choose from gets larger and the *probability* that the interface will generate a longer backoff time increases. If a collision happens again for that frame attempt, the process continues with the value of k (and hence, the range of the number r) exponentially increasing for the first 10 retries of a given frame transmission attempt.

After ten retries, the value of k stops increasing, which represents the truncation of the algorithm. At this point 2^k is equal to 1024, so that r is being chosen from the range of numbers from 0 through 1023. If the frame continues to encounter collisions after 16 retries, the interface will give up. The interface discards the frame, reports a transmission failure for that frame to the high-level software, and proceeds with the next frame, if any.

On a network with a reasonable load, a station will typically acquire the channel and transmit its frame within the first few tries. Once the station has done so, it clears its backoff counter. If a station encounters a collision on its next frame transmission attempt, it will calculate a new backoff time.

Since an idle channel is instantly available to the first station that wants to send a frame, the MAC protocol provides very low access time when the offered load on the Ethernet channel is light. Stations wishing to transmit frames will experience longer wait times as the load on the channel increases based on the retransmission times generated by the backoff algorithm.

In effect, each station makes an estimate of the number of other stations that are providing a load on the channel. The backoff algorithm provides a way for stations to do this by allowing the stations to base the estimate on the one property of the network traffic that each station can easily monitor. That property is the number of times that a station has tried to send a given frame and has detected a collision. Table 3-1 shows the estimates that a station makes and the range of backoff times that may occur on a 10 Mbps channel.

Table 3-1. Maximum Backoff Times on a 10 Mbps System

Collision on Attempt Number	Estimated Number of Other Stations	Range of Random Numbers	Range of Backoff Times[a]
1	1	0...1	0...51.2 μs
2	3	0...3	0...153.6 μs
3	7	0...7	0...358.4 μs
4	15	0...15	0...768 μs
5	31	0...31	0...1.59 ms
6	63	0...63	0...3.23 ms
7	127	0...127	0...6.50 ms
8	255	0...255	0...13.1 ms
9	511	0...511	0...26.2 ms
10–15	1023	0...1023	0...52.4 ms
16	too high	N/A	discard frame

[a] Backoff times are shown in microseconds (μs) and milliseconds (ms).

As Table 3-1 shows, a station exponentially increases its estimate of the number of other stations that are transmitting on the network. After the range reaches 1023, the exponential increase is stopped, or truncated. The truncation provides an upper limit on the backoff time that any station will need to deal with. The truncation has another effect, since it means that there are 1024 potential "slots" for a station to transmit. This number leads to the inherent limit of 1024 stations that can be supported by a half-duplex Ethernet system.

After 16 tries, the station gives up the frame transmission attempt and discards the frame. By the sixteenth attempt, the network is considered to be overloaded or broken—there is no point in retrying endlessly.

All of the numbers used in the collision and backoff mechanism were chosen as part of worst-case traffic and population calculations for an Ethernet system. The goal was to determine reasonable time expectations for a single station to wait for network access. On smaller Ethernets with smaller host populations, the stations detect collisions faster. This leads to smaller collision fragments and more rapid resolution of collisions among multiple stations.

Now that we've seen how the Ethernet half-duplex timing works for 10 and 100 Mbps Ethernet, we'll look next at half-duplex operation for Gigabit Ethernet.

Gigabit Ethernet Half-Duplex Operation

The Gigabit Ethernet half-duplex mode uses the same basic CSMA/CD access mechanism as the 10 and 100 Mbps varieties of Ethernet, with the major exception of the slot time. The slot time in Gigabit Ethernet was modified to accommodate the special timing constraints which arise from the speed of the system.

Currently, all Gigabit Ethernet equipment is based on the full-duplex mode of operation described in Chapter 4. To date, none of the vendors have plans to develop equipment based on half-duplex Gigabit Ethernet operation. Nonetheless, a half-duplex CSMA/CD mode for Gigabit Ethernet has been specified, if only to insure that Gigabit Ethernet met the requirements for inclusion in the IEEE 802.3 CSMA/CD standard. For the sake of completeness, a description of Gigabit Ethernet half-duplex mode is provided here.

Gigabit Ethernet Half-Duplex Network Diameter

A major challenge for the engineers writing the Gigabit Ethernet standard was to provide a sufficiently large network diameter in half-duplex mode. As we've seen, the maximum network diameter (i.e., cable distance) between any two stations largely determines the slot time, which is an essential part of the CSMA/CD MAC mechanism.

Repeaters, transceivers and the interfaces have circuits that require some number of bit times to operate. The combined set of these devices used on a network takes a significant number of bit times to handle frames, respond to collisions, and so on. It also takes a small amount of time for a signal to travel over a length of fiber optic or metallic cable. All of this results in the total timing budget for signal propagation through a system, which determines the maximum cabling diameter allowed when building a half-duplex Ethernet system.

In Gigabit Ethernet, the signaling happens ten times faster than it does in Fast Ethernet, resulting in a bit time that is one-tenth the size of the bit time in Fast Ethernet. Without any changes in the timing budget, the maximum network diameter of a Gigabit Ethernet system would be about one-tenth of that for Fast Ethernet, or in the neighborhood of 20 meters (65.6 feet).

Twenty meters is usable within a single room, such as a machine room equipped with a set of servers. However, one of the goals for the Gigabit Ethernet system is to support a large enough half-duplex network diameter to reach from a Gigabit Ethernet hub to the desktop in a standard office building. Desktop cabling for office buildings is typically based on structured cabling standards, which require the ability to reach 100 meters from a hub port. This means that the total network diameter may reach a maximum of 200 meters when connecting two stations to a Gigabit Ethernet repeater hub.*

Looking for Bit Times

To meet the 200 meter half-duplex network diameter goal, the designers of the Gigabit Ethernet system needed to increase the round-trip timing budget to accommodate longer cables. If it was somehow possible to speed up the internal operations of devices, such as repeaters, then it might be possible to increase the bit timing budget. The idea is that you could save some bit times that are consumed when signals are sent through repeater hubs. Unfortunately, with today's technology, it is not possible to produce repeaters and other components with ten times less delay than equivalent Fast Ethernet devices.

The next place you might think of looking to save bit times is in the cable propagation delays. However, it turns out that the signal propagation delay through the cables cannot be reduced, as the delay is fundamentally based on the speed of light (which is notoriously difficult to improve).

Another way to gain time and achieve longer cable distance was in the minimum frame transmission specification. If the minimum frame time was extended then the Ethernet signal would stay on the channel longer. This would extend the round-trip time of the system and make it possible to achieve the 200 meter goal for the cabling diameter over twisted-pair cable. The problem with this scheme, however, is that changing the minimum frame length would make the frame incompatible with the other varieties of Ethernet—all of which use the same standard minimum frame length.

---

* Repeaters can only be used in a half-duplex, shared Ethernet channel. By definition, anything connected to a repeater hub must be operating in half-duplex mode.

Carrier Extension

The solution to this conundrum is to extend the amount of time occupied by the signal carrier associated with a minimum frame transmission, without actually modifying the minimum frame length or other frame fields. Gigabit Ethernet does this by extending the amount of time a frame signal is active on a half-duplex system with a mechanism called carrier extension, as shown in Figure 3-2. The frame signal, or *carrier*, is extended by appending non-data signals, called extension bits. Extension bits are used when sending short frames so that the frame signal stays on the system for a minimum of 512 bytes (4,096 bit times), which is the new slot time for Gigabit Ethernet. This slot time makes it possible to use longer cables, and is also used in the collision backoff calculations on Gigabit Ethernet systems.

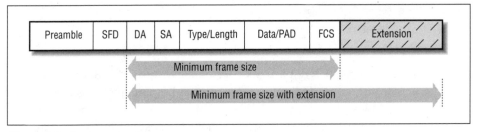

Figure 3-2. Carrier extension

The use of carrier extension bits assumes that the underlying physical signaling system is capable of sending and receiving non-data symbols. Signaling for all fiber optic and metallic cable Gigabit Ethernet systems is based on signal encoding schemes that provide non-data symbols that will trigger carrier detection in all station transceivers. This makes it possible to use these non-data symbols as carrier extension bits without having the extension bits confused with real frame data. These encoding schemes are described in more detail in Chapter 6.

With carrier extension, a minimum size frame of 64 bytes (512 bits) is sent on a Gigabit Ethernet channel along with 448 extension bytes (3,584 bits), resulting in a carrier signal that is 512 bytes in length. Any frame less than 4,096 bits long will be extended as much as necessary to provide carrier for 4,096 bit times (but no more).

Carrier extension is a simple scheme for extending the collision domain diameter; however, it adds considerable overhead when transmitting short frames. A minimum-size frame carrying 46 bytes of data is 64 bytes in length. Carrier extension adds another 448 bytes of non-data carrier extension bits when the frame is transmitted, which significantly reduces the channel efficiency when transmitting short frames.

The total impact on the channel efficiency of a network will depend on the mix of frame sizes seen on the network. As the size of the frame being sent grows, the number of extension bits needed during transmission of the frame is reduced. When the frame being sent is 512 bytes or more in length, no extension bits are used. Therefore, the amount of carrier extension overhead encountered when sending frames will vary depending on the frame size. Carrier extension is only used in half-duplex Gigabit Ethernet. In full-duplex mode the CSMA/CD MAC protocol is not used, which removes any concern about the slot time. Therefore, full-duplex Gigabit Ethernet links do not need carrier extension, and are able to operate at full efficiency.

Frame Bursting

The Gigabit Ethernet standard defines an optional capability called frame bursting to improve performance for short frames sent on half-duplex channels. This makes it possible for a station to send more than one frame during a given transmission event, improving the efficiency of the system for short frames. The total length of a frame burst is limited to 65,536 bit times plus the final frame transmission, which sets a limit on the maximum burst transmission time. Figure 3-3 shows how frame bursting is organized.

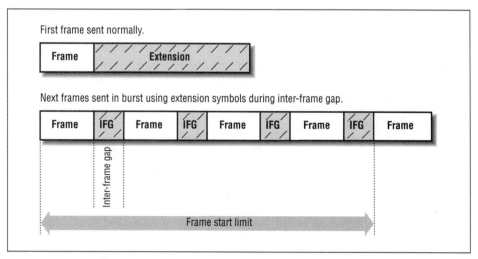

Figure 3-3. Frame bursting

Here's how the frame bursting system works. The first frame of the transmission is always sent normally, so that the first frame is sent by itself, and will be extended if necessary. Because collision always occurs within the first slot time, only this frame can be affected by a collision, requiring it to be retransmitted. This frame may encounter one or more collisions during the transmission attempt.

However, once the first frame (including any extension bits) is transmitted without a collision, then a station equipped with frame bursting can keep sending additional frames until the 65,536 bit time burst limit is reached. To accomplish this, the transmitting station must keep the channel from becoming idle between frame transmissions. If the station became idle during frame transmission, other stations would try to acquire the channel, leading to collisions.

The frame bursting station keeps the channel active by transmitting special symbols that are understood by all stations to be non-data symbols during the interframe gap times of the frames. This causes all other stations to continue to sense carrier (*activity*) on the channel. This, in turn, causes the other stations to continue deferring to passing traffic, allowing the frame bursting station to continue sending frames without concern that a collision will occur.

In essence, the first frame transmission clears the channel for the subsequent burst frames. Once the first frame has been successfully transmitted on a properly designed network, the rest of the frames in a burst are guaranteed not to encounter a collision. Frames sent within a burst do not require extension bits. The transmitting station is allowed to continue sending frames in a burst until the *Frame Burst Limit* (FBL) is reached, which is the time to the start of the last frame in the burst.

For short frames, the optional frame bursting mechanism can improve the utilization rate of the channel. However, this can only occur if the station software is designed to take advantage of the ability to send bursts of frames. Without frame bursting, a half-duplex Gigabit Ethernet channel is less than twice as fast as a Fast Ethernet channel for the shortest frame size. With frame bursting, the Gigabit Ethernet channel is slightly over nine times faster than the Fast Ethernet system for a constant stream of short frames.

Frame bursting and channel efficiency

Without frame bursting the channel efficiency is low for a Gigabit Ethernet channel carrying a constant stream of 64-byte frames (512 bits). It requires an overhead of one slot time to carry the 512 bit minimum size frame, which is 4096 bit times in the Gigabit Ethernet system. To this we add 64 bit times of preamble and 96 bit times of interframe gap, for a total of 4,256 bits of overhead. Dividing the 512 bit payload by the overhead of 4,256 bits reveals a 12 percent channel efficiency.

With frame bursting the Gigabit Ethernet channel is considerably more efficient for small frames, since a whole series of frames can be sent in a burst without overhead for the slot time once the channel is acquired. Theoretically, you could send 93 small frames in a single burst, with a channel efficiency of over 90 percent. However, it is unlikely that the smallest possible frames will dominate the traffic flow in the real world. Nor is it likely that a given station will have so many small frames to send that it can pack a frame burst full of them on a constant basis.

Remember, these limits only occur in half-duplex mode due to the round-trip timing requirements. Carrier extension is not needed in full-duplex mode, since full-duplex mode does not use CSMA/CD and is unconcerned about round-trip timing. A full-duplex Gigabit Ethernet system can operate at the full frame rate for all frame sizes, or ten times faster than a full-duplex Fast Ethernet system. Gigabit Ethernet performs quite well, particularly since the vendors of Gigabit Ethernet equipment support only the full-duplex mode of operation.

Collision Domain

A useful concept to keep in mind while working with Ethernet is the notion of *collision domain*. This term refers to a single half-duplex Ethernet system whose elements (cables, repeaters, station interfaces and other network hardware) are all part of the same signal timing domain. In a single collision domain, if two or more devices transmit at the same time a collision will occur. A collision domain may encompass several segments, as long as they are linked together with repeaters, as shown in Figure 3-4.

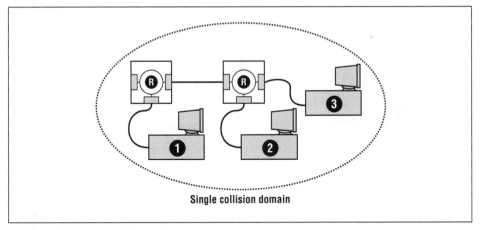

Figure 3-4. Ethernet collision domain

A repeater is a signal-level device that enforces the collision domain on the segments to which it is connected. The repeater only concerns itself with individual Ethernet signals; it does not make any decisions based on the addresses of the frame. Instead, a repeater simply retransmits the signals that make up a frame.

Repeaters make sure that the repeated media segments are part of the same collision domain by enforcing any collisions seen on any segment attached to the repeater. For example, a collision on segment A is enforced by the repeater sending a jam sequence onto segment B. As far as MAC protocol (including the collision detection scheme) is concerned, a repeater makes multiple network cable segments function like a single cable. Repeaters are described in more detail in Chapter 17, *Ethernet Repeater Hubs*.

On a given Ethernet composed of multiple segments connected with repeaters, all of the stations are involved in the same collision domain. The collision algorithm is limited to 1024 distinct backoff times. Therefore, the maximum number of stations allowed in the standard for a multi-segment LAN linked with repeaters is 1024. However, that doesn't limit your site to 1024 stations, because Ethernets can be connected together with packet switching devices such as switching hubs or routers.

As Figure 3-5 illustrates, the repeaters and computers are connected by means of a *switching hub*. These Ethernets are in separate collision domains since switching hubs do not forward collision signals from one segment to another. Switching hubs contain multiple Ethernet interfaces. They operate by receiving a frame on one Ethernet port, moving the data through the hub, and transmitting the data out another Ethernet port in a new frame.

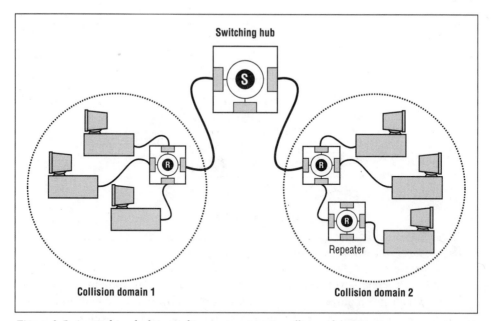

Figure 3-5. A switching hub is used to create separate collision domains

When you use a switching hub to link Ethernets, the linked Ethernets will each have their own separate collision domain. Unlike Ethernet repeaters, switching hubs do not enforce collisions onto their attached segments. Instead, individual

Ethernet systems attached to a switching hub function as separate network systems. Each Ethernet connected to a switch port can be as large as the standard allows. This means that you can use switches to link multiple Ethernets without being concerned about the sum of all stations attached to all of the Ethernets exceeding 1024 stations.

As long as switching hubs or routers are used to link the Ethernets, then the round-trip times and collision domains of those Ethernets are kept separate. This allows you to link a whole campus of Ethernet LANs without worrying about exceeding the guidelines for a single collision domain. You can use switching hubs to build large network systems by interconnecting individual Ethernet systems. The operating details of switching hubs are described in Chapter 18.

Ethernet Channel Capture

The Ethernet MAC protocol is a reliable, low overhead access control system that has proved its worth in millions of Ethernets. However, the MAC protocol is not perfect, and there are aspects of its operation that are not always optimal.

The best known example of this is an effect called *Ethernet channel capture*. Channel capture results in short-term unfairness, during which a station tends to consistently lose the competition for channel access. There must be one or more stations with a lot of data to send for channel capture to occur, causing them to contend for access the channel.

The sending station must also be able to continually transmit data at the maximum rate supported by the channel for short periods of time. Continuously sending data in this way sets up the collision and backoff conditions required for channel capture to occur. If the sending station does not have enough performance to continuously send data at the full rate supported by the channel, then the capture effect will not occur.

Operation of Channel Capture

An example of *channel capture* works as follows. If you look at all the stations on a channel when several active stations are simultaneously contending for access, you would expect to see collisions. Each station will possess a nonzero collision counter. As soon as one of the stations acquires the channel and delivers its frame, it clears its collision counter and starts over with a new frame transmission. The rest of the stations trying to transmit will still have nonzero collision counters.

If the *winning* station immediately returns to the channel contention with a collision counter of zero, it has an advantage over the other stations which have higher collision counters. The stations with higher collision counters will tend to choose longer backoff times before retrying their frame transmissions. The station that wins will return to the fray with a zero collision counter, and therefore tend to continue winning. This station will effectively *capture* the channel for a brief period.

This can only occur if the winning station can rapidly and continually transmit data, which requires a high-performance station with a lot of data to send. This is not a common scenario, since most stations typically send data in short bursts. This helps explain why channel capture was first noticed when artificially high network loads were created using performance test software. Another place channel capture may be seen is when a file server is generating large bulk data flows doing backups while various user machines are trying to access the same channel.

Let's look at a worst-case example of channel capture. Consider the case of two high-performance workstations which both have a significant amount of data to send. Both computers also have Ethernet interface cards and computer busses that permit them to send frames as fast as the Ethernet channel allows. On their first transmission they collide and choose a backoff of zero or one. Let's say Station A chooses backoff 0 and Station B chooses 1. In this case, A would transmit the frame while B waits for its 1 slot time. At the end of A's frame transmission, both A and B are ready to transmit again. They both wait for the interframe gap period, then transmit, collide, and backoff. This is A's first collision for this frame transmission attempt, so A will choose a backoff of 0 or 1. Assuming this is B's second collision, then B will choose a backoff integer from between 0 and 3.

There is a five in eight chance that A will pick a lower number than B; a two in eight chance that they choose the same number and collide again; and a one in eight chance that B will choose a lower number than A. Therefore, A will most likely win by picking a lower backoff time and transmit its frame. If they pick the same number and collide again, the odds get even worse for B.

Since we're assuming that these two stations have a lot of data to send, the process repeats again. Only this time it is still A's first attempt to transmit a new frame and poor station B is on attempt number three for its frame transmission. Each time station A succeeds, station B's disadvantage increases. Once A has transmitted three or four frames, then A will pretty much be able to transmit at will. B will continue losing the channel contentions until B's transmission attempts counter reaches 16 and station B discards the frame and starts over. At this point A and B are back on even terms, and the contention is fair again.

Long-Term Fairness

If you look at the channel arbitration during the 16 retries that B makes trying to send a frame, then the channel appears to be unfair. But over a period of several minutes both A and B will get about equal shares of the channel, since sometimes B will be the winner that gets to send a burst of packets. For most stations it does not appear that channel capture often results in a frame discard. Instead, the typical network application will tend to have less than 16 frames worth of data to send at any given time, and the channel capture will be of shorter duration.

Stations with slower network interfaces that cannot sustain a constant train of back-to-back frame transmissions will tend to break up the capture effect. As soon as a station ever pauses in its transmission attempts, then another station will be able to access the channel. Further, networks with high-performance computers are often segmented into smaller pieces using switching hubs, and the smaller populations on these segmented network channels are less likely to get involved in channel capture.

To really see channel capture at work may take an artificially high load, which is why channel capture may be seen with applications that test network throughput using a constant stream of data being sent between network test programs. For example, if channel capture occurs while measuring network performance using IP software, you could try setting the size of the "window" in the IP network software down to something around 8 Kbytes. This has the effect of reducing the total number of packets that will be sent at any given time, while not making any significant difference in throughput over a 10 Mbps channel. This, in turn, breaks up the capture effect and allows the network test program to provide the high throughput results that everyone was expecting.

A Fix for Channel Capture?

Over the years, channel capture has been studied intensely because of the potential bottlenecks it could create. Subsequently, a mechanism called Binary Logarithmic Arbitration Method (BLAM) was developed as a way to avoid channel capture. The BLAM mechanism eliminates the capture effect by changing the backoff rules to make access to the channel more fair. The result is to smooth the flow of packets on a busy network. The BLAM algorithm was designed to be backward compatible with existing Ethernet interfaces, so that mixed networks with standard Ethernet and BLAM-equipped interfaces could interoperate. A complete description of Ethernet channel capture and the BLAM algorithm can be found in a paper by Mart L. Molle, titled *A New Binary Logarithmic Arbitration Method for Ethernet.*[*]

An IEEE project called 802.3w was launched to study the implementation of BLAM and to decide whether to add BLAM to the official Ethernet standard. For a variety

---

[*] This paper is Technical Report CSRI-298 of the Computer Systems Research Institute, University of Toronto, Toronto, Canada, M5S 1A1. The paper is available online in PostScript format via anonymous FTP from *ftp://ftp.cs.toronto.edu/csri-technical-reports/298/* in two files: *paper.ps* and *figures.ps.*

of reasons it was decided not to standardize BLAM. For one thing, vendors were nervous about deploying a new Ethernet operational mode into the field. Despite simulations and lab tests of BLAM, the new algorithm had not been deployed extensively. What if unforeseen complications occurred? There are many millions of Ethernet nodes already in use, which makes vendors understandably conservative when it comes to changing how Ethernet works.

Meanwhile, reports from the field indicated that most customers were not encountering the capture effect, so it appeared that vendors would be going to significant effort and risk to solve a relatively rare problem. Many networks these days are segmented with switching hubs, thereby limiting the number of machines that are contending for access on any given channel and making it harder for channel capture to occur. It's also the case that higher speed Ethernet makes it more difficult for channel capture to occur. A given application and set of stations that can cause channel capture on a 10 Mbps network has to work ten times harder to capture the channel on a 100 Mbps network.

For that matter, high-performance computers and server systems in today's networks are typically connected directly to an Ethernet switch, with full-duplex mode of operation enabled on the link. Full-duplex mode does not use the Ethernet MAC protocol, which means the capture effect can never occur on these links. In the end, the shrinking benefits of adding BLAM appeared to be outweighed by the risks, and the BLAM spec was shelved.

High-level Protocols and the Ethernet Frame

A wide range of computers can use the same Ethernet system, with each computer "speaking" several different high-level network protocols. The process of identifying which high-level network protocol suite is being carried in the data field of the frame is called *multiplexing*. Multiplexing simply means that multiple sources of information can be placed onto a single system. In this case, multiple high-level protocols can be carried over the same Ethernet system.

Multiplexing Data in Frames

The original system of multiplexing for Ethernet is based on using the type field in the Ethernet frame. For example, the high-level protocol software can create a packet of IP data, and then hand the packet to the software on the computer that understands how to create Ethernet frames with type fields. The framing software inserts a hexadecimal value in the type field of the frame that corresponds to the type of high-level protocol being carried by the frame, and then hands the data to the interface driving software.

Best Effort Delivery

This is a good place to point out that the Ethernet MAC protocol does not provide a guaranteed data delivery service. Like most other LAN systems, Ethernet does not provide strict guarantees for the reception of all data. Instead, the Ethernet MAC protocol makes a "best effort" to deliver the frame without errors. If the channel becomes congested and the collision retry limit is reached, or if bit errors occur during transmission, then a frame may be dropped. Ethernet was designed this way to keep the basic frame transmission system as simple and inexpensive as possible, by avoiding the complexities of establishing guaranteed reception mechanisms at the link layer.

It is assumed that higher layers of network operation, such as TCP/IP, will provide the mechanisms needed to establish and maintain reliable data connections when required. Despite all this, the vast majority of Ethernets operate with very few bit errors or dropped frames. The physical signaling system is designed to provide a very low bit error rate. As long as the channel is not continually overloaded, the odds that the frame will make it to its destination without problems are quite high.

The Ethernet interface driver deals with the details of interacting with the Ethernet interface to send the frame over the Ethernet channel. When carrying packets from IP, the type field will be assigned the hexadecimal value 0x0800. The receiving station then uses the value in the type field to demultiplex the received frame.

In Figure 3-6, two computer systems, Michelson and Morley, are sending data to one another over an Ethernet. Each system supports both TCP/IP and AppleTalk. The TCP/IP system uses the type field. AppleTalk, on the other hand, uses a method of identifying frame data based on the LLC standard, which is described later in this chapter.

In the figure, Michelson wants to send data to Morley via a TCP/IP-based application (such as an email application or some automatic network software that the OS runs). The application hands the data to the TCP/IP software. The TCP/IP software creates a high-level protocol packet to transport the data, and hands the packet to the interface driver software for the particular network technology that Michelson is connected to: in this case, an Ethernet system. The interface driver software creates an Ethernet frame, containing the TCP/IP packet in the data field of the frame.

At this point we'll ignore the issue of how to find Morley's Ethernet address, and just assume that this has been accomplished. (The details of the address discovery process using the address resolution protocol (ARP) are described in Chapter 2.) The frame is then sent over the Ethernet, where it is received by the physical

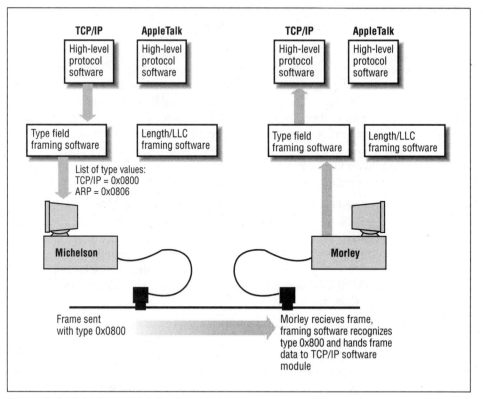

Figure 3-6. Multiplexing high-level protocols

network interface on Morley. The received frame is then handed to software that recognizes the type field, and hands the high-level protocol data carried by the frame to the appropriate high-level protocol software (such as TCP/IP). This is known as *demultiplexing*.

Each layer of the network system is substantially independent of the other layers. This independence is called *encapsulation*. By encapsulating the task performed by each layer, the complex system of network software can be broken down into more manageable chunks. By providing standardized operating system interfaces to the network programmers, the complexity of each network layer is effectively hidden from view.

The programmer is free to write software that hands the completed high-level protocol packet to the appropriate computer system software interface. The details of placing the protocol packet into the data field of an Ethernet frame are automatically dealt with. In this way, an IP-based application, and the IP software itself, can function without major changes regardless of which physical network system the computer happens to be attached to.

Things are made somewhat more complex because of the presence of two methods of identifying data in a frame: one using a type field to identify data, and one using the IEEE 802.2 Logical Link Control (LLC) standard. As you might expect, the mechanism used to identify data in the frame must be agreed upon by all the computers running the network software in question.

The most widely used high-level protocol today is TCP/IP, which uses the type field in the Ethernet frame. IP network software was originally developed on computers using the DIX Ethernet standard, which specified the use of a type field. IP network software continues to use the type field to the present day. By sticking with the type field, the IP software can continue to interoperate with other IP systems already in the field. Newer network protocols developed since the creation of the IEEE 802.2 LLC standard (e.g., AppleTalk), use the length field and LLC mechanisms for multiplexing and demultiplexing frame data.

Multiplexing Data with LLC

Since some network protocols use the LLC standard, you may encounter these frames when looking at the output of a network analyzer. To see how they work, we'll look next at the operation of a frame that uses the length/type field as a length field along with the LLC protocol.

As we've seen, the value of the identifier in the length/type field determines which way the field is being used. When used as a length field, the task of identifying the type of high-level protocol being carried in the frame is moved to the 802.2 LLC fields carried in the first few bytes of the data field. Let's look at the LLC fields in a little more detail (see Figure 3-7, below).

Figure 3-7 shows an IEEE 802.2 LLC protocol data unit, or PDU. The LLC PDU contains a Destination Service Access Point (DSAP), which identifies the high-level protocol that the data in the frame is intended for, much like the type field does. After a Source Service Access Point (SSAP) and some control data, the actual user data (the data that makes up the high-level protocol packet) follows the LLC fields.

When you are using the 802.2 LLC fields, multiplexing and demultiplexing work in the same way that they do for a frame with a type field. The difference is that the identification of the type of high-level protocol data is shifted to the SSAP, which is located in the LLC PDU. The whole LLC PDU fits inside the first few bytes of the data field of the Ethernet frame. In frames carrying LLC fields, the actual amount of high-level protocol data that can be carried is a few bytes less than in frames that use a type field.

You may be wondering why the IEEE went to all the trouble of defining the 802.2 LLC protocol to provide multiplexing when the type field seems to be able to do the job just as well. The reason is that the IEEE 802 committee was created to

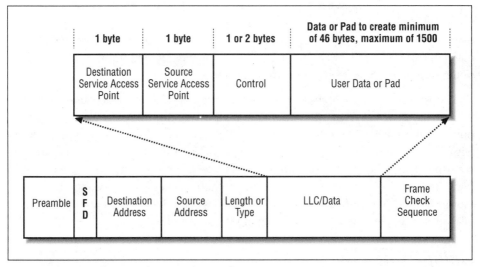

Figure 3-7. LLC PDU carried in an Ethernet frame

standardize a whole set of LAN technologies, and not just the 802.3 Ethernet sys-tem. To do that, they needed something that would work no matter which LAN technology was in use.

Since there was no guarantee that all LAN frames would have a type field, the IEEE 802 committee moved the task of identifying the type of data being carried by the frame into a LLC protocol. The LLC protocol defines a set of fields that are placed in the first few bytes of the data field. All LAN systems have a data field, which makes it easy enough to write network protocol software that can look at the first few bytes of data in the data field. The first few bytes of data are then interpreted in terms of the LLC specifications.

The interpretation of LLC fields is therefore identical no matter which LAN system is used. High-level network protocol implementations that were developed since the creation of the 802.2 standard in the 1980s typically use the LLC mechanisms. Therefore, if your site has a mix of computers running IP and, say, AppleTalk pro-tocols, you can expect to see both frames with type fields, and frames with length fields and LLC data, traveling over your Ethernet.

LLC Sub-Network Access Protocol

Just to make things more interesting, the 802.2 LLC protocol can also be used to carry type identifiers. In other words, when you send a frame on a non-Ethernet LAN technology that does not provide a type field in its frame, there's a way to use the LLC fields to provide a type identifier. The rationale for this approach comes from the fact that the LLC fields are not large. Given that limitation, the

IEEE didn't want to use up the limited number of bits in the LLC fields to provide identifiers for all of the older high-level protocol types. Instead, a method was created to preserve the existing set of high-level protocol type identifiers, and to reuse them in the IEEE LLC system.

This approach provides yet another set of bytes in the data field of the frame, known as LLC Sub-Network Access Protocol (SNAP) encapsulation. In SNAP, the contents of the LLC fields of the frame are used to identify another set of bits in the data field that are organized according to the SNAP specification. The SNAP fields are used to carry the older protocol type identifiers. The standard for the use of SNAP encapsulation via IP is documented in RFC 1042. Access to RFC documents is described in Appendix A, *Resources.*

If you're writing network protocol software, then SNAP encapsulation is a handy way to continue using the same high-level protocol type identifiers when sending frames over other LAN systems. In the Ethernet system itself, of course, you can simply use a frame with the type field, and you don't need to concern yourself with any of this. However, you will probably encounter SNAP encapsulation if you deal with multiple LAN systems at this level of detail.

As a network user, you don't need to lose sleep over which frame format your computers may be using. The choice of frame format is typically built into your networking software, in which case there's nothing you need to do about it.

4

In this chapter:
- Operation of Full-Duplex
- Ethernet Flow Control

Full-Duplex Ethernet

Full-duplex is an optional mode of operation allowing simultaneous communication between a pair of stations. The link between the stations must use a point-to-point media segment, such as twisted-pair or fiber optic media, to provide independent transmit and receive data paths. With full-duplex mode enabled, both stations can simultaneously transmit and receive, which doubles the aggregate capacity of the link. For example, a half-duplex Fast Ethernet twisted-pair segment provides a maximum of 100 Mbps of bandwidth. When operated in full-duplex, the same 100BASE-TX twisted-pair segment can provide a total bandwidth of 200 Mbps.

Another major advantage of full-duplex operation is that the maximum segment length is no longer limited by the timing requirements of shared channel half-duplex Ethernet. In full-duplex mode, the only limits are those set by the signal-carrying capabilities of the media segment. This is especially useful for fiber optic segments.

The optional full-duplex mode is specified in the 802.3x supplement to the standard, which formally describes the methods used for full-duplex operation. This supplement was approved for adoption into the IEEE 802.3 standard in March 1997. The 802.3x supplement also describes an optional set of mechanisms used for flow control over full-duplex links. The mechanisms used to establish flow control are called MAC Control and PAUSE. First we'll describe how full-duplex mode works, and then we'll show how the MAC Control and PAUSE mechanisms can be used to provide flow control over a full-duplex link.

Operation of Full-Duplex

The following requirements, as stated in the 802.3x standard, must be met for full-duplex operation:

- The media system must have independent transmit and receive data paths that can operate simultaneously. Such data paths are typically found on twisted-pair and fiber optic links.

- There are exactly two stations connected with a full-duplex point-to-point link. Since there is no contention for use of a shared medium, the multiple access algorithms (i.e., Carrier Sense with Multiple Access and Collision Detect, or CSMA/CD) are unnecessary.

- Both stations on the LAN are capable of, and have been configured to use, the full-duplex mode of operation. This means that both Ethernet interfaces must have the capability to simultaneously transmit and receive frames.

The original mode of Ethernet operation is half-duplex, based on CSMA/CD. The operation of CSMA/CD is described in detail in Chapter 3, *The Media Access Control Protocol.* In the CSMA/CD-based half-duplex mode of operation, only one station can transmit at any given time; other stations must defer until that transmission is complete.

Ethernet repeaters as defined in the IEEE 802.3 standard are not stations and cannot be operated in full-duplex mode. Ethernet repeaters simply pass Ethernet signals between attached segments, and a repeater can only operate in half-duplex mode.

Beware of confusing terms that you may find in advertising or network trade journals, such as "full-duplex repeater." Vendors have created devices which they call "buffered repeaters," "buffered distributors," and "full-duplex repeaters," but these are not true repeaters. The operation and configuration of these devices is not described in the Ethernet standard and system configuration guidelines. Instead, these devices typically operate as switching hubs. Switching hubs are described in Chapter 18, *Ethernet Switching Hubs.*

Figure 4-1 shows two stations simultaneously sending and receiving over a full-duplex link segment. The segment provides independent data paths so that both stations can be active without interfering with one another's transmissions. To provide full-duplex operation, both the station interface (*controller*) and the transceiver at each station must support and be configured for full-duplex operation.

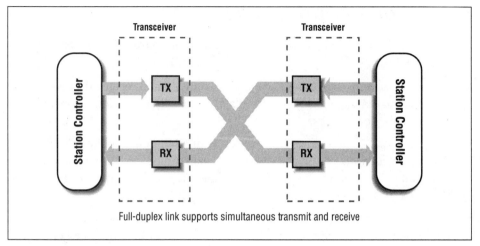

Figure 4-1. Full-duplex operation

When sending a frame in full-duplex mode, the station ignores carrier sense and does not defer to traffic being received on the channel. However, the station still waits for an interframe gap period between frame transmissions as Ethernet interfaces are designed to expect an interframe gap between each frame. Providing the interframe gap ensures that the interfaces at each end of the link can keep up with the full frame rate of the link. In full-duplex mode, the stations at each end of the link ignore any collision detect signals that come from the transceiver. If the transceiver has a collision detect light, then placing the transceiver in full-duplex mode means that the significance of the collision detect light is undefined, and the light should be ignored.

The CSMA/CD algorithm used on shared half-duplex Ethernet channels is not used on a link operating in full-duplex mode. A station on a full-duplex link sends whenever it likes, ignoring *carrier sense* (CS). There is no *multiple access* (MA) since there is only one station at each end of the link and the Ethernet channel between them is not the subject of access contention by multiple stations. Since there is no access contention, there will be no collisions either, so the station at each end of the link is free to ignore *collision detect* (CD).

Effects of Full-Duplex Operation

While full-duplex operation has the potential to double the bandwidth of an Ethernet link segment, it usually won't result in a large increase in performance on a link that connects to a user's computer. That's because most network protocols are designed to send data and then wait for an acknowledgment. This leads to asymmetric data patterns, in which most of the data is sent in one direction, and smaller amounts of data (in the form of acknowledgments) return in the other direction.

On the other hand, full-duplex links between switching hubs in a network backbone system will typically carry multiple conversations between many computers. Therefore, the aggregated traffic on backbone channels will be more symmetric, with both the transmit and receive channels seeing roughly the same amount of traffic. For that reason, the largest benefit of a full-duplex bandwidth increase is usually seen in backbone links.

Nonetheless, configuring a link to a user's computer for full-duplex operation can still be useful. For example, if it's a modern computer capable of placing a heavy load on an Ethernet channel, it might encounter the Ethernet capture effect described in Chapter 3. Configuring full-duplex mode shuts off the CSMA/CD algorithm and avoids any problems with capture effect.

Configuring Full-Duplex Operation

It is essential that both ends of a link operating in full-duplex mode are configured correctly, or the link will have serious data errors. To ensure correct configuration, the standard recommends that Ethernet Auto-Negotiation (see Chapter 5, *Auto-Negotiation*) be used whenever possible to automatically configure full-duplex mode.

However, using Auto-Negotiation to configure full-duplex operation on a link may not be as simple as it sounds. For one thing, support for Auto-Negotiation is optional for most Ethernet media systems, in which case the vendor is not required to provide Auto-Negotiation capability. Furthermore, Auto-Negotiation was originally developed for twisted-pair Ethernet devices only, and thus it is not supported on all Ethernet media types. The 10 Mbps and 100 Mbps fiber optic media systems do not support the Auto-Negotiation standard, while Gigabit Ethernet fiber optic systems have their own auto-configuration scheme. Therefore, you may find that you have to manually configure full-duplex support on the station at each end of the link.

On a manually configured link, it is essential that both ends of the link be properly configured for full-duplex operation. If only one end of the link is in full-duplex mode, and the other is in half-duplex mode, then the half-duplex end of the link will lose frames due to errors, such as late collisions. Data will still flow across the link, but as the full-duplex end will be sending data whenever it pleases, it will not be obeying the same CSMA/CD rules as the half-duplex end. Because the misconfigured link will still support the flow of data (despite the errors), it is possible that this problem may not be detected right away. Therefore, you need to be aware that this condition can occur, and make absolutely sure that both ends of a manually configured link are set for the same mode of operation.

At each end of the link, you must also ensure that *both* the Ethernet interface and the transceiver are configured for full-duplex operation. This can be difficult in some cases, since the 10 Mbps Attachment Unit Interface (AUI) used between an Ethernet interface and an external transceiver was designed before full-duplex mode was developed and does not support automatic full-duplex configuration.[*]

For this reason, the standard recommends that only 10 Mbps Ethernet interfaces with built-in transceivers be used for full-duplex segments. That's because the 15-pin AUI connector used to connect to external transceivers does not provide any way for the Ethernet interface in the station to discover the capabilities of the external transceiver and to correctly set the mode of the transceiver. As a result, when using an external transceiver with a 15-pin connection, you could end up with a transceiver in half-duplex mode connected to an interface in full-duplex mode. On the other hand, the newer 40-pin Medium Independent Interface (MII), which supports both 10 and 100 Mbps Ethernet systems, makes it possible for the interface to detect and set the operational mode of an external transceiver.

If an external transceiver is used, then it is essential that the mode of operation of the Ethernet interface and the transceiver at a given station match. There can be problems if an Ethernet interface in full-duplex mode is connected to a transceiver in half-duplex mode, or if the station interfaces are not in the same mode. The standard notes that this sort of confusion

> …can lead to severe network performance degradation, increased collisions, late collisions, CRC errors, and undetected data corruption.[†]

Full-Duplex Media Support

Table 4-1 provides a complete list of Ethernet media systems, and shows which ones can support the full-duplex mode of operation.

Full-Duplex Media Segment Distances

When a segment is operating in full-duplex mode, the CSMA/CD-based MAC is shut off. As a result, cable length limits imposed by the round-trip timing constraints of the CSMA/CD algorithm no longer exist. Since there is no round-trip timing limit, the only limit on the length of the cabling is the one imposed by the signal transmission characteristics of the cable. For that reason, some full-duplex segments can be much longer than the same segments operated in half-duplex mode.

---

[*] Media system connectors are described in detail in Chapter 6, *Ethernet Media Fundamentals*.

[†] 802.3x Full-Duplex supplement to IEEE Std 802.3 (1996), p. 57.

Table 4-1. Full-Duplex Media Support

Media System	Cable Type	Full-Duplex Support?
10BASE5	50 ohm thick coaxial cable	No
10BASE2	50 ohm thin coaxial cable	No
10BASE-T	2-pair Category 3/4/5 twisted-pair	Yes[a]
10BASE-FL	2 multimode optical fibers (MMF)	Yes[a]
10BASE-FB[b]	2 multimode optical fibers	No
10BASE-FP[c]	2 multimode optical fibers	No
10BROAD36[b]	75 ohm coaxial cable	No
100BASE-TX	2-pair Category 5 twisted-pair	Yes
100BASE-FX	2 multimode optical fibers	Yes
100BASE-T4[b]	4-pair Category 3 twisted-pair	No
100BASE-T2[c]	2-pair Category 3/4/5 twisted-pair	Yes
1000BASE-SX	2 multimode optical fibers	Yes
1000BASE-LX	2 MMF or single-mode optical fibers	Yes
1000BASE-CX	2-pair shielded twisted-pair	Yes
1000BASE-T	4-pair Category 5 twisted-pair	Yes

[a] Although the media system supports full-duplex mode, an external transceiver with a 15-pin AUI interface must be specifically configured for full-duplex operation. More modern external transceivers with 40-pin MII interfaces are automatically configured by the station interface.

[b] The 10BASE-FB, 10BROAD36 and 100BASE-T4 equipment was sold only by a few vendors, and these media systems are not widely used.

[c] The 10BASE-FP and 100BASE-T2 media systems were never developed by any vendor, and are not deployed.

Twisted-pair segments are limited in distance due to the signal carrying characteristics of the cable, and cannot be extended in length when operated in full-duplex mode. A maximum cabling distance recommendation of 100 meters (328 feet) for unshielded twisted-pair cable is common to the 10BASE-T, 100BASE-TX and 1000BASE-T media systems. Due to the restricted signal carrying capability of twisted-pair cable, the maximum limit for a twisted-pair cable segment is the same whether the segment is operated in full-duplex or half-duplex mode.

Fiber optic segments, on the other hand, have very good signal carrying characteristics and are mostly limited in length by the timing constraints of half-duplex operation. For that reason, a full-duplex mode fiber optic segment can be considerably longer than the same segment type operating in half-duplex mode. As an example, a 100BASE-FX fiber optic segment using a typical multimode fiber optic cable is limited to segment lengths of 412 meters (1351.6 feet) in half-duplex mode. However, the same media system can reach as far as 2 km (6561.6 feet) when operated in full-duplex mode.

Single-mode fiber optic media can carry signals over longer distances than multi-mode fiber. Therefore, a full-duplex fiber link can be stretched considerably further if single mode fiber media is used. In the case of a 100BASE-FX link, single-mode fiber can provide link distances of 20 km or more. For full-duplex links, you need to consult the equipment vendor for specifications on the maximum length of the segment.

Ethernet Flow Control

The rate of traffic on network backbones is always growing, and as a result backbone switches connected together with full-duplex links can be heavily loaded with traffic. A switching hub typically has a fixed set of resources, in the form of internal switching bandwidth and packet buffers, which it apportions to its switching ports. Resources like packet buffer memory are expensive, and many low-cost switches limit these resources. To keep these limited resources from being overwhelmed, a variety of non-standard flow control mechanisms were developed by switching hub vendors for use on half-duplex segments. These include the use of a short burst of carrier signal sent by the switching hub to cause stations on a half-duplex segment to stop sending data when the buffers on a switching port are full. These mechanisms are described in more detail in Chapter 18.

This sort of mechanism is based on the half-duplex mode of operation—it will not work on a full-duplex segment that is not using the CSMA/CD algorithm and ignores things like carrier. As a result, a switching hub connected to full-duplex segments needs a new mechanism to send a flow control message. To that end, an explicit flow control message is provided by the optional MAC Control and PAUSE specifications in the 802.3x Full-Duplex supplement.

MAC Control Protocol

The optional MAC Control portion of the 802.3x supplement provides a mechanism for real-time control and manipulation of the frame transmission and reception process in an Ethernet station. In normal Ethernet operation, the media access control (MAC) protocol defines how to go about transmitting and receiving frames. In the optional Ethernet flow control system, the MAC Control protocol provides mechanisms to control when Ethernet frames are sent.

When implemented, the MAC Control system provides a way for the station to receive a MAC Control frame and act upon it. The operation of the MAC Control system is transparent to the normal media access control functions in a station. MAC Control is not used for a non-real-time function like configuring interfaces, which is handled by network management mechanisms. Instead, MAC Control is designed to allow stations to interact in real time to control the flow of traffic. New functions beyond flow control may be added in the future.

MAC Control frames are identified with a type value of 0x8808 (hex). A station equipped with optional MAC Control receives all frames using the normal Ethernet MAC functions, and then passes the frames to the MAC Control software for interpretation. If the frame contains the hex value 0x8808 in the type field, then the MAC Control function reads the frame, looking for MAC Control operation codes carried in the data field. If the frame does not contain the 0x8808 value in the type field, then MAC Control takes no action, and the frame is passed along to the normal frame reception software on the station.

MAC Control frames contain operational codes (*opcodes*) in the data field of the frame. The frame size is fixed at the minimum frame size allowed in the standard, which is 46 bytes. The opcode is contained in the first two bytes of the data field. There is no reliable transport mechanism, so MAC Control must be able to deal with the fact that MAC Control frames may be lost, discarded, damaged, or delayed.

PAUSE Operation

The PAUSE system of flow control on full-duplex link segments is defined in 802.3x and uses MAC Control frames to carry the PAUSE commands.* The MAC Control opcode for a PAUSE command is 0x0001 (hex). A station that receives a MAC Control frame with this opcode in the first byte of the data field knows that the control frame is being used to implement the PAUSE operation, for the purpose of providing flow control on a full-duplex link segment. Only stations configured for full-duplex operation may send PAUSE frames.

When a station equipped with MAC Control wishes to send a PAUSE command, it sends a PAUSE frame to the 48-bit destination multicast address of 01-80-C2-00-00-01. This particular multicast address has been reserved for use in PAUSE frames. The use of a well-known multicast address simplifies the flow control process by making it unnecessary for a station at one end of the link to discover and store the address of the station at the other end of the link.

Another advantage of using this multicast address arises from the use of flow control on full-duplex segments between switching hubs. The particular multicast address used is selected from a range of addresses which have been reserved by the IEEE 802.1D standard (which specifies the operation of switching hubs).

---

* "PAUSE" is not an acronym. Instead, PAUSE is written in uppercase letters to indicate that the word is a formally defined function in the full-duplex Ethernet standard. This is common practice for formally defined words and phrases in the standard.

Normally, a frame with a multicast destination address that is sent to a switch will be forwarded out all other ports of the switching hub. However, this range of multicast addresses is special and will not be forwarded by an 802.1D-compliant switch. Instead, frames sent to this address are understood by the switch to be frames meant to be acted upon within the switch.

A station sending a PAUSE frame to the special multicast address includes the PAUSE opcode, and also includes the period of pause time being requested, in the form of a two byte integer. This number contains the length of time for which the receiving station is requested to stop transmitting data. The pause time is measured in units of pause "quanta," where each unit is equal to 512 bit times. The range of possible pause time requests is from 0 through 65,535 units.

Figure 4-2 shows what a PAUSE frame looks like. The PAUSE fields are carried in the data field of the MAC Control frame. The MAC Control opcode of 0x0001 indicates that this is a PAUSE frame. The PAUSE frame carries a single parameter, defined as the *pause_time* in the standard. In this example, the contents of *pause_ time* is 2, indicating a request that the device at the other end of the link stop transmitting for a period of two slot times.

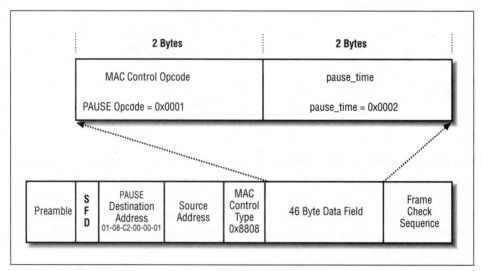

Figure 4-2. PAUSE frame

By using MAC Control frames to send PAUSE requests, a station at one end of a full-duplex link can request the station at the other end of the link to stop transmitting data for a period of time. This provides real-time flow control between switching hubs, or even between a switching hub and a server which are equipped with the optional MAC Control software and connected by a full-duplex link.

5

Auto-Negotiation

Automatic configuration of Ethernet equipment is provided by the Auto-Negotiation protocol, which is defined in the Ethernet standard. This chapter describes the Auto-Negotiation protocol, and shows how automatic configuration functions. The need for an automatic configuration system becomes obvious when you consider the challenge facing someone who is installing a desktop computer and connecting it to an Ethernet system.

Among the things the installer needs to know are which speed should be set on the Ethernet interface and whether full-duplex mode should be enabled. However, these features are embedded in the network equipment and are invisible to the installer. One twisted-pair port looks a lot like another, and it is not obvious which network options may be supported. The Auto-Negotiation protocol allows Ethernet equipment to automatically select the correct speed and other features, thus relieving the installer of this configuration task.

Development of Auto-Negotiation

The specifications for Auto-Negotiation were first published in 1995 as part of the 802.3u Fast Ethernet supplement to the IEEE standard. These specifications were based on an automatic configuration system called *NWay*, which was invented by National Semiconductor. Engineers working on the standard found that an automatic configuration signaling system could be readily developed that would work on twisted-pair links. Therefore, all Ethernet media systems that use twisted-pair media can also support the Auto-Negotiation signals. However, fiber optic links use a variety of light sources and optical wavelengths, which do not interoperate.

That, in turn, makes it impossible to develop an automatic configuration signaling system that works on all fiber optic links.

For that reason, there is no IEEE standard Auto-Negotiation support for most fiber optic link segments. The only exception is the Gigabit Ethernet fiber optic automatic configuration system, which is described later in this chapter. Given that the vast majority of desktop computers are connected to twisted-pair link segments, the Auto-Negotiation standard is still very useful even without a 10- or 100 Mbps fiber optic link negotiation capability.

Basic Concepts of Auto-Negotiation

Auto-negotiation makes it possible for Ethernet stations to exchange information about their capabilities over a link segment. This, in turn, allows the stations to perform automatic configuration to achieve the best possible mode of operation over a link. At a minimum, Auto-Negotiation can provide automatic speed matching for Ethernet devices at each end of a link. By using this mechanism, an Ethernet-equipped computer can take advantage of the highest speed offered by a multi-speed switching hub port.

The Auto-Negotiation standard includes automatic sensing of other capabilities as well. For example, a switching hub capable of supporting full-duplex operation on some or all of its ports can advertise that fact using Auto-Negotiation. Stations connected to the hub that also support full-duplex operation can then automatically configure themselves to use the full-duplex mode in interaction with the hub.

Automatic configuration makes it possible to build twisted-pair Ethernet interfaces that can automatically support several speeds. Many switching hubs now support multiple Ethernet speeds on their twisted-pair ports, with the most common configuration being a combination of 10BASE-T and 100BASE-TX. Most twisted-pair Ethernet interfaces for computers are also being provided with this capability. With the development of the twisted-pair Gigabit Ethernet standard, vendors are now building twisted-pair ports and interfaces that can automatically configure themselves to operate at any one of three speeds: 10-, 100-, and 1000 Mbps.

Operation of the Auto-Negotiation system includes the following basic concepts:

- *Operation over link segments.* Auto-Negotiation is designed to work over link segments only. A link segment can only have two devices connected to it—one at each end.

- *Auto-Negotiation occurs at link initialization.* When a device is turned on, or an Ethernet cable is connected, the link is initialized by the Ethernet devices at each end of the link. Link initialization and Auto-Negotiation occurs once, prior to any data being sent over the link.

- *Auto-Negotiation uses its own signaling system.* Each Ethernet media system has a particular method of sending signals over the cable. However, the Auto-Negotiation system uses its own, independent signaling system designed for twisted-pair cabling. These signals are sent once, at link initialization time.

When describing the operation of Auto-Negotiation, the device at the opposite end of a link from a local device is called the *link partner.* Figure 5-1 shows two link segments. Each link segment has two devices: a computer at one end and a switching hub at the other.

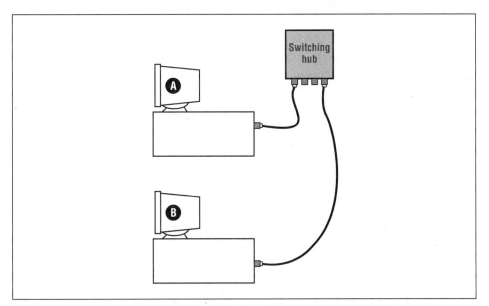

Figure 5-1. Auto-Negotiation link partners

Using the Auto-Negotiation protocol, each device advertises its capabilities to the link partner at the other end of the link. The protocol then selects the highest common denominator between the devices at each end of the link. Let's assume that station A only supports 10BASE-T operation and station B only supports 100BASE-TX. Let's further assume that the ports on the switching hub can support both 10BASE-T and 100BASE-TX. With Auto-Negotiation, both computers can automatically configure themselves for the highest performance possible over their respective links to the hub.

Auto-Negotiation Signaling

The Auto-Negotiation protocol uses *Fast Link Pulse* (FLP) signals to carry information between the devices at each end of a link. These signals are a modified version of the *Normal Link Pulse* (NLP) signals used for verifying link integrity in the 10BASE-T system.

The FLPs used to carry Auto-Negotiation information are specified for the following twisted-pair media systems:

- 10BASE-T

- 100BASE-TX (using unshielded twisted-pair)

- 100BASE-T4

- 100BASE-T2

- 1000BASE-T

With the exception of the fiber optic Gigabit Ethernet system, there is no IEEE Auto-Negotiation standard for any other fiber optic Ethernet segments. Also, a 100BASE-TX segment based on shielded twisted-pair cable and 9-pin connectors (allowed in the 100BASE-TX specifications) will not support Auto-Negotiation.

FLP Operation

Fast link pulses are sent in bursts, consisting of 33 short pulses. Each pulse is 100 nanoseconds wide. The timing between each burst is the same as the timing between NLPs. This timing, along with the fact that an individual FLP pulse looks like a NLP, convinces a 10BASE-T device that it is receiving an NLP. This provides backward compatibility with older 10BASE-T equipment that does not support Auto-Negotiation.

The burst of FLP signals is used to send information about device capabilities. An FLP burst contains 33 pulse positions, of which the 17 odd-numbered pulse positions each contain a link pulse that represent clock information. The 16 even-numbered pulse positions carry data, where the presence of a pulse in an even-numbered pulse position represents a logic 1, and the absence of a pulse represents a logic 0. This encoding scheme is used to transmit 16-bit *Link Code Words*, or messages, that contain the Auto-Negotiation information.

When link initialization occurs, the Auto-Negotiation protocol sends as many 16-bit messages as are needed. However, many media systems can complete the negotiation in the first message, or *base page*. Figure 5-2 shows what the base page message looks like. The 16 bits are labeled D0 through D15. Bits D0 through D4 are used as a *Selector Field* which identifies the type of LAN technology in use. This field allows the Auto-Negotiation protocol to be extended to other LANs in the future. For Ethernet, the S0 position of the Selector Field is set to 1, and all other Selector Field positions are set to 0.

D0	D1	D2	D3	D4	D5	D6	D7	D8	D9	D10	D11	D12	D13	D14	D15
S0	S1	S2	S3	S4	A0	A1	A2	A3	A4	A5	A6	A7	RF	Ack	NP

Figure 5-2. Auto-Negotiation base page message

The 8-bit field from D5 through D12 of the base page message is called the *Technology Ability Field*. The bits in this field are identified as A0 through A7, and are used to indicate support for various technologies, as shown in Table 5-1. If a device supports one or more of these capabilities, it sets the corresponding bit to 1. An auto-negotiating device uses these bits to advertise all of its capabilities in a single base page message.

Table 5-1. Base Page Technology Ability Field

Bit	Technology
A0 (D5)	10BASE-T
A1 (D6)	10BASE-T full-duplex
A2 (D7)	100BASE-TX
A3 (D8)	100BASE-T full-duplex
A4 (D9)	100BASE-T4
A5 (D10)	PAUSE operation for flow control
A6 (D11)	Reserved
A7 (D12)	Reserved

Bit D13 of the base page message is the *Remote Fault Indicator*. This bit may be sent by the remote link partner to indicate that the partner has detected a fault at the remote end. For example, Station "B" in Figure 5-1 could set the RF bit to 1 to signal to the switching hub that the receive side of the link to the station had failed.

Bit D14 is the *Ack* bit, and is used to acknowledge receipt of the 16-bit message. Negotiation messages are sent repeatedly until the link partner acknowledges them, which completes the Auto-Negotiation process. The link partner sends an acknowledgement after three consecutive messages are received that contain identical information. This helps ensure that the Auto-Negotiation process will receive messages correctly even if some bit errors are encountered during the negotiation process.

The final bit in the base page message is D15, which is used to signal the *Next Page*. Capabilities that are not listed in the base page Technology Ability Field may be advertised in one or more additional Next Page messages. The Next Page protocol provides the ability to send vendor-specific commands, or any new configuration commands that may be required as the Ethernet system evolves. For example, the 1000BASE-T Gigabit Ethernet system uses the Next Page protocol to advertise and configure twisted-pair Gigabit Ethernet capabilities.

If a device implements the Next Page ability and wishes to send a Next Page message, it sets the NP bit to a value of 1. The Next Page protocol consists of a two message sequence. The "Message Page" indicates the number and type of "Unformatted Pages" which may follow. The Unformatted Pages contain the data being exchanged between the link partners. Two acknowledgement messages are provided as part of the Next Page exchange. The first acknowledges receipt of the messages, and the second indicates whether the receiver was able to act upon the information or perform the task defined in the Next Page message.

Once the stations have completed the Auto-Negotiation process, additional bursts of FLPs will not be sent over the link. The Auto-Negotiation system continuously monitors the link status, and can detect when a link goes down and comes back up, as when, for example, a link outage is caused by disconnecting the patch cord to a station. Once a link comes back up, the Auto-Negotiation process will take place again using a burst of FLPs.

As we've just seen, Auto-Negotiation is performed automatically when the equipment is powered on, as well as at any time that link status has indicated that the link is up. Auto-Negotiation can also be triggered manually at any time through the management interface to an Auto-Negotiation device. This is done by toggling the link status, which causes the link to re-initialize.

Auto-Negotiation Operation

The Auto-Negotiation protocol contains a set of priorities which result in the devices selecting their highest common set of abilities. When two Auto-Negotiation devices with multiple capabilities are connected, they find their highest common denominator (HCD) based on a priority table that is specified in the standard. The priority is assigned by technology type, and is not based on the bit ordering in the Technology Ability Field of the base message.

The priorities defined in the standard are listed below, ranking from the highest to the lowest priority:

- 1000BASE-T full-duplex
- 1000BASE-T
- 100BASE-T2 full-duplex
- 100BASE-TX full-duplex

- 100BASE-T2
- 100BASE-T4
- 100BASE-TX
- 10BASE-T full-duplex
- 10BASE-T

All IEEE twisted-pair Ethernet technologies are listed, whether or not they have been successful in the marketplace. Therefore, you will find media systems listed here that are not widely deployed, or that have never been sold. The rationale for the ranking of priorities is based on finding the highest performance among the common set of technologies supported at each end of the link. For example, the full-duplex mode of operation for a given media system is always given higher priority, since the full-duplex system can send more data than a half-duplex link operating at the same speed. If auto-negotiating devices at both ends of the link can support full-duplex operation, then they will automatically configure themselves for the higher-performance full-duplex mode.

The above priority list shows that if both devices on the link advertise that they can support 10BASE-T and 100BASE-TX, then the Auto-Negotiation protocol in the link partners will connect using the 100BASE-TX mode instead of 10BASE-T. If both link partners also advertise full-duplex capability, then the 100BASE-TX full-duplex mode will be selected.

If both link partners support the use of PAUSE frames for Ethernet flow control, and if the link is enabled for full-duplex operation, then PAUSE operation will also be enabled at each end of the link. PAUSE operation can be configured via Auto-Negotiation over twisted-pair or Gigabit Ethernet fiber optic segments, but only if the segments are using the full-duplex mode of operation. Since the use of PAUSE is independent of data rate or link technology, it is not included in the priority resolution table.*

If there is no common technology detected at either end of the link, then the Auto-Negotiation protocol will not make a connection. In this case, the port will be left in the off position. For example, if a device that only supports 10BASE-T is connected to a port on a switch that only supports 100BASE-TX, then no connection will be established on that link.

Most twisted-pair switching hub ports now support multiple speed operation, with the most common support including 10BASE-T and 100BASE-TX. However,

---

* "The use of PAUSE Operation for Full-Duplex links (as indicated by bit A5) is orthogonal to the negotiated data rate, medium, or link technology. The setting of this bit indicates the availability of additional DTE capability when full-duplex operation is in use.... There is no priority resolution associated with the PAUSE operation." Annex 28B.3, IEEE 802.3z Specification for Full Duplex Operation (1996), p 82.

repeater hubs have a special situation, since all ports on a repeater must operate at the same speed. The following example helps illustrate some of the conditions that can occur with repeater hubs.

Repeater Hubs and Auto-Negotiation

The Auto-Negotiation protocol allows hub ports, and Ethernet devices connected to those ports, to negotiate their highest common denominator of performance over a given link. However, the protocol does not specify the behavior of repeater hub ports that may be connected to interfaces with differing capabilities. A repeater is used to create a shared half-duplex signal channel for all attached devices. That shared signal channel must operate at the same speed for all ports on the repeater hub.

Consider the case of an auto-negotiating repeater hub with one port connected to a device that only supports the 10BASE-T media system. The rest of the ports on the hub are attached to interfaces that support both 10 Mbps and 100 Mbps operation. In this case, the hub may take several approaches to resolve the speed mismatch.

One approach might be to negotiate a lower speed on all ports, to accommodate the 10 Mbps interface. However, this drops the link speed for all other stations connected to ports on the repeater hub to 10 Mbps. Rather than reduce the link speed for other stations, the designer of a 100BASE-T repeater hub may decide not to allow a fixed-speed 10 Mbps interface to make a connection. Instead the port would be shut down and the hub could send a message to its management interface reporting the failed connection attempt.

Yet another approach suitable for a higher cost repeater hub is to design a hub with multiple repeaters, each operating at a different speed. The Auto-Negotiation protocol could be used in combination with management software running on the hub to set things up correctly. The ports operating at 10 Mbps would be automatically connected to the 10 Mbps repeater in the hub. The 100 Mbps ports would be automatically connected to a separate 100 Mbps repeater. The two repeaters in the hub could communicate through a two-port Ethernet switch located inside the hub. A hub equipped with an internal two-port switch and the dynamic configuration system we've just described can simultaneously support 10 Mbps operation on one port and 100 Mbps operation on another port at the same time.

Auto-Negotiation and Cable Type

The Auto-Negotiation system is designed so that a link will not become operational until matching capabilities exist at each end. However, the Auto-Negotiation protocol is not able to test the quality of the cable used on the link. Therefore, it is up to the installer to make sure that the correct cable type is in place.

Let's assume that we have a link with a switching hub at one end, a station at the other end, and Auto-Negotiation in operation in both devices. Both the hub port and the station can support 10BASE-T and 100BASE-TX operation. Let's further assume that a Category 3 "voice-grade" cable is used in this link. In that case, auto-negotiating 100BASE-TX over this link would be a problem since the 100BASE-TX system requires higher performance Category 5 "data-grade" cable.* When power is applied or a connection is first made, the hub and station will use Auto-Negotiation to determine the capabilities at each end of the Category 3 link.

Auto-Negotiation will choose to operate at the highest-performance mode the devices have in common, which is 100BASE-TX. The Auto-Negotiation link pulses are simply bursts of the same link pulses used in 10BASE-T. This means that the pulses will successfully travel over Category 3 wire, since 10BASE-T signals were designed to work over Category 3 or better cable. As a result, the negotiation process will function correctly, resulting in a 100BASE-TX link. However, once the Auto-Negotiation protocol is finished, the signaling switches over to the higher speed 100BASE-TX data rate, which requires the use of Category 5 cable. This means that this link will either operate marginally with a high rate of errors, or not at all.

Modern structured cabling systems are based on Category 5 cabling throughout, thus avoiding this kind of problem with higher speed Ethernet systems. However, Category 5 cabling was not available when the 10BASE-T standard was first developed in the early 1990s, and older cabling plants designed to support 10 Mbps Ethernet systems may be based on lower quality Category 3 cabling.

While Auto-Negotiation is a handy feature that allows the highest-performance mode to be selected automatically on a given link, it still requires that the correct cable type be in place for the highest speed mode that may be selected. It's up to you to ensure that the correct cable is in use. If your site has been cabled with Category 5 cabling everywhere, then this is not an issue. All current twisted-pair Ethernet systems will work over Category 5 cable.

If you have lower quality cabling, then you can manually set the correct mode of operation for a given link. By manually setting the configuration, you can make sure that a link does not negotiate a mode of operation that exceeds the capabilities of the cabling for that link. There is no standard for manual configuration, which means that manual configuration operates differently, depending on the equipment and vendor involved. For example, an Ethernet interface in a computer

---

* The Category system for classifying cable quality is described in Chapter 14, *Structured Cabling*.

may be configured by running special configuration software provided by the manufacturer. Ethernet ports on a switching hub can often be configured using commands accessed by way of an ASCII terminal interface on the switch. Some vendors may also provide a management software application that you can run on a remote computer, which uses commands sent over the network to set the configuration of a switching hub.

Parallel Detection

The Auto-Negotiation feature was designed after many of the twisted-pair media systems were invented. Therefore, support for the Auto-Negotiation protocol is optional for most media systems. For that reason, the Auto-Negotiation system must be compatible with interfaces that do not support Auto-Negotiation, as well as with older interfaces built before Auto-Negotiation existed. If Auto-Negotiation only exists at one end of the link, the Auto-Negotiation protocol is designed to detect that condition and respond correctly using a mechanism called *Parallel Detection.*

The absence of FLPs from a link partner indicates that the link partner does not support Auto-Negotiation. In that case, parallel detection can use the presence of 10BASE-T NLP signals to determine whether the link partner is based on 10BASE-T or not. Other media systems (e.g., 100BASE-TX and 100BASE-T4) have sufficiently different signal characteristics to make it possible for *Parallel Detection* to determine which media system is in use. Once it determines which media system is being used, *Parallel Detection* will set the port for that particular media system.

For example, let's assume that station A in Figure 5-1 is an older 10BASE-T device that isn't aware of Auto-Negotiation. When station A is powered on, the switching hub in Figure 5-1 will see NLPs coming from the station. The *Parallel* Detection portion of the Auto-Negotiation protocol will detect the presence of NLPs only and automatically set the port for half-duplex 10BASE-T mode.

Problems with Parallel Detection

You can encounter problems with parallel detection if the device at one end of the link does not support Auto-Negotiation and has been manually configured for full-duplex operation. As we've just seen, a device equipped with Auto-Negotiation can detect the correct speed by listening to the characteristic signals coming from a link partner that does not support Auto-Negotiation. However, the auto-negotiating device cannot detect the duplex or other capabilities of the device at the other end of the link. Therefore, when an auto-negotiating device uses Parallel

Detection to set the speed, the standard requires that it also set the half-duplex mode of operation.*

If the device at the other end of the link does not support Auto-Negotiation and has been manually configured for full-duplex operation, then this link will be mis-configured. The manually configured end of the link will be using full-duplex mode, and the auto-negotiating end will use half-duplex mode. This leads to frame errors, late collisions and dropped frames—all of which can have a severe impact on network performance. To avoid these problems, you must ensure that links with an auto-negotiating device at one end and a manually configured device at the other have the correct duplex settings. If you need full-duplex support on this link, then you will have to disable the Auto-Negotiation feature at one end of the link, and configure the speed and duplex manually for both ends of the link.

Reports from the field indicate that some Auto-Negotiation devices using Parallel Detection incorrectly set their end of the link for full-duplex operation. The standard requires that only the half-duplex mode be selected when Parallel Detection is used. Therefore, any device that uses Parallel Detection and selects full-duplex mode instead fails to meet the requirements of the standard. More often what happens is that a computer enabled for full-duplex support that does not support Auto-Negotiation is moved to a switching hub port that has Auto-Negotiation enabled. The result is a misconfigured link, as described above. This looks strange at first glance, since the switching port says it supports Auto-Negotiation and yet the link isn't configured correctly. However, once you understand that one end of the link is not supporting Auto-Negotiation, then this failure mode becomes clear.

Because of the problems with duplex negotiation, some network managers have chosen to disable Auto-Negotiation support on their hub ports and computers, and prefer to set the port characteristics by hand. Other network managers report that their problems were resolved by upgrading the Ethernet driver software on their computers so that they can support Auto-Negotiation. You should also make sure that your network hubs are running the most recent versions of software. Upgrading the software can make it possible for the devices at each end of the link to use the Auto-Negotiation protocol instead of depending on Parallel Detection. Running the Auto-Negotiation protocol at both ends of the link configures both speed and duplex correctly, avoiding any problems with incorrect mode selection.

---

* Parallel Detection on twisted-pair links applies only to 10/100 equipment. The 1000BASE-T twisted-pair Gigabit Ethernet system requires that Auto-Negotiation be implemented as part of the signaling specifications. Therefore, all 1000BASE-T equipment is capable of Auto-Negotiation and does not use Parallel Detection.

Management Interface

An optional management interface may be included that allows you to manually disable Auto-Negotiation, or to force the negotiation process to take place. This may be in the form of a program you run on a computer to set up the Ethernet interface. Alternatively, it can be a set of commands supported on an Ethernet hub, which are accessed through a terminal interface or over the network. The management interface also allows you to manually select a specific operational mode for a given hub port or Ethernet interface. When using a management interface to manually set the configuration, you need to make sure that the equipment at both ends of the segment is configured identically, and that the correct mode of operation has been chosen.

Manually overriding the configuration of an Ethernet interface can be dangerous. For example, if a user with a computer connected to a repeater hub mistakenly decides to set the Ethernet interface in their computer to full-duplex operation it can cause serious problems for all stations connected to the hub. A user might decide to do this because they've heard that full-duplex mode provides more bandwidth, and they've found a configuration program that will allow them to set the interface in their computer to full-duplex. Without knowing any more about the operation of their network, forcing the full-duplex mode to be selected might seem like a good idea.

However, in practice this is a very bad idea for stations connected to repeaters. Repeaters are by definition half-duplex devices, and every segment connected to them must be set to the traditional half-duplex mode for correct operation. If someone mistakenly sets their computer to full-duplex operation it will still send and receive data through the repeater hub more or less successfully. It will also cause problems in interaction with other stations connected to the hub that are correctly operating in half-duplex mode. The correctly configured half-duplex stations will encounter problems because the full-duplex station sends data without obeying the CSMA/CD rules. One symptom of this behavior can be late collisions detected on the repeater ports connected to half-duplex stations. Late collisions are serious problems on a network, since they cause signal errors and lost frames. Each lost frame must be detected and retransmitted by the network applications involved. This, in turn, causes lower network performance, and may cause some applications to fail.

1000BASE-X Auto-Negotiation

The 1000BASE-T twisted-pair Gigabit Ethernet system uses the same Auto-Negotiation system used by all other twisted-pair Ethernet systems. However, the 1000BASE-X Gigabit Ethernet system has its own system of Auto-Negotiation, which operates over the 1000BASE-X media segments. As noted earlier, the various fiber optic Ethernet media systems use such different signaling and wavelengths of light that there is no way to send Auto-Negotiation signals that all systems could detect.

Nonetheless, the designers of 1000BASE-X decided to develop an Auto-Negotiation system that was specific to the three media segment types defined in the 1000BASE-X standard. These systems are 1000BASE-SX and 1000BASE-LX fiber optic segments, as well as the 1000BASE-CX short copper segment.

The 1000BASE-X Auto-Negotiation system only works over these three media types. Since these media types only operate at 1000 Mbps, there is no need to automatically set the speed. Consequently, the 1000BASE-X Auto-Negotiation system only advertises and configures capabilities such as full or half-duplex operation and support for flow control PAUSE frames.

II

Ethernet Media Systems

Part II covers the Ethernet media systems in detail. The basic media components common to all media systems are described in Chapter 6, *Ethernet Media Fundamentals*. It is highly recommended that you read this chapter before reading any of the six media chapters that follow.

Information found in the set of six media chapters describes the most commonly used Ethernet media systems. Each of the media chapters is based on an identical format to help organize and clearly present the entire range of Ethernet media systems. However, the identical format leads to some unavoidable repetition, which is especially noticeable if you read several of the media chapters in a row.

Part II concludes with a description of the half-duplex configuration guidelines that apply when media segments are combined using repeater hubs. Part II contains these chapters:

- Chapter 6, *Ethernet Media Fundamentals*
- Chapter 7, *Twisted-Pair Media System (10BASE-T)*
- Chapter 8, *Fiber Optic Media System (10BASE-F)*
- Chapter 9, *Fast Ethernet Twisted-Pair Media System (100BASE-TX)*
- Chapter 10, *Fast Ethernet Fiber Optic Media System (100BASE-FX)*
- Chapter 11, *Gigabit Ethernet Twisted-Pair Media System (1000BASE-T)*
- Chapter 12, *Gigabit Ethernet Fiber Optic Media System (1000BASE-X)*
- Chapter 13, *Multi-Segment Configuration Guidelines*

6

Ethernet Media Fundamentals

To send Ethernet signals from one station to another, stations are connected to one another with a media system based on a set of standard components. Some of these are hardware components specific to each media cabling system, such as the media cables and connectors. These media-specific components are described in the individual media chapters and cabling chapters that follow. Other components, such as Ethernet interfaces, are common to all media systems. Reading this chapter will provide the background you need to understand the components that connect to each of the Ethernet systems: 10-, 100-, or 1000 Mbps.

As the Ethernet system has evolved, it has developed a set of *medium-independent* attachments. Medium independence means that the Ethernet interface does not have to know anything about the media system. These attachments allow an Ethernet interface to be connected to any type of media system. With this system, multiple media systems can be developed without requiring any changes in the Ethernet interface controllers.

The first medium-independent attachment was developed for the 10 Mbps Ethernet system, and is called the *attachment unit interface* (AUI). The AUI supports the 10 Mbps media systems only. The next medium-independent attachment was developed as part of the Fast Ethernet standard, and is called the *medium-independent interface* (MII). The MII provides support for both 10 and 100 Mbps media segments. Finally, a *gigabit medium-independent interface* (GMII) was developed as part of the Gigabit Ethernet system. The GMII accommodates the increased speed of the Gigabit Ethernet system by providing a wider data path to the Ethernet interface. We'll look at all three of these medium-independent attachments, so that you can see how they are used to connect a station to an Ethernet.

This chapter also describes other elements of the Ethernet system that may be found in all media types. These include transceivers—both internal and external—

as well as transceiver cables and *network interface cards* (NICs). Finally, we will look at the block encoding schemes and signaling mechanisms used to send Ethernet signals over cables.

Attachment Unit Interface

The AUI was developed as part of the original 10 Mbps Ethernet system. Ethernet originated as a 10 Mbps system, operating over coaxial cable.* Later, new media systems based on twisted-pair and fiber optic link segments were invented for the 10 Mbps system. In the early 1990s, the 10BASE-T twisted-pair system became a popular method of connecting desktop computers, which lead to the widespread adoption of Ethernet as the networking system of choice.

The AUI makes it possible to connect an Ethernet interface to any one of the several 10 Mbps media systems while isolating the interface from any details of the specific media system in use. The development of a medium-independent attachment was actually a side effect of the design of the original thick coaxial cabling system. The thick coaxial system requires the use of external transceivers connected directly to the coax cable. Providing a connection between the Ethernet interface in the station and the external transceiver on the coaxial cable led to the development of the AUI. The AUI, in turn, made it possible to develop other cabling systems for 10 Mbps Ethernet without requiring any changes in the Ethernet electronics in the station.

Figure 6-1 illustrates how the AUI is used in the 10 Mbps system. This figure shows the complete set of components that can be used to implement a twisted-pair 10 Mbps Ethernet connection. Both internal and external transceiver connections are shown.

This set of components and their three-letter acronyms might seem like alphabet soup at first glance. However, it is useful to know these acronyms as they are found in vendor literature and are printed on Ethernet devices. Starting with the DTE, we will then discuss the AUI connector and AUI cable, and finish with the transceiver.

Data Terminal Equipment or Repeater Port

To begin with, there is the networked device, which can be a station or a repeater port. A station, more formally called *data terminal equipment* (DTE) in the

---

* Ethernet coaxial cable systems provide only a single 10 Mbps channel, and coaxial cable systems can be difficult to install and operate. For that reason, they are no longer the first choice for implementing a network that must support more than a few stations. The details of coaxial Ethernet media systems (10BASE5 and 10BASE2) are covered in Appendix B, *Thick and Thin Coaxial Media Systems.*

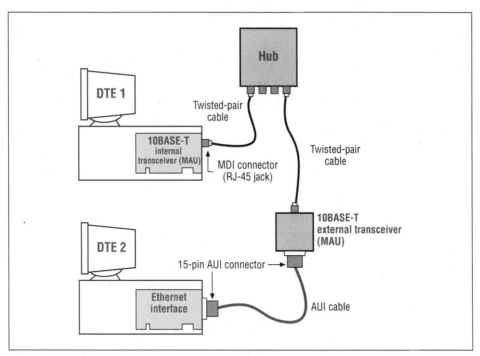

Figure 6-1. AUI connection for a 10 Mbps Ethernet system

standard, is a unique, addressable device on a network. A DTE is a device that serves as an originating or terminating point for data. For example, each Ethernet-equipped computer or port on a switching hub is a DTE, since each is equipped with an Ethernet interface. The Ethernet interface contains the electronics needed to perform the *media access control* (MAC) functions required to send and receive Ethernet frames over the Ethernet channel.

Ethernet ports on repeater hubs are *not* DTEs and do not use an Ethernet interface. A repeater port connects to an Ethernet media system using standard components, such as a transceiver. However, repeater ports operate at the individual bit level for Ethernet signals, moving the signals through the repeater so that they can travel from one segment to another. Therefore, repeater ports do not contain Ethernet interfaces since they do not operate at the level of Ethernet frames.

Attachment Unit Interface and Cable

The AUI is the medium-independent attachment that allows an Ethernet interface to be connected to one of several media systems. In Figure 6-1, DTE 2 has an AUI connector and external transceiver that, in turn, is connected to a twisted-pair cable. The AUI connector on DTE 2 makes it possible for that station to be connected to any of several 10 Mbps Ethernet media systems, by using the appropriate external transceiver. Figure 6-1 also shows DTE 1, which has a built-in 10BASE-T transceiver. Since this station does not have a 15-pin AUI connector, it cannot be connected to any other media system; it connects only to a twisted-pair cable.

AUI Connector

The 15-pin AUI connector provides an external transceiver connection for a station. This connector provides power to the external transceiver, and provides a path for Ethernet signals to travel between the Ethernet interface and the media system. The AUI connector uses a slide latch mechanism to make an attachment between male and female 15-pin connectors. The slide latch mechanism is described in Appendix C, *AUI Equipment: Installation and Configuration*. Figure 6-2 lists the signals provided by the 15-pin AUI connector.

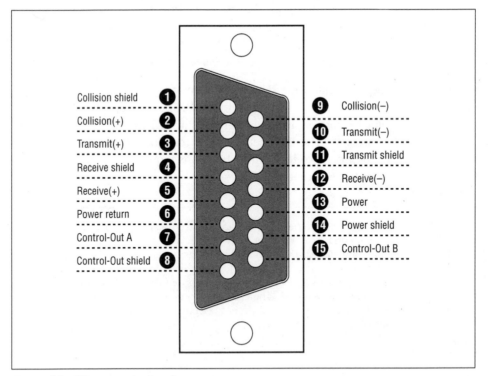

Collision shield ❶
Collision(+) ❷
Transmit(+) ❸
Receive shield ❹
Receive(+) ❺
Power return ❻
Control-Out A ❼
Control-Out shield ❽

❾ Collision(−)
❿ Transmit(−)
⓫ Transmit shield
⓬ Receive(−)
⓭ Power
⓮ Power shield
⓯ Control-Out B

Figure 6-2. AUI connector signals

The signals sent by the transceiver and received by the Ethernet interface are low voltage differential signals. There are two wires for each signal, with one wire for the positive (+) and one wire for the negative (–) portions of the signal. The voltage level on these wires varies from +0.7 volts to –0.7 volts, providing a nominal total of 1.4 volts peak-to-peak for the entire signal.

> The "Control-Out" signal was provided to send optional control signals from an Ethernet interface to the transceiver. This option was never implemented by any vendor and is not used.

AUI Transceiver Cable

The 10 Mbps transceiver cable, formally known as an AUI cable, is built like an electrical extension cord: there's a plug (*male connector*) on one end and a socket (*female connector*) on the other. The transceiver cable carries three data signals between a 10 Mbps Ethernet interface and the external transceiver:

*   *Transmit data*, from the Ethernet interface to the transceiver.

*   *Receive data*, from the transceiver to the interface.

*   A *collision presence signal*, from the transceiver to the interface.

Each signal is sent over twisted-pair wires. Another pair of wires is used to carry 12-volt DC power from the Ethernet interface to the transceiver. The standard transceiver cable uses fairly heavy-duty stranded wire to provide good flexibility and low resistance.

The AUI transceiver cable, shown in Figure 6-3, is equipped with a 15-pin female connector on one end that is provided with a sliding latch; this is the end that is attached to the outboard transceiver. The other end of the transceiver cable has a 15-pin male connector, equipped with locking posts; this is the end that attaches to the Ethernet interface. Some 15-pin AUI connectors on Ethernet interfaces have been equipped with screw posts instead of the sliding latch fastener described in the standard, requiring a special transceiver cable with locking screws on one end instead of sliding latch posts.

The AUI transceiver cable described in the IEEE standard is relatively thick (approximately 1 cm or 0.4 inch diameter), and may be up to 50 meters (164 feet) long. There is no minimum length standard for a transceiver cable, and external transceivers are sold that are small enough to fit directly onto the 15-pin AUI connector of the Ethernet interface, dispensing with the need for a transceiver cable.

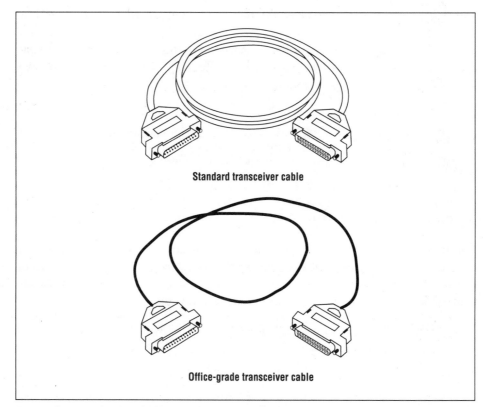

Figure 6-3. Standard and office-grade AUI transceiver cables

"Office-grade" transceiver cables (shown at the bottom of Figure 6-3), are thinner and more flexible than the standard cable. The thinner wires used in office grade transceiver cables also have higher signal loss than standard cables, which limits the length of office grade cables. The maximum allowable length for an office grade transceiver cable, which has four times the amount of signal attenuation as standard cables, is 12.5 meters (41 feet).

Theoretically, you could connect several transceiver cables together to make up a single longer cable. However, this may not be a good idea, since the sliding latch connectors may not hold the cable ends together very well, and you could end up with intermittent connections.

Medium Attachment Unit

The next component shown in the DTE 2 connection in Figure 6-1 is the *medium attachment unit* (MAU), more commonly known as a *transceiver*. The transceiver gets its name because it *trans*mits and re*ceives* signals on the physical medium. The AUI transceiver is the link between the different types of electrical signaling used over the media systems, and the signals that are sent through the AUI inter-face to the Ethernet interface in the station. Each 10 Mbps media system has a spe-cific transceiver designed to perform the type of electrical signaling used for that medium. There are coaxial, twisted-pair, and fiber optic transceivers, each equipped with the components it takes to send and receive signals over that par-ticular medium.

The external AUI transceiver is a small box, typically a few inches on each side. There's no specified shape; some are long and thin, and some are almost square. The transceiver electronics typically receive their power over the transceiver cable from the Ethernet interface in the station. According to the standard, an AUI trans-ceiver may draw up to 500 milliamps ($\frac{1}{2}$ amp) of current.

The transceiver transmits signals from the Ethernet interface onto the media, and receives signals from the media which it sends to the Ethernet interface. The sig-nals that transceivers send vary according to the type of media in use. On the other hand, signals that travel between the transceiver and the Ethernet-equipped device over the AUI interface are the same, no matter which media type is in use. That's why you can make a connection between any 10 Mbps media system and a 15-pin connector on an Ethernet device. The signaling over the 15-pin interface is the same for all transceivers; only the media signals are different.

AUI transceiver jabber protection

The jabber protection function senses when a broken Ethernet device has gone berserk and is continuously transmitting a signal—a condition known as *jabber-ing*. Jabbering causes a continual carrier sense on the channel, jamming the chan-nel and preventing other stations from being able to use the network. If that happens, the jabber protection circuit enables a *jabber latch*, which will shut off the signal to the channel.

The AUI transceiver specification allows two methods of resetting the jabber latch: power-cycling or by automatically restoring operation one-half second after the jabbering transmission ceases. In some very old AUI transceivers, the jabber latch would not reset until the transceiver was power-cycled, which required the net-work administrator to disconnect and reconnect the transceiver cable to get the transceiver to work again. Needless to say, this approach was not very popular with network administrators. Modern AUI transceivers are built using a single chip design that automatically comes out of jabber latch mode once an overlong trans-mission has ceased.

The SQE Test signal

The earliest Ethernet standard, DIX V1.0, did not include a signal for testing the operation of the collision detection system. However, in the DIX V2.0 specifications, the AUI transceiver was provided with a new signal, called the *collision presence test* (CPT). The name for the collision signal changed to *signal quality error* (SQE) in the IEEE 802.3 standard, and the CPT signal was also changed to SQE Test. The purpose of the SQE Test signal is to test the collision detection electronics of the transceiver, and to let the Ethernet interface know that the collision detection circuits and signal paths are working correctly.

> When you install an external AUI transceiver on your Ethernet system it is extremely important to correctly configure the SQE Test signal. The SQE Test signal *must be disabled* if the transceiver is attached to a repeater hub. For all other devices that may be attached to an external 10 Mbps transceiver, the standard recommends that the SQE Test signal be enabled.

You may find that some vendors do not label things correctly, which can lead to some confusion. For example, you may find that the switch on the transceiver for enabling the SQE Test signal will be labeled "SQE" instead of "SQE Test." Since "SQE" is the name of the actual collision signal, the last thing you'd want to do is disable the collision detection signal in Ethernet. Nonetheless, this confusion of terms is very widespread. The operation and configuration of the SQE Test signal is described in detail in Appendix C.

Medium-Dependent Interface

The actual connection to the network medium (e.g., twisted-pair cable) is made by way of a component that the standard calls the *medium-dependent interface*, or MDI. In the real world, this is a piece of hardware used for making a direct physical connection to the network cable.

In Figure 6-1, the MDI is an eight-pin connector, also referred to as an RJ-45–style jack. The MDI is actually a part of the transceiver, and provides the transceiver with a direct physical and electrical connection to the twisted-pair wires used to carry network signals in the 10 Mbps twisted-pair media system.

In the case of thick coaxial Ethernet, the most commonly used MDI is a type of coaxial cable clamp that is installed directly onto the coaxial cable. For fiber optic Ethernet, the MDI is a fiber optic connector.

Medium-Independent Interface

The invention of the 100 Mbps Fast Ethernet system was also the occasion for the development of a new attachment interface, called simply the *medium-independent interface* (MII). The MII can support operation at both 10 and 100 Mbps. Figure 6-4 shows the same two stations as Figure 6-1, but this time an MII is being used.

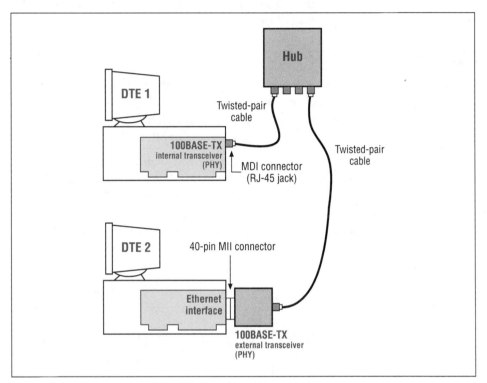

Figure 6-4. MII connection for a 100 Mbps Fast Ethernet system

The other major difference between this diagram and the one shown in Figure 6-1 is that a transceiver with an MII is called a *physical layer device* (PHY) instead of a MAU. In essence, the MII is an updated and improved version of the original 10 Mbps–only AUI. The MII can be embedded inside equipment, as in the twisted-pair interface shown on DTE 1. In this case, the transceiver and MII are inside the computer. All the user sees is the twisted-pair connector, which connects the twisted-pair media to the internal transceiver.

An Ethernet device can also be provided with a 40-pin MII connector, which allows connections to external transceivers, as shown attached to DTE 2 in Figure 6-4. The external transceiver provides maximum flexibility, since you can provide either a twisted-pair or fiber optic transceiver. This allows a connection to either twisted-pair or fiber optic media types operating at 10 or 100 Mbps speeds.

The MII is designed to make the signaling differences among the various media segments transparent to the Ethernet electronics inside the networked device. The

MII does this by converting the signals received from the various media segments by the transceiver (PHY) into standardized digital format signals. The digital signals are then provided to the Ethernet electronics in the networked device over a 4-bit wide data path. The same standard digital signals are provided to the Ethernet interface no matter what kind of media signaling is used.

MII Connector

The 40-pin MII connector and optional MII cable provide a path for the transmission of signals between an MII interface in the station and an external transceiver. The vast majority of MII transceivers are designed for direct connection to the MII connector on the networked device, and do not use an MII cable.

Figure 6-5 shows two MII transceivers, one equipped with an MII cable (at top), and the other (below) equipped with jack screws for direct connection to the mating screw locks on the DTE. The jack screws replace the much-maligned slide latch mechanism used for the 15-pin AUI in the original 10 Mbps Ethernet system. If an optional MII cable is used, the end of the MII cable will be equipped with a 40-pin connector and a pair of jack screws that fasten into the mating screw locks on the networked device.

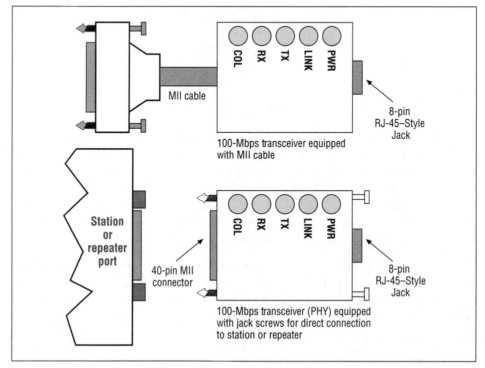

Figure 6-5. MII connector and transceiver

MII connector signals

The signals provided on the MII connector are different from the ones found on the 15-pin AUI connector in the 10 Mbps system.

The 40-pin MII connector is small and the pins are densely packed, so care should be taken to avoid damaging the pins when connecting and disconnecting network components. Note that the MII pins can be easily bent and that the +5 volt pins on the lower row are right next to ground pins.

If the +5 volt pins or ground pins bend and touch against one another during installation, it is possible to blow a fuse in the network equipment, which will cause the MII port to stop working. The prudent network manager may wish to power off the equipment while connecting or disconnecting MIIs, just to be safe.

Figure 6-6 shows the 40 pins of the MII connector, with the signals carried by the pins indicated. The MII defines a 4-bit wide data path for transmit and receive data that is clocked at 25 MHz to provide a 100 Mbps transfer speed, or 2.5 MHz for 10 Mbps operation. According to the standard, the electronics attached to each MII connector (male and female) should be designed to withstand connector insertion and removal while the power is on.

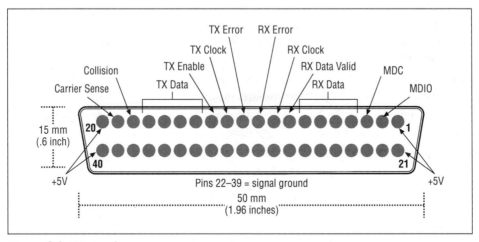

Figure 6-6. MII signals

The MII provides for a set of control signals that make it possible for the Ethernet interface in the networked device to interact with the external transceiver to set and detect various modes of operation. This management interface can be used to place the transceiver into loopback mode for testing, to enable full-duplex operation if the transceiver supports it, to select the transceiver speed if the transceiver supports dual speed mode, and so on. The MII signals are as follows:

+5 volts

Pins 1, 20, 21, and 40 are used to carry +5 volts at a maximum current of 750 milliamps, or $\frac{3}{4}$ amp.

Signal ground

Pins 22 through 39 carry signal ground wires.

Management Data I/O

Pin 2 carries the Management Data Input/Output signal, a bi-directional signal used to carry serial data representing control and status information between the transceiver and the DTE. The management interface provides various functions, including resetting the transceiver, setting the transceiver into full-duplex mode, and enabling a test of the electronics and signal paths involved in the collision signal.

Management Data Clock

Pin 3 carries the Management Data Clock, which is used as a timing reference for serial data sent on the management data interface.

RX Data

Pins 4, 5, 6, and 7 provide the 4-bit Receive Data path from the transceiver to the DTE.*

RX Data Valid

Pin 8 carries the Receive Data Valid signal, which is generated by the transceiver while receiving a valid frame.

RX Clock

Pin 9 carries the Receive Clock which runs at 25 MHz in 100 Mbps Fast Ethernet systems and at 2.5 MHz in 10 Mbps systems, to provide a timing reference for receive signals.

RX Error

Pin 10 carries this signal, which is sent by the transceiver upon detection of received errors.

TX Error

Pin 11 carries this signal, which can be used by a repeater to force the propagation of received errors. This signal may be used by a repeater under certain circumstances and is never used by a station.

---

* A 4-bit chunk of data is also called a *nibble*, to distinguish it from an 8-bit byte.

TX Clock

> Pin 12 carries the Transmit Clock, which runs continuously at a frequency of 25 MHz for 100 Mbps Fast Ethernet systems and at 2.5 MHz for 10 Mbps systems. The purpose of this signal is to provide a timing reference for transmit signals.

TX Enable

> Pin 13 carries the Transmit Enable signal from the DTE to the transceiver to signal the transceiver that transmit data is being sent.

TX Data

> Pins 14, 15, 16, and 17 provide the 4-bit wide transmit data path from the DTE to the transceiver.

Collision

> Pin 18 carries this signal from the transceiver. It indicates a collision detected on the network segment. If a transceiver is in full-duplex mode, then this signal is undefined by the standard and the collision light on the transceiver may glow steadily or erratically when full-duplex mode is enabled. See the instructions that came with the transceiver you are using for details.

Carrier Sense

> Pin 19 carries this signal, which indicates activity on the network segment from the transceiver to the DTE.

MII Transceiver and Cable

The PHY shown in Figure 6-4 performs approximately the same function as a transceiver in the 10 Mbps Ethernet system. However, unlike the original 10 Mbps MAU, the PHY, or transceiver, also performs the media system signal encoding and decoding. In addition, an MII transceiver can be automatically configured to operate in full- or half-duplex mode, and can operate at either 10 or 100 Mbps.

The transceiver may be a set of integrated circuits inside the Ethernet port of a network device and therefore invisible to the user, or it may be a small box like the external transceiver used in 10 Mbps Ethernet. An external MII transceiver is equipped with a 40-pin MII plug designed for direct connection to the 40-pin MII jack on the networked device, as shown in Figure 6-5. This connection may include a short MII transceiver cable, although in practice these are not easily found.

According to the standard, an MII cable consists of 20 twisted pairs with a total of 40 wires. The twisted-pair cable also has a 40-pin plug on one end equipped with male jackscrews that connect to mating female screw locks. The cable can be a maximum of 0.5 meters in length (approximately 19.6 inches). However, the vast majority of external transceivers attach directly to the MII connector on the device with no intervening cable.

MII jabber protection

An MII transceiver operated at 10 Mbps has a jabber protection function, which provides a jabber latch similar to the one in the AUI transceiver described earlier in this chapter. In the 100 Mbps Fast Ethernet system, the jabber protection feature was moved to the Fast Ethernet repeater ports. This change was made possible because all Fast Ethernet segments are link segments and must be connected to a repeater hub for communication with other stations. Moving the circuitry for jabber protection to the repeater hub offloads that requirement from the transceiver and provides the same level of protection for the network channel. Therefore, transceivers operating at 100 Mbps Fast Ethernet do not provide the jabber latch function. Instead, each Fast Ethernet repeater port monitors the channel for long transmissions and shuts the port down if the carrier signal persists for anywhere from 40,000 to 75,000 bit times.

MII SQE Test

The SQE Test signal is provided on AUI-based equipment to test the integrity of the collision detect electronics and signal paths. However, there is no SQE Test signal provided in the MII. SQE Test can be removed from the MII since all media systems connected to an MII are link segments. Collisions are detected on link segments by the simultaneous occurrence of data on the receive and transmit data circuits. As such, the link monitor function in MII transceivers ensures that the receive data circuits are working correctly.

Additionally, the MII provides a loopback test of the collision detect signal paths from an external transceiver to the Ethernet device. Taken together, this provides a complete check of collision detect signal paths, making the SQE Test signal unnecessary for the MII.

Gigabit Medium-Independent Interface

The development of 1000 Mbps Gigabit Ethernet system led to the development of yet another attachment interface, called the *gigabit medium-independent interface* (GMII). Because of the higher speeds used in Gigabit Ethernet, an externally exposed interface is too difficult to engineer reliably. For this reason, the GMII does not support an exposed connector for attaching a transceiver or an outboard transceiver cable. Therefore, unlike the AUI or MII, the GMII only provides a standard way of interconnecting integrated circuits on circuit boards. At most, the GMII can be used as a motherboard-to-daughterboard interface inside a piece of equipment.

Since there is no exposed GMII, there is no way to attach an external transceiver to a Gigabit Ethernet system. If a station is equipped with a GMII, all the user will see is an MDI connector, such as the 8-pin RJ-45–style jack used for making the connection to a twisted-pair segment.

Like the MII, the GMII provides media independence by making the signaling differences among media segments transparent to the Ethernet electronics inside the networked device. The GMII converts the various media line signals received by the embedded Gigabit Ethernet transceiver (PHY) into standardized digital data signals. These signals are then provided to the Ethernet controller chip, which is responsible for creating Ethernet frames for transmission, and for assembling received data into Ethernet frames for reception. While the MII provides 4-bit data paths, the GMII uses a byte-wide interface, providing an 8-bit data path between the transceiver chip and the Ethernet controller chip inside the equipment. By transferring twice as much data for a given data interface clock rate, the GMII makes it easier for an Ethernet controller to handle gigabit data speeds.

The GMII is designed to support only 1000 Mbps operation, with 10 and 100 Mbps operation provided by the MII. Transceiver chips are available that simultaneously implement both the MII and GMII circuits on a given Ethernet port. This provides 10/100/1000 Mbps support over twisted-pair cabling with automatic configuration via the Auto-Negotiation protocol.

Gigabit Ten-Bit Interface

For Gigabit Ethernet devices that only support the 1000BASE-X media family, the media independence provided by the GMII is not required. The 1000BASE-X system is based on signaling and media systems originally developed for the ANSI Fibre Channel standard. If only 1000BASE-X support is needed, then another internal interface, called the *Ten-Bit Interface* (TBI), is provided by the standard. This interface is ten code bits wide, to accommodate the 8B/10B signal encoding used in the 1000BASE-X media system, described later in this chapter.

The TBI is used in commercial Fibre Channel serializer/deserializer (SERDES) components, and has been adopted by Ethernet chip manufacturers for use in 1000BASE-X systems. Like the GMII, the TBI is also hidden inside the equipment— only equipment designers need to deal with it. In practice, you will only see a fiber optic or copper Gigabit Ethernet port on the outside of the equipment. The exact details of which internal signaling interface is used and how the port is wired up inside the device are not important to the user of Gigabit Ethernet equipment.

GMII Transceiver

A Gigabit Ethernet transceiver (PHY) consists of one or more integrated circuit chips located inside the Gigabit Ethernet device. Since there is no exposed signaling interface for Gigabit Ethernet, there are also no external transceivers. However, some of the media signaling components used in a transceiver may be exposed to the user as part of the Gigabit Interface Converter (GBIC), which is described in the next section.

Like the MII transceiver, the Gigabit Ethernet PHY also performs media system signal encoding and decoding, and can be automatically set to operate in full- or half-duplex mode. Unlike the MII transceiver, the GMII transceiver is not capable of multi-speed operation, and is designed to only operate at 1000 Mbps.

Gigabit Interface Converter

As mentioned above, some of the media signaling components used to perform transceiver functions are exposed to the user as part of the GBIC. The GBIC was originally developed for use in the Fibre Channel system, and is referred to as a *serial transceiver module* in that system. Gigabit Ethernet vendors have adopted the Fibre Channel language and refer to GBICs as transceivers. Strictly speaking, the GBIC module only provides the transmitter and receiver components needed to send signals over Gigabit Ethernet, and does not function as a complete Gigabit Ethernet transceiver. Nonetheless, you will see the phrase "Gigabit Ethernet transceiver" used in reference to GBICs.

The GBIC is a small module that can be plugged into the Gigabit Ethernet port on a switch or an interface card and is hot-swappable. The GBIC and the components inside a GBIC port on the switch are static sensitive, so be sure to use a static grounding strap when handling or installing a GBIC.

The GBIC is a widely adopted way of providing the transmitter and receiver components needed to send signals over Gigabit Ethernet fiber optic media segments. Vendors also expect to provide 1000BASE-T GBICs as the twisted-pair Gigabit equipment evolves. Fiber optic GBIC modules make it possible for a given Gigabit Ethernet port to be equipped with either 1000BASE-SX or 1000BASE-LX fiber optic media signaling components as needed by the customer.

Figure 6-7 shows a GBIC designed for connection to a 1000BASE-LX Gigabit Ethernet fiber optic segment. There are two SC connectors on the front of the GBIC for connecting the fiber optic cables. The back of the GBIC has a 20-pin connector (called the "SC-20" connector in the GBIC standard), for connection to the electronics in the Gigabit Ethernet port. The GBIC snaps into place when fully inserted into a port on an Ethernet hub or interface card.

Figure 6-7. A Gigabit Interface Converter (GBIC)

Whether or not a Gigabit Ethernet switching hub or network interface port is equipped with a GBIC is entirely up to the vendor. Where cost or port density is a concern, the vendor may choose to use built-in SC or MT-RJ fiber optic connectors. On the other hand, if a vendor wants to provide maximum flexibility on a switching hub port, for example, then they may choose to use a GBIC.

GBICs are available from a number of sources. However, some major vendors of Gigabit Ethernet switches note that they will not support third-party suppliers. In that case, you must buy your GBICs from the same vendor that made the network equipment. In general, this is probably a good practice as the vendor can certify that the GBICs they sell for use in their equipment meet all of their requirements.

Ethernet Signal Encoding

A number of encoding schemes are used for sending Ethernet signals over the various types of media. Signal encoding is a means of combining both clocking and data information into a self-synchronizing stream of signals sent over a media system. Each media system presents a certain challenge to the engineer in terms of sending Ethernet signals that can make it from one end of the cable to another.

As higher speed Ethernet systems have evolved, more complex block encoding schemes have been used. All of these signaling systems have the same set of goals. One goal is to include sufficient clocking information along with the signals to ensure that the signal decoding circuitry can function correctly. Other goals are to ensure that the error rate is kept very low, and that the Ethernet signals have a very high probability of surviving their trip over the media system.

AUI Signal Encoding

Signals sent over all 10 Mbps media systems—these include the 10 Mbps coaxial, twisted-pair and fiber optic media systems—use a relatively simple encoding scheme called Manchester encoding.* Manchester encoding combines data and clock into *bit symbols*, which provide a clocking transition in the middle of each bit. As shown in Figure 6-8, each Manchester-encoded bit is sent over the network in a *bit period* which is split into two halves, the polarity of the second half always being the reverse of the first half.

The rules for Manchester encoding define a 0 as a signal that is high for the first half of the bit period and low for the second half. A 1 is defined as a signal that is low for the first half of the bit period, and high for the second half. Figure 6-8 shows a station sending the bit pattern 001.

One result of Manchester encoding is to provide a clock transition in each digital bit sent. This transition is used by the receiving station to synchronize itself with the incoming data. While Manchester encoding makes it easy for a receiver to synchronize with the incoming signal and to extract data from it, a drawback of the scheme is that the worst-case signaling rate is twice the data rate. In other words, a 10 Mbps stream of all ones or all zeroes results in a Manchester encoded signaling rate of 20 MHz on the cable.

Different *physical line signaling* methods are used to send the Manchester encoded signals over the media cable, depending on the media system involved. For example, Manchester encoded signals are sent over the original thick coax media system by transmitting an electrical current. Actually, a 10BASE5 transceiver sends two currents onto the coax: a steady DC offset current and a signaling current that changes in amplitude to represent ones and zeroes. The offset current provides a baseline around which the signals are sent. Should you look at thick coax signals with an oscilloscope, you might see something like the signals shown in Figure 6-8.

The line signaling current generates a signal voltage that ranges from 0 to –2 volts. Other line signaling schemes are used for 10 Mbps twisted-pair or fiber optic media systems. Manchester encoding is used for all 10 Mbps media systems, with the only difference being the line signaling system used to send the encoded bits over the cables. The specifics of each physical line signaling system are described in the individual media chapters.

---

* This system is named for its origin at Manchester University in England.

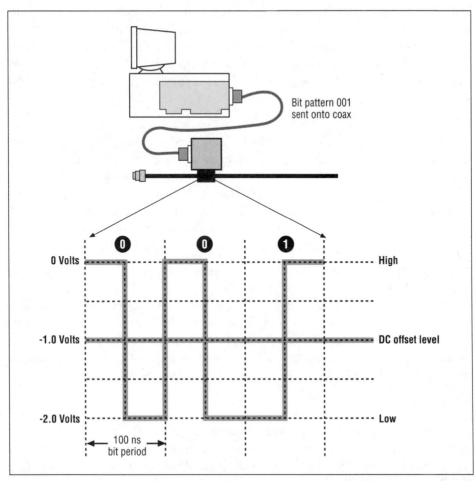

Figure 6-8. Manchester signals over 10BASE5

MII Signal Encoding

The MII transceivers are designed to deal with several signal encoding schemes. A twisted-pair MII transceiver can deal with both the Manchester encoding found on 10 Mbps systems, and the signal encoding used on 100 Mbps twisted-pair media systems. The MII transceiver turns these signals into standard 4-bit chunks of data, which are sent to the Ethernet controller.

The signal encoding used on Fast Ethernet systems is based on block encoding, which is more complex than Manchester encoding. Block encoding takes a group, or block, of data bits and encodes them into a larger set of code bits. The data stream is divided into a fixed number of bits per block, typically 4 or 8 bits. Each data block is translated into a set of code bits, also called *code symbols*. For example, a 4-bit data block (16 possible bit patterns) may be translated into a 5-bit code symbol (32 possible symbols). The expanded set of code symbols is arbitrarily chosen, and is designed to help improve line signaling by providing a better balance between ones and zeroes. The extra code symbols are also used for control purposes, such as signaling the start-of-frame and end-of-frame, as well as carrier extension and error signaling.

Depending on the media system, the block encoded symbols may be transmitted using a simple two-level signaling system, or more complex multi-level line signaling. Multi-level line signaling can transmit more than one bit of information at a time. This effectively compresses the number of bits being transmitted into a smaller number of signal transitions on the cable. Using more complex line signaling schemes results in signal transition rates that can be supported on typical twisted-pair cable, which has limits on how fast it can transmit data.

The 100BASE-TX and 100BASE-FX Fast Ethernet systems (collectively known as 100BASE-X) both use the same block encoding scheme. The 100BASE-T4 and 100BASE-T2 systems use different encoding schemes and physical line signaling to provide Fast Ethernet signaling over twisted-pair cable that is lower quality and not rated to meet Category 5 specifications. However, since Category 5 cabling is widely adopted, there is no need for these two systems, and they never caught on in the marketplace; therefore, they will not be discussed here.

100BASE-X encoding

Rather than re-invent the wheel when it came to sending signals at 100 Mbps, the 100BASE-X media systems adopted portions of the block encoding and physical line signaling originally developed for the ANSI Fiber Distributed Data Interface (FDDI) network standard. FDDI is a 100 Mbps Token Ring network that was popular in the early 1990s. The block encoding used in FDDI and the 100BASE-X media types relies on a system called *4B/5B*, which divides the data into 4-bit blocks. The 4-bit blocks are translated into 5-bit code symbols for transmission over the media system. The encoded symbols are transmitted over fiber optic cables as two-level signals. The addition of a fifth bit means that the 100 Mbps data stream becomes a 125 Mbaud stream of signals on a fiber optic media system.[*]

The 5-bit encoding scheme allows for the transmission of 32 5-bit symbols, including 16 symbols that carry the four-bit data values from zero through F, along with a further set of 16 symbols used for control and other purposes. These other

---

[*] A *baud* is a unit of signaling speed per second. Mbaud = one million baud.

symbols include the IDLE symbol which is continually sent when no other data is present.* For this reason, the signaling system used in Fast Ethernet is continually active, sending IDLE symbols at 125 Mbaud if nothing else is going on.

Table 6-1 shows 9 of the 32 5-bit symbols that can be sent over the channel. Each five-bit symbol transmitted on the channel is mapped to a four-bit nibble of data, which is sent over the MII interface. There are a number of non-data symbols, some of which are given letter names (*J* and *K*) and used for special purposes such as indicating the start of preamble in a frame.

Table 6-1. Five-Bit Symbols

Five-Bit Code Group as Sent on the Channel	Data on MII interface	Interpretation
11110	0000	Data 0
01001	0001	Data 1
10100	0010	Data 2
10101	0011	Data 3
01010	0100	Data 4
Etc.	Etc.	Etc.
11101	1111	Data F
11111	Undefined	IDLE
11000	0101	*J*, always paired with *K*
10001	0101	*K*, always paired with *J*
Etc.	Etc.	Etc.

Carrier detection in MII transceivers ignores the IDLE symbols, so the carrier detect signal only becomes active when actual frame data symbols are seen on the channel. The pair of symbols called *J* and *K* are used together to indicate the start of the preamble in an Ethernet frame. A further pair of symbols called *T* and *R* are used to indicate the end of frame. The MII transceiver (PHY) deals with the task of recognizing these five-bit symbols, removing the special symbols, and delivering standard Ethernet frame data to the station interface or repeater port.

Each Fast Ethernet media system uses a different line signaling scheme to send the block encoded signals over the physical media. The details of each Fast Ethernet physical line signaling system are described in the individual media chapters.

---

* "IDLE" is not an acronym. Instead, IDLE is in uppercase in the Ethernet standard to show that the word is formally defined. The IDLE symbol is used to keep the signaling system active when there is no other data to send.

GMII Signal Encoding

The signaling techniques developed for the Fibre Channel standard and the twisted-pair Fast Ethernet media systems have been adapted and extended for Gigabit Ethernet. The fiber optic versions of Gigabit Ethernet are based on block encoding originally developed for the Fibre Channel standard. The details of this signal encoding are described in Chapter 12, *Gigabit Ethernet Fiber Optic Media System (1000BASE-X)*.

Development of 1000BASE-T twisted-pair Gigabit Ethernet led to another set of block encoding and line signaling techniques based on work done for Fast Ethernet media systems. The following is an example of GMII block encoding for 1000BASE-T Ethernet.

Sending 1 billion bits per second over a twisted-pair media system is a daunting engineering challenge, and pushes the state of the art when it comes to signal encoding and transceiver chips. The 1000BASE-T system uses a block encoding scheme called 4D-PAM5, which transmits signals over four wire pairs. This coding scheme translates an 8-bit byte of data into a simultaneous transmission of four code symbols (4D) over four pairs of wire. The code symbols are sent over the media system using 5-level Pulse Amplitude Modulated (PAM5) signals. The five-level line signaling system includes an error correction signal to improve the signal to noise ratio on the cable.

The block encoding scheme and the line signaling systems used for Gigabit Ethernet media are quite complex, and of primary interest to designers of transceiver chips. Anyone who wants to examine the details can find the complete block encoding and line signaling specifications listed in many pages of dense engineering detail in the Gigabit Ethernet standard.

Ethernet Network Interface Card

In the earliest days of Ethernet, the NIC was a fairly large board covered with chips wired together to implement the necessary functions. Nowadays, an Ethernet interface is typically contained in a single chip that incorporates the required functions, including the MAC protocol. Ethernet interface chips are designed to keep up with the full rate of the Ethernet system.

However, the Ethernet interface is only one of an entire set of entities that must interact to make network services happen. Various elements have an effect on how many Ethernet frames a given computer can send and receive within a specified period of time. These include the speed with which your computer system can respond to signals from the Ethernet interface chip and the amount of available buffer memory for storing frames. The efficiency of the interface driver software also has an effect.

This is an important point to understand. For example, all Ethernet interface chips are capable of sending and receiving a frame at the full frame rate for the media system they support. However, the total performance of the computer system, buffer memory and software that interacts with the Ethernet interface is not specified in any standard. These days, most computers are more than capable of sending and receiving a constant stream of Ethernet frames at the maximum frame rate of a 10 or 100 Mbps Ethernet system.

Slower computers with lower performance Ethernet interfaces and insufficient buffer memory may not be able to keep up with the full frame rate. When Ethernet frames are not acknowledged and read by the computer, they are simply dropped by the interface. This is acceptable behavior as far as the standard is concerned, since no attempt is made to standardize computer performance.

Ethernet Interface Buyer's Guide

The Ethernet NICs are built into most desktop computers these days, so you probably won't have to concern yourself with buying one. A computer or workstation with built-in Ethernet is designed to get the best possible performance from that interface. The manufacturer of the computer will have done all the work of integrating the interface hardware and software. The network software loaded on the computer will already know how to work with the built-in interface.

However, some computers do not come with built-in Ethernet, requiring you to purchase a NIC separately. If you have to add an Ethernet card to a computer, the task can be fairly complex. It's up to you to find the right Ethernet card to meet your needs. There are buyer's guides and test reports in the major computer magazines (both in print and online), which evaluate the performance of various cards to help you make an informed decision. The decision can be difficult, since there are many Ethernet cards for sale at a wide range of prices and performance in terms of bus speed, buffer memory, and so on. When you buy an add-on interface, you need to determine which interface will work well with the network software you intend to run, as well as with your existing computer hardware.

These days you can buy interface cards that come with circuitry capable of operating at 10-, 100-, and 1000 Mbps, which often support multiple speeds in various combinations. These are referred to in vendor literature as 10/100 cards, 100/1000 cards, or even 10/100/1000 cards depending on the speeds supported. Multi-speed cards typically support the Auto-Negotiation standard, which allows the cards to automatically configure themselves for operation at the correct speed (see Chapter 5, *Auto-Negotiation*). Another option that is typically supported by multi-speed NICs is full-duplex operation. A useful feature to look for is the presence of status lights on the Ethernet card to indicate transmit and receive data, collisions, the status of the link test signal, and so on. These lights are useful when trouble-shooting a network connection.

Gigabit Ethernet interfaces

Many computers are currently using a significant percentage of their CPU power to generate heavy loads on a Fast Ethernet channel. These machines will not suddenly be able to go ten times faster just because they are connected to a Gigabit Ethernet channel. Gigabit Ethernet speeds and frame rates push the limits of what is possible today. As of this writing, most desktop computers and even many high performance server computers cannot keep up with the full frame rate of a Gigabit Ethernet channel.

Current PCI computer buses appear to have enough bandwidth to make significant use of a Gigabit Ethernet channel. However, interfaces will require special design to help speed up network protocol software, and to improve data rates in and out of a Gigabit Ethernet interface. Some vendors provide interfaces which provide high-level protocol packet processing onboard, to speed the flow of packets between the computer and the network. Another approach involves buffering several packets before interrupting the computer's CPU.

7

Twisted-Pair Media System (10BASE-T)

The 10BASE-T system was the first popular twisted-pair Ethernet system. The invention of 10BASE-T in the early 1990s led to the widespread adoption of Ethernet for desktop computers.

The 10BASE-T system is designed to support the transmission of 10 Mbps Ethernet signals over "voice-grade" Category 3 twisted-pair cables. However, the vast majority of twisted-pair cabling systems in use today are based on Category 5 twisted-pair cables. Category 5 cables have higher quality signal carrying characteristics and work very well with the 10BASE-T system.

In this chapter we discuss the signaling and media components used in the 10BASE-T system. We also provide the basic configuration guidelines for a single 10BASE-T segment.

10BASE-T Signaling Components

The following signaling components may be used in the 10BASE-T system to send and receive signals over the media system:

- Ethernet interface with a built-in 10BASE-T transceiver.

- AUI transceiver cable.

- External 10BASE-T AUI-based transceiver, also called a medium attachment unit (MAU).

- Repeater hub equipped with 10BASE-T ports.

10BASE-T Ethernet Interface

A 10BASE-T Ethernet interface typically includes a built-in 10BASE-T transceiver that is used to make a direct connection to the twisted-pair segment. Figure 7-1 shows a NIC designed for installation in a desktop computer.

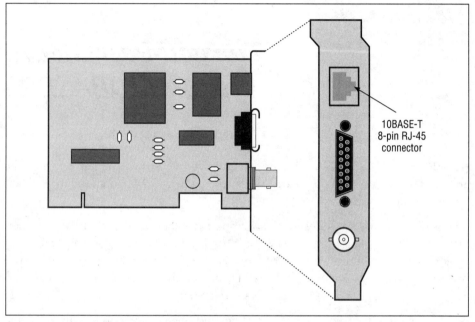

Figure 7-1. 10BASE-T Ethernet interface

This particular card is equipped with three connectors that allow an attachment to a variety of 10 Mbps Ethernet media systems. The card can be connected to a 10BASE-T segment using the built-in 10BASE-T transceiver and the RJ-45–style jack that connects to a twisted-pair cable. It can also be connected to a 10BASE-T segment using the 15-pin AUI connector and an external 10BASE-T transceiver. These days, many twisted-pair NICs typically have only an RJ-45–style connector on them, and use internal transceivers to support operation at multiple speeds. On such a multi-speed interface, the Auto-Negotiation standard is typically used to automatically configure the speed of operation.

Transceiver Cable

For 10BASE-T cards equipped with an AUI interface, an AUI transceiver cable may be used to make a connection between the AUI connector on the interface and the AUI connector on an external 10BASE-T transceiver. A transceiver cable is not necessary when a built-in 10BASE-T transceiver is used.

External 10BASE-T Transceiver

A station interface that only has a 15-pin AUI connector can be connected to a 10BASE-T Ethernet segment using an external 10BASE-T Ethernet transceiver. Figure 7-2 shows an external 10BASE-T transceiver equipped with an 8-pin RJ-45–style jack.

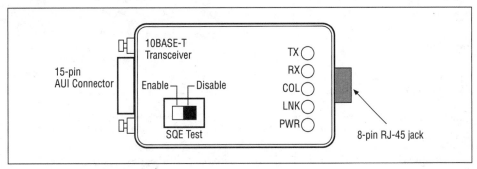

Figure 7-2. External 10BASE-T transceiver

Signal Polarity and Polarity Reversal

The transmit and receive data signals on each wire pair of a 10BASE-T twisted-pair segment are polarized, with one wire of each wire pair carrying the positive (+) signal, and the other carrying the negative (–) signal. Many 10BASE-T transceivers support an optional feature called *polarity reversal*, which can automatically detect and correct wiring errors that result in incorrect polarity in a given wire pair.

Polarity reversal refers to swapping the position of the two wires within a given wire pair. This is different from a wiring crossover error, which involves swapping the position of wire pair 2 with wire pair 3, for example.

10BASE-T Signal Encoding

Signals sent over the 10BASE-T media system are encoded using the Manchester encoding system described in Chapter 6, *Ethernet Media Fundamentals*. 10BASE-T transceivers are designed to send and receive signals over a segment that consists of four wires: one pair of wires for transmitting data and another pair for receiving data.

Physical line signaling

The 10BASE-T line signals are sent over the twisted-pair wires as balanced differential currents. In each wire pair, one wire is used to carry the positive amplitude of the differential signal (from 0 volts to +2.5 volts), and one wire carries the negative amplitude of the signal (from 0 volts to –2.5 volts). The peak signal carried by each of the wires is approximately 2.5 volts, which provides a total of 5 volts peak-to-peak measured across both wires in the pair.

Differential signaling provides its own zero reference point, around which the electrical signals swing positive or negative. There is no need to reference the signals on a 10BASE-T segment to a common ground level shared by the equipment at both ends. By not referencing the signals to a common ground, the 10BASE-T system is isolated from variations in ground voltage that can occur in a twisted-pair cabling system. This eliminates problems with ground currents and improves the reliability of the system.

10BASE-T Media Components

The following set of media components are used to build a 10BASE-T twisted-pair segment:

- Unshielded twisted-pair (UTP) cable, Category 3 or better.
- Eight-position RJ-45–style modular connector.

UTP Cable

The 10BASE-T system operates over two pairs of UTP wires; one pair receives data signals into the station or hub port, and the other pair is used for transmitting data signals from the station or hub port. The 10BASE-T standard was designed to accommodate twisted-pair cabling systems based on ordinary voice-grade telephone wire rated to meet the TIA/EIA Category 3 specifications (see Chapter 14, *Structured Cabling*). The target length in the standard for a 10BASE-T segment based on voice-grade cabling and components is 100 meters (328 feet). More details on installing and using twisted-pair cables and connectors can be found in Chapter 15, *Twisted-Pair Cables and Connectors.*

A 10BASE-T segment can be longer than 100 meters as long as the signal quality specifications are met. Most of the time this will not matter, since the vast majority of all office and work areas are within 100 meters of a telecommunications closet. However, on occasion, you may need a 10BASE-T segment that is longer than 100 meters to reach equipment that's further away from the closet. The next section will discuss ways to increase the length of your 10BASE-T segments.

10BASE-T Segments Longer than 100 Meters

The major limiting factor on a 10BASE-T segment is the strength of the signal, or signal attenuation. The receiver circuit in a typical 10BASE-T transceiver has a signal squelch level set at 300 millivolts (mV), which helps prevent the faint signals induced by signal crosstalk between wire pairs from becoming a problem, by lim-iting the level at which signals are received. Once a signal sinks below this level, it will not be received by a 10BASE-T transceiver. With this approach, signals induced by crosstalk below 300 mV are simply ignored. However, this also means that when signal attenuation over a long segment lowers the real signal level to below 300 mV, the segment will stop working.

10BASE-T attenuation specifications

The maximum signal attenuation allowed in the specifications for a 10BASE-T seg-ment is 11.5 decibels (dB) as measured from one end of the segment to the other with a cable testing device. A typical Category 5 cable has an attenuation of 10 dB per 500 feet at 10 MHz frequencies. Therefore, 500 feet of this kind of twisted-pair cable would use up the majority of the 11.5 dB signal loss that is allowed on a 10BASE-T segment.

You can expect that at least 1.5 dB of the loss budget will be used up by the sig-nal losses that occur in RJ-45–style connectors, patch panels, and patch cables. Taken all together, even if you use Category 5 cable it will be difficult to achieve a segment any longer than approximately 150 meters (roughly 490 feet) while stay-ing within the signal quality specifications found in the standard.

Special signaling equipment

Some vendors have designed hubs and transceivers that allow you to stretch things by lowering the squelch level. If your segment is built using high-quality twisted-pair cable, it will typically have very low levels of crosstalk. In that case, by lowering the squelch level of the receiver circuit you will be able to send sig-nals further before the signal level drops too low to be received.

A 10BASE-T segment will be more likely to function over distances greater than 100 meters if you use high quality low-attenuation twisted-pair cable and keep the number of connectors and patch panels to a minimum. The further you go beyond 100 meters, however, the greater the total amount of signal attenuation will be. Eventually it will be impossible even for transceivers equipped with a low squelch setting to accurately receive the signal.

Twisted-Pair Impedance Rating

For best results, you should use twisted-pair cable with a 100 ohm characteristic impedance rating. However, the standard notes that it is possible to build seg-ments using twisted-pair cable with a 120 ohm characteristic impedance, a type of cable commonly used in certain European countries. If you must use cable with a 120 ohm impedance, then you should check with the vendor of your transceiver and repeater equipment to see if the equipment is designed to function adequately with twisted-pair cables at that impedance level.

Eight-Position RJ-45–Style Jack Connector

The 10BASE-T media system uses two pairs of wires, which are terminated in an eight-position (RJ-45–style) connector. This means that four pins of the eight-pin connector are used. Table 7-1 lists the 10BASE-T signals used on the 8-pin connector.

Table 7-1. 10BASE-T 8-Pin Connector Signals

Pin Number	Signal
1	TD+ (Transmit Data)
2	TD– (Transmit Data)
3	RD+ (Receive Data)
4	Unused
5	Unused
6	RD– (Receive Data)
7	Unused
8	Unused

A typical twisted-pair segment will have all eight wires connected to the RJ-45–style connector in the standard configuration used for structured cabling systems, even though the 10BASE-T media system only uses four of the eight wires.

The TIA/EIA 568A structured cabling standard recommends installing two twisted-pair cables for each office: one for data service and another for telephone or other service. A conservative design reserves a four-pair cable for data service, uses a cable rated to meet the Category 5 or better specifications, and connects all eight wires of the cable. That way, the network can provide a 10 Mbps 10BASE-T connection to the desktop today and then be upgraded to faster Ethernet systems (100- and 1000 Mbps) in the future.

Connecting a Station to 10BASE-T Ethernet

Now that we've seen the components that make up a 10BASE-T Ethernet system, let's look at how these components are used to connect a station to a twisted-pair segment.

Figure 7-3 shows two computers (stations). The one on the top of the figure has a 10BASE-T network interface card (NIC) installed. The NIC has an RJ-45 connector, to which the 10BASE-T segment is directly attached. The computer on the bottom has an interface with an AUI connector, and is attached to the 10BASE-T twisted-pair segment with an external transceiver. A signal crossover is required in each twisted-pair segment to ensure that the Ethernet signals are connected properly. Signal crossover for twisted-pair cables and connectors is described in Chapter 15.

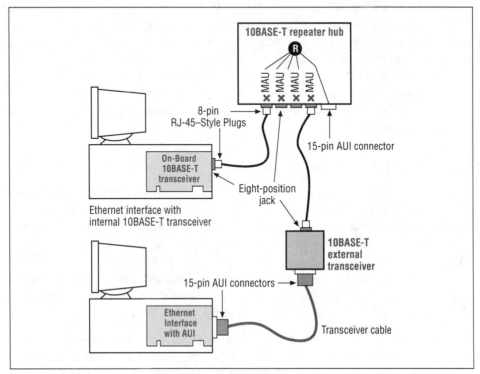

Figure 7-3. Connecting a station to a 10BASE-T Ethernet system

A 10BASE-T Ethernet interface with built-in transceiver electronics includes the transceiver chip on the same board as the Ethernet interface, eliminating the external transceiver and transceiver cable. The interface board is provided with an RJ-45–style jack connector which provides a direct connection between the transceiver on the interface and the 10BASE-T repeater hub. The external transceiver is equipped with both an RJ-45–style jack and a 15-pin AUI connector. The twisted-pair cable from the repeater hub is connected to the RJ-45–style jack on the transceiver. A transceiver cable is used to make the connection between the station and the 15-pin AUI on the external transceiver.

The repeater hub is shown with four 10BASE-T ports equipped with built-in transceivers (MAUs). The crossover wiring inside the repeater hub is indicated with an "X." (The standard notes that all ports with internal crossover wiring should be marked with an "X.") The repeater hub also comes equipped with a 15-pin AUI connector that allows a connection to any external transceiver, making it possible to connect this port of the hub to any of the 10 Mbps Ethernet media systems.

The least expensive connection to a 10BASE-T Ethernet segment is achieved by using 10BASE-T Ethernet interfaces with a built-in transceiver so that you don't need to purchase an external transceiver and transceiver cable. However, as this figure shows, you can also accommodate stations with 15-pin AUI connectors by using an external transceiver equipped with an RJ-45 jack. You can also find small external transceivers that may be attached directly to the 15-pin AUI connector on an Ethernet station. This eliminates the need for a transceiver cable, making it even easier for a station with a 15-pin AUI connector to be attached to a 10BASE-T Ethernet segment.

10BASE-T Link Integrity Test

10BASE-T transceivers continually monitor the receive data path for activity as a means of checking whether the link is working correctly. The transceivers also send a link test signal to one another to verify the integrity of both twisted-pair links. The link signal is only sent when there is no other data on the network, so there is no performance impact caused by sending link signals. Vendors can optionally provide a link light on the transceiver. If the link lights on the transceivers at both ends of a segment are lit when you connect a segment, then you have an indication that the segment is wired correctly.

The presence of a link light at both ends indicates that the transceivers are powered on, that basic transceiver functions are working, and that a signal path exists between the transceivers. It's important that the link lights on both transceivers be lit, since the lights indicate if both signal paths between the two devices are wired correctly.

The link test signal pulse operates more slowly than actual Ethernet signals, so the presence of link lights won't guarantee that Ethernet signals will work over the segment. Odds are good that a correctly wired segment will work, but if the signal crosstalk on the segment is too high, then it may not work despite the presence of the link lights.

10BASE-T Configuration Guidelines

The Ethernet standard contains guidelines for building a single 10BASE-T twisted-pair segment, as well as guidelines for linking multiple segments into a larger half-duplex system. Table 7-2 lists the guidelines for a 10BASE-T segment. The configuration rules for linking multiple 10 Mbps segments with repeater hubs are described in Chapter 13, *Multi-Segment Configuration Guidelines*.

Table 7-2. 10BASE-T Single Segment Guidelines

Media Type	Maximum Segment Length	Maximum Number of Transceivers (per segment)
Twisted-Pair 10BASE-T	100 m (328 feet)[a,b]	2

[a] 100 meters is the target length set in the standard for 10BASE-T segments based on Category 3 (voice grade) cable and components. 10BASE-T segments may be longer while still meeting the electrical specifications in the standard, depending on the quality of the twisted-pair segment.

[b] There is no minimum length specification for a 10BASE-T segment. In practice you can purchase ready-made patch cables as short as 1 foot, which can be used to connect 10BASE-T equipment together. However, you may find that if you want to test the cable with a hand-held cable tester, there may be a minimum cable length that the tester requires for an accurate test of cable parameters.

8

Fiber Optic Media System (10BASE-F)

The 10BASE-F fiber optic media system uses pulses of light to send Ethernet signals. This approach has several advantages. For one thing, a fiber optic link segment can carry Ethernet signals for considerably longer distances than metallic media can. For example, a 10BASE-FL fiber optic link segment allows you to connect Ethernet hubs over distances as long as two kilometers (6,561.6 feet). Full-duplex fiber optic links sent over single-mode fiber can connect over considerably longer distances, as described later in this chapter.

Fiber optic media is widely used as the backbone cabling in a structured cabling system. It allows you to link Ethernet hubs located on each floor of the building with a media system that can travel longer distances than twisted-pair segments. Fiber optic media can also support higher speed Ethernet systems. This means that the fiber optic media you install to support a 10 Mbps Ethernet channel today can be used as a Fast or Gigabit Ethernet channel in the future.

In this chapter we discuss the evolution of the 10BASE-F system. We also discuss the signaling and media components used in 10BASE-F, and provide the basic configuration guidelines for a single 10BASE-F segment.

Old and New Fiber Link Segments

There are two 10 Mbps fiber optic link segment types in use, the original Fiber Optic Inter-Repeater Link (FOIRL) segment, and the newer 10BASE-FL segment. The original FOIRL specification described a link segment of up to 1,000 meters to be used between repeaters only. As the cost of repeaters dropped and repeater hubs with higher port density were used, it became cost-effective to link individual computers to fiber optic ports on a repeater hub. Vendors created external

FOIRL transceivers to allow this, although a fiber connection from a repeater to an Ethernet station was not specifically described in the FOIRL standard.

To deal with this issue and to update the set of fiber optic media standards, a new standard called 10BASE-F was developed. The new standard provides a set of fiber media specifications including a new link segment to allow direct attachments between repeater ports and stations. The 10BASE-F standard includes three fiber optic segment types:

10BASE-FL

The *fiber link* (FL) standard replaces the older FOIRL link segment. 10BASE-FL signaling equipment is designed to interoperate with existing FOIRL-based equipment. 10BASE-FL provides a fiber optic link segment that may be up to 2,000 meters long, provided that the segment only uses 10BASE-FL devices.

If older FOIRL equipment is mixed with 10BASE-FL equipment then the maximum segment length may only be 1,000 meters. A 10BASE-FL segment may be used to connect two computers, or two repeaters, or a computer and a repeater port. The 10BASE-FL specs are the most widely used portion of the entire set of 10BASE-F fiber optic specifications. 10BASE-FL equipment is available from a large number of vendors.

10BASE-FB

The 10BASE-FB specification describes a synchronous signaling *fiber backbone* (FB) segment. This media system allows many Ethernet repeaters to be linked in series, exceeding the usual limit on the total number of repeaters that may be used in a given 10 Mbps Ethernet system. 10BASE-FB links—typically attached to repeater hubs—are used to link 10BASE-FB synchronous signaling repeater hubs together in a repeated backbone system that can span long distances. Individual 10BASE-FB links may be up to 2,000 meters in length. The 10BASE-FB system was not widely adopted. For the first few years after the standard was developed, equipment was available from a very few vendors. Currently there do not appear to be any vendors selling 10BASE-FB devices.

10BASE-FP

The *fiber passive* (FP) standard provides a set of specifications for a "passive fiber optic mixing segment." This was based on a non-powered device that acted as a fiber optic signal coupler, linking multiple computers on a fiber optic media system. According to the standard, 10BASE-FP segments may be up to 500 meters long; a single 10BASE-FP fiber optic passive signal coupler may link up to 33 computers. This system does not appear to have been developed by any vendor, and equipment based on this standard doesn't exist.

Next, we will describe the 10BASE-FL fiber link segment and the older FOIRL segment, since these segments are the most widely used of fiber optic segments.

10BASE-FL Signaling Components

The following signaling components may be used in the 10BASE-FL system to send and receive signals over the media system:

- Ethernet interface equipped with a 10BASE-FL transceiver. A 10BASE-FL connection is most often provided as an external transceiver which is attached to a 15-pin AUI connector on the interface.

- Transceiver cable, also called an *attachment unit interface* (AUI).

- External 10BASE-FL transceiver, also called a fiber optic *medium attachment unit* (MAU).

10BASE-FL Ethernet Interface

As discussed in the previous chapter, the vast majority of Ethernet connections to the desktop these days are made using twisted-pair media. Consequently, there is not a large market demand for an Ethernet interface with a built-in fiber optic transceiver to allow a direct 10 Mbps fiber optic connection.

As such, most vendors do not offer an interface with a built-in fiber optic transceiver. Instead, fiber optic segments are typically connected by using an external 10BASE-FL transceiver connected to a 15-pin AUI port on the Ethernet interface.

Transceiver Cable

In the 10BASE-F system, a transceiver cable may be used to make a connection between the Ethernet interface and an external 10BASE-F transceiver. If the 10BASE-F transceiver is small enough to fit directly onto the 15-pin AUI connector on the Ethernet interface, the transceiver cable is not needed.

10BASE-FL Transceiver

The typical connection to a fiber optic segment is made with an Ethernet interface that connects to an external 10BASE-FL transceiver using a 15-pin AUI connector.

Figure 8-1 shows a 10BASE-FL external transceiver, equipped with ST fiber optic connectors. A number of 10BASE-FL transceivers are small enough to fit directly onto the 15-pin connector on an Ethernet interface.

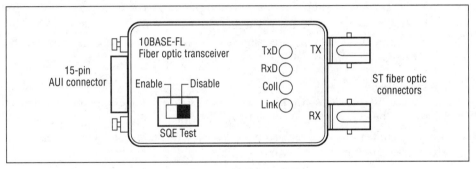

Figure 8-1. 10BASE-FL transceiver

10BASE-FL Signal Encoding

Signals sent over the 10BASE-FL media system use the Manchester encoding system described in Chapter 6, *Ethernet Media Fundamentals*.

Physical line signaling

10BASE-FL transceivers send and receive signals as light pulses over a fiber optic segment that consists of two fiber optic cables: one cable for transmitting data and one cable for receiving data. This is done using a very simple line signaling scheme called *Non-Return-to-Zero* (NRZ). NRZ results in a light pulse being transmitted for a logic one (1) and no light pulse for logic zero (0).

Signals are sent over a 10BASE-FL segment by turning the light on and off to indicate the Manchester-encoded signals representing ones and zeroes. The Manchester encoding ensures that there are enough logic transitions in the signal stream to provide clocking information for the signal decoding circuits.

10BASE-FL Media Components

The following media components are used to build a fiber optic segment:

- Fiber optic cable.
- Fiber optic connectors.

Fiber Optic Cable

The fiber optic cable specified in the standard for a fiber link segment consists of a graded-index multimode fiber cable (MMF) with a 62.5 micron (µm) fiber optic core and 125 µm outer cladding. The shorthand designation for this kind of fiber is 62.5/125. Each fiber optic link segment requires two strands of fiber, one to transmit data and one to receive data. There are many kinds of fiber optic cables available, ranging from simple two-strand jumper cables with a plain PVC outer jacket material on up to large inter-building cables carrying many fibers in a bundle. More details on installing and using fiber optic cables and connectors can be found in Chapter 16, *Fiber Optic Cables and Connectors*.

A major advantage of fiber optic cable is that the use of light pulses instead of electrical currents provides complete electrical isolation for equipment located at each end of a fiber optic link. This isolation provides immunity from hazards such as lightning strikes, and from the effects caused by different levels of electrical ground currents found in separate buildings.

For safe and reliable operation of your Ethernet system, electrical isolation of the sort provided by a fiber optic segment is essential when Ethernet segments are installed between buildings. Fiber optic media is also useful in environments such as manufacturing floors, since fiber optic segments are unaffected by the high levels of electrical noise that can be generated by heavy motors, welders, or other kinds of manufacturing equipment.

Fiber Optic Connector

The fiber connector used on 10BASE-FL link segments is generally known as an ST connector.* The formal name of this connector in the ISO/IEC international standards is *BFOC/2.5*. Figure 8-2 shows a pair of fiber optic cables equipped with ST plug connectors.

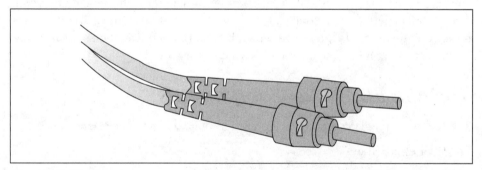

Figure 8-2. ST connectors

The ST connector is a spring-loaded bayonet connector whose outer ring locks onto the connection. The ST connector has a key on an inner sleeve along with the outer bayonet ring. To make a connection, you line up the key on the inner sleeve of the ST plug with a corresponding slot on the ST receptacle. You then

---

* ST stands for *straight tip* fiber optic connector.

push in the connector and lock it in place by twisting the outer bayonet ring. This provides a tight connection with precise alignment between the two pieces of fiber optic cable being joined.

Connecting a Station to 10BASE-FL Ethernet

Figure 8-3 shows a computer (station) equipped with an Ethernet network interface card (NIC). The NIC comes with a 15-pin AUI connector, which is used to make a connection to an external 10BASE-FL transceiver. The 10BASE-FL transceiver is connected over a fiber optic cable to a repeater hub with built-in 10BASE-FL transceivers.

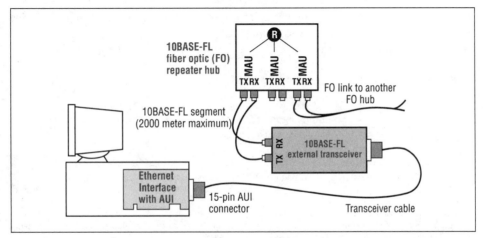

Figure 8-3. Connecting a station to a 10BASE-FL Ethernet system

A signal crossover is required to make a connection between the 10BASE-FL transceiver at the station, and a 10BASE-FL transceiver located in each repeater or switching hub port. Signal crossover is described in Chapter 16.

10BASE-FL Link Integrity Test

10BASE-FL transceivers and older FOIRL transceivers monitor the light level on the fiber optic link segment to provide a link integrity test. Vendors can optionally provide a link light on the fiber optic transceiver to give you a visual indication of the link's integrity status. If the link lights on the transceivers at each end of the link are lit when you connect them to the segment, then you know that both transceivers are powered up and working. The lights also indicate that the segment is connected properly, and that the optical loss is within acceptable limits.

To provide continual link detection, the transceivers send a 1 MHz idle signal during periods when no data is being sent. If the light level on the link drops below that required for reliable data reception, the transceivers will detect this condition and stop sending or receiving data over the link. However, transmission of the idle signal will continue, which provides a way to detect the link when the light level over the fiber optic link returns to an acceptable value.

10BASE-FL Configuration Guidelines

The Ethernet standard contains guidelines for a single 10BASE-FL fiber optic segment, as well as guidelines for linking multiple segments into a larger half-duplex system. Table 8-1 lists the single segment guidelines for a 10BASE-FL segment. The configuration rules for linking multiple 10 Mbps segment types with repeater hubs are described in Chapter 13, *Multi-Segment Configuration Guidelines*.

Table 8-1. 10BASE-FL Single Segment Guidelines

Media Type	Maximum Segment Length	Maximum Number of Transceivers (per segment)
10BASE-FL	2,000 m (6,561 feet)[a,b]	2
FOIRL	1,000 m (3,280 feet)[b]	2

[a] If 10BASE-FL transceivers are used at each end of the segment, then the segment may be up to 2,000 m. If one end of the segment uses an FOIRL transceiver, then the segment is limited to a maximum of 1,000 m.

[b] There is no minimum length specified for this segment type. However, some vendors offer "extended length" versions of this equipment which require a vendor-specific minimum length segment to prevent signal errors caused by over-driving the fiber optic receiver.

Longer 10 Mbps Fiber Segments

Longer fiber segments are possible when the link is operated in full-duplex mode. As explained in Chapter 4, *Full-Duplex Ethernet*, the use of full-duplex mode on a link segment means that the segment length is no longer restricted by the round trip timing limits of a shared Ethernet channel. Instead, the segment length is only limited by the signal carrying characteristics of the media—in this case, the optical power loss (signal attenuation) and signal dispersion over the fiber optic cable. Transceivers are available that can achieve distances of up to 5 km over full-duplex segments built using multimode fiber optic cables.

Single-mode fiber optic cable transceivers can be purchased to drive a full-duplex 10 Mbps link for distances of up to 40 km. However, a single-mode fiber system is more expensive and difficult to use than multimode. The single-mode fiber optic core is typically 8 or 9 μm in diameter, compared to the 62.5 μm core in multi-mode cable. Coupling a light source into the small core of single-mode cable requires a more expensive laser light source and precise connectors. Therefore, while much longer full-duplex fiber optic segments are possible, you must be prepared to deal with more complex fiber optic design and installation issues.

9

Fast Ethernet Twisted-Pair Media System (100BASE-TX)

The 100BASE-TX twisted-pair media system is the most widely used Fast Ethernet media type. The 100BASE-TX standard is based on the twisted-pair specifications first developed for the FDDI TP-PMD (Twisted-Pair Physical Medium Dependent) standard. The system operates over two pairs of twisted-pair wires: one pair to receive data signals and the other pair to transmit data signals.

This chapter describes the signaling and media components used in the 100BASE-TX system. We also describe how a station is connected to a 100BASE-TX segment, and provide the basic configuration guidelines for a single segment.

100BASE-TX Signaling Components

The following signaling components may be used in the 100BASE-TX system to send and receive signals:

- Ethernet interface with a built-in 100BASE-TX transceiver.
- Medium-Independent Interface (MII).
- External 100BASE-TX transceiver, also called a *physical layer device* (PHY).

100BASE-TX Ethernet Interface

A 100BASE-TX interface may be equipped with a built-in 100BASE-TX transceiver used to make a direct connection to the twisted-pair segment. If the interface is equipped with a 40-pin MII connector, external transceivers can be used. Figure 9-1 shows a network interface card designed to be installed in a desktop computer.

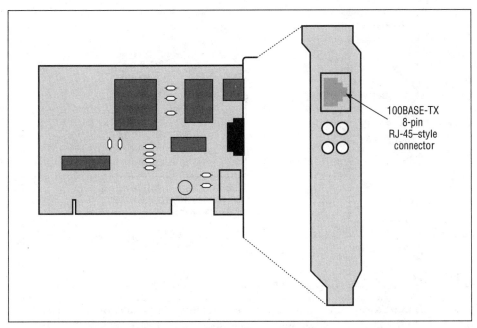

Figure 9-1. 100BASE-TX Ethernet interface

The card is equipped with an RJ-45–style jack that makes a direct connection to a twisted-pair cable. Many twisted-pair NICs typically have only an RJ-45–style connector on them. These NICs may use internal transceivers to support operation at multiple speeds. On such a multi-speed interface, the Auto-Negotiation standard is typically used to automatically configure the speed of operation.

Medium-Independent Interface

The MII is a 40-pin connector that allows an external 100BASE-TX transceiver to be connected to the Ethernet interface. An external transceiver is typically connected directly to the MII connector on the interface.

100BASE-TX Transceiver

A 100BASE-TX interface with a built-in transceiver is connected directly to the twisted-pair Ethernet segment; there is no need for an outboard transceiver since the transceiver is built into the interface card. However, if an Ethernet device is equipped with a 40-pin MII connector, then it can be connected to a twisted-pair Ethernet segment using an external 100BASE-TX Ethernet transceiver.

Figure 9-2 shows an external 100BASE-TX transceiver equipped with an 8-pin RJ-45–style jack, which allows for connection of the twisted-pair cable.

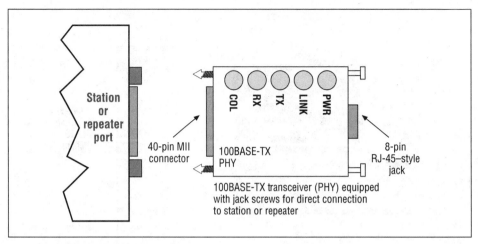

Figure 9-2. 100BASE-TX external transceiver

100BASE-TX Signal Encoding

The 100BASE-TX system is based on the signaling originally developed for the ANSI X3T9.5 FDDI standard, which includes both fiber optic and twisted-pair media. The signal encoding used in FDDI and 100BASE-TX relies on the *4B/5B* system, described in Chapter 6, *Ethernet Media Fundamentals.*

Physical line signaling

The physical signaling used to transmit the five-bit symbols over twisted-pair cables is based on a system called multilevel threshold-3 (MLT-3). This means that at each signal transition the signal can have one of three levels. During each clock transition, a change from one level to the next marks a logical one (1), where a constant signal level indicates a logical zero (0). Since the signal level doesn't change when a zero is transmitted, this reduces the total signaling rate on the wire.

In the 100BASE-TX transceiver the 4B/5B block encoded data is first scrambled, to spread out the electromagnetic emission patterns in the data. It is then transmitted onto the twisted wire pairs as a series of three voltages with a signal transition rate of 125 Mbaud. The differential voltages swing from approximately zero to +1 volts on the positive wire, and from zero to –1 volts on the negative wire of the wire pairs.

Even though the MLT-3 signaling system reduces the signaling rate, the 100BASE-TX system is still doing a lot of high frequency signaling over the twisted-pair cables. Therefore, it's important that all twisted-pair cables—including patch cords and other components used in a 100BASE-TX segment—meet or exceed the Category 5 signal-carrying specifications needed to handle the signals. If lower-quality cable and components are used, the signal error rate will increase, causing frame loss and reduced network performance.

100BASE-TX Media Components

The following set of media components are used to build a 100BASE-TX twisted-pair segment:

- Unshielded or shielded twisted-pair cable.

- Eight-position RJ-45–style modular connectors that meet Category 5 specifications.

Unshielded Twisted-Pair Cable

The 100BASE-TX system operates over two pairs of unshielded twisted-pair (UTP) wires; one pair receives data signals, while the other pair transmits data signals. The maximum segment length is 100 meters (328 feet) of unshielded twisted-pair cable that has a 100 ohm characteristic impedance rating and that meets or exceeds the TIA/EIA Category 5 specifications. Additional details on installing and using UTP cables and connectors can be found in Chapter 15, *Twisted-Pair Cables and Connectors.*

Shielded Twisted-Pair Cable

The TP-PMD standard supports the option of sending FDDI signals over shielded twisted-pair cable. Since the 100BASE-TX standard is based on TP-PMD, it also provides the option of support for shielded twisted-pair (STP) cabling with characteristic impedance of 150 ohms. This type of cabling may be found in certain building cabling systems, particularly older 802.5 Token Ring systems. The maximum segment length for a STP segment is also 100 meters.

The vast majority of 100BASE-TX interfaces are based on the RJ-45 connector. However, if a vendor wishes to include the 150-ohm media connection option on a 100BASE-TX adapter board or transceiver, then the medium-dependent interface (MDI) used to connect to the shielded twisted-pair medium must use a 9-pin "D-type." The 9-pin connector is wired according to the ANSI TP-PMD specifications: Pin 1: Receive (+), Pin 5: Transmit (+), Pin 6: Receive (–), Pin 9: Transmit (–).

Eight-Position RJ-45–Style Jack Connector

The unshielded twisted-pair version of the 100BASE-TX media system is the most widely used. In this system, the two pairs of wires are terminated in an eight-position (RJ-45–style) connector, which means that four pins of the eight-position connector are used. The 100BASE-TX signals used on the 8-pin connector are the same as the 10BASE-T signals shown in Table 7-1 in Chapter 7, *Twisted-Pair Media System (10BASE-T)*.

The pin numbers used in the eight-pin connector for 100BASE-TX were changed from the ones defined in the ANSI TP-PMD standard, in order to conform to the wiring scheme already in use in the 10BASE-T standard. The ANSI standard uses pins 7 and 8 for receive data, whereas 100BASE-TX uses the same pins as the 10BASE-T system: 3 and 6. That way, a 100BASE-TX Ethernet adapter can replace a 10BASE-T adapter in a station, and be plugged into the same Category 5 cable system without changing the wires.

According to the structured cabling standards, a typical Category 5 twisted-pair segment built will have all eight wires connected to the RJ-45–style connector, even though the 100BASE-TX media system only uses four of the eight wires. The other wires should not be used to support any other services, as the 100BASE-TX system is not designed to tolerate the increased signal crosstalk that occurs when sharing the cable with other signals.

Connecting a Station to 100BASE-TX Ethernet

Figure 9-3 shows two computers connected to 100BASE-TX twisted-pair segments. The top computer is equipped with an Ethernet NIC with a built-in 100BASE-TX transceiver. The card comes with an RJ-45–style jack connector, to which the twisted-pair cable is connected. The computer on the bottom is connected with an external transceiver, which is attached to the 40-pin MII interface on the Ethernet card.

A signal crossover is required in each twisted-pair segment to ensure that the Ethernet signals are connected properly. Signal crossover for twisted-pair cables and connectors is described further in Chapter 15. The repeater hub is shown with four 100BASE-TX connectors with built-in transceivers. The crossover wiring is done inside the hub as indicated by the "X" on the hub port.

100BASE-TX Link Integrity Test

The 100BASE-TX transceiver circuits (PHY) continually monitor the receive data path for activity as a means of checking that the link is working correctly. The signal encoding on 100BASE-TX segments sends signals continually, even during idle periods. Therefore, activity on the receive data path is sufficient to provide a continual check of link integrity.

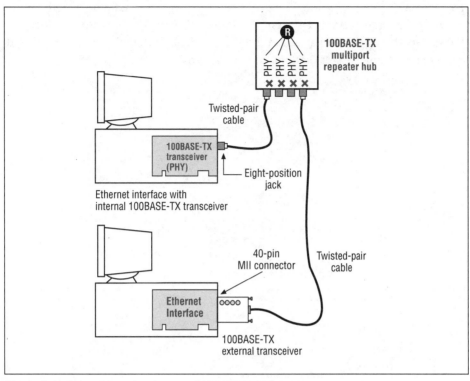

Figure 9-3. Connecting a station to a 100BASE-TX Ethernet system

100BASE-TX Configuration Guidelines

The Ethernet standard contains guidelines for building a single 100BASE-TX twisted-pair segment, as well as guidelines for linking multiple segments into a larger system. Table 9-1 lists the single segment guidelines for a 100BASE-TX segment. Multiple 100 Mbps segments can be connected together in half-duplex mode with a single Class I or Class II repeater. The configuration rules for linking multiple 100 Mbps segment types with repeater hubs are described in Chapter 13, *Multi-Segment Configuration Guidelines*.

Table 9-1. 100BASE-TX Single Segment Guidelines

Media Type	Maximum Segment Length	Maximum Number of Transceivers (per segment)
Twisted-Pair 100BASE-TX	100 m (328 feet)[a]	2

a There is no minimum length specification for a 100BASE-TX segment. In practice, you can purchase ready-made patch cables as short as 1 foot and use them to connect 100BASE-TX equipment together. However, you may find that if you want to test the cable with a hand-held cable tester, there may be a minimum cable length that the tester requires for an accurate test of cable parameters.

The 100BASE-TX specifications allow a segment with a maximum length of 100 meters. Unlike the 10BASE-T system, 100BASE-TX segments cannot be longer than 100 meters due to the limitations in the signal timing budget that result from sending signals ten times faster than the original Ethernet system.

10

Fast Ethernet Fiber Optic Media System (100BASE-FX)

The 100BASE-FX fiber optic media system provides all of the advantages of a 10BASE-FL fiber optic link segment, while operating ten times faster. Distances of 2 km (6561.6 feet) over multimode fiber optic cables are possible when operating 100BASE-FX segments in full-duplex mode. Considerably longer distances are possible when using single mode fiber segments. This is why the 100BASE-FX media system is a popular choice for Ethernet backbone networks.

In this chapter we describe the signaling and media components used in the 100BASE-FX system. We also show how a station is connected to a 100BASE-FX segment. Finally, we describe the basic configuration guidelines for a single 100BASE-FX segment.

100BASE-FX Signaling Components

The following signaling components may be used in the 100BASE-FX system to send and receive signals over the media system:

- Ethernet interface with a built-in 100BASE-FX fiber optic transceiver.

- Media-Independent Interface (MII).

- External 100BASE-FX transceiver, also called a Physical Layer Device (PHY).

100BASE-FX Ethernet Interface

A 100BASE-FX interface may be equipped with a built-in 100BASE-FX transceiver, which is used to make a direct connection to the fiber optic segment. If the interface is equipped with a 40-pin MII connector, then external transceivers can be used.

Figure 10-1 shows a network adapter card designed for installation in a desktop computer. The card is equipped with a duplex SC fiber optic connector that makes a direct connection to the fiber optic cables in the segment.

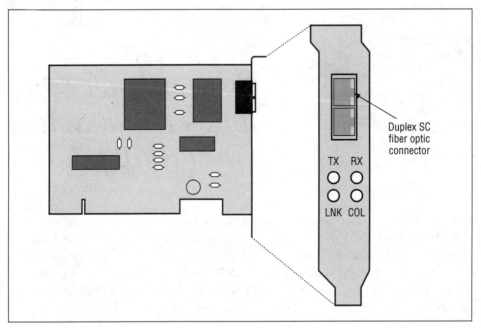

Figure 10-1. 100BASE-FX Ethernet interface

Media-Independent Interface

The MII is a 40-pin connector that allows an external 100BASE-FX transceiver to be connected to the Ethernet interface. The transceiver is typically connected directly to the MII connector on the interface.

100BASE-FX Transceiver

A 100BASE-FX interface with a built-in transceiver is connected directly to the fiber optic Ethernet segment; there is no need for an outboard transceiver since the transceiver is on the interface card.

However, if an Ethernet device is equipped with a 40-pin MII connector, then it can be connected to a fiber optic Ethernet segment using an external 100BASE-FX Ethernet transceiver. Figure 10-2 shows an external 100BASE-FX transceiver equipped with a duplex SC fiber optic connector.

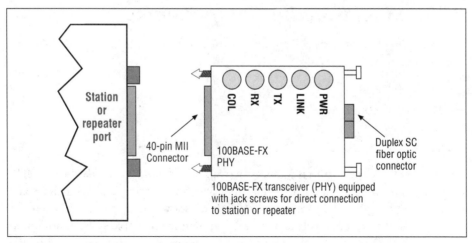

Figure 10-2. 100BASE-FX external transceiver

100BASE-FX Signal Encoding

The 100BASE-FX system is based on block encoded signaling originally developed for the ANSI X3T9.5 FDDI standard, which includes both fiber optic and twisted-pair media. The block encoding used in FDDI and 100BASE-FX relies on a system called *4B/5B*, described in Chapter 6, *Ethernet Media Fundamentals*.

Physical line signaling

The physical signaling used to transmit 100BASE-FX signals is accomplished by sending light pulses over the fiber optic cables. The 100BASE-FX system uses a variant of the Non-Return-to-Zero (NRZ) scheme, which is called Non-Return-to-Zero, Invert-on-ones (NRZI). This system makes no change in the signal level when sending a logic zero (0), and inverts the signal from its previous state for a logic one (1). The goal is to ensure a minimum number of logic transitions in the signal to provide clocking information for the signal decoding circuits.

The peak optical transmission power from a 100BASE-FX transceiver is between 200 and 400 microwatts (µW). Given an approximately equal number of ones and zeroes sent over the segment, the average power sent over a fiber optic link is between 100 and 200 µW. These figures are for light being coupled into a standard 62.5/125 micron (µm) fiber. Since there are no electromagnetic emissions on a fiber optic link, there is no need to scramble the data, as done with 100BASE-TX systems to limit the level of electromagnetic emissions.

100BASE-FX Media Components

The following set of media components are used to build a 100BASE-FX fiber optic segment:

- Fiber optic cable.

- Fiber optic connectors.

Fiber Optic Cable

The 100BASE-FX specification requires two strands of *multimode fiber optic* (MMF) cable per link, one for transmit data, and one for receive data, with the signal crossover (TX to RX) performed in the link as shown in Figure 10-4. There are many kinds of fiber optic cables available, ranging from simple two-strand jumper cables with PVC plastic for the outer jacket material on up to large inter-building cables carrying many fibers in a bundle.

The typical fiber optic cable used for a 100BASE-FX fiber link segment consists of a *graded-index* MMF cable. These fibers optic cables have a 62.5 μm fiber optic core and 125 μm outer cladding (62.5/125). The wavelength of light used on a 100BASE-TX fiber link segment is 1350 nanometers (nm). Signals sent at that wavelength over MMF fiber can provide segment lengths of up to 2,000 meters (6,561 feet) when operating the link in full-duplex mode. More details on installing and using fiber optic cables and connectors can be found in Chapter 16, *Fiber Optic Cables and Connectors.*

Fiber Optic Connector

The *medium-dependent interface* (MDI) for a 100BASE-FX link may be one of three kinds of fiber optic connectors. Of the three, the duplex SC connector shown in Figure 10-3 is the recommended alternative in the standard and is the one most widely used by vendors. The SC connector is designed for ease of use; the connector is pushed into place and automatically snaps into the connector housing to complete the connection.

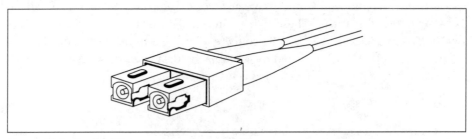

Figure 10-3. Duplex SC connector

The ST connector may also be used. This is the same connector used for a 10BASE-FL link. It is a spring-loaded bayonet-type connector that has a key on an inner sleeve and an outer bayonet ring. To make a connection, you line up the key on the inner sleeve of the ST plug with a corresponding slot on the ST receptacle, then push the connector in and lock it in place by twisting the outer bayonet ring.

According to the standard, the FDDI fiber optic *media interface connector* (MIC) may also be used on 100BASE-FX equipment; however, this optional connector has not been adopted by equipment vendors.

Connecting a Station to 100BASE-FX Ethernet

Figure 10-4 shows a computer equipped with a 100BASE-FX Ethernet adapter. In this example, the adapter card comes with an SC duplex connector, which makes a connection to the fiber cables that connect to the repeater hub.The repeater hub in the figure is shown with three pairs of 100BASE-FX SC connectors and built-in transceivers. A signal crossover is required to make a connection between the 100BASE-FX transceiver in the station, and the 100BASE-FX transceiver located in each repeater or switching hub port. Signal crossover is described in Chapter 16.

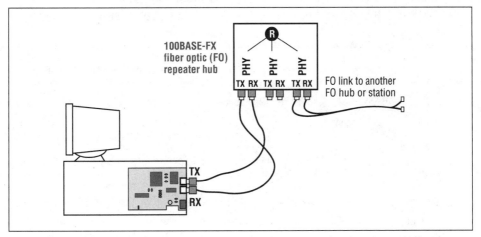

Figure 10-4. Connecting a station to a 100BASE-FX Ethernet system

100BASE-FX Link Integrity Test

The 100BASE-FX transceiver circuits (PHY) continually monitor the receive data path for activity as a means of checking that the link is working correctly. The signaling system used for 100BASE-FX segments is based on the ANSI FDDI signaling system, which sends signals continually even during idle periods of no network traffic. Therefore, activity on the receive data path is sufficient to provide a continual check of link integrity.

An optional link integrity check on 100BASE-FX fiber optic segments is called the *Far End Fault* function. In operation, Far End Fault detection occurs when the constant stream of IDLE symbols is no longer detected on a 100BASE-FX link. At this point, the device that has seen the failure of the IDLE symbols on its receive side of the link will then transmit a constant stream of Far End Fault signals. A device equipped with optional Far End Fault capability will interpret the incoming Far End Fault signals as a link failure, and will be able to signal that failure to a management interface in the device.

The Far End Fault detection feature is useful since fiber links can be very long. A system that can detect that a link is working in one direction but not the other can save a lot of time when troubleshooting links. In addition, vendors can build hubs with Far End Fault detection that allows the hubs to automatically enable a backup link to replace the failed link.

100BASE-FX Configuration Guidelines

The Ethernet standard contains guidelines for building a single 100BASE-FX fiber optic segment, as well as guidelines for linking multiple segments into a larger system. Table 10-1 lists the single segment guidelines for a 100BASE-FX segment.

Table 10-1. 100BASE-FX Single Segment Guidelines

Media Type	Maximum Segment Length	Maximum Number of Transceivers (per segment)
Fiber optic 100BASE-FX	412 m (1351 feet)[a, b]	2

[a] This maximum segment length is for a half-duplex segment connected between two stations. If a repeater is used to link two fiber optic segments, then the maximum distance allowed will be less than 412 m. Consult the multi-segment configuration rules in Chapter 13 for details.
[b] There is no minimum length specified for this segment type. Two 100BASE-FX stations can be linked with a patch cable that is as short as practicable.

Multiple 100 Mbps segments can be connected together in half-duplex mode with a single Class I or Class II repeater. A half-duplex network based on repeaters can provide a network with a maximum total cable diameter of 200 meters between stations. The configuration rules for linking multiple 100 Mbps segment types with repeater hubs are fully described in Chapter 13, *Multi-Segment Configuration Guidelines.*

Longer Fiber Segments

Longer fiber segments are possible when the link is operated in full-duplex mode. Full-duplex mode on a link segment means that the segment length is no longer restricted by the round-trip timing limits of a shared Ethernet channel. Instead, the segment length is limited by the optical power loss (signal attenuation) and signal dispersion over the fiber optic cable. Typical fiber optic transceivers can achieve distances of 2 km over 100BASE-FX segments built using multimode fiber optic cables. Longer distances can be achieved when using single-mode fiber for a full-duplex segment.

While single-mode 100BASE-FX links can achieve distances of 20 km or more, this type of fiber is more expensive and difficult to use than multimode fiber. The single-mode fiber core may typically be 8 or 9 μm in diameter, compared to the 62.5 μm core in multimode. Coupling a light source into the small core of single-mode fiber requires a more expensive laser light source and very precise connectors.

You may be able to find a 100BASE-FX transceiver equipped with single-mode fiber optics. Another approach is to connect a standard, multimode 100BASE-FX transceiver to an outboard conversion device. The conversion device converts the standard 100BASE-FX multimode signals to a proprietary signal sent over single-mode fiber for distances of from 20 to 40 km or more when operated in full-duplex mode.

11

Gigabit Ethernet Twisted-Pair Media System (1000BASE-T)

The specifications for the 1000BASE-T media system were developed in the 802.3ab supplement to the IEEE standard, which was formally adopted in July 1999. Supporting 1 billion bits per second over unshielded twisted-pair (UTP) cable is a remarkable achievement. To make it happen, the 1000BASE-T media system uses a mix of signaling and encoding techniques that were originally developed for the 100BASE-TX, 100BASE-T2 and 100BASE-T4 media standards. While 100BASE-T2 and 100BASE-T4 were not widely adopted in the marketplace, their technology was used in developing the 1000BASE-T standard.

The 100BASE-T2 Fast Ethernet standard is based on a complex signal encoding system used to send 100 Mbps signals over two pairs of Category 3 cable. These techniques were adopted and extended by the 1000BASE-T standard for use over four pairs of Category 5 cable. From the 100BASE-T4 system, the 1000BASE-T standard adopted the technique of simultaneously sending and receiving signals over the same wire pairs. The 1000BASE-T system also adopted the line signaling rate of the very popular 100BASE-TX Fast Ethernet system. Maintaining the same line signaling rate makes it possible for 1000BASE-T to work over the same widely used Category 5 cabling that supports a 100BASE-TX link.

This chapter describes the signaling and media components used in the 1000BASE-T system. We also show how a station is connected to a 1000BASE-T segment, and provide the basic configuration guidelines for a single 1000BASE-T segment.

1000BASE-T Signaling Components

Unlike other Ethernet systems that provide an exposed AUI or MII connector which supports an external transceiver and transceiver cable, the 1000BASE-T Gigabit Ethernet system requires an Ethernet interface with a built-in Gigabit Ethernet transceiver. There is no exposed transceiver connector in the Gigabit Ethernet system, and therefore no support for an external transceiver.

The 1000BASE-T interface comes equipped with a built-in transceiver used to make a direct connection to the 1000BASE-T twisted-pair segment. The interface electronics can either be built into the computer at the factory, or can be an adapter card that is installed in one of the computer's expansion slots. An Ethernet interface is also found in every switching hub port. Figure 11-1 shows a network interface card designed to be installed in a desktop computer.

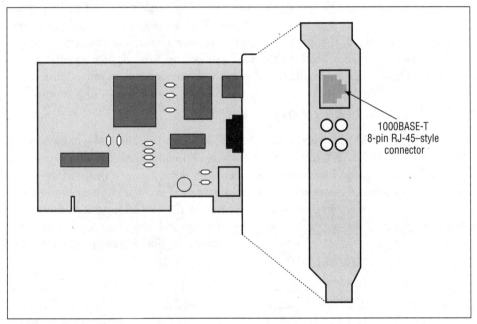

Figure 11-1. 1000 BASE-T Ethernet interface

This particular card is equipped with an RJ-45–style jack that makes a direct connection to the twisted-pair segment. Many twisted-pair NICs typically have only an RJ-45–style connector on them. These NICs may use a combination of internal GMII and MII transceivers to support operation at multiple speeds. On such a multi-speed interface, the Auto-Negotiation standard is typically used to automatically configure the speed of operation.

1000BASE-T Signal Encoding

As mentioned earlier, signaling techniques that were originally developed for the 100BASE-T2, -T4, and -TX standards have been adopted and extended for Gigabit Ethernet. To this pre-existing set of technologies, the 1000BASE-T system adds its own set of digital signaling processing techniques.

Signal encoding on a 1000BASE-T link is based on a complex block encoding scheme called 4D-PAM5, which is described in Chapter 6, *Ethernet Media Fundamentals*. The encoded signals are transmitted using a five-level symbol that carries two bits of data in each symbol. Four such encoded symbols represent an 8-bit byte of data in the portion of the encoding called 4D. The encoding scheme and the complete set of encoded symbols used are quite complex, and of primary interest only to designers of transceiver chips.*

The encoded symbols are transmitted over the wire pairs using a five-level *pulse amplitude modulation* system called PAM5. The five-level line signaling system includes error correction signals to improve the signal to noise ratio on the cable. The differential voltages used on the wire pair swing from approximately zero to +1 volts on the positive wire and from zero to −1 volts on the negative wire.

Signaling and Data Rate

A 1000BASE-T link transmits and receives data on all four wire pairs simultaneously. The 1000BASE-T transceivers at each end of the link contain four identical transmit sections and four identical receive sections. Each of the four wire pairs in the link segment is connected to both transmit and receive circuitry in the transceiver. A special circuit known as a hybrid makes it possible for the transceiver to deal with the task of simultaneously transmitting and receiving signals on each wire pair. Figure 11-2 is a schematic drawing of two transceivers connected together over four twisted pairs of wire.

This drawing shows the basic data paths through the hybrid circuits in each transceiver. Two bits of Ethernet data are encoded and sent per signal transition on each wire pair and all four wire pairs are simultaneously used to send and receive data. The result is a total of eight bits of information sent across all four pairs for each signal transition. A transition rate of 125 Mbaud therefore achieves a total data rate of 1000 Mbps. Using a five-level line signaling system maintains approximately the same signaling rate on the cable as 100BASE-TX Fast Ethernet.

---

* Anyone who wants to examine the details of the encoding scheme and bit-to-symbol mapping can find the specifications listed in Clause 40 of the Gigabit Ethernet standard. Directions for acquiring a copy of the Gigabit Ethernet standard can be found in Appendix A, *Resources*.

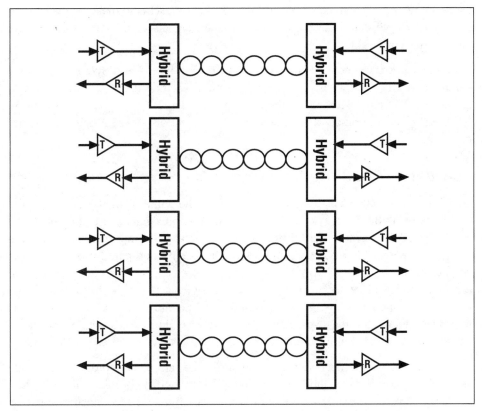

Figure 11-2. 1000BASE-T signal transmission

The continuous signaling in both directions on all four wire pairs generates signal echo and crosstalk, which the 1000BASE-T system must handle. To help with these issues, the 1000BASE-T system uses a set of *digital signal processing* (DSP) techniques. These include echo cancellation, *near-end crosstalk* (NEXT) cancellation and *far-end crosstalk* (FEXT) cancellation. Another DSP technique is *signal equalization*, to help compensate for signal distortion over the channel. The 1000BASE-T transceiver also scrambles the signal to spread out the electromagnetic emission patterns in the data to help avoid signal emission from the cable.

Signal Clocking

Auto-Negotiation support is mandatory in the 1000BASE-T standard and is embedded in the transceiver (PHY). To help improve signal processing, 1000BASE-T includes a *master-slave system* of synchronous signal clocking for each wire pair. The Auto-Negotiation mechanism is used to decide which transceiver becomes the master or the slave. The master and slave ends of a given wire pair synchronize their signaling using the clock signal provided by the master. This allows the transceiver circuits linked over each wire pair to differentiate between the signals they are sending and alien signals sent on other pairs. This scheme makes it possible to more easily detect and suppress alien crosstalk signals coming from other wire pairs in the same cable.

The signal encoding scheme provides both data symbols and symbols used for control and other purposes. These other symbols include the IDLE symbol which is continually sent when no other data is present. The signaling system in 1000BASE-T is continually active, sending IDLE symbols at 125 Mbaud if nothing else is going on.

1000BASE-T Cabling Requirements

Signaling for a 1000BASE-T system operates at the same signaling rate over the cable as the 100BASE-TX system. However, the complex signaling techniques used in 1000BASE-T are more sensitive to certain signal performance issues on Category 5 segments. Therefore, it's important that all twisted-pair cables and other components used in a 1000BASE-T segment meet or exceed the Category 5 signal carrying specifications to properly handle the signals. If you want to exceed the Category 5 specifications, you can purchase Category 5e cable, which has improved signal carrying capabilities. You can also find cables with even higher signal quality ratings being sold by cable vendors.

Reliable Gigabit Ethernet operation requires that all patch cords be correctly assembled using high quality components. The twisted pairs must maintain their twists as close as possible to the RJ-45 connectors, and the connectors must be high quality for the best signal carrying capabilities. It can actually be quite difficult to build homemade patch cords that meet these requirements. Homemade patch cables that don't meet Category 5 specifications can cause problems on a 1000BASE-T segment. For the best results, you should purchase high quality patch cords that have been manufactured under carefully controlled conditions and that are tested and rated to meet or exceed Category 5 specifications.

New cable testing standards have been developed to verify that a Category 5 cabling system can support Gigabit Ethernet signals. These new standards are described in Chapter 14, *Structured Cabling*.

1000BASE-T Media Components

The following media components are used to build a 1000BASE-T twisted-pair segment:

- Category 5 UTP cable.

- Eight-position RJ-45–style modular connectors that meet or exceed Category 5 specifications.

UTP Cable

The 1000BASE-T system operates over four pairs of Category 5 UTP wires. The maximum segment length is 100 meters (328 feet) of UTP cable with a 100 ohm characteristic impedance rating and that meets or exceeds the TIA/EIA Category 5 specifications. More details on installing and using twisted-pair cables and connectors can be found in Chapter 15, *Twisted-Pair Cables and Connectors.*

Eight-Position RJ-45–Style Jack Connector

The 1000BASE-T media system uses four pairs of wires that are terminated in an eight-position (RJ-45–style) connector. Since a 1000BASE-T system uses four pairs of wires, all eight pins of the connector will be used. Table 11-1 lists the 1000BASE-T signals used on the 8-pin connector.

Table 11-1. 1000BASE-T RJ-45 Signals

Pin Number	Signal
1	BI_DA+
2	BI_DA–
3	BI_DB+
4	BI_DC+
5	BI_DC–
6	BI_DB–
7	BI_DD+
8	BI_DD–

As shown in Table 11-1, the four wire pairs are used to carry four bi-directional data signals (BI_D). The four bi-directional data signals are called BI_DA, BI_DB, BI_DC and BI_DD. The data signals on each pair of a 1000BASE-T twisted-pair segment are polarized, with one wire of each signal pair carrying the positive (+) signal, and the other carrying the negative (–) signal. The signals are connected so that both wires associated with a given signal are members of a single wire pair.

The 1000BASE-T transceivers typically include circuits that can detect incorrect signal polarity in a wire pair (*polarity reversal*). These circuits can correct polarity reversal by automatically moving the signals to the correct circuits inside the transceiver. However, not all Ethernet devices may be able to correct a polarity reversal, and it is not a good idea to depend on this ability. Instead, all cables should be wired so that correct signal polarity is observed.

Connecting a Station to 1000BASE-T Ethernet

Figure 11-3 shows a computer equipped with a 1000BASE-T Ethernet adapter. The adapter card comes with an RJ-45–style jack connector. A Category 5 twisted-pair cable is used to make a connection to a switching hub.

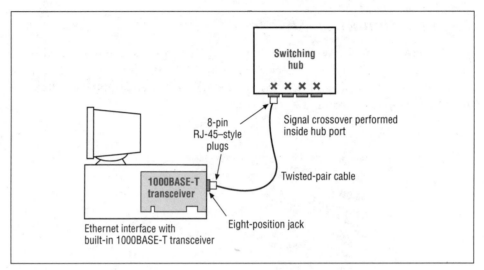

Figure 11-3. Connecting a station to a 1000BASE-T Ethernet system

The switching hub is shown with four 1000BASE-T connectors with built-in transceivers and interfaces. A signal crossover is required between devices connected to a 1000BASE-T segment. Signal crossover for twisted-pair cables and connectors is described in Chapter 15. The crossover wiring is done inside the hub as indicated by the X on the hub port.

The 1000BASE-T standard mandates Auto-Negotiation capability, as described in Chapter 5, *Auto-Negotiation*. Multi-speed Ethernet controller and transceiver chips make it possible for vendors to build twisted-pair Ethernet interfaces that can automatically configure themselves for operation at all three speeds: 10-, 100-, and 1000 Mbps. With this capability, vendors can build Ethernet interfaces that automatically operate at the highest speed supported by the devices at each end of the twisted-pair link.

1000BASE-T Link Integrity Test

The Gigabit Ethernet transceiver circuits continually monitor the receive data path for activity as a means of verifying whether the link is working correctly. The signaling system used for 1000BASE-T segments continually sends signals—even during idle periods where there isn't any traffic on the network. Therefore, activity on the receive data path is sufficient to provide a check of link integrity.

1000BASE-T Configuration Guidelines

The Ethernet standard contains guidelines for building a single 1000BASE-T twisted-pair segment, as well as guidelines for linking multiple segments into a larger system. Table 11-2 lists the single segment guidelines for a 1000BASE-T segment.

Table 11-2. 1000BASE-T Single Segment Guidelines

Media Type	Maximum Segment Length	Maximum Number of Transceivers (per segment)
Twisted-pair 1000BASE-T	100 m (328 feet)[a]	2

[a] There is no minimum length specification for a 1000BASE-T segment. In practice, you can purchase ready-made patch cables as short as 1 foot and use them to connect 1000BASE-T equipment together. However, you may find that if you want to test the cable with a hand-held cable tester, there may be a minimum cable length that the tester requires for an accurate test of cable parameters.

Multiple 1000 Mbps segments can be connected together in half-duplex mode with a single Gigabit Ethernet repeater, providing a network with a maximum total cable length of 200 meters between stations. Configuration rules for linking multiple 1000 Mbps segment types with repeater hubs are described in Chapter 13, *Multi-Segment Configuration Guidelines*.

The 1000BASE-T specification allows a segment with a maximum length of 100 meters. Unlike the 10BASE-T system, 1000BASE-T segments cannot be longer than 100 meters due to signal transmission limits.

12

Gigabit Ethernet Fiber Optic Media System (1000BASE-X)

The specifications for the 1000BASE-X system were developed in the 802.3z supplement to the IEEE standard. 1000BASE-X is a collective identifier for three media segments: two fiber optic segments and a short copper jumper. Of these three, the fiber optic segments are widely used, while the short copper jumper has not been adopted by the marketplace. Therefore, this chapter describes the two fiber optic segments in detail, with coverage of the short copper jumper included for completeness. The two fiber optic segments consist of a 1000BASE-SX (short wavelength) segment and a 1000BASE-LX (long wavelength) segment. The third segment type is called the 1000BASE-CX short copper jumper.

The 1000BASE-X media system is based on specifications first published in the ANSI X3T11 Fibre Channel standard. Fibre Channel is a high-speed network technology that was developed to support bulk data applications such as linking file servers and providing high speed image transport for video editing. The 1000BASE-X standard adapted the signal encoding and physical medium signaling from the Fibre Channel standard, with the only major change being an increase in the data rate from 800 Mbps to 1000 Mbps.

The first part of this chapter provides a brief look at 1000BASE-X components and signaling, followed by a more detailed look at the three 1000BASE-X media segments, with an emphasis on the widely used fiber optic segments.

1000BASE-X Signaling Components

As with the 1000BASE-T system, the 1000BASE-X Gigabit Ethernet system requires an Ethernet interface with a built-in Gigabit Ethernet transceiver. The 1000BASE-X interface is equipped with a built-in transceiver used to make a direct connection to one of the 1000BASE-X media segments.

Figure 12-1 shows a Gigabit Ethernet network interface card for installation in a server or high performance workstation. The card is equipped with a duplex SC fiber optic connector that connects to the fiber optic cables in the segment.

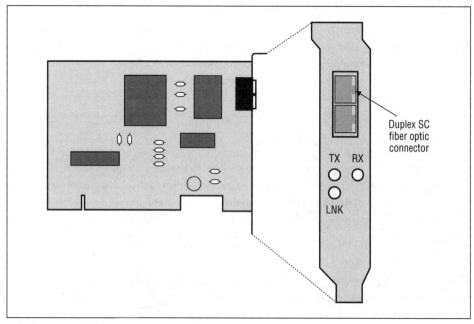

Figure 12-1. 1000BASE-SX Ethernet interface

The most widely available 1000BASE-X NICs are designed for connection to a 1000BASE-SX media segment, and support full-duplex mode only. The 1000BASE-SX system uses less expensive short-distance lasers designed for connection to relatively short lengths of multimode fiber optic segments. Therefore, the 1000BASE-SX system is often used inside buildings, and for connections to high performance servers and workstations. The lengths of the fiber segments that each media system can accommodate are described later in this chapter.

A 1000BASE-X interface in a switching hub port may support either 1000BASE-SX or 1000BASE-LX segments, depending on what market segment the hub was designed for. High performance backbone switching hubs typically support both 1000BASE-SX and 1000BASE-LX media types, since that results in the maximum flexibility. Smaller hubs intended for use inside a single building are usually equipped with 1000BASE-SX ports. The 1000BASE-CX short copper jumper was included in the standard for connections such as those inside a single machine room. However, it has not been adopted by the marketplace, and 1000BASE-CX equipment does not appear to be available.

A signal crossover is required to make the data flow correctly between two 1000BASE-X hub ports, or between a computer and a hub. Signal crossover is described in Chapter 16, *Fiber Optic Cables and Connectors.*

1000BASE-X Link Integrity Test

The Gigabit Ethernet transceiver circuits continually monitor the receive data path for activity to verify whether the link is working correctly or not. The signaling system used for 1000BASE-X segments sends signals continually, even during idle periods of no network traffic. Therefore, activity on the receive data path is sufficient to provide a check of link integrity.

1000BASE-X Signal Encoding

The 1000BASE-X system is based on signaling originally developed for the Fibre Channel standard. The Fibre Channel standard defines five layers of operation (FC0 through FC4). The FC0 and FC1 layers are the ones adapted for use in Gigabit Ethernet. FC0 defines the basic physical link, including media interfaces that operate at various bit rates; FC1 defines signal encoding and decoding as well as error detection.

The signal encoding used in Fibre Channel and 1000BASE-X is called 8B/10B. In this encoding system, 8-bit bytes of data are turned into 10-bit code-groups for transmission over the media system. The 10-bit encoding scheme allows for the transmission of 1,024 10-bit code-groups. There are 256 code-groups that carry the 8-bit data sent over the link and another set of code-groups that are used for special control characters.

The set of 1,024 10-bit code-groups makes it possible to choose a specific set of 256 data code-groups that contain sufficient signal transitions to ensure adequate clock recovery at the receiver end of the link. The code-groups used to send data also ensure that the number of ones and zeroes sent over time are approximately equal. This helps prevent any cumulative signal bias in the electronic components along the signal path that might otherwise be caused by the transmission of long strings of ones or zeroes.

Special code-groups are used for encoding the IDLE signal, which is continually sent when no other data is present, and to send carrier extension bits and signals that define the start and end of frame. The complete set of data code-groups and special code-groups used are complex, and of primary interest only to designers of transceiver chips. Anyone who wants to examine the complete set of code-groups can find them listed in Clause 36 of the Gigabit Ethernet standard.

Physical line signaling

The physical signaling used to transmit the ten-bit code-groups is based on the basic *non-return-to-zero* (NRZ) line code. This is a simple line signaling code in which a logical one results in a high voltage level or high light level, and a logical zero results in a low voltage level or low light level. Using 10 bits to encode every 8-bit byte and transmitting the signals with an NRZ line code causes the 1000 Mbps Gigabit Ethernet data rate to become a 1.250 Mbaud rate of signals on the media system. The 1.250 Mbaud signal transition rate means that the 1000BASE-X system is doing a lot of high-frequency signaling over the fiber optic cables. Since the maximum frequency at which light emitting diodes (LEDs) can operate is about 622 MHz, 1000BASE-X fiber optic transceivers must use lasers to handle the high-frequency signals.

1000BASE-X Media Components

Gigabit Ethernet fiber optic segments use pulses of laser light instead of electrical currents to send Ethernet signals. This approach has several advantages. For one thing, a fiber optic link segment can carry Gigabit Ethernet signals for considerably longer distances than twisted-pair media can. The standard specifies that a full-duplex 1000BASE-LX segment can reach as far as 5000 meters (16,404 feet, or a little over 3 miles).

However, many vendors sell "long haul" versions of 1000BASE-LX equipment which are designed to reach as far as 10 km (6.2 miles) on single-mode fiber. Vendors have also developed "extended reach" versions of 1000BASE-LX single-mode interfaces that can send signals over distances of 70–100 kilometers or more. In large multi-building campuses, the fiber distances can add up fast, as the fiber cables may not be able to take the most direct route between buildings on the campus and a central switching location. Therefore, these long-reach transceivers can be quite useful. The LX interfaces are essential when it comes to building metropolitan area network (MAN) links, in which Gigabit Ethernet is used to provide network services between sites on a city-wide basis.

1000BASE-SX and 1000BASE-LX Media Components

The following set of media components are used to build both 1000BASE-SX and 1000BASE-LX fiber optic segments:

- Multimode or single-mode fiber optic cable.
- Fiber optic connectors.

Fiber Optic Cable

Both 1000BASE-SX and 1000BASE-LX fiber optic media segments require two strands of cable: one for transmitting and one for receiving data. The required signal crossover, in which the transmit signal (TX) at one end is connected to the receive signal (RX) at the other end, is performed in the fiber optic link.

Maximum segment lengths for 1000BASE-SX and 1000BASE-LX are dependent on a number of factors. If a Gigabit Ethernet segment is operated in half-duplex mode, then there are limits imposed by the round-trip timing. Gigabit Ethernet half-duplex segment lengths are described in Chapter 13, *Multi-Segment Configuration Guidelines.*

The half-duplex cable distance limits described in Chapter 13 are based on round-trip timing calculations that assume ideal signal propagation behavior over the media cables. However, sending signals over fiber optic cables at 1.25 GHz is a difficult engineering task. Complex signal propagation and attenuation issues place length limits on some types of fiber optic cable. Therefore, fiber optic segment lengths in the Gigabit Ethernet system will vary depending on the cable type and wavelength used by the media type. Complete information on these issues, as well as details on how to build multimode and single-mode fiber optic segments, can be found in Chapter 16, *Fiber Optic Cables and Connectors.*

Fiber Optic Connectors

The standard recommends the use of the duplex SC fiber optic connector for both 1000BASE-SX and 1000BASE-LX fiber optic media segments, as shown in Figure 12-2.

However, there is nothing to prevent vendors from using other fiber optic connectors. For example, you may find vendors using the more compact MT-RJ connector on 1000BASE-SX ports. The MT-RJ connector is shown in Figure 12-3.

The MT-RJ connector provides both fiber connections in a space the size of an RJ-45 connector. Since the MT-RJ connector takes up about half the space required

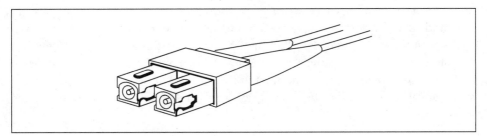

Figure 12-2. Duplex SC connector

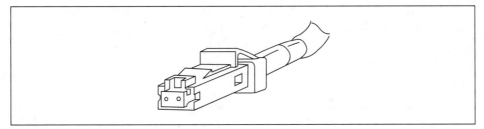

Figure 12-3. MT-RJ connector

by the SC connectors, this allows vendors to provide more 1000BASE-SX ports on a switching hub.

Gigabit Interface Converter

Some vendors use the Gigabit Interface Converter (GBIC), which allows the customer to support either the 1000BASE-SX or 1000BASE-LX media types on a single port. The GBIC is a small, hot-swappable module that provides the media system signaling components for a Gigabit Ethernet port. The GBIC is described in Chapter 6, *Ethernet Media Fundamentals*.

1000BASE-CX Media Components

A 1000BASE-CX segment consists of a short "jumper" cable based on high-quality shielded twisted-pair cable. The cable can be up to 25 meters (82 feet) in length. The *short-haul jumper* is intended for linking equipment in small areas such as switch closets and computer rooms. This media standard has not been adopted in the marketplace, which means that 1000BASE-CX equipment is not available from any vendor today. The following information is provided to complete the coverage of the entire 1000BASE-X system.

The 1000BASE-CX segment type is based on a shielded cable containing balanced wire pairs and rated at a characteristic impedance of 150 ohms. A CX jumper cable requires a "passive network" of components (capacitors, resistors, inductors) to improve the signal carrying capability of the cable. Therefore, these cables are built and sold as assemblies of a certain length, with all components and the passive equalization networks installed at the factory. Such cables are designed to operate over a specified length, and cannot be connected together like extension cords to extend their length in the field. If these cables are connected together, the signal equalization will not be correct, leading to increased error rates and frame loss.

1000BASE-CX Connectors

There are two connectors defined in the standard for use on the ends of a CX jumper cable. The preferred connector is an 8-pin High Speed Serial Data Connector (HSSDC or Fibre Channel Style 2), which is shown in Figure 12-4. This provides better electrical characteristics and a smaller size than the alternative connector does.

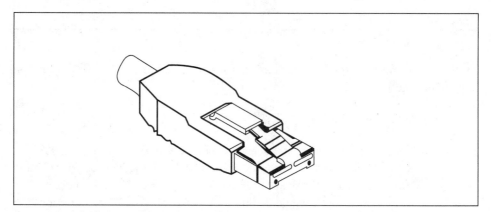

Figure 12-4. Style 2 HSSDC connector

The 1000BASE-CX signals on the Style 2 HSSDC connector are connected as follows:

- Transmit+ on pin 1.
- Transmit− on pin 3.
- Receive− on pin 6.
- Receive+ on pin 8.

The alternative connector is a 9-pin shielded D-subminiature connector, shown in Figure 12-5. This is the same DB-9 connector used in Token Ring systems with 150 ohm shielded cable.

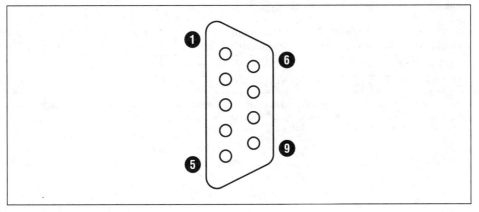

Figure 12-5. 9-pin D-subminiature connector

The 1000BASE-CX signals on the 9-pin connector are connected as follows:

- Transmit+ on pin 1.

- Transmit– on pin 6.

- Receive+ on pin 5.

- Receive– on pin 9.

Signal crossover must be provided in the cable segment. The Transmit+ signal on one end of the cable must be connected to Receive+ at the other end and vice versa. Similarly, the Transmit– signal must be connected to Receive– and vice versa. The end result is that both transmit signal pins on one end of the cable are connected to the receive signal pins at the other end of the cable, while maintaining the correct signal polarity.

1000BASE-SX and 1000BASE-LX Configuration Guidelines

Table 12-1 lists the single segment guidelines for 1000BASE-SX and 1000BASE-LX segments. Multiple 1000 Mbps segments can be connected together in half-duplex mode with a repeater, providing a network with a maximum total cable diameter of 200 meters between stations. The configuration rules for linking multiple 1000 Mbps segment types with repeater hubs are described in Chapter 13.

Table 12-1. 1000BASE-SX and 1000BASE-LX Single Segment Guidelines

Media Type	Minimum Segment Length	Maximum Segment Length	Maximum Number of Transceivers (per segment)
1000BASE-SX	2 m (6.5 feet)	220 m (1,351 feet)[a]	2
1000BASE-LX	2 m (6.5 feet)	5,000 m (16,404 feet)[b]	2

[a] The maximum cable length shown is for a commonly used multimode fiber optic cable. Other cable types will provide different maximum lengths, as described in Chapter 16.

[b] The maximum cable length shown is for a commonly used single-mode fiber optic cable. Other cable types will provide different maximum lengths, as described in Chapter 16.

13

Multi-Segment Configuration Guidelines

The individual media chapters you've just read covered the basic configuration guidelines for a single segment media system. However, when it comes to building a more complex half-duplex Ethernet system based on repeater hubs, you need to know what the multi-segment guidelines have to say.

The official configuration guidelines provide two approaches for verifying the configuration of a half-duplex shared Ethernet channel: Transmission System Model 1 and Transmission System Model 2. Model 1 provides a set of "canned" configuration rules. As long as your half-duplex network system meets these basic rules, it will function correctly in terms of the essential timing specifications. Model 2 provides a set of calculation aids that make it possible for you to evaluate more complex network topologies that aren't covered under the Model 1 configuration rules.*

This chapter describes the rules for combining multiple segments with repeater hubs to build complex half-duplex Ethernet systems operating at 10-, 100- and 1000-Mbps. We begin by looking at the scope of the configuration guidelines. To help make it clear how the guidelines apply to a single Ethernet system, we then need to describe the function of a collision domain. Following that, we describe the Model 1 and Model 2 rules as they apply to each Ethernet system.

---

* The Gigabit Ethernet standard includes a set of configuration guidelines for half-duplex operation based on repeater hubs. However, since there are no half-duplex Gigabit Ethernet repeater hubs available on the market, you probably won't get much opportunity to use this part of the book. Instead, all current Gigabit Ethernet links are operated in full-duplex mode, which is described in Chapter 4, *Full-Duplex Ethernet.*

Scope of the Configuration Guidelines

The configuration guidelines apply to the Ethernet equipment described in the IEEE 802.3 standard. Further, the Ethernet media segments must be built according to the recommendations in each media system standard. If your half-duplex network system includes Ethernet equipment or media segments that are not described in the standard, you may not be able to use the configuration guidelines to verify its operation.

The engineers in the IEEE committee developed the configuration rules based on the known signal timing and electrical performance specifications of Ethernet equipment that fully conforms to the published standard. That way, they could predict what the behavior of the Ethernet equipment would be, and how the signal timing would function across multiple segments.

Using non-compliant equipment and media segments makes it impossible to evaluate the timing of the network. Linking media segments together with equipment not described in the standard also makes it impossible to evaluate the timing. In both cases, there is no way for the design engineers to know how such equipment and media segments will behave. While such an Ethernet may function perfectly well, it will be "outside the standard," and you will not be able to use the official IEEE configuration guidelines to verify that such a system meets the half-duplex timing specifications.

Network Documentation

When it comes to evaluating the configuration of your network and for later troubleshooting, you should document each network link in your system when it is installed. The documentation should include the length of each cable segment in the link, including any transceiver cables and patch cables. Also included should be the cable type used in each segment and any information you can collect on the cable manufacturer, the cable ID numbers printed on the outer sheath, and the cable delay in bit times provided by the manufacturer. The standard recommends that you create your own forms based on Table 13-1 for use in collecting information and documenting your network.

Collision Domain

The multi-segment configuration guidelines apply to a half-duplex Ethernet *collision domain* described in Chapter 3, *The Media Access Control Protocol.* A collision domain is formally defined as a single Carrier Sense Multiple Access with Collision Detection (CSMA/CD) network in which there will be a collision if two computers attached to the system transmit at the same time.

Table 13-1. Sample Cable Segment Documentation Form

	Horizontal Cabling	Transceiver Cables	Wiring Closet Patch Cord(s)	Station Patch Cords
Length				
Type (e.g., Category 5)				
Cable Manufacturer				
Cable Code/ID				

An Ethernet system composed of a single segment or of multiple segments linked with repeater hubs constitutes a single collision domain. Figure 13-1 shows two repeater hubs connecting three computers. Since only repeater connections are used between the segments in this network, all of the segments and computers are in the same collision domain.

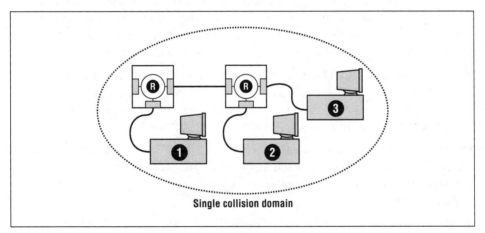

Single collision domain

Figure 13-1. Repeater hubs create a single collision domain

Another important point is that all segments within a given collision domain must operate at the same speed. That's because repeater hubs assume that all segments connected to the repeater are operating at the same speed and have the same round-trip timing constraints. This is also why there are three sets of half-duplex configuration guidelines, one each for 10-, 100-, and 1000 Mbps Ethernet. Each of the three Ethernet speeds has its own round-trip timing constraints and its own set of configuration guidelines.

The configuration guidelines described in this chapter are taken directly from the IEEE 802.3 standard, which describes the standards for the operation of a single half-duplex Ethernet local area network (LAN). Therefore, these guidelines only apply to a single collision domain, and have nothing to say about combining multiple Ethernet collision domains with packet switching devices such as switching hubs or routers. Switching hubs enable you to create new collision domains on each port, allowing you to link many networks together. You can also link segments operating at different speeds with switching hubs. The operation and configuration of switching hubs are described in Chapter 18, *Ethernet Switching Hubs.*

Model 1 Configuration Guidelines for 10 Mbps

The first configuration model provided in the 802.3 standard describes a set of multi-segment configuration rules for combining various 10 Mbps Ethernet segments. **Bold text** is taken directly from the IEEE standard.[*]

- **Repeater sets are required for all segment interconnection.** A "repeater set" is a repeater and its associated transceivers (i.e., medium attachment units, or MAUs) and attachment unit interface (AUI) cables, if any. Repeaters must comply with all IEEE specifications in clause 9 of the 802.3 standard, and are used for signal retiming and reshaping, preamble regeneration, etc.

- **MAUs that are part of repeater sets count toward the maximum number of MAUs on a segment.** Twisted-pair, fiber optic and thin coax repeater hubs typically use internal MAUs located inside each port of the repeater. Thick Ethernet repeaters use an outboard MAU to connect to the thick coax.

- **The transmission path permitted between any two DTEs may consist of up to five segments, four repeater sets (including optional AUIs), two MAUs, and two AUIs.** The repeater sets are assumed to have their own MAUs, which are not counted in this rule.

- **AUI cables for 10BASE-FP and 10BASE-FL shall not exceed 25 m.** (Since two MAUs per segment are required, 25 m per MAU results in a total AUI cable length of 50 m per segment.)

- **When a transmission path consists of four repeaters and five segments, up to three of the segments may be mixing and the remainder must be link segments. When five segments are present, each fiber optic link segment (FOIRL, 10BASE-FB, or 10BASE-FL) shall not exceed 500 m, and each 10BASE-FP segment shall not exceed 300 m.** A mixing segment is defined in the standard as one that may have more than two medium dependent interfaces attached to it

---

(e.g., a coaxial cable segment). A link segment is defined as a point-to-point full-duplex medium that connects two and only two MAUs.[*]

- When a transmission path consists of three repeater sets and four segments, the following restrictions apply:

  — The maximum allowable length of any inter-repeater fiber segment shall not exceed 1000 m for FOIRL, 10BASE-FB, and 10BASE-FL segments and shall not exceed 700 m for 10BASE-FP segments.

  — The maximum allowable length of any repeater to DTE fiber segment shall not exceed 400 m for 10BASE-FL segments and shall not exceed 300 m for 10BASE-FP segments and 400 m for segments terminated in a 10BASE-FL MAU.

  — There is no restriction on the number of mixing segments in this case. In other words, when using three repeater sets and four segments, all segments may be mixing segments if desired.

Figure 13-2 shows an example of one possible maximum Ethernet configuration that meets the canned configuration rules. The maximum packet transmission path in this system is between station 1 and station 2, since there are four repeaters and five media segments in that particular path. Two of the segments in the path are mixing segments, and the other three are link segments.

While the canned configuration rules are based on conservative timing calculations, you shouldn't let that lead you to believe that you can bend these rules and get away with it. Despite the allowances made in the standards for manufacturing tolerances and equipment variances, there isn't a lot of engineering margin left in maximum-sized Ethernets. If you want maximum performance and reliability, then you need to stick to the published guidelines.

In addition, while the configuration guidelines emphasize the maximum limits of the system, you should beware of stretching things as far as they can go. Ethernets, like many other systems, work best when they aren't being pushed to their limits.

Model 2 Configuration Guidelines for 10 Mbps

The second configuration model provided by the IEEE provides a set of calculation aids that make it possible for you to check the validity of more complex

---

[*] The phrase *full-duplex medium* means that the cable segment provides independent transmit and receive data paths. It does not mean that the segment is operating in full-duplex mode.

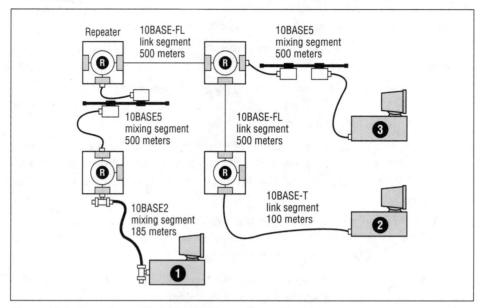

Figure 13-2. A maximum Model 1 10 Mbps configuration

Ethernet systems. We will be describing the network models and segment timing values provided in the standard for making the Model 2 calculations.

While the detailed description of this calculation method may seem complex, in reality the calculation method is a very straightforward process based on simple multiplication and addition. You may find the following description of the network models and timing values confusing at first glance. If so, you may wish to skip ahead to the section, *Simple 10 Mbps Model 2 Configuration,* to see how easy the actual calculations can be.

There are two sets of calculations provided in the standard that must be performed for each Ethernet system you evaluate. The first set of calculations verifies the round-trip signal delay time, while the second set verifies that the amount of interframe gap shrinkage is within normal limits. Both calculations are based on network models that evaluate the worst-case path through the network.

Network Models and Delay Values

The network models and the delay values provided in the Model 2 guidelines were deliberately designed to hide a lot of complexity while still making it possible for you to calculate the timing values for any Ethernet system. Each component in an Ethernet system provides a certain amount of delay, all of which are listed in the 802.3 standard in excruciating detail.

The "5-4-3" Rule

An over-simplified version of the 10 Mbps Model 1 rules, called the "5-4-3" rule, has been circulating for some years. Various forms of the 5-4-3 rule have been published, and some of them include misleading terms that are incorrect. To quote from one widely distributed configuration guide, the 5-4-3 rule means that there may be as many as five segments connected in series in a network. This guide further states that up to four repeaters may be used, and up to three "populated segments." A populated segment is defined as a segment that is "attached to PCs."

While this may sound like an easy to remember rule of thumb, the "5-4-3" rule is an over-simplification of the actual configuration rules described above. Worse, the use of the term "populated segment" is misleading. This definition means that a coax segment could be regarded as an "unpopulated" segment in a network system as long as two conditions were met. First, the coax segment was not used to support PCs and, second, the segment was only used as a link segment to connect to a repeater at each end. However, this is incorrect.

A link segment is specifically defined in the 802.3 standard as a segment based on a point-to-point full-duplex media type that connects two—and only two—MAUs. A full-duplex medium means that the medium provides separate transmit and receive data paths. This is important, since collision detection occurs faster on a full-duplex medium than it does on coaxial segments. This difference in timing is factored into the total round-trip timing delays that are incorporated in the Model 1 configuration guidelines. That's why the notion of an "unpopulated" coax segment that could be used as a link segment is misleading and incorrect.

To recast the 5-4-3 rule into something closer to reality, we can define it to mean that you can have up to five segments in series, with up to four repeaters, and no more than three "mixing" segments. If three mixing segments are used, then the remaining two segments must be link segments as defined in 802.3. Actually, you can have up to four mixing segments under some circumstances as described in the real 802.3 rules above, so even our corrected 5-4-3 rule is still an over-simplification.

As the Ethernet signal moves through the system, it also encounters startup delays that vary depending on which kind of equipment is involved. If you were an expert, you could use a calculator and a copy of the 802.3 standard to calculate the total of all of the bit time delays. You could also calculate the complex timing delays involved in detecting and signaling collisions, all of which differ depending on the media type involved and even the direction in which the signal travels. Fortunately, the IEEE standard has provided a better way to do things.

In the Model 2 configuration guidelines, the standard provides a set of network models and *segment delay values* that incorporate all of the complex delay calculations and other considerations we've just mentioned. All you need to do is to use the network models provided and follow the rules for the calculations involved. Although the network models and the rules for using them may seem arbitrary at first glance, by following the rules you can quickly and simply evaluate the round-trip timing for a complex Ethernet system.

If you are curious as to exactly what goes into the segment delay values and the path delay calculations, you can refer to the IEEE 802.3 standard. The standard lists every delay component used, and explains why the calculation rules are set up the way they are.

Figure 13-3 shows the network model which is used in the standard for calculating the round-trip timing of the worst-case path. The worst-case path is the path through your network system that has the longest segments and the most repeaters between any two stations. The calculation model includes a left and right end segment, and as many middle segments as needed.

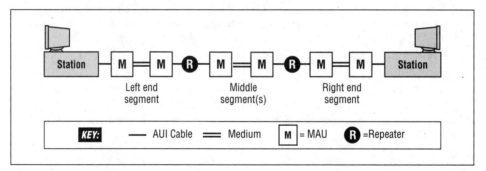

Figure 13-3. Network model for round-trip timing

To check the round-trip timing on your network, you make a similar model of the worst-case path in your system. We will show how the round-trip timing model is used by evaluating two sample networks later in this chapter. The network model used for interframe gap shrinkage is very similar to the round-trip timing model, as you will see in the section on calculating interframe gap shrinkage.

Finding the Worst-Case Path

You begin the process of checking an Ethernet system by finding the path in the network with the maximum delay. This is the path with the longest round-trip time and largest number of repeaters between two stations. In some cases, you may decide that you have more than one candidate for worst-case path in your system. If that's the case, then you should identify all the paths through your network that look like they meet the worst-case definition. Following this, you can do the calculations for each worst-case path you have found, and if any path exceeds the limits for round-trip timing or interframe gap, then the network system does not pass the test.

You should have a complete and up-to-date map of your network on hand that you can use to find the worst-case path between two stations. However, if your system is not well documented then you will have to investigate and map the network yourself. The information you need includes:

- The type of segments being used (twisted pair, fiber optic, coax).
- How long the segments are.
- The location of all repeaters in the system.
- How the segments and repeaters in the system are laid out.

Once you have this information then you can determine what the maximum path between any two stations is, and what kinds of segments are used in the maximum path.

After you've found your worst-case path(s), the next thing you need to do is make a model of your path based on the network model shown in Figure 13-3. You do this by assigning the segment at one end of your worst-case path to be a left end segment, leaving a right end segment and possibly one or more middle segments.

To help you do this, draw a sketch of your worst-case path, noting the segment types and lengths. Then arbitrarily assign one of the end segments to be the left end; it doesn't matter which kind of segment it is. This leaves you with a right end segment; all other segments in the worst-case path become middle segments.

Calculating Round-Trip Delay Time

One goal of the configuration guidelines is to make sure that any two stations on a half-duplex Ethernet LAN can contend fairly for access to the shared Ethernet channel if they happen to transmit at the same time. When this happens, each station attempting to transmit must be notified of channel contention (collision) by receiving a collision signal within the correct collision timing window.

The way to verify whether your Ethernet system meets the limits is by calculating the total path delay, or *round-trip timing*, of the worst-case path in your system. This is done using segment delay values, which are provided in terms of bit time values for each Ethernet media type. A bit time is the amount of time required to send one data bit on the network, which is 100 nanoseconds (ns) for a 10 Mbps

Ethernet system. Table 13-2 shows the segment delay values provided in the standard for use in calculating the total worst-case path delay.

Table 13-2. Round-trip Delay Values in Bit Times

Segment Type	Max Length (in meters)	Left End		Middle Segment		Right End		RT Delay/meter
		Base	Max	Base	Max	Base	Max	
10BASE5	500	11.75	55.05	46.5	89.8	169.5	212.8	0.0866
10BASE2	185	11.75	30.731	46.5	65.48	169.5	188.48	0.1026
FOIRL	1000	7.75	107.75	29	129	152	252	0.1
10BASE-T	100a	15.25	26.55	42	53.3	165	176.3	0.113
10BASE-FL	2000	12.25	212.25	33.5	233.5	156.5	356.5	0.1
Excess AUI	48	0	4.88	0	4.88	0	4.88	0.1026

a Actual maximum segment length depends on cable characteristics.

Calculating the total round-trip delay is a matter of adding up the delay values found on the worst case path in your network. Once you have calculated the segment delay values for each segment in the worst-case path on your LAN, you then add the segment delay values together to find the total path delay. The standard recommends that you add a margin of 5 bit times to this total. *If the result is less than or equal to 575 bit times, the path passes the test.*

This value ensures that a station at the end of a worst-case path will be notified of a collision and stop transmitting within 575 bit times. This includes 511 bits of the frame plus the 64 bits of frame preamble and start frame delimiter (511 + 64 = 575). Once you know that the round-trip timing for the worst-case path in your network is okay, then you can be sure that all other paths must be okay as well.

There is one more item to check in the calculation for total path delay. If the path you are checking has left and right end segments of different segment types, then you must check the path twice. The first time through, you must use the left end path delay values of one of the segment types, and the second time through you must use the left end path delay values of the other segment type. The total path delay must pass the delay calculations no matter which set of path delay values are used. We will show how this is done in the complex network example later in this chapter.

Calculating the Interframe Gap Shrinkage

The interframe gap is a 96 bit time delay provided between frame transmissions to allow the network interfaces and other components some recovery time between frames. As frames travel through an Ethernet system, the variable timing delays in network components combined with the effects of signal reconstruction circuits in the repeaters can result in an apparent shrinkage of the interframe gap. Too small a gap between frames can overrun the frame reception capability of network interfaces, leading to lost frames. Therefore, it's important to ensure that a minimum interframe gap is maintained at all receivers (stations).

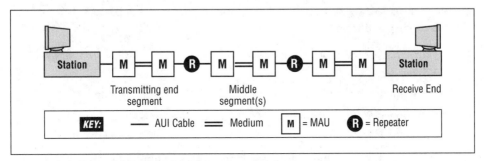

Figure 13-4. Network model for interframe gap shrinkage

The network model for checking the interframe gap shrinkage is shown in Figure 13-4. As you can see, it looks a lot like the round-trip path delay model, except that it includes a *transmitting end* segment. When you are doing the calculations for interframe gap shrinkage, only the transmitting end and the middle segments are of interest, since only signals on these segments must travel through a repeater to reach the receiving end station. The final segment connected to the receiving end station does not contribute any gap shrinkage and is therefore not included in the interframe gap calculations. Table 13-3 provides the values used for calculating interframe gap shrinkage.

Table 13-3. Interframe Gap Shrinkage in Bit Times

Segment Type	Transmitting End	Mid-Segment
Coax	16	11
Link segment	10.5	8

When the receive and transmit end segments are not the same media type, the standard says to use the end segment with the largest number of shrinkage bit times as the transmitting end for the purposes of this calculation. This will provide the worst-case value for interframe gap shrinkage. *If the total is less than or equal to 49 bit times, then the worst-case path passes the shrinkage test.*

Model 1 Configuration Guidelines for Fast Ethernet

Transmission System Model 1 of the Fast Ethernet standard provides simplified configuration guidelines. The goal of the configuration guidelines is to make sure that the important Fast Ethernet timing requirements are met, so that the medium access control (MAC) protocol will function correctly. The basic rules for Fast Ethernet configuration include:

- All copper (twisted-pair) segments must be less than or equal to 100 meters in length.

- Fiber segments must be less than or equal to 412 meters in length.

- If medium independent interface (MII) cables are used, they must not exceed 0.5 meters each.

When it comes to evaluating network timing, delays attributable to the MII do not need to be accounted for separately, since these delays are incorporated into station and repeater delays.

With these rules in mind, Table 13-4 shows the maximum collision domain diameter for segments using Class I and Class II repeaters. These repeaters are described in Chapter 17, *Ethernet Repeater Hubs*. The maximum collision domain diameter in a given Fast Ethernet system is the longest distance between any two stations (DTEs) in the collision domain.

Table 13-4. Model 1—Maximum Fast Ethernet Collision Domain in Meters

Repeater Type	All Copper	All Fiber	Copper and Fiber Mix (e.g., T4 and FX)	Copper and Fiber Mix (TX and FX)
DTE-DTE Single Segment	100	412	N/A	N/A
One Class I Repeater	200	272	231[a]	260.8[a]
One Class II Repeater	200	320	N/A[b]	308.8[a]
Two Class II Repeaters	205	228	N/A[b]	216.2[c]

[a] Assumes 100 m of twisted-pair cabling and one fiber link.

[b] Not Applicable. FX fiber and T4 copper segments cannot be linked in a Class II repeater.

[c] Assumes 105 m of twisted-pair cable and one fiber link.

The first row in Table 13-4 shows that a DTE-to-DTE (station-to-station) link with no intervening repeater may be made up of a maximum of 100 meters of copper, or 412 meters of fiber optic cable. The next row provides the maximum collision domain diameter when using a Class I repeater, including the case of all twisted-pair and fiber optic cables, or a network with a mix of twisted-pair and fiber cables. The third row shows the maximum collision domain length with a single Class II repeater in the link.

The last row of Table 13-4 shows the maximum collision domain allowed when two Class II repeaters are used in a link. In this last configuration, the total twisted-pair segment length is assumed to be 105 meters on the mixed fiber and twisted-pair segment. This includes 100 meters for the segment length from the repeater port to the station, and five meters for a short segment that links the two repeaters together in a wiring closet.

Figure 13-5 shows an example of a maximum configuration based on the 100 Mbps simplified guidelines we've just seen. Note that the maximum collision domain diameter includes the distance:

```
A (100 m) + B (5 m) + C (100 m)
```

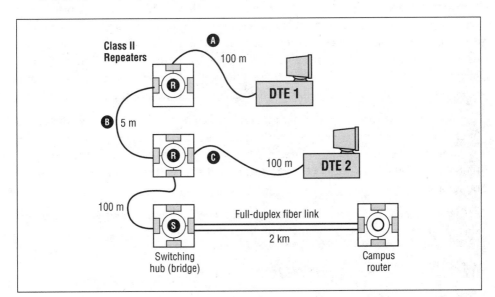

Figure 13-5. One possible maximum 100 Mbps configuration

The inter-repeater segment length can be longer than 5 m as long as the maximum diameter of the collision domain does not exceed the guidelines for the segment types and repeaters being used. Segment *B* in Figure 13-5 could be 10 meters in length, for instance, as long as other segment lengths are adjusted to keep the maximum collision diameter to 205 meters. While it's possible to vary the length of the inter-repeater segment in this fashion, you should be wary of doing so and carefully consider the consequences. Next we'll describe the major reason why you want to avoid using inter-repeater segments longer than 5 meters.

Longer Inter-Repeater Links

The chief problem with using longer inter-repeater links is that this makes your network timing rely on the use of shorter than standard segments from the repeater ports to the stations, which could cause confusion and problems later on. These days everyone assumes that twisted-pair segment lengths can be up to 100 meters long. Because of that, a new segment that's 100 meters long could be attached to a system with a long inter-repeater link later. In this case, the maximum diameter between some stations could then become 210 meters. If the signal delay on this long path exceeds 512 bit times, then the network may experience problems, such as late collisions. You can avoid this by keeping the length of inter-repeater segments to five meters or less.

A switching hub is just another station (DTE) as far as the guidelines for a collision domain are concerned. The switching hub shown in Figure 13-5 provides a way to link separate network technologies—in this case, a standard 100BASE-T segment and a full-duplex Ethernet link. The switching hub is shown linked to a campus router with a full-duplex fiber link that spans up to two kilometers. This makes it possible to provide a 100 Mbps Ethernet connection to the rest of a campus network using a router port located in a central section of the network.

Figure 13-6 shows an example of a maximum configuration based on a mixture of fiber optic and copper segments. Note that there are two paths representing the maximum collision domain diameter. This includes the distance A (100 m) + C (208.8 m), or the distance B (100 m) + Ċ (208.8 m), for a total of 308.8 meters in both cases.

A Class II repeater can be used to link the copper (TX) and fiber (FX) segments, since these segments both use the same encoding scheme.

Model 2 Configuration Guidelines for Fast Ethernet

Transmission System Model 2 for Fast Ethernet segments provides a set of calculations for verifying the signal timing budget of more complex half-duplex Fast Ethernet LANs. These calculations are much simpler than the Model 2 calculations used in the original 10 Mbps system, since the Fast Ethernet system uses only link segments.

The maximum diameter and the number of segments and repeaters in a half-duplex 100BASE-T system are limited by the round-trip signal timing required to ensure that the collision detect mechanism will work correctly. The Model 2 configuration calculations provide the information you need to verify the timing bud-

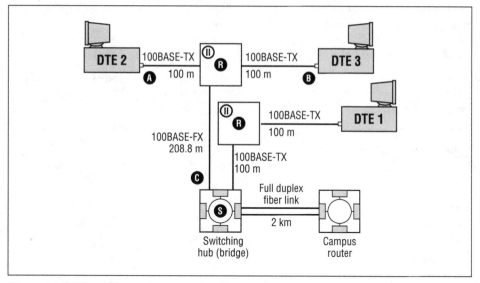

Figure 13-6. Mixed fiber and copper 100 Mbps configuration

get of a set of standard 100BASE-T segments and repeaters. This ensures that their combined signal delays fit within the timing budget required by the standard.

You may notice that these calculations appear to have a different round-trip timing budget than the timing budget provided in the 10 Mbps media system. This is because media segments in the Fast Ethernet system are based on different signaling systems than 10 Mbps Ethernet, and because the conversion of signals between the Ethernet interface and the media segments consumes a number of bit times.

You may also notice that there is no calculation for interframe gap shrinkage, unlike the one found in the 10 Mbps Model 2 calculations. That's because the maximum number of repeaters allowed in a Fast Ethernet system is limited, thus eliminating the risk of excessive interframe gap shrinkage.

Calculating Round-Trip Delay Time

Once you have determined the worst-case path (see *Finding the Worst-Case Path* in the *Model 2 Configuration Guidelines for 10 Mbps* section), your next step is to calculate the total round-trip delay. This can be accomplished by taking the sum of all the delay values for the individual segment in the path, plus the station delays and repeater delays. The calculation model in the standard provides a set of delay values measured in bit times, as shown in Table 13-5. Note that the *Round-Trip Delay in Bit Times per Meter* only applies to the cable types in the table. The device types in the table (DTE, repeater) have only a maximum round-trip delay through each device listed.

Table 13-5. 100BASE-T Component Delays

Component	Round-Trip Delay in Bit Times per Meter	Maximum Round-Trip Delay in Bit Times
Two TX/FX DTEs	N/A	100
Two T4 DTEs	N/A	138
One T4 and one TX/FX DTE[a]	N/A	127
Category 3 Cable	1.14	114 (100 meters)
Category 4 Cable	1.14	114 (100 meters)
Category 5 Cable	1.112	111.2 (100 meters)
Shielded Twisted-Pair Cable	1.112	111.2 (100 meters)
Fiber Optic Cable	1.0	412 (412 meters)
Class I Repeater	N/A	140
Class II Repeater with all ports TX/FX	N/A	92
Class II Repeater with any T4 port	N/A	67

[a] Worst case values are used.

To calculate the round-trip delay value, you multiply the length of the segment (in meters) times the *Round-Trip Delay in Bit Times per Meter* listed in the table for the segment type. This results in the round-trip delay in bit times for that segment. If your segment is at the maximum length you can use the *Maximum Round-Trip Delay in Bit Times* value listed in the table for that segment type. If you're not sure of the segment length, you can also use the maximum length in your calculations just to be safe.

Once you have calculated the segment delay values for each segment in the worst-case path, you then add the segment delay values together. You also add the delay values for two stations (DTEs), and the delay for any repeaters in the path, to find the total path delay. Your vendor may provide values for cable, station, and repeater timing, which you can use instead of the ones in the table.

To this total path delay value, you should add a safety margin of zero to four bit times, with four bit times of margin recommended in the standard. This helps account for unexpected delays, such as those caused by long patch cables between a wall jack in the office and the computer. *If the result is less than or equal to 512 bit times, the path passes the test.*

Calculating Your Own Segment Delay Values

The segment delay value varies depending on the kind of segment used, and on the quality of cable in the segment if it is a copper segment. More accurate cable delay values may be provided by the manufacturer of the cable. If you know the propagation delay of the cable you are using, you can also look up the delay for that cable in Table 13-6.*

Table 13-6. Conversion Table for Cable Propagation Times

Speed Relative to c	Nanoseconds/Meter	Bit Time/Meter	
		100 Mbps Fast Ethernet	1000 Mbps Gigabit Ethernet
0.4	8.34	0.834	8.34
0.5	6.67	0.667	6.67
0.51	6.54	0.654	6.54
0.52	6.41	0.641	6.41
0.53	6.29	0.629	6.29
0.54	6.18	0.618	6.18
0.55	6.06	0.606	6.06
0.56	5.96	0.596	5.96
0.57	5.85	0.585	5.85
0.58	5.75	0.575	5.75
0.5852	5.70	0.570	5.70
0.59	5.65	0.565	5.65
0.6	5.56	0.556	5.56
0.61	5.47	0.547	5.47
0.62	5.38	0.538	5.38
0.63	5.29	0.529	5.29
0.64	5.21	0.521	5.21
0.65	5.13	0.513	5.13
0.654	5.10	0.510	5.10
0.66	5.05	0.505	5.05
0.666	5.01	0.501	5.01
0.67	4.98	0.498	4.98
0.68	4.91	0.491	4.91
0.69	4.83	0.483	4.83
0.7	4.77	0.477	4.77
0.8	4.17	0.417	4.17
0.9	3.71	0.371	3.71

---

* The lowercase *"c"* used in the table is standard scientific notation for the speed of light.

Table 13-6 is taken from the standard and provides a set of delay values in bit times per meter, listed in terms of the speed of signal propagation on the cable. The speed (*propagation time*) is provided as a percentage of the speed of light; this is also called the *Nominal Velocity of Propagation,* or NVP, in vendor literature.

If you know the NVP of the cable you are using, then this table can provide the delay value in bit times per meter for that cable. Calculate the total delay value for your cable by multiplying the *Bit Time/Meter* value by the length of your segment. The result of this calculation must be multiplied by two to get the total round-trip delay value for your segment. The only difference between 100 Mbps Fast Ethernet and 1000 Mbps Gigabit Ethernet in the above table is that the bit time in Fast Ethernet is ten times longer than the bit time in Gigabit Ethernet. For example, since the bit time is one nanosecond in Gigabit Ethernet, a propagation time of 8.34 nanoseconds per meter translates to 8.34 bit times.

Typical Propagation Values for Cables

As an example of vendor NVP specifications, Table 13-7 lists some typical propagation rates for Category 5 cable provided by two major vendors. These values apply to both 100 Mbps Fast Ethernet and 1000 Mbps Gigabit Ethernet systems.

Table 13-7. Typical Vendor-Supplied Cable Propagation Times

Vendor	Part Number	Jacket	NVP
AT&T	1061	non-plenum	70%
AT&T	2061	plenum	75%
Belden	1583A	non-plenum	72%
Belden	1585A	plenum	75%

Model 1 Configuration Guidelines for Gigabit Ethernet

Transmission System Model 1 of the Gigabit Ethernet standard provides simplified configuration guidelines. The goal of the configuration guidelines is to ensure that the timing requirements for Gigabit Ethernet are met so that the medium access control (MAC) protocol will function correctly. The rules for half-duplex Gigabit Ethernet configuration are:

- The system is limited to a single repeater.

- Segment lengths are limited to the lesser of 316 meters (1,036.7 feet) or the maximum transmission distance of the segment media type.

The maximum length in terms of bit times for a single segment is 316 meters. However, any media signaling limitations which reduce the maximum transmission distance of the link to below 316 meters take precedence. The fiber optic media signaling limitations can be found in Chapter 16, *Fiber Optic Cables and Connectors.* Table 13-8 shows the maximum collision domain diameter for a Gigabit Ethernet system for the segment types shown. The maximum diameter of the collision domain is the longest distance between any two stations (DTEs) in the collision domain.

Table 13-8. Model 1—Maximum Gigabit Ethernet Collision Domain in Meters

Configuration	Category 5 UTP	1000BASE-CX	Fiber Optic 1000BASE-SX/LX	Category 5 and Fiber Optic	1000BASE-CX and 1000BASE-SX/LX
DTE-DTE Single Segment	100	25	316[a]	N/A	N/A
One Repeater	200	50	220	210[b]	220[c]

[a] May be limited by the maximum transmission distance of the link.

[b] Assumes 100 m of Category 5 unshielded twisted-pair (UTP) cable and one optical fiber link of 110 m.

[c] Assumes 25 m of 1000BASE-CX and one optical fiber link of 195 m.

The first row in Table 13-8 shows the maximum lengths for a DTE-to-DTE (station-to-station) link. With no intervening repeater the link may be up of a maximum of 100 m of copper, 25 m of 1000BASE-CX cable, or 316 m of fiber optic cable. Some of the Gigabit Ethernet fiber optic links described in Chapter 12, *Gigabit Ethernet Fiber Optic Media System (1000BASE-X),* are limited to quite a bit less than 316 m due to signal transmission considerations. In those cases, you will not be able to reach the 316 m maximum allowed by the bit timing budget of the system.

The row labeled *One Repeater* provides the maximum collision domain diameter when using the single repeater allowed in a half-duplex Gigabit Ethernet system. This includes the case of all twisted-pair cable (200 m), all fiber optic cable (220 m) or a mix of fiber optic and copper cables.

Model 2 Configuration Guidelines for Gigabit Ethernet

Transmission System Model 2 for Gigabit Ethernet segments provides a set of calculations for verifying the signal timing budget of more complex half-duplex Gigabit Ethernet LANs. These calculations are much simpler than the Model 2 calculations for either the 10 Mbps or 100 Mbps Ethernet systems, since Gigabit

Ethernet only uses link segments and only allows one repeater. Therefore, the only calculation needed is the worst-case *path delay value* (PDV).

Calculating the Path Delay Value

Once you have determined the worst-case path (see "Finding the Worst-Case Path" in the "Model 2 Configuration Guidelines for 10 Mbps" section), you then calculate the total round-trip delay value for the path, or PDV. The PDV is made up of the sum of segment delay values, repeater delay, DTE delays, and a safety margin.

Segment Delay Value

The calculation model in the standard provides a set of delay values measured in bit times, as shown in Table 13-9. To calculate the round-trip delay value, you multiply the length of the segment (in meters) times the *Round-Trip Delay in Bit Times per Meter* listed in the table for the segment type. This results in the round-trip delay in bit times for that segment.

Table 13-9. 1000BASE-T Component Delays

Component	Round-Trip Delay in Bit Times per Meter	Maximum Round-Trip Delay in Bit Times
Two DTEs	N/A	864
Category 5 UTP Cable Segment	11.12	1112 (100 m)
Shielded Jumper Cable (CX)	10.10	253 (25 m)
Fiber Optic Cable Segment	10.10	1111 (110 m)
Repeater	N/A	976

The result of this calculation is the round-trip delay in bit times for that segment. You can use the *Maximum Round-Trip Delay in Bit Times* value listed in the table for that segment type if your segment is at the maximum length. The max delay values can also be used if you're not sure of the segment length and want to use the maximum length in your calculations just to be safe. To calculate cable delays, you can use the conversion values provided in right-hand column of Table 13-6.

To complete the PDV calculation, you add the entire set of segment delay values together, along with the delay values for two stations (DTEs), and the delay for any repeaters in the path. Your vendor may provide values for cable, station and repeater timing, which you can use instead of the ones in the tables provide here.

To this total path delay value, you add a safety margin of from zero to 40 bit times, with 32 bit times of margin recommended in the standard. This helps account for any unexpected delays, such as those caused by extra long patch cords between a wall jack in the office and the computer. *If the result is less than or equal to 4,096 bit times, the path passes the test.*

Sample Network Configurations

Next, we'll look at a few sample network configurations to show how the configuration rules work in the real world. The 10 Mbps examples will be the most complex, since the 10 Mbps system has the most complex set of segments and timing rules. Following that we will show a single example for the 100 Mbps system, since the configuration rules are much simpler for Fast Ethernet. There is no need for a Gigabit Ethernet example, as the configuration rules are extremely simple, allowing for only a single repeater hub. In addition, all Gigabit Ethernet equipment being sold today only supports full-duplex mode, which means there are no half-duplex Gigabit Ethernet systems.

Simple 10 Mbps Model 2 Configuration

Let's look at how the 10 Mbps Model 2 calculations work with a very simple example first. Figure 13-7 shows a network with three 10BASE-FL segments connected to a fiber optic repeater. Two of the segments are 2 km (2,000 m) in length, and one is 1.5 km in length.

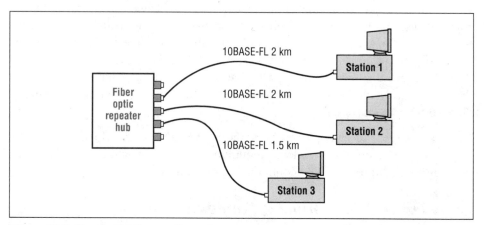

Figure 13-7. Simple 10 Mbps configuration example

Although this is a simple network, it is a configuration that is not described in the Model 1 configuration rules. Therefore, the only way to verify its operation is to perform the Model 2 calculations. By looking at Figure 13-7, we see that the worst-case delay path is between Station 1 and Station 2, as this path has the longest distance between any two stations. Next, we will evaluate this worst-case path for total round-trip delay and interframe gap shrinkage.

Round-trip delay

Since there are only two media segments in the worst-case path, the network model for round-trip delay only has a left and right end segment. There are no middle segments to deal with. We'll assume for the purposes of this example that the fiber optic transceivers are connected directly to the stations and repeater, which eliminates the need to add extra bit times for transceiver cable length. Both segments in the worst-case path are the maximum allowable length, which means we can simply use the "Max" values from Table 13-2.

According to the table, the Max left end segment delay value for a 2 km 10BASE-FL link is 212.25 bit times. For the 2 km right end segment, the Max delay value is 356.5 bit times. Add them together, plus the five bit times margin recommended in the standard, and the total is: 573.75 bit times. This is less than the 575 maximum bit time budget allowed for a 10 Mbps network, which means that the worst-case path is okay. All shorter paths will have smaller delay values, so all paths in this Ethernet system meet the requirements of the standard as far as round-trip timing is concerned. To complete the interframe gap calculation, we need to compute the gap shrinkage in this network system.

Interframe gap shrinkage

Since there are only two segments, we only have to look at a single transmitting end segment when calculating the interframe gap shrinkage. There are no middle segments to deal with, and the receive end segment does not count in the calculations for interframe gap. Since both segments are of the same media type, finding the worst-case value is easy. According to Table 13-3, the interframe gap value for the link segments is 10.5 bit times, and that becomes our total shrinkage value for this worst-case path. This is well under the 49 bit times of interframe shrinkage allowed for a 10 Mbps network.

As you can see, the example network meets both the round-trip delay requirements and the interframe shrinkage requirements, thus it qualifies as a valid network according to the Model 2 configuration method.

Complex 10 Mbps Model 2 Configuration

The next example is more difficult, comprised of many different segment types, extra transceiver cables, etc. All these extra bits and pieces also make the example more complicated to explain, although the basic process of looking up the bit times and adding them together is still quite simple.

For this complex configuration example, please refer back to Figure 13-2 earlier in the chapter. This figure shows one possible maximum-length system using four repeaters and five segments. According to the Model 1 rule-based configuration method, we've already seen that this network complies with the standards. To check that, we'll evaluate this network again, this time using the calculation method provided for Model 2.

As usual, we start the process by finding the worst-case path in the sample network. By examination, you can see that the path between Stations 1 and 2 in Figure 13-2 is the maximum delay path. It contains the largest number of segments and repeaters in the path between any two stations in the network. Next, we make a network model out of the worst-case path. Let's start the process by arbitrarily designating the thin Ethernet end segment as the left end segment. That leaves us with three middle segments composed of a 10BASE5 segment and two fiber optic link segments, and a right end segment comprised of a 10BASE-T link segment.

Next, we need to calculate the segment delay value for the 10BASE2 left end segment. This can be accomplished by adding the left end base value for 10BASE2 coax (11.75) to the product of the round-trip delay times the length in meters (185 × 0.1026 = 18.981) results in a total segment delay value of 30.731 for the thin coax segment. However, since 185 m is the maximum segment length allowed for 10BASE2 segments, we can simply look up the Max left hand segment value from Table 13-2, which, not surprisingly, is 30.731. The 10BASE2 thin Ethernet segment is shown attached directly to the DTE and repeater, and there is no transceiver cable in use. Therefore, we don't have to add any excess AUI cable length timing to the value for this segment.

Calculating separate left end values

Since the left and right end segments in our worst-case path are different media types, the standard notes that we need to do the path delay calculations twice. First calculate the total path delay using the 10BASE2 segment as the left end segment and the 10BASE-T segment as the right end. Then swap their places and make the calculation again, using the 10BASE-T segment as the left end segment this time, and the 10BASE2 segment as the right end segment. The largest value that results from the two calculations is the one we must use in verifying the network.

AUI delay value

The segment delay values provided in the table include allowances for a transceiver cable (AUI) of up to two meters in length at each end of the segment. This allowance helps takes care of any timing delays that may occur due to wires inside the ports of a repeater.

Media systems with external transceivers connected with transceiver cables require that we account for the timing delay in these transceiver cables. You can find out how long the transceiver cables are, and use that length multiplied by the round-trip delay per meter to develop an extra transceiver cable delay time which is then added to the total path delay calculation. If you're not sure how long the transceiver cables are in your network, you can use the maximum delay shown for an transceiver cable, which is 4.88 for all segment locations, left end, middle, or right end.

Calculating middle segment values

Let's continue the process of finding the total round-trip delay time by doing the calculations for the middle segments. In the worst-case path for the network in Figure 13-2, there are three middle segments composed of a maximum length 10BASE5 segment, and two 500 m long 10BASE-FL fiber optic segments. By looking in Table 13-2 under the *Middle Segments* column, we find that the 10BASE5 segment has a Max delay value of 89.8.

Note that the repeaters are connected to the 10BASE5 segment with transceiver cables and outboard MAUs. That means we need to add the delay for two transceiver cables. Let's assume that we don't know how long the transceiver cables are. Therefore, we'll use the value for two maximum-length transceiver cables in the segment, one at each connection to a repeater. That gives us a transceiver cable delay of 9.76 to add to the total path delay.

We can calculate the segment delay value for the 10BASE-FL middle segments by multiplying the 500 meter length of each segment by the *RT Delay/meter* value, which is 0.1, giving us a result of 50. We then add 50 to the middle segment base value for a 10BASE-FL segment, which is 33.5, for a total segment delay of 83.5.

Although it's not shown in Figure 13-2, fiber optic links often use outboard fiber optic transceivers and transceiver cables to make a connection to a station. Just to make things a little harder, let's assume we used two transceiver cables, each being 25 m in length, to make a connection from the repeaters to outboard fiber optic transceivers on the 10BASE-FL segments. That gives us a total of 50 m of transceiver cable on each 10BASE-FL segment. Since we have two such middle segments, we can represent the total transceiver cable length for both segments by adding 9.76 extra bit times to the total path delay.

Completing the round-trip timing calculation

We started our calculations with the 10BASE2 segment assigned to the left end segment, which leaves us with a 10BASE-T right end segment. This segment is 100 m long, which is the length provided in the "Max" column for a 10BASE-T segment. Depending on the cable quality, a 10BASE-T segment can be longer than 100 m, but we'll assume that the link in our example is 100 m. That makes the

Max value for the 10BASE-T right end segment 176.3. Adding all the segment delay values together, we get the result shown in Table 13-10.

Table 13-10. Round-Trip Path Delay with 10BASE2 Left End Segment

Link	Media	Bit-Time Delay
Left End	10BASE2	30.731
Mid-segment	10BASE5	89.8
Mid-segment	10BASE-FL	83.5
Mid-segment	10BASE-FL	83.5
Right End	10BASE-T	176.3
Excess Length AUI	Quan. Four	19.52
	Total Path Delay =	483.351

To complete the process, we need to perform a second set of calculations with the left and right segments swapped. In this case, the left end becomes a maximum length 10BASE-T segment, with a value of 26.55, and the right end becomes a maximum length 10BASE-2 segment with a value of 188.48. Note that the excess length AUI values do not change. As shown in Table 13-2, the bit time values for AUI cables are the same no matter where the cables are used. Adding the bit time values again, we get the following result in Table 13-11.

Table 13-11. Round-Trip Path Delay with 10BASE-T Left End Segment

Link	Media	Bit-Time
Left End	10BASE-T	26.55
Mid-segment	10BASE5	89.8
Mid-segment	10BASE-FL	83.5
Mid-segment	10BASE-FL	83.5
Right End	10BASE2	188.48
Excess Length AUI	Quan. Three	19.52
	Total Path Delay =	491.35

The second set of calculations shown in Table 13-11 produced a larger value than the total from Table 13-10. According to the standard we must use this value for the worst-case round-trip delay for this Ethernet. The standard also recommends adding a margin of five bit times to form the total path delay value. We are allowed to add anywhere from zero to five bits margin, but five bit times is recommended.

Adding five bit times for margin brings us up to a total delay value of 496.35 bit times, which is less than the maximum of 575 bit times allowed by the standard. Therefore, our complex network is qualified in terms of the worst-case round-trip timing delay. All shorter paths will have smaller delay values, which means that all paths in the Ethernet system shown in Figure 13-2 meet the requirements of the standard as far as round-trip timing is concerned.

Interframe gap shrinkage

We finish the evaluation of the complex network example shown in Figure 13-2 by calculating the worst-case interframe gap shrinkage for that network. This is done by evaluating the same worst-case path we used in the path delay calculations. However, for the purposes of calculating gap shrinkage we only evaluate the transmitting and mid-segments.

Once again we start by applying a network model to the worst-case path, in this case the network model for interframe gap shrinkage. To calculate interframe gap shrinkage, the transmitting segment should be assigned the end segment in the worst-case path of your network system that has the largest shrinkage value. As shown in Table 13-3, the coax media segment has the largest value, so for the purposes of evaluating our sample network we will assign the 10BASE2 thin coax segment to the role of transmitting end segment. That leaves us with middle segments consisting of one coax and two link segments, and a 10BASE-T receive end segment which is simply ignored. The totals are seen in Table 13-12.

Table 13-12. Total Interframe Gap Shrinkage

Media/Link	Shrinkage in Bit Times
Transmitting End Coax	16
Mid-segment Coax	11
Mid-segment Link	8
Mid-segment Link	8
Total PVV =	43

As you can see, the total path variability value for our sample network equals 43. This is less than the 49 bit time maximum allowed in the standard, which means that this network meets the requirements for interframe gap shrinkage.

100 Mbps Model 2 Configuration

For this example, you'll need to refer back to Figure 13-5, which shows one possible maximum length network. As we've seen, the Model 1 rule-based configuration method shows that this system is okay. To check that, we'll evaluate the same system using the calculation method provided in Model 2.

Worst-case path

In the sample network, the two longest paths are between Station 1 and Station 2, and between Station 1 and the switching hub. Signals from Station 1 must go through two repeaters and two 100 m segments, as well as a 5 m inter-repeater segment to reach either Station 2 or the switching hub. As far as the configuration guidelines are concerned, the switching hub is considered as another station.

Both of these paths in the network include the same segment lengths and number of repeaters, so we will evaluate one of them as the worst-case path. Let's assume that all three segments are 100BASE-TX segments, based on Category 5 cables. By looking up the Max Delay value in Table 13-5 for a Category 5 segment, we find 111.2 bit times.

The delay of a 5 m inter-repeater segment can be found by multiplying the round-trip Delay per Meter for Category 5 cable (1.112) times the length of the segment in meters (5). This results in 5.56 bit times for the round-trip delay on that segment. Now that we know the segment round-trip delay values, we can complete the evaluation by following the steps for calculating the total round-trip delay for the worst-case path.

To calculate the total round-trip delay, we use the delay times for stations and repeaters found in Table 13-5. As shown in Table 13-13, the total round-trip path delay value for the sample network is 511.96 bit times when using Category 5 cable. This is less than the maximum of 512 bit times, which means that the network passes the test for round-trip delay.

Table 13-13. Round-Trip Delay in Sample Network, Default Timing Values

Two TX DTEs	100
100 meter Cat 5 segment	111.2
100 meter Cat 5 segment	111.2
5 meter Cat 5 segment	5.56
Class II repeater delay[a]	92
Class II repeater delay[a]	92
Total Delay =	511.96

[a] All repeater ports TX or FX.

Note, however, that there is no margin of up to 4 bit times provided in this calculation. There are no spare bit times to use for margin, because the bit time values shown in Table 13-5 are all worst-case maximums. This table provides worst-case values that you can use if you don't know what the actual cable bit times, repeater timing, or station timing values are.

For a more realistic look, let's see what happens if we work this example again, using actual cable specifications provided by a vendor. In Table 13-14, let's assume that the Category 5 cable is AT&T type 1061 cable, a non-plenum cable which has an NVP of 70 percent as shown in Table 13-7. If we look up that speed in Table 13-6, we find that a cable with a speed of 0.7 is rated at 0.477 bit times per meter. The round-trip bit time will be twice that, or 0.954 bit times. Therefore, timing for 100 m will be 95.4 bit times, and for 5 m it will be 4.77 bit times. Again, refer to Table 13-14 to see how things add up using these different cable values.

Table 13-14. Round-Trip Delay Using Vendor Timing for Cable

Two TX DTEs	100
100 m Cat 5 segment	95.4
100 m Cat 5 segment	95.4
5 m Cat 5 segment	4.77
Class II repeater delay[a]	92
Class II repeater delay[a]	92
Margin	4
Total Delay =	483.57

[a] All repeater ports TX or FX.

When real-world cable values are used instead of the worst-case default values in Table 13-5, there is enough timing left to provide for 4 bit times of margin. This meets the goal of 512 bit times, with bit times to spare.

Working with bit time values

Some vendors note that their repeater delay values are smaller than the value listed in Table 13-5, which will make it easier to meet the 512 bit time maximum. While these extra bit times could theoretically be used to provide an inter-repeater segment longer than five meters, this approach could lead to problems.

While providing a longer inter-repeater link might appear to be a useful feature, you should consider what would happen if that vendor's repeater failed and had to be replaced with another vendor's repeater whose delay time was larger. If that were to occur, then the worst-case path in your network might end up with excessive delays due to the bit times consumed by the longer inter-repeater segment you had implemented. You can avoid this problem by designing your network conservatively and not pushing things to the edge of the timing budget.

It is possible to use more than one Class I or two Class II repeaters in a given collision domain. This can be done if the segment lengths are kept short enough to provide the extra bit time budget required by the repeaters. However, the majority of network installations are based on building cabling systems with 100 m segment lengths (typically implemented as 90 m "in the walls" and 10 m for patch cables). A network design with so many repeaters that the segments must be kept very short to meet the timing specifications is not going to be useful in most situations.

III

Building Your Ethernet System

Now that we've looked at the various Ethernet media systems, this section covers how to build Ethernet local area networks. The chapter on structured cabling describes the structured cabling standards and how structured cabling systems are organized. The chapters on twisted-pair and fiber optic media explain how the cables and connectors work, and how to use them. The twisted-pair and fiber optic chapters include specific information that applies to each of the Ethernet media systems. The chapters on repeater and switching hubs describe how these devices function, and provide some basic examples of how to use them in your network designs.

Part III contains these chapters:

- Chapter 14, *Structured Cabling*
- Chapter 15, *Twisted-Pair Cables and Connectors*
- Chapter 16, *Fiber Optic Cables and Connectors*
- Chapter 17, *Ethernet Repeater Hubs*
- Chapter 18, *Ethernet Switching Hubs*

14

Structured Cabling

An essential truth of networking is that a network system can never be better than its cabling. Providing high-quality cabling can be easy enough for a small Ethernet based on a single twisted-pair hub that supports just a few stations. You can connect all of these devices together with a few high-quality patch cords and your network will be complete. However, the majority of networks support more than just a few stations. Indeed, most office buildings these days require a network system that connects to practically every room in the building. Providing a high-quality cabling system for an entire building is a much more complex task. That's where a structured cabling system can help.

A structured cabling system is based on point-to-point cable segments that are installed according to the detailed guidelines and specifications published in the structured cabling standards. This provides a very reliable and manageable cabling system. A structured cabling system based on industry standards and high-quality components allows your network to function at its best, delivering stable network services for your users day-in and day-out.

You can think of the cabling system as the essential skeleton of your network. Like most skeletons, it's typically hidden out of sight, which means that it can be easily overlooked.* Overlooking your cabling system can be dangerous, however,

---

* Network cabling skeletons are hidden in the time-honored place for skeletons: a closet (in this case, a wiring closet).

since the lack of a solid and well-designed cabling system makes network growth and management much harder to accomplish.

Despite the importance of building a high-quality media system, you won't find any advice on how to proceed with this task in the Ethernet standard. That's because the specifications for cabling systems are outside the scope of that standard. However, cabling systems are very much inside the range of things a network designer must accomplish in order to build a reliable and manageable network system. This chapter provides an introduction and overview of the structured cabling standards, and shows how Ethernet cabling fits within those standards. The basic elements of a structured cabling system are described, with emphasis on the horizontal cabling segment used to connect Ethernet stations to hubs. We also described the new cable specifications and testing standards that have been developed to support Gigabit Ethernet.

Note that this chapter can only provide a brief overview of a very large topic. There are many standards involved when cabling a building, including the whole set of structured cabling standards as well as electrical safety standards, fire safety standards, and so on. A full treatment of structured cabling practices, rules and regulations would occupy an entire bookshelf. As discussed later in this chapter, it is strongly recommended that large cabling projects should be installed by trained professionals who are aware of all the standards and practices and who have been trained to do the job correctly.

Structured Cabling Systems

A set of cables installed without any particular plan and without any regard for the industry guidelines might appear to work well enough at first. However, the lack of structure will make it difficult to accommodate network growth and to troubleshoot the system when problems occur. Unstructured cabling systems built without reference to industry standards are often prone to intermittent network failures which can come and go depending on the time of day and the traffic load. Troubleshooting a cable system that "just grew" without any particular structure can be a time-consuming process of tracing cables to their source while your users are sitting unproductively at their desks waiting for the network to come back up. A structured cabling system can help you avoid these problems.

When designing a cabling system, it's important to plan. The goal is to come up with a plan that scales well, and that will accommodate constant growth while still maintaining order. You also want to make sure that the cabling used in your system can accommodate higher network speeds as required. Network systems are almost always growing and changing to accommodate new technology, add new connections, and to allow people to move around. Accommodating new technology, adding users, and moving connections around is referred to as "moves, adds, and changes" (MAC) and you may hear references to the "MAC cycle" by facilities managers.* A major advantage of a structured cabling system is that it is deliberately designed to make it easier to deal with the constant task of moves, adds, and changes.

A structured cabling system provides a flexible cabling plan that can support multiple computer and telephone systems purchased from any vendor. Structured cabling systems involve a hierarchy based on backbone cables that carry signals between telecommunications closets on various floors of a building, and on horizontal cables that deliver services from the telecommunications closet to the work area. The ease with which such a system can be expanded and rearranged helps manage the constant moves, adds, and changes that can occur. A network media system based on a structured cabling system results in a more reliable network that is also easier to troubleshoot.

TIA/EIA Cabling Standards

A widely used set of vendor-independent structured cabling specifications has been developed by the Telecommunications Industry Association (TIA) and the Electronic Industries Association (EIA). The most recent version of the cabling specifications is officially called the *TIA/EIA-568-A Commercial Building Telecommunications Cabling Standard*. Both the TIA and the EIA are members of the American National Standards Institute (ANSI), which is the coordinating body for voluntary standards groups within the United States. Web sites providing copies of these standards for sale are listed in Appendix A, *Resources*.

The goal of the TIA/EIA cabling standards is to provide a generic, vendor-independent cabling system supporting both voice and data requirements. Before the creation of the TIA/EIA standards, there was no non-proprietary standard you could turn to for guidance when it came to installing a cabling system in your building. In the 1980s, building cabling systems were primarily designed to support telephones, and included only voice-grade twisted-pair cable suitable for telephone communications. If you wanted to support data communications, you typically had to install a proprietary cabling system from a computer vendor.

In many cases, your building ended up with a ceiling stuffed full of bulky cables installed to support equipment from several different computer vendors. Each vendor's cable system used non-compatible cables and connectors. In those days, it

---

* Since this is easily confused with the Medium Access Control (MAC) layer of the Ethernet standards, this particular piece of jargon is best left to facilities managers.

seemed that every vendor had a different approach to cabling for their computer network equipment. Facilities managers were forced to invent their own procedures and policies for dealing with the unholy tangle of cables that could result.

The TIA/EIA standards helped solve this problem by providing a single source of specifications and recommendations whose goal was a set of structured cables capable of handling everything your building needs to support. For example, the TIA/EIA 568-A cabling standard for commercial buildings specifies component requirements, cabling distances and outlet and connector configurations. The standard also provides recommended cabling topologies. By using these standards, you can design structured cabling systems to support all manner of telecommunications including voice, data, and video.

The complete TIA/EIA standard for structured cabling systems is comprised of a series of documents, and like all standards there is a constant process of revision and change. The horizontal cabling specifications provided in TIA/EIA 568 are the portion of the standard that you will encounter most often when connecting Ethernet equipment. Therefore, we will provide a detailed description of the horizontal segment later in this chapter. Before describing the horizontal segment, we will provide a brief tour of the complete set of TIA/EIA cabling standards and components. The TIA/EIA standards include the following:

Commercial Building Telecommunications Cabling Standard, ANSI/TIA/EIA-568-A-95.

> This standard provides specifications for building a structured cabling system, including standards for horizontal cables, backbone cables, cable spaces, interconnection equipment, etc.

Commercial Building Standard for Telecommunications Pathways and Spaces, ANSI/EIA/TIA-569-A-98.

> This standard specifies the design and construction practices to be used for supporting structured cabling systems. Included are specifications for telecommunications closets, equipment rooms, cable pathways and so on.

Residential and Light Commercial Telecommunications Wiring Standard, ANSI/EIA/TIA-570-91.

> This standard describes a premises wiring system for connecting cables in homes or small offices.

Administration Standard for the Telecommunications Infrastructure of Commercial Buildings, ANSI/TIA/EIA-606-93.

> This standard provides a uniform administration scheme for structuring and recording information on all components of the cabling system.

Commercial Building Grounding and Bonding Requirements for Telecommunications, ANSI/TIA/EIA-607-94.

This standard defines the grounding practices needed to support the equipment used in a cabling system.

You should also know that there is an international cabling standard developed by the International Organization for Standardization (ISO) and the International Electrotechnical Commission (IEC), called *ISO/IEC 11801:1995, Generic Cabling for Customer Premises.* This standard covers the same range of topics as the TIA/EIA-568 standard, and includes the category rating system for cables. The ISO standard qualifies the performance of a link with the term *class*, and lists four classes of performance from class A through class D. ISO class C and D links are similar to the TIA/EIA Category 3 and Category 5 links.

Six Elements of Structured Cabling

The TIA/EIA 568 cabling standard lists six basic elements of a structured cabling system. We'll quickly list these elements, since you will often encounter these terms when dealing with cabling systems. Following this, we show how these basic elements are used in a star topology, which is the basis of the structured cabling standards.

Building entrance facilities

The cables, surge protection equipment, and connecting hardware that may be used to link the cabling inside your building with the campus data network or public telephone network are located here.

Equipment room

This is a space reserved for more complex equipment than may be found in telecommunications closets. Equipment rooms may be used for major cable terminations and for any grounding equipment needed to make a connection to the campus data network and public telephone network.

Building backbone cabling

Building backbone cabling based on a star topology is used to provide connections between telecommunications closets, equipment rooms and the entrance facilities.

Telecommunications closet

The primary function of the telecommunications closet, also called a wiring closet, is to provide a location for the termination of the horizontal cable on a given floor of a building. This closet houses the mechanical cable terminations and any cross-connects for the horizontal and backbone cabling system. It may also house interconnection equipment including Ethernet hubs and switches.

Horizontal cabling

The horizontal cabling system extends from the telecommunications closet to the communications outlet located in the work area. Horizontal cabling components include the horizontal link cables installed between the telecommunications closet and the outlet in the work area. They also include the work area outlets and cable termination equipment such as patch panels located in the telecommunications closet. Further, any patch cables required for cross-connects between hub equipment in the closet and the horizontal cabling system are included as well.

Work area

The work area may be an office space or any other area where computers and other equipment are located. The work area components of a structured cabling system include any patch cables required to connect the user's computer, telephone or other device to the communications outlet on the wall.

Star Topology

The structured cabling system described in the TIA/EIA 568 standard is based on a star topology. A star topology is a set of point-to-point links originating from a central hub; the links appear to radiate out from the hub like rays from a star. Figure 14-1 illustrates the basic elements of a structured cabling system, and shows how these elements are arranged in a star topology.

The standard specifies a backbone system with a star cabling topology that has no more than two levels of hierarchy within a building. This means that a cable should not go through more than one intermediate cross-connect device between the *main cross-connect* (MC) located in an equipment room and the *horizontal cross-connect* (HC) located in a wiring closet.

There are many advantages to the star topology:

- Central wiring hubs ease the task of managing moves, adds, and changes.

- Central cabling points provide faster troubleshooting.

- Independent point-to-point links prevent cable problems on any given link from affecting other links.

- Central equipment hubs can provide easier migration to new technologies. You can increase the speed of a network by upgrading hub equipment without having to re-cable the entire building.

- Physical security (e.g., door locks) can be provided for critical equipment that could cause widespread network failure if tampered with.

A star topology is also a major advantage for an installer or troubleshooter. Someone holding on to one end of a network connection in an office can know exactly

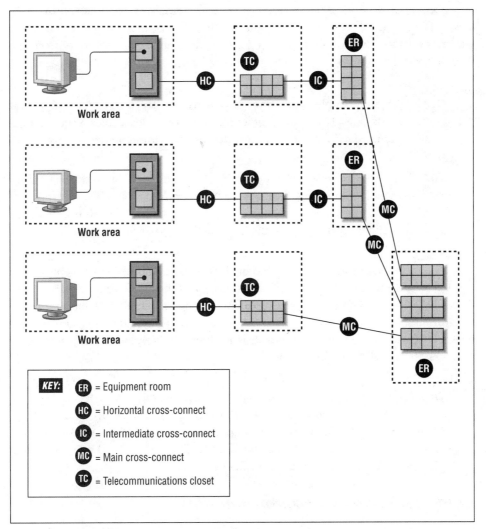

Figure 14-1. Elements of a structured cabling system

where the other end is located. That also means they can easily determine what equipment is connected to each end. This makes installing, testing, and troubleshooting a segment much easier and less time consuming.

Twisted-Pair Categories

The TIA/EIA 568 standard rates twisted-pair cable in terms of which *category* of cable specifications it meets. The category specifications in this standard are widely used in the network industry to identify which types of twisted-pair cable can accommodate 10-, 100-, or 1000 Mbps data signals. What follows are brief descriptions of the basic TIA/EIA categories that do not include the actual signal specifications needed to meet the category requirements. All quotes are from the TIA/EIA 568 standard.

Category 1 and 2

"Category 1 and 2 cables and connecting hardware are not recognized as part of this standard..." These two categories are for older cables used in telephone systems; they are not recommended for carrying Ethernet signals.

Category 3

"This designation applies to 100 ohm UTP (unshielded twisted pair) cables and associated connecting hardware whose transmission characteristics are specified up to 16 MHz." Category 3 UTP cables with a 100 ohm impedance rating are capable of supporting the 10BASE-T Ethernet media system.

Category 4

"This designation applies to 100 ohm UTP cables and associated connecting hardware whose transmission characteristics are specified up to 20 MHz." Category 4 cables with a 100 ohm impedance rating are capable of supporting the 10BASE-T Ethernet media system. This cable was originally designed to support 16-Mbps token ring systems. It is no longer widely used, since most sites prefer to install Category 5 cables.

Category 5

"This designation applies to 100 ohm UTP cables and associated connecting hardware whose transmission characteristics are specified up to 100 MHz." Category 5 cables with a 100 ohm impedance rating are capable of supporting all Ethernet media systems that use unshielded twisted-pair, including 10BASE-T, 100BASE-TX, and 1000BASE-T.

Category 5 and 5e Recommendation

The current TIA/EIA-568-A cabling standard recommends the use of Category 5 cabling for any new horizontal cable installations. As of this writing, a new version of the standard is being developed, which specifies Category 5e cable (the "e" stands for *enhanced*). The Category 5e standard is described later in this chapter. The new cable standard specifies improved cable characteristics, which were instigated by the development of Gigabit Ethernet. When the new standard is formally approved, then Category 5e cable will become the official recommendation for all new cabling installations. Meanwhile, Category 5e cable is already available from vendors, and cable installers should use it for all new installations.

Category 6

A Category 6 cable standard is under development by the ISO and other standards agencies which will provide significantly higher signal performance on twisted-pair cable than Category 5e. However, providing a large improvement over the Category 5e specifications is a major engineering challenge, and the development of a new Category 6 standard based on UTP cable and RJ-45–style connectors has been slow. Meanwhile, the Category 5 and 5e standards are perfectly capable of carrying signals for all Ethernet systems, including Gigabit Ethernet. Since the Category 5 and 5e cable market is highly competitive, the cost of this cable is also quite reasonable.

Of course, vendors are free to develop and sell better cables and connectors. It is up to you to decide whether you want to spend more money to install a cabling system with higher quality signal carrying capabilities. Until the Category 6 standard is eventually formalized and adopted by the standards committees, you also need to carefully evaluate claims of compliance with the new standard. You should also be aware that the Category 6 cable standard is evolving. Conservative network managers who want stable and reliable network systems may wish to wait until the technical issues have been resolved, and the standard has been formally adopted.

Ethernet and the Category System

The Ethernet specifications for twisted-pair Ethernet media systems were written with the Category system in mind. All Ethernet twisted-pair media systems can be supported over Category 5 twisted-pair cables and connecting equipment. When the 10BASE-T twisted-pair Ethernet standard was developed, it was designed to work over lower quality Category 3 "voice grade" cables. With the development of higher speed networks, the structured cabling standard was extended to include specifications for Category 5 and 5e cables. Category 5e cable is now the preferred cable, since it offers greater flexibility and a wider range of networking possibilities. The following is a list of the commonly available twisted-pair Ethernet standards and the cable categories that they are specified to work with:

- The 10BASE-T system is specified for two pairs of Category 3 or better cables, including Category 3 or better connecting hardware, patch cables, and jumpers. A Category 3 25-pair cable may be used in the segment as long as the signal specifications for multiple disturber crosstalk are met. Multiple disturber crosstalk is described in Chapter 20, *Troubleshooting*.

- The 100BASE-TX system requires two pairs of Category 5 cable and Category 5 connecting hardware, patch cables, and jumpers.

- The 1000BASE-T system requires four pairs of Category 5 or better cabling and hardware.

Horizontal Cabling

A horizontal cable is one that extends from the communications outlet in the office or *work area* to the telecommunications closet. The list of components that may be found in a standard horizontal cabling system include:

Horizontal link cabling

A horizontal link, described in detail later in this chapter, may extend a maximum distance of 90 meters (295 feet). There are three types of cables recognized in TIA/EIA-568-A as options for use in horizontal links:[*]

- Four-pair (eight wires), 100 ohm impedance UTP (24 AWG solid conductors, Category 5 recommended). Connector type is an eight-position RJ-45–style modular jack terminating all eight wires of the four-pair cable.

- Two-pair 150 ohm *shielded twisted-pair* (STP) using an IEEE 802.5 four-position shielded token ring connector.

- Two-fiber, 62.5/125 multimode optical fiber cable. The specified fiber optic connector type, formally called an SCFOC/2.5 duplex connector, is generally known as an SC connector. The "SC" stands for "Subscriber Connector," and FOC stands for "Fiber Optic Connector."

Telecommunications outlet/connector

A minimum of two *work area outlets* (WAOs) is specified for each work area; each work area is connected directly to a telecommunications closet. One outlet should connect to one four-pair (eight wire) UTP cable. The other outlet may connect to either another four-pair UTP cable, an STP cable, or a fiber optic cable, as required to meet the needs of your work area. Any active or passive adapters needed at the work area should be external to the outlet.

Cross-connect patch cables

Equipment cable and patch cables used in telecommunications closets should not exceed 6 meters (19.6 feet) in length. An allowance of 3 meters (9.8 feet) is provided for the patch cable from the telecommunications outlet to the workstation. A total allowance of 10 meters (32.8 feet) is provided for all patch cables and equipment cables in the entire length from the closet to the workstation. This, combined with the maximum of 90 meters of horizontal link

---

[*] While the 50 ohm coaxial cables used for thick and thin Ethernet are still recognized cable types in the current TIA/EIA-568-A standard, they are not recommended for new cabling installations. Coaxial-based systems are expected to be removed from the next revision of the standard.

cable distance, makes a total of 100 meters (328 feet) for the maximum horizontal channel distance from the network equipment in the closet to the computer in the office.

Horizontal Channel and Basic Link

The TIA/EIA bulletin, *Telecommunications System Bulletin 67 (TSB-67)*, details requirements for testing and certifying installed UTP horizontal cabling. TSB-67 defines a basic link and a channel for testing purposes, as shown in Figure 14-2. The basic link consists of the fixed cable that travels between the wall plate in the office or work area and the wire termination point in the wiring closet. The basic link is limited to a maximum length of 90 meters (295 feet). A cabling contractor can install this portion of the cabling system in a building and test it according to the guidelines in TSB-67. This provides a way to certify the installed cabling in a new cabling system before any network or telephone equipment is hooked up.

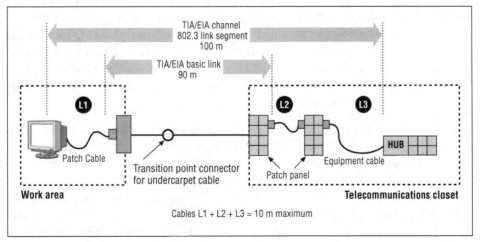

Figure 14-2. Basic link and channel

The standard includes an allowance for an additional maximum length of 10 meters (32.8 feet) for patch cables and equipment cables. These cables can be located between the hub and the patch panel or cross-connect located in the closet. They can also be located between the wall outlet and the computer located in the office or work area.

The total horizontal cable segment including all patch cables and equipment cables is called the *channel*, and may be a maximum of 100 meters (328 feet) in length. TSB-67 includes test specifications for the complete channel to allow end-to-end testing that includes all patch cords and equipment cords. The link segment specifications in the IEEE 802.3 standard for UTP Ethernet segments are

---

The 100 Meter Design Goal

Both the TIA/EIA standard and the twisted-pair Ethernet specifications are written with a 100 meter length design goal for segments. The 100 meter goal comes from studies that show that the vast majority of the desktops in the average office building are within 100 meters of cable length from the nearest telecommunications closet.

---

based on the entire end-to-end channel as well. For example, the maximum amount of signal attenuation specified for a 10BASE-T segment is 11.5 dB, which is the amount of signal loss allowed for the entire horizontal segment from one end of the channel to the other.

The cabling standard notes that horizontal cabling systems contain the greatest number of individual cables in your building, and are often much more difficult to replace than backbone cabling. That's because horizontal cabling is pulled through the ceilings and walls of the building to reach each work area, making the installation costs of horizontal cabling much higher. For this reason, Category 5e cabling and components should be used in the horizontal cabling system. A cabling system based on Category 5e cabling and components can accommodate everything from telephones on up to high-speed data communications.

The horizontal link cable is just one component of a horizontal cabling system. You also need to make sure that all of the components used are rated to meet Category 5 or better specifications. The horizontal channel will typically include a jumper or patch cable from the Ethernet hub in the telecommunications closet to a wire termination patch panel of some sort. The horizontal link cable will usually terminate in an eight-position (RJ-45–style) connector in another patch panel located in the closet. From that patch panel, the horizontal link cable travels over ceilings and through the walls until it reaches the work area, typically an office.

In the office, the horizontal link cable terminates in another eight-position jack connector installed in a wall plate. To make a connection to a workstation in the office, you need to connect another patch cable from the modular jack connector in the wall plate to the modular jack connector in the network interface of the computer. Every one of these components must be rated for Category 5 signal performance in order to end up with a complete horizontal channel rated at Category 5. If all of the cables and components in a segment are not at the Category 5 level of quality, then you may experience slow network performance caused by increased frame loss due to signal errors.

New Twisted-Pair Standards

New cabling standards are being developed in response to the creation of Gigabit Ethernet. Signaling for the 1000BASE-T Gigabit Ethernet twisted-pair media system operates at roughly the same rate over the cable as the 100BASE-TX system. The major difference is that the 1000BASE-T system uses all four wire pairs in the cable, whereas 100BASE-TX uses only two wire pairs. Additionally, the complex signaling techniques and bi-directional signaling used in 1000BASE-T are more sensitive to certain signal performance issues on Category 5 segments.

These issues include the amount of signal reflections caused by cable connectors, as well as the amount of signal crosstalk on the cable. Some of these signal performance issues were not precisely defined in the original Category 5 cabling or testing specifications. To help ensure that a Category 5 cabling system will support 1000BASE-T signals, new testing and cabling standards have been developed by the TIA. The approach has been twofold. First, new specifications have been published for existing Category 5 cable systems. Second, a new cabling standard has been developed to enhance the original Category 5 standard.

Additional Category 5 Specifications

The 1000BASE-T system is more sensitive to the amount of signal reflections caused by cable connectors, as well as to the amount of signal crosstalk on the cable. This means that existing cable plants should be checked to ensure that they meet the 1000BASE-T requirements. To assist in the process of checking existing Category 5 cabling systems, the TIA/EIA created an advisory document called *Technical Systems Bulletin 95: Additional Transmission Specifications for 4-Pair 100 ohm Category 5 Cabling.*

The intent of TSB95 is to provide guidelines and additional specifications for currently installed Category 5 cabling. The specifications describe additional signaling parameters that were not included in the original Category 5 cable specifications, and that became more important with the development of Gigabit Ethernet. TSB95 was developed as a way of taking official notice of these additional parameters, and of providing some guidelines for testing the parameters.

The 1000BASE-T standard states:

> 1000BASE-T signaling requires four pairs of Category 5 balanced cabling as specified in ISO/IEC 11801:1995 and ANSI/EIA/TIA-568-A (1995) and tested for the additional performance parameters...using testing procedures defined in (proposed) ANSI/TIA/EIA TSB95.*

---

* Clause 40.1, 802.3ab draft supplement to IEEE Std 802.3, March 25, 1999.

In other words, existing Category 5 cabling plants that meet the current cabling standards and that are currently supporting Fast Ethernet systems should be able to carry 1000BASE-T signals without difficulty. However, you need to retest the installed cable segments to make sure that they meet all signal parameters. TSB95 includes testing specifications for signal parameters that are important for 1000BASE-T but that were not included in the original Category 5 cabling standard. Testing can be done with hand-held cable testers that automatically cycle through the series of tests required to certify links for performance standards such as Cat5, TSB-95, and Cat5e.

Cabling experts predict that some small percentage of Category 5 cabling systems will be found to have been installed incorrectly or with substandard components. These systems are unlikely to be able to support either Fast Ethernet or Gigabit Ethernet signals. If testing uncovers a link that does not meet the specifications, there are several things you can do to take corrective action. The link should be re-tested after each corrective action is applied:

- Replace the patch cord at the work area end of the link with a patch cord that meets or exceeds the Category 5e specification.

- Reconfigure the link to eliminate wiring closet cross-connect cables and connectors.

- Replace any transition point connector with equipment that meets or exceeds the Catgeory 5e specification.

- Replace the work area outlet with an outlet that meets or exceeds the Category 5e specification.

- Replace the wiring closet interconnect equipment (patch panel) with equipment that meets or exceeds the Category 5e specification.

Enhanced Category 5 Cable Standard

A revised TIA/EIA cabling standard is under development which provides an expanded set of specifications for both twisted-pair cable and cable testing equipment. The enhanced testing specifications and the enhanced Category 5 specifications are both part of revision 5 of the 568-A standard, called TIA/EIA 568-A-5. Formal adoption of the revised standard is expected in early 2000.

For new cabling installations, the revised standard provides specifications for an enhanced version of Category 5 cabling, called Category 5e. The enhancements include improvements in the performance of a cable segment. New cabling installations should be based on Category 5e cable and components that meet the enhanced standard. The improved performance of the Category 5e spec helps ensure that a new cabling installation will meet all the specifications for 1000BASE-T.

However, note that Gigabit Ethernet does not require a Category 5e cabling system. The 1000BASE-T standard has been designed to work over any Category 5 cable installation that meets the current (non-enhanced) Category 5 specifications. A rule of thumb is that if the cabling system currently supports 100BASE-TX Fast Ethernet, then it will support 1000BASE-T Gigabit Ethernet. To ensure that the segment meets the requirements, you need to test the segment with test equipment that complies with the specifications in TSB95.

Identifying the Cables

A cable identification scheme is essential in any network that contains more than a few stations. A complete floor or building network can quickly get out of hand without a coherent cable labeling scheme. There's no particular magic to coming up with a cable labeling system; you simply need to establish a few naming conventions and stick to them. The challenge is to get the labels onto the cables as they are installed.

Another difficulty is to find labels that will stick to the cables and not fall off over time. For that reason, it's best to use labels that are specifically designed for cable systems. If the cables aren't labeled when they are installed, you will find that it's almost impossible to get around to labeling them later. The memory of where the cables go fades more quickly than you might imagine, and before you know it, you're left with a network system that consists of a maze of twisty little cables that all look alike.

There are a variety of schemes for identifying cables based on the major components of a cabling system. Since the wire distribution equipment is installed in equipment frames—also known as *telco* or *equipment racks*—the telephone industry calls the cable termination points *distribution frames*. The *horizontal distribution frame,* or HDF, may be one or more telecommunication closets on a floor. The *main distribution frame* (MDF) is the main equipment room where the backbone cabling of the building is terminated.

Figure 14-3 shows a cable identification system provided by Panduit Corporation. The Panduit system is designed to provide as much information as possible on the cabling system itself, in an effort to minimize the need to keep and refer to external documentation. Your facilities manager may prefer another approach; there is no single system that meets all local requirements.

In this labeling scheme, each closet is identified by three characters indicating the floor number and the closet number. If your building has more than 99 floors, you will need to expand the number of characters used. In our example, closet B on the third floor is identified as 03B. Each equipment rack in the closet is identified by a unique character, so that rack C is identified with the letter C. Each row of

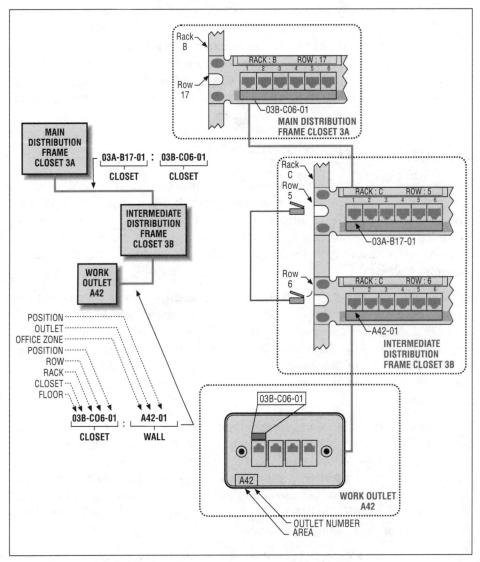

Figure 14-3. Cable administration

equipment on the rack is given a two-digit number and each position on the row is given a two-digit number as well. Therefore, the label 03B–C06–01 identifies a patch panel as being on the third floor in closet B, rack C, equipment row 6, position 1.

The work area outlet in this scheme is given a unique zone and identification number. To do this, divide your floor plan into zones as needed, and then assign a unique ID number for each wall outlet. Each connector in the wall outlet is given a unique position number as well. Therefore, the label A42-01 identifies wall out-let number 42 in zone A, outlet connector position 1. With this organizational scheme, you can create labels for the cabling and equipment in your system that provide a great deal of information. For example, a cable with the label 03B-C06-01/A42-01 tells you which wiring closet the cable comes from. It also tells you exactly where, in all of the equipment located in the closet, the cable is terminated. Further, it tells you which wall outlet the cable goes to and the specific connector on the wall outlet to which the cable is attached.

By uniquely identifying the cables and labeling the cables as they are installed, you provide the information required to manage the cabling system in your network. A technician working on the office end of a connection can locate the cabling closet that each cable comes from. The technician can perform network tests or make changes to the system without having to spend any time tracing cables or disrupting other users while hunting for the right cable. There are several companies that sell cable labels and printing software or standalone printers for the label. These tools help to automate the labeling process in a large cable plant. The online buyer's guides listed in Appendix A are a useful resource for locating suppliers of cable labels.

Documenting the Cable System

An essential feature of a cabling system is documentation. For small networks that cover a single floor or a small set of floors, you can get by with an annotated copy of the building floor plan. While building your network, you should draw each cable installation on your copy of the floor plan and identify it. A separate note-book or a spreadsheet with an explanation of your cable identification system should be kept as well.

Cables should be identified when they are installed, and a label should be attached to each end of the cable. After you've done this, an entry should be made in the cabling notebook or spreadsheet application. It takes some discipline to ensure that this is done each time a network installation is made. However, over time you can create a document that will be quite valuable when it comes time to redesign the network, add new connections, or troubleshoot the system.

For larger systems, covering entire buildings or sets of buildings, you may wish to consider a commercial software package designed to help manage cables. There are several packages designed for managing telecommunications cabling. Some of these packages are based on computer-aided design (CAD) software, and may include a database for handling the thousands of entries that a large cabling system can generate. Such packages are typically expensive and take a fair amount of time to set up and use. Nevertheless, if you are trying to manage large amounts of cable, a good cable management software package may be the only thing that can keep the system under some semblance of control.

While all of these systems may seem like extra work, they are really essential tools for your network. Unlike most tools, a structured cabling system and adequate documentation can be easily overlooked in the rush to design and install a network. However, by providing a cabling plan and documentation of your cabling system you will create a powerful tool for network management, and one that will pay real dividends when it comes to managing and troubleshooting the network.

Building the Cabling System

Once you've decided to install a structured cabling system, your next decision to make is: Who will build the system? The logical choices are build it yourself or hire a professional contractor. Which approach you choose depends on the size and complexity of your cabling system, your budget, and the hardware skills of your staff.

At one extreme, a twisted-pair cabling system for a small workgroup is easy to set up and run. Twisted-pair Ethernet components can be very easy to work with. You can buy a small repeater or switching hub and some ready-made twisted-pair patch cables with eight-position plugs already connected. The patch cables are used to hook the stations to the hub ports, resulting in a complete network. If you need to install twisted-pair cabling for a whole floor or an entire building, however, things get more complex.

For large cable installations there are several arguments in favor of hiring a professional cabling contractor. For one thing, a large cabling design can bring up a number of issues that you may have never heard of before. For instance, cables that are installed in office buildings and other public spaces must meet a variety of stringent building safety and fire codes. Many people prefer to hire a contractor who will see to it that things are done correctly. This may include installing conduits, or making sure that any holes drilled through walls and floors are filled with fire-retardant material. A contractor who specializes in dealing with these issues can make sure that compliance with building standards and cabling standards is maintained when the cabling is installed.

There can be other, more critical, problems as well when trying to install your network. For example, a network being installed in an older building may face the challenge of dealing with asbestos. In the United States and other countries, there are strict regulations in place that apply when disturbing these materials in any way. Regulations on these and other topics vary from state to state in the U.S., and from country to country worldwide. Professional contractors can bring the expertise needed to deal with the special problems in your building, and with the regulations that may apply to your site.

Even if you decide to hire a cabling contractor to do the design and installation, you still need to make sure that the contractor knows exactly what your needs are. You also need to make sure that a careful cabling plan is followed, so that the cable installation is well documented and expanded in the future. The contractor should also test each installed cable and provide certification that the cabling meets the rated performance specifications. Some contractors will deal with these issues for you automatically, and some won't.

A cabling system for an entire building is a major project. When cabling a building, it is strongly recommended that professional cabling contractors be used. A cabling contractor knows how to design cable layouts for buildings, and how to estimate cabling and installation costs, and should be able to help you with the planning for your system. A contractor can also evaluate your site for special problems, and develop estimates for asbestos abatement, if required. When evaluating a cabling contractor, you can ask the contractor for the names of previous customers. You can then ask the customers whether the contractor completed their job on time and within budget, and whether the customer was happy with the resulting cabling system.*

For a smaller design involving a limited area, you may decide to forgo using outside contractors. This assumes that you have access to technicians with the appropriate training, skills and tools, or that you're willing to install and test the cables yourself. Chapter 15, *Twisted-Pair Cables and Connectors*, and Chapter 16, *Fiber Optic Cables and Connectors*, provide more details on these cables. Note that while these chapters provide guidelines and instructions on how to build horizontal cable segments, they do not describe how to install an entire building-wide cabling system.

---

* The Building Industry Consultants Service International (BICSI) offers a course on cabling system basics, how to develop a cabling design and proposal, and how to work with cabling contractors. Access information for course DD100: "Introduction to Voice/Data Cabling" is listed in Appendix A.

15

Twisted-Pair Cables and Connectors

The cables and components used to build a Category 5 twisted-pair horizontal cable segment are based on the TIA/EIA 568-A structured cabling specifications, which are designed to support all three twisted-pair Ethernet media systems. The TIA/EIA specifications are described in Chapter 14, *Structured Cabling*.

In this chapter, we'll show how a Category 5 cable segment is wired and describe the components that are typically used. This can be useful even if you don't build your own horizontal cable segment. Knowing the components and wiring standards used in a cable segment can help you make sure that your cabling system is assembled properly. Being able to find your way around a cabling system is also a major benefit when it comes to troubleshooting network problems.

Following the section on a Category 5 cable segment, you'll learn how to install an RJ-45 connector on a twisted-pair patch cable. The chapter concludes with special twisted-pair cabling considerations for the three twisted-pair Ethernet media systems, including the signal crossover wiring required by each system.

Category 5 Horizontal Cable Segment

A horizontal cable segment is one that travels from a wiring closet to a work area, connecting an Ethernet hub with a station. This is the most widely used cable segment type in a structured cabling system. Building a Category 5 twisted-pair segment involves the following set of components and specifications:

- Category 5 twisted-pair cable.

- Eight-position connector.

- Four-pair wiring schemes.

- Modular patch panel used to hold 8-position jacks.

- Work area wall outlet.

- Twisted-pair patch cables and equipment cables with 8-position plugs.

We will look at each of these items in turn and see how they can be used to build a Category 5 cable segment.

Telephone Industry Jargon

The components and techniques used in a structured cabling system were first developed in the telephone industry. Therefore, it helps to know some telephone industry jargon when it comes to dealing with the components and techniques used for building horizontal cables. In the telephone industry, to *terminate* a wire means to attach the wire to a connector or wiring panel of some sort. A wire termination panel is a set of connectors to which the eight wires in a four-pair twisted-pair cable are attached.

The word *termination* in this case has nothing to do with the signal terminating resistor that is used on the end of an Ethernet coaxial cable segment. Instead, termination in the telephone industry simply means that a wire comes to an end and that it is connected to a wire termination device. Wire termination devices are widely used in the telephone industry and include patch panels, cross-connect blocks (also called *punch-down blocks*), and cable jacks and plugs.

Category 5 Twisted-Pair Cable

Twisted-pair cable is quite different from the thick or thin coaxial cables used in the original Ethernet media systems (see Appendix B, *Thick and Thin Coaxial Media Systems*). The major difference is that the electrical characteristics of twisted-pair cable are not as tightly controlled as they are with coaxial cable. This makes transmitting high frequency electrical signals over twisted-pair cabling a more difficult engineering task, since the signals have to deal with a harsher electrical environment. That, in turn, is the primary reason why the Ethernet specifications for twisted-pair segments call for much shorter segment lengths than coaxial cable segments. The shorter segment length limits the negative effects on the signal caused by the harsher signal environment of twisted-pair media.

The twisted-pair cable specified for building a horizontal link consists of a set of solid wires surrounded by a thin layer of insulation. The solid wire is low cost and makes it easy to install the individual wires in the punch-down connectors widely used in structured cabling systems. This type of connector is also called an *insulation displacement connector*, or IDC.

An IDC allows a solid wire to be "punched down" into the connector without stripping off the insulation. Instead, the sharp edges of the connector components displace the insulation and grip the metal core of the wire as it is pushed into the connector with a punch-down tool. The punch-down tool cuts off any excess wire at the same time that it punches the wire down, making the task of connecting twisted-pair wires to connectors quick and easy.

Figure 15-1 shows an office outlet with two 8-position RJ-45–style jacks equipped with 110-type punch-down wire terminators. A side view of a single 110-type wire terminator is shown in exaggerated scale below the office outlet to illustrate how a wire is terminated using this type of punch-down block. The twisted-pair wire is placed in the jaws of the metal terminals and a punch-down tool is used to force the wire into the narrow space between the metal terminals of the wire terminator. The metal terminals automatically cut through the outer insulation of the wire and tightly grip the solid metal core, providing an electrical connection to the wire. There are a variety of punch-down blocks and other kinds of wire terminators available in the cabling industry; however, they all use this same basic technique for making wire connections.

Twisted-Pair Cable Signal Crosstalk

When it comes to transmitting signals over twisted-pair cable, one of the most important cable characteristics is signal crosstalk. Signal crosstalk (also called *Near End Crosstalk*, or NEXT) occurs when the signals in one wire are electromagnetically coupled, or cross over, into another wire. This happens because wires in close proximity to one another can pick up each other's signal. In a twisted-pair Ethernet segment, excessive crosstalk can result in the signals from the transmit wires being coupled into the receive wires. This increases electrical noise levels and signal error rates, and can also cause problems with collision detection.

A twisted-pair transceiver, for example, detects a collision by the simultaneous occurrence of a signal on both the transmit and receive wire pairs. An excessive amount of signal crosstalk can result in the generation of spurious or *phantom collisions* being detected on the twisted-pair segment. If the phantom collision occurs outside the specified timing window, then it is a late collision, which results in lost frames and late collision errors being reported by the interface.

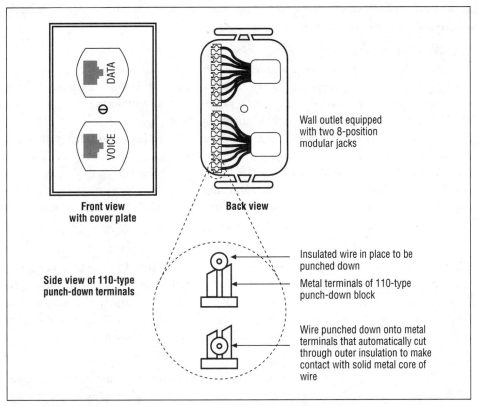

Wall outlet equipped
with two 8-position
modular jacks

Front view
with cover plate

Back view

Side view of 110-type
punch-down terminals

Insulated wire in place to be
punched down

Metal terminals of 110-type
punch-down block

Wire punched down onto metal
terminals that automatically cut
through outer insulation to make
contact with solid metal core of
wire

Figure 15-1. Punch-down connector

The way to avoid crosstalk is to use the correct type of twisted-pair cable, and to ensure that each pair of wires in a twisted-pair segment are twisted together for the entire length of the segment. Twisting the two wires of a wire pair together minimizes the effect of electromagnetic signal coupling between pairs of wire in the cable. This helps make sure that any interference between the wire pairs is below the level of crosstalk that the twisted-pair transceivers are designed to ignore.

Twisted-Pair Cable Construction

A major difference in construction between the various categories of twisted-pair cable has to do with how many twists per foot the wire pairs have been given. The wire pairs in a voice-grade Category 3 cable typically have two twists per foot. This is lightly twisted wire, and you may have to strip back a good bit of outer insulation on a Category 3 cable to reveal the twists. The wire pairs in Category 4 and Category 5 cables have progressively more twists per foot. Category 5 is tightly twisted which results in superior crosstalk performance at higher frequencies. For instance, one vendor specifies the wire pairs in a Category 5 cable as having from 19 to 25 twists per foot.

Another characteristic of twisted-pair cables is the type of insulation used on the wires and the cable jacket. Plenum-rated insulation is more stable at high temperatures and provides superior electrical characteristics. Standard PVC insulation will perform as rated for normal room temperatures, but at temperatures above 40°C (104°F) the signal attenuation of PVC insulated cable increases markedly. Therefore, plenum-rated cables provide better temperature stability and help insure that the signal quality of your cabling system will remain high. A form of Teflon® called fluorinated ethylene propylene (FEP), is typically used for the outer jacket of plenum cables. FEP, the most common form of Teflon, is also used as insulation on the individual wires inside cables to improve signal quality and stability.

Plenum-rated cables are typically required for installation in air handling spaces (also called plenums) to meet fire regulations. The reason for this is that different kinds of plastic cable insulation behave differently in a fire. PVC insulation is "fire retardant" in comparison to plain polyethylene plastic, but PVC will still burn and produce smoke and heat. Teflon FEP insulation produces much less smoke and heat when burning, and does not support the spread of flames. The *National Electric Code* (NEC) provides three identifiers for communications wires and cables:

CMP

> Cables with a CMP identifier are plenum-rated, and are suitable for installation in ducts and plenums without the use of conduit. These cables are designed for fire resistance and low smoke-producing characteristics.

CMR

> Cables with a CMR identifier are not plenum-rated. However, they are engineered to prevent the spread of fire from floor to floor and are suitable for riser use and vertical shaft applications.

CM

> Cables with a CM identifier are specified for general building wiring use, in areas other than plenums and risers.

By looking on the cable for these cable marks, you can tell if a particular cable is suited for a given installation. There is no major difference between CM and CMR cables, since they are both based on PVC insulation; CMR cables simply have more fire retardant material in them, to help slow down the spread of flames.

Twisted-Pair Installation Practices

Most structured cabling systems are installed by professional cabling contractors. A cable contractor has the expertise and equipment required to correctly and safely install the hundreds of twisted-pair cables that a typical office building can require. Cable contractors are also familiar with the structured cable standards and will ensure that the cabling systems that they install meet the specifications.

The currents and voltages used to carry Ethernet signals over twisted-pair wires are small and pose no threat to the user of Ethernet equipment. However, the twisted-pair wires used for telephone services or to power circuit repeaters used in high-speed data lines may carry large currents and voltages used for ringing circuits.

Before handling any wire in a cabling system, you should test the cable with a voltmeter to make sure that the wire is not carrying dangerous voltages or currents. Always observe standard safety practices when working on any type of wire, and take all necessary precautions to avoid electrical shock.

Should you decide to install a small twisted-pair cable system or a few horizontal segments, the TIA/EIA standards provide the following cable installation guidelines:

Maintain the minimum bending radius
> The minimum bending radius for a 4-pair cable should be four times the cable radius. If the cable diameter is 0.5 cm (0.20 inches); the minimum bend radius will be about 2.0 cm (0.80 inches).

Minimize jacket twisting and compression
> Install cable ties loosely and use Velcro® fasteners that allow the cable bundle to move around a bit. Take precautions to avoid tightly compressing the jacket of the cable. Do not use staple guns to fasten the cable to backboards. All of these guidelines are intended to minimize any effect on the wire twists inside the cable. To support high speed signals, the wire twists in a Category 5 cable must remain tightly twisted and not be disturbed anywhere along the length of the cable. Cable ties and fasteners that are too tight, or outer cable jackets that are excessively twisted, can affect the wire twists inside the cable.

Avoid stretching the cable
> Do not exceed 25 lbs. of pulling tension when installing the cable.

Keep wire twists intact to within 1.3 cm (0.5 inch) of any wire termination point for Category 5 systems
> For example, when making a wire termination in an 8-position jack, do not untwist any further back than 0.5 inches from the end of the wire pairs in the cable.

Avoid close proximity to power cables or other electrical equipment

A distance of 30.5 cm (12 inches) is recommended between horizontal cables and fluorescent lighting fixtures. A distance of 1.02 m (40 inches) is recommended for transformers and electrical motors. If the horizontal cable is in a metal conduit, then a distance of 6.4 cm (2.5 inches) is recommended for unshielded power lines carrying less than 2,000 volts. If the horizontal cable is in an open or non-metal pathway, then a distance of 12.7 cm (5 inches) is recommended for unshielded power lines carrying less than 2,000 volts.

Eight-Position (RJ-45–Style) Jack

The 8-position connector used in the TIA/EIA 568 standard is formally described as one that meets the requirements specified in the IEC 603-7 standard for 8-way connectors. You will often hear the 8-position connector referred to as an RJ-45–style connector, since this is what an 8-position connector was originally called by the telephone industry. The RJ-45 name comes from *Registered Jack*, which is an official U.S. telephone industry designation for an 8-position connector.[*]

To make sure that the entire segment can carry high frequency signals without excessive signal distortion, crosstalk, or signal loss, *all* of the connection components in the horizontal channel must be correctly installed and rated to meet Category 5 specifications. Simply installing Category 5 cable is not enough; all of the other components used in the segment must also meet the Category 5 specifications. Standard telephone-type voice-grade RJ-45 connectors are widely available, but they do not meet the Category 5 specifications. Instead, to provide a segment that meets the Category 5 specifications, you must be sure to use 8-position connectors and other components that are specifically designed for use in Category 5 cable systems.

Four-Pair Wiring Schemes

For a horizontal cable segment, the TIA/EIA 568 standard recommends the use of four-pair cables with all eight wires terminated in 8-position jack connectors at each end of the link. The entire twisted-pair cabling system should be wired "straight through." This means that pin 1 of the connector at one end of a horizontal cable is wired to pin 1 of the connector at the other end, and so on for all eight connections. This keeps the structured cabling system very simple and straightforward.

---

[*] The U.S. telephone industry organizes its operation in terms of services that are registered with various public utilities commissions. The specifications for these services include such things as the jack connectors used to provide wire termination for the services, hence the name *Registered Jack*.

Tip and Ring

The words *tip* and *ring* are used to identify wires in a wire pair. Most single telephone circuits require just two wires to deliver what is known in the telephone industry as *plain old telephone service* (POTS). These two wires are identified as "tip" and "ring" by the industry. These names date from the earliest days of manual telephone switchboards, when operators made connections between telephone lines using patch cables with plugs on the end. The plugs had a tip and a ring conductor on them; hence the names for the two wires still used to make a basic telephone connection. Each pair of wires in a modern communications cable are still considered to have a designated tip conductor and ring conductor, labeled T1 and R1 for the first pair, T2 and R2 for the second pair, and so on.

Color Codes

To help identify all the wires found in a multi-pair communications cable, the telephone industry has developed a widely used system of color coding. This system uses a pair of colors to identify the individual wires in each wire pair. The primary color group consists of white, red, black, yellow and violet. The secondary group uses the colors blue, orange, green, brown and slate. These colors are used to identify the wires in the majority of twisted-pair communications cables, from two-pair cables on up to larger cables.

A primary color is paired with one of the secondary colors for each wire in the cable. For large cables, the primary color is used until it has been combined with each of the five secondary colors. Then the next primary color is paired with each of the five secondary colors, and so on. In a typical four-pair cable, the primary color is white, and no other primary color is needed, since there are only four pairs.

Starting with the first wire in the first wire pair of a cable (T1), the insulation is given a base coat of the first primary color, white, with a stripe or dash of the secondary color blue. This is written as "white/blue" and is abbreviated as W-BL. The second wire in the first wire pair (R1) is given a base coat of the secondary color, blue, with a stripe or dash of the primary color white, written as "blue/white" and abbreviated as BL-W or sometimes just BL. In the first wire pair, then, the T1 wire is white with a blue stripe, and the R1 wire is blue with a white stripe. In the second wire pair, wire T2 is white with an orange stripe, and R2 is orange with a white stripe, etc.

Wiring Sequence

The term *wiring sequence* refers to the order in which the wires are terminated on a connector. There are two wiring sequence options provided in the TIA/EIA 568 standard. The *preferred* wiring sequence according to the standard is called T568A, and the *optional* wiring sequence is called T568B. Figure 15-2 shows the preferred and optional wiring sequence for an 8-position jack connector. Which sequence you use is a local decision. Note that the words "preferred" and "optional" may not reflect reality at your site.

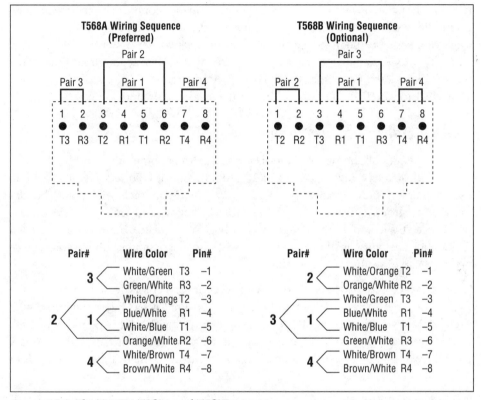

Figure 15-2. The TIA-EIA T568A and T568B wiring sequence

The optional wiring sequence is widely used in the United States, and many cable installers use it as their default cabling standard. That's because the optional T568B sequence is also known as the AT&T 258A wiring sequence, and has been widely used for years in AT&T cabling systems. It's up to you to find out what wiring sequence is widely used at your site, and to make sure that your cabling system adheres to the local standard to avoid confusion.

The center two positions in both wiring sequences, pins 4 and 5, are always used for pair 1—this is where telephone voice circuits are wired if the link is used for voice service. That's why the 10BASE-T standard originally specified the use of positions 1, 2, 3 and 6, avoiding the use of pins 4 and 5. That way you could run a 10BASE-T service and voice service over the same four-pair cable if you wished.

Most installations prefer to keep the voice and data services on separate cables to avoid the problem of noise from telephone ringing circuits affecting the data service. Subsequent Ethernet twisted-pair media standards based on two pairs have followed the 10BASE-T wiring scheme for cabling compatibility.

Keeping the wires correctly paired together for the entire length of the horizontal channel is critically important to maintain signal quality for Ethernet signals. As it happens, there is an older wiring sequence that you may encounter in existing cabling systems that does not provide the correct wire pairing and can lead to problems for Ethernet signals. The older wiring sequence that results in incorrect wire pairing is called the *Universal Service Order Code* system, or USOC. Despite the name, this is not a universally adopted system, but it shows up in many older telephone systems. The USOC system deals with the pairs differently, and the wire identification used in the old USOC system is often based on an older color scheme as well.

Because of the way the pairs are wired in the USOC scheme, you will end up with a *split pair* if you try to install a twisted-pair Ethernet segment on a cable using this wiring sequence. Figure 15-3 shows an 8-position connector with USOC wiring based on the older color coding scheme that is frequently used with USOC systems. For comparison, the T568A wiring sequence is also shown.

Notice that the wires connected to pins 1 and 2, which are paired together in both the T568A and T568B wiring sequence, are not paired together in the USOC scheme. If you plug a twisted-pair Ethernet station into a cabling system that is wired using the USOC scheme, the Ethernet segment can end up with excessive signal noise and crosstalk because of the split pair wiring. It might not be immediately obvious that there's a problem with the segment, since a simple wiring test of the connection would show that basic wire connectivity from end-to-end is okay—but checking for connectivity between the pins at each end of the link will not detect the problem. The USOC wiring sequence provides wires between every pin of the eight-pin connectors located at each end of the link. What USOC doesn't provide is the *correct pairing* of the wires on the wire pairs used to carry Ethernet signals.

It may seem odd that just twisting the wires together in a pair would make this much difference, but it does. Ethernet signals operate at high frequency, and at the frequencies involved, the lack of twists on a pair of wires makes a big difference in the electrical characteristics of those wires. The twisted-pair Ethernet segment will experience excessive signal noise and crosstalk, and can fail to operate properly if the correct wires are not twisted together for the full length of the segment.

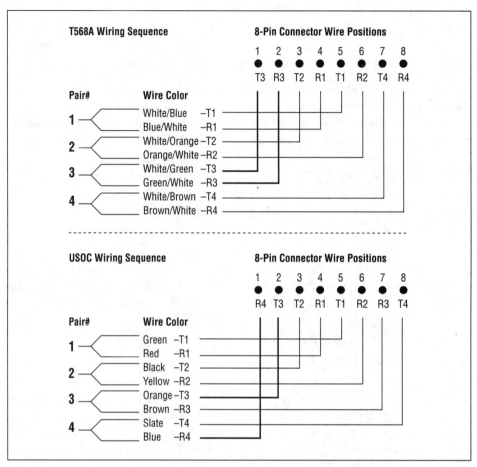

Figure 15-3. Split pairs in USOC wiring

Modular Patch Panel

Modular patch panels are panels designed to hold a number of RJ-45–style jack connectors. The eight wires of the horizontal link cable are terminated in the jack connector, and the connector is installed in the patch panel, which is located in the telecommunications closet. You then use a patch cable to connect the jack in the patch panel to another patch panel or to hub equipment located in the closet, depending on how your cabling system is organized. You can buy patch panels that come fully populated with connectors, or you can get blank panels and simply add the number of connectors you need.

Figure 15-4 shows a modular patch panel of the sort used in telecommunications closets. From the patch panel, a horizontal link cable travels to the work area wall outlet, where the link cable is terminated in an 8-position modular jack. A patch cable is shown connected to the work area outlet. The other end of the patch cable could be connected to a computer in the office. Modular patch panels provide a great deal of flexibility. You can also use several different patch panels in a given wiring closet, dedicated to different services. When you add new network equipment, you can provide separate patch panels for that equipment and easily connect different offices to different network equipment in the wiring closet, depending on what the user requires.

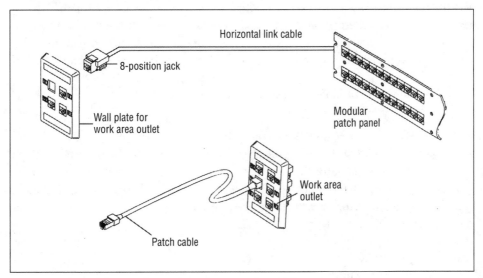

Figure 15-4. Modular patch panel, work area outlet, and patch cable

Work Area Outlet

The eight wires of each horizontal link cable are terminated in a modular 8-position jack connector mounted in a wall plate of the office space or work area. The telephone industry has had years of experience in wiring offices, and consequently there are a wide variety of wall plates available for terminating twisted-pair cables.

You can buy wall plates that range from a fixed pair of simple 8-position jacks to a more complex modular system that allows a wide variety of connectors to be installed in the same wall plate. A modular wall outlet makes it an easy task to provide a neat, low-cost, and reliable office connection to the horizontal cabling system.

Twisted-Pair Patch Cables

Each end of the horizontal link is connected to equipment such as Ethernet hubs or computers using patch and equipment cables. At the wiring closet end of the link, patch and equipment cables are used to connect the link to an Ethernet hub, for example, or into the backbone cabling system. At the work area end of the link, a patch cable is used to make the connection between the computer in the office and the jack in the wall outlet.

Patch cables must be very flexible to allow lots of movement, and for that reason they must use stranded twisted-pair wire instead of the solid kind. If you repeatedly bend solid conductor cable, the solid conductor inside the insulation of the cable will eventually crack and break, which can result in an intermittent failure that can be very hard to track down. Stranded cable, on the other hand, can withstand large amounts of bending and twisting without problems.

You can buy ready-made patch cables from cable suppliers at reasonable cost. Since it's easy to buy ready-made patch cables, many sites choose to avoid the problems with building their own patch cables and purchase them from suppliers. This also takes advantage of the fact that a good quality manufactured patch cable will be built using the correct connectors and stranded cable and according to standardized manufacturing and test procedures. There are a lot of patch cables on the market, so you need to make sure that the patch cables you buy are rated to meet Category 5 or better specifications. Very low-cost or generic patch cables may not be carefully built with quality components and may not meet the specifications or may not maintain their rating over time.

Telephone-Grade Patch Cables

Beware of using standard telephone-grade patch cables for twisted-pair segments. One common patch cable used in the telephone industry goes by the name of *silver satin*, which describes the outside color of the cable. This is the flat patch cable you will often see being used to connect a telephone to a wall jack, and this cable is widely stocked in ordinary hardware or office supply stores. The wide availability of silver satin is unfortunate, since it's not suitable for use in a network cable system.

The biggest problem with this type of patch cable is that the conductors in silver satin cords are not twisted together, leading to excessive levels of crosstalk on the wires in this cable. High levels of signal crosstalk can lead to spurious frame errors and the occurrence of phantom collisions on your segment. Another problem with silver satin is that the conductors are quite small, which causes higher signal attenuation. Therefore, using silver satin significantly reduces the distance that a signal may travel.

One of the worst problems with silver satin cable is that despite all the signal errors, it may seem to work okay at first when it is used in an Ethernet segment. That often leads people to think they can get away with using this kind of patch cable. However, the silver satin patch cable may still be generating problems on the network due to phantom collisions, late collision errors, and other signal problems.

These problems can be masked since the Ethernet system will keep trying to function despite errors, and the problems on a single segment may not cause the rest of the network to fail. That, coupled with the fact that each station's high-level protocol software will keep retransmitting frames until something gets through, tends to hide the effects of a poorly functioning media system. However, the higher the traffic rate gets, the more these errors will occur, often leading to complaints of a slow network.

As things progressively get worse, you will be forced to find all of the silver satin patch cables and replace them with the right kind of twisted-pair patch cable. A better approach is to simply forbid the use of any wire or other component in a horizontal cabling system that does not meet Category 5 specifications. Also, make sure everyone understands that silver satin patch cables are something that must be avoided in any structured cabling system designed to carry data signals.

Equipment Cables

In the telecommunications closet, the *equipment cable* is the cable that connects the active equipment, such as an Ethernet hub to the patch panel. The equipment cable might be as simple as a patch cable, or may include cables that are more complex. For Ethernet hubs with RJ-45–style jacks on the front, you simply connect patch cables from each jack on the hub to the appropriate jack on the patch panel in the wiring closet and you're done. However, some hubs come with high-density 50-pin connectors and cables.

50-Pin Connectors and 25-Pair Cables

You may encounter 10BASE-T Ethernet hubs that are equipped with 50-pin connectors instead of RJ-45–style jacks. This approach is often used when a manufacturer needs to accommodate a large number of connections on a single interface board and there isn't enough room on the board to accommodate all of the RJ-45–style jack connectors required. In that case, a single 50-pin connector can provide twelve 4-wire connections, and manufacturers can support 24 connections on a single interface board with just two 50-pin connectors. The 50-pin connectors, and the 25-pair cables they are connected to, have traditionally have been used in voice-grade cabling systems and are typically rated for Category 3 performance.

However, newer versions of these cables and connectors have been developed and are rated for Category 5 use.

You can also purchase pre-wired 25-pair cables with 50-pin connectors on each end. In this scheme, you just plug the 50-pin connector into the hub and plug the other end into a pre-wired patch panel that provides a set of RJ-45–style jacks. You then connect a patch cable from the jack in this panel to a jack in a patch panel that supports your horizontal link cables. This makes a complete connection from the wall plate in the office to a port on your Ethernet hub. This approach can greatly reduce the amount of time you spend building cables, but this type of cabling is usually limited to 10 Mbps 10BASE-T equipment. That's because it's hard to achieve the low levels of signal crosstalk required in higher speed data systems in a 25-pair cable that is designed to carry multiple active signal pairs.

50-pin wiring sequence and mounting hardware

One thing to watch out for when using pre-wired 25-pair cables and 50-pin connectors is the wiring sequence used. These sorts of cables can be wired several different ways. Therefore, you need to find out how the hub vendor has wired the 50-pin connector on their hub, and then find a 25-pair cable and cross-connect block that is wired so everything works properly.

There are also several kinds of mounting hardware available for the 50-pin connector. You will sometimes discover that one vendor's 50-pin connector plug may not attach well to another vendor's 50-pin socket connector due to different locking mechanisms, or the location of a fastening screw. Before buying 25-pair cables and 50-pin connectors, it's a good idea to check with the vendor of the hub you are using. They can often provide a list of connectors that are known to work well with the connector on the hub.

50-pin multiple disturber crosstalk

A short length of 25-pair cable from the hub equipment to a nearby patch panel will typically work for a 10 Mbps data service such as 10BASE-T. However, if you use 25-pair cable at both ends of the link, or even make the entire link out of 25-pair cable, you may encounter something called *multiple disturber near end crosstalk* (MDNEXT). This refers to the fact that the more active wires you have in close proximity with one another, the greater the chances are for signal crosstalk. In a 4-pair cable, there is usually only one data service being supported, so crosstalk is limited. On the other hand, there are more active wires, or *disturbers,* in close proximity to one another in a 25-pair cable, which increases the chances for crosstalk.

Multiple disturber crosstalk may not show up immediately, but instead could occur when things get busy enough. For example, if you use a 25-pair cable to connect a 10BASE-T hub to a lab full of stations, you may not notice any problems until all of the stations are active. When all of the stations are active, you then have the largest number of active pairs, and hence the highest probability of multiple disturber crosstalk in a 25-pair cable. To check for this problem, you need test equipment that can simultaneously place signals on all transmit pairs of a 25-pair cable while measuring for excessive crosstalk.

While using pre-wired 25-pair cables for connections to patch panels and hub equipment can minimize the amount of wiring you have to do in a wiring closet, there are also some drawbacks. For one thing, they are often limited in signal quality, and cannot support higher speed versions of Ethernet. Also, it can be more difficult to troubleshoot a network problem in this kind of installation because there is no easy way to move a connection from port to port of the Ethernet hub. Since all connections are wired simultaneously with the 25-pair cable, you can't pull one connection out and try it on another hub port as a test. This makes it much more difficult to isolate a problem to a particular horizontal cable.

Harmonica connectors

A cable *harmonica* is a small plastic housing equipped with a strip of RJ-45–style jacks in a row, so named since the row of RJ-45 holes on the housing make it look somewhat like the musical instrument. The harmonica terminates one end of a 25-pair cable whose other end is equipped with a 50-pin connector for connection to an Ethernet hub. This system typically supports up to 12 RJ-45–style jacks per harmonica.

If you buy a hub that uses this scheme, you need to make sure that the harmonica you get is wired correctly. RJ-45–style harmonicas are used in the telephone industry, and are therefore sold by telephone equipment vendors. However, they often come wired for standard telephone service by default. Therefore, a typical harmonica from a telephone supplier may not have the correct wiring scheme needed by the ports on your Ethernet hub.

Building a Twisted-Pair Patch Cable

This is a quick reference guide to the installation of an RJ-45 plug onto a patch cable. Before building your own cable, you should know that the task of properly installing connectors on cables is more complex than it might appear at first glance. While many people can crimp a connector onto the end of a cable, it takes special care to make sure that the connector is installed as well as possible.

There are good reasons why high quality cable assemblies purchased from a reputable company with the connectors already installed will typically be more reliable than ones you make yourself. Reputable cable and connector manufacturers employ engineers who ensure that all components and tooling used in the manufacturing process are correct, and that every connector is installed in a consistent manner. These engineers put samples of the manufactured cable assemblies through tests to ensure that critically important characteristics, such as pull strength and electrical resistance, are being correctly maintained. The result of the manufacturing process is a cable that is correctly mated to the connector, and a connector that is correctly installed using the right tool with the correct amount of pressure.

Duplicating the carefully controlled manufacturing process yourself can be quite difficult. Without careful attention to a number of important issues, the result may be a cable with a connector that doesn't really fit the cable correctly, and that may have been crimped onto the cable with the incorrect tool. Although such a cable may initially pass when tested with a cable tester, these problems can eventually lead to intermittent connections and network outages.

It's not impossible to build a good homemade cable; it just takes a lot more attention to detail, and may cost more than you might expect to do the job correctly. For example, while all RJ-45 connectors may look alike at first glance, there are small differences in the way they are built and the way they may fit into a crimping tool. Finding the exact match between the crimping tool and the connector you use can be difficult. There are a lot of RJ-45 crimping tools on the market too, and a number of them are of low quality with flimsy plastic or lightweight metal frames which may not provide enough force to produce a really solid crimp. High quality crimping tools are expensive, and often require special crimping dies designed for specific versions of RJ-45 connectors.

Therefore, it's a good idea to consider buying high quality patch cables ready-made from a reputable manufacturer. This is especially true for any system that will be supporting 1000BASE-T twisted-pair Gigabit Ethernet. The Gigabit Ethernet standard sends signals over all four wire pairs simultaneously. Marginal patch cables will very likely cause signal errors when used on a Gigabit Ethernet link.

Twisted-pair patch cables should only be made using stranded wire cable. Solid wire cable is unacceptable for patch cables, since it will break when flexed, causing intermittent connections. If you choose to build your own patch cables, you need to buy stranded twisted-pair cable and the correct RJ-45–style plugs for terminating stranded wire.

Since solid conductor cable is specified for use in the horizontal cable segment, many RJ-45 connectors are designed for use on solid conductor cable and may cause problems when crimped onto a stranded patch cable. Using the wrong connector on stranded twisted-pair could cut too deeply into the conductors of the wire and weaken them so that they may break easily, which could result in an intermittent connection. To avoid this, you need to make sure that you are using plugs that have been specifically designed for stranded wire.

Installing an RJ-45 Plug

Building a patch cable is a process of installing RJ-45 plug connector on each end of a stranded cable. Here we describe the process of installing the RJ-45 connectors.

Attaching cable connectors involves the use of very sharp knives for stripping cable insulation as well as crimping tools that can be dangerous to operate. Many crimping tools incorporate a ratchet mechanism that, once engaged, prevents the tool from being opened until it has first closed completely. Anything caught in the crimping tool, including your fingers, will be crushed.

1. Carefully strip away a few inches of the outer insulation from the twisted-pair cable, revealing the individually insulated twisted-pair conductors inside. Each twisted-pair conductor consists of a set of thin stranded wires surrounded by insulation. *Do not cut into the insulation of the twisted-pair conductors.*

2. Orient the conductors according to the colors of the insulation.

3. Straighten out the twisted-pair conductors, arrange them as shown in Figure 15-5, and cut the conductors to a length of about 12 mm (1/2 inch). Leave the insulation in place on the individual twisted-pair conductors. Make sure that the conductors are all cut to the same length, providing a square end to the cut.

4. If you wish to use the TIA/EIA 568A preferred wiring sequence, then arrange the conductors in the following order from top to bottom. The wire colors, and the pin numbers to which they connect, are as follows:

   - Pin 8: Brown/White

   - Pin 7: White/Brown

   - Pin 6: Orange/White

   - Pin 5: White/Blue

   - Pin 4: Blue/White

   - Pin 3: White/Orange

   - Pin 2: Green/White

   - Pin 1: White/Green

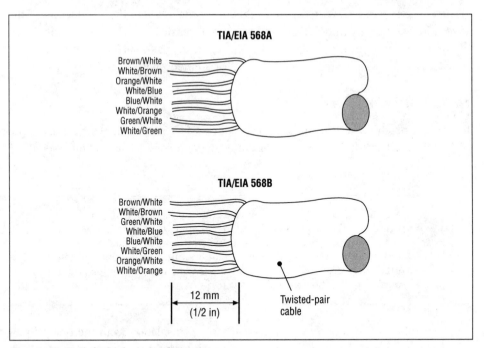

Figure 15-5. Arrange the twisted-pair wires

If you wish to use the TIA/EIA 568B optional wiring sequence (also known as the AT&T 258A wiring sequence), then arrange the conductors in the following order from top to bottom:

- Pin 8: Brown/White

- Pin 7: White/Brown

- Pin 6: Green/White

- Pin 5: White/Blue

- Pin 4: Blue/White

- Pin 3: White/Green

- Pin 2: Orange/White

- Pin 1: White/Orange

5. Hold the RJ-45 connector with the bottom (contact side) facing you. The blunt end of the connector (which gets inserted into an RJ-45 jack) should be pointing to the left and the open end of the connector should point to the right.

While holding the connector in this orientation, the pin 8 position is on the top edge, and the pin 1 position is on the bottom edge. Hold the twisted-pair cable firmly in your other hand. Insert the insulated twisted-pair conductors into the connector as shown in Figure 15-6. Make sure to keep the conductors in the correct sequence.

6. Slide the conductors all the way into the connector, so that they are firmly seated against the inside front of the connector shell. When the conductors are all the way into the connector, you should be able to see the ends of the conductors through the front of the connector (see Figure 15-7). The outer insulation of the cable should be under the strain relief clamp.

7. While holding the cable and connector firmly together, insert them all the way into the crimping tool (see Figure 15-8). The connector will go all the way into the crimp tool only if it is inserted from the correct side. Before crimping, verify that the conductors are still properly seated inside the connector.

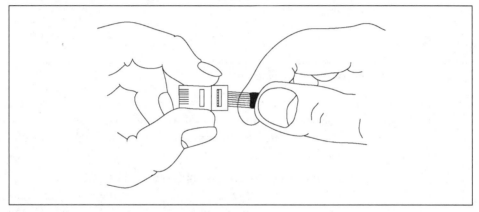

Figure 15-6. Insert conductors into the connector

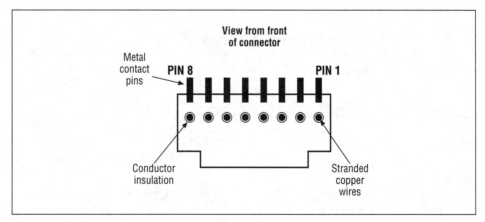

Figure 15-7. Conductors properly inserted inside the connector

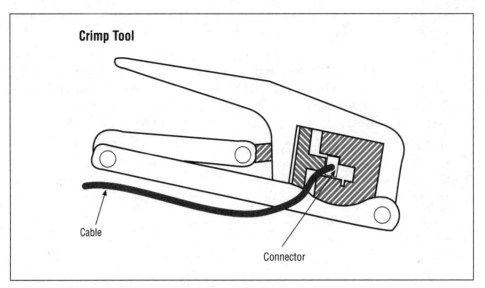

Figure 15-8. Insert connector into crimping tool

8. Place the flat base of the crimp tool on a solid surface, such as a table or floor. Press down the handle of the crimp tool until it comes into contact with the stop. This forces the contacts inside the connector to bite through the insulation on the conductors.

   This also forces the cable strain relief assembly into place. The strain relief block is important, since it clamps the cable into place in the connector. This prevents stresses on the cable from pulling the conductors out of the connector.

9. Figure 15-9 shows a connector before and after crimping. After crimping, the plug contacts bite through the insulation and into the copper wire portion of the twisted pair conductors. The strain relief block is forced into place to hold the cable into the connector.

Ethernet Signal Crossover

To make the data flow when connecting two twisted-pair Ethernet transceivers together over a twisted-pair link segment, the transmit data signals of one transceiver must end up on the receive data pins of the other transceiver, and vice versa. The crossover wiring may be accomplished in one of two ways: with a crossover cable or inside the hub.

If you are only networking two computers, then you can provide the signal crossover by using a crossover patch cable. The crossover cable is built with the transmit pins on one end of the cable connected to the receive data pins on the other end of the crossover cable, and vice versa.

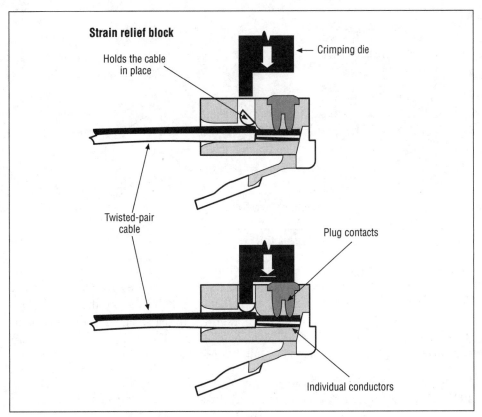

Figure 15-9. Connector before and after crimping

However, most networks support more than two computers, and the multiple network segments communicate by connecting the segments to repeater or switching hubs. That's why the Ethernet standard recommends that the signal crossover wiring be accomplished at one point in the cabling system—inside the hub. Figure 15-10 shows how signal crossover works inside an Ethernet hub.

When the signal crossover wiring is done inside the hub ports, you are relieved of the task of supplying a crossover cable for every Ethernet segment in your cabling system. Instead, each twisted-pair segment is wired straight through as recommended in the structured cabling standards.

10BASE-T and 100BASE-T Crossover Cable

In the fairly unusual case of networking only two machines, the two machines can be linked together with a single cable. This eliminates the need for an Ethernet hub, but also eliminates the automatic signal crossover that is done inside the hub ports. Therefore, when linking two machines with a patch cable, you can either

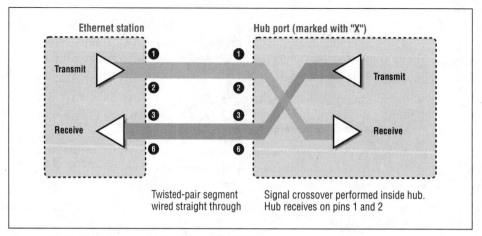

Figure 15-10. *Signal crossover inside a 10BASE-T hub port*

purchase a ready-made crossover cable or build a crossover cable to make the signals work properly. Another use for a crossover cable arises when you need to link hub ports together between two hubs that already have done the signal crossover inside their ports. In this case, there are one too many signal crossovers being done, and this connection will not work with a straight-through cable. Therefore, you need to use a crossover cable to link the two hub ports.

Figure 15-11 shows the crossover cable wiring required for 10BASE-T and 100BASE-T systems. Since both of these media systems use the same four wires, a Category 5 crossover patch cable wire in this fashion will work on both systems.

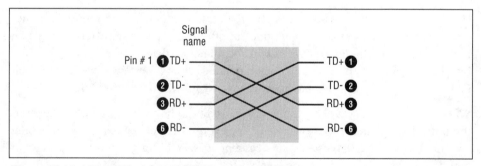

Figure 15-11. *10BASE-T and 100BASE-T crossover cable wiring*

1000BASE-T Crossover Cable

The 1000BASE-T Gigabit Ethernet system uses four pairs of wires, and requires that all four wires be crossed-over correctly to operate. To make this easier, the Gigabit Ethernet standard includes an optional automatic crossover function. The optional automatic crossover function appears to be supported in most Gigabit Ethernet transceiver chips.

In the automatic crossover system, the transceiver automatically moves the link signals to the correct logic gates inside the transceiver chip. Once a transceiver has moved the signals to different gates, it waits for approximately 60 milliseconds while checking the link for link pulses or data. This provides a mechanism for each end of the link to automatically configure the crossover function as needed. A random startup time is used to ensure that the ends of the link will not start moving the signals in synchronization, and thereby never achieve a correct crossover.

If neither or both of the ports you are connecting implement an internal crossover, then you can provide an external crossover to make the link work. External crossover when linking just two machines is required for 10- and 100 Mbps Ethernet links, since only the 1000BASE-T standard has an automatic crossover feature. You can provide the signal crossover for a 1000BASE-T link by building a crossover patch cable as shown in Figure 15-12. This crossover cable will work for all other Ethernet twisted-pair media systems as well.

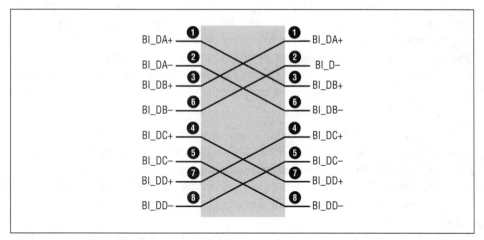

Figure 15-12. 1000BASE-T crossover cable

Identifying a Crossover Cable

There are a several ways to tell the difference between a normal, straight-through cable, and a crossover cable. Ideally, a crossover cable will be labeled as such at one or both ends of the cable, making identification easy. However, if there are no labels, then there are a couple of approaches you can take.

A hand-held cable tester can be used to generate a "wiremap" of the cable, which typically provides a display that shows which wires are connected to which pins.

You can also try looking at the wire colors inside the RJ-45–style plugs on each end of the cable, assuming that the plugs are made of transparent plastic. If you hold the two plugs together—side by side—you can see that the wire colors on the pins at each end of the cable are the same for a straight-through cable. On a crossover cable, the wire colors connected to pins 1 and 2 at one end of the cable will be connected to pins 3 and 6 at the other end.

Twisted-Pair Ethernet and Telephone Signals

A twisted-pair Ethernet transceiver is typically attached to a twisted-pair segment with a patch cord connected to an RJ-45–style modular jack in a wall outlet. One RJ-45 modular jack looks a lot like another, and it's possible to mistakenly connect a transceiver to a telephone outlet instead of the correct data outlet. The center two pins of the RJ-45 jack (pins 4 and 5) are typically used by standard telephone services. Therefore, to avoid a conflict with telephone services, the 10BASE-T and 100BASE-T systems do not use pins 4 and 5.

However, if the local telephone wiring does not follow standard conventions, or if a port is miswired, it is possible to connect telephone services to the pins used by the 10- or 100 Mbps Ethernet systems. There is also a possibility that the twisted-pair transceiver could be damaged by the voltages used for ringing a telephone. The standard notes that while the Ethernet transceiver may be damaged by a ringing voltage, the manufacturer must ensure that there will be no safety hazard to the user from the ringing voltage.

The 1000BASE-T twisted-pair standard uses all four pairs, with wires connected to all eight pins on the RJ-45 connector. This makes it much likelier that a Gigabit Ethernet cable mistakenly installed in a telephone jack will receive telephone signals. The standard notes that telephone battery voltage is generally 56 VDC. Telephone ringing voltage includes an AC signal of up to 175 V peak with large transient voltages at the start and end of each ring interval. There is a possibility that the 1000BASE-T transceiver could be damaged by these voltages.

The standard also notes that the 1000BASE-T equipment is not required to survive such wiring hazards without damage. However, the manufacturer of Ethernet equipment must ensure that there will be no safety hazard to the user from the telephone voltages. According to the standard, a 1000BASE-T transceiver typically appears as an *off-hook* telephone to the telephone system, meaning that the telephone is in use. Since the telephone system will not send ringing voltages to an off-hook telephone, this should help prevent any damage to an incorrectly connected 1000BASE-T transceiver.

16

Fiber Optic Cables and Connectors

Fiber optic Ethernet systems are based on multimode and single-mode fiber optic cables and connectors. Depending on the speed of the Ethernet media system and the type and wavelength of fiber optic transmitters used in the system, the behavior of fiber optic media can vary. This is especially true for the Gigabit Ethernet fiber optic system, which sends very high frequency signals over fiber optic cable.

This chapter begins with a description of the fiber optic cable issues that are common to all fiber optic Ethernet media systems. Following that is a description of the fiber optic issues specific to each Ethernet media system. The Gigabit Ethernet media section is the largest, since this system has the widest variety of fiber optic characteristics to describe.

Fiber Optic Cable

There are a wide variety of fiber optic cable types, which are used according to the task at hand. Fiber optic patch cords typically consist of two fibers, either multimode or single-mode depending on your requirements. Patch cords can be equipped with whatever fiber optic connector you need at each end of the cable. There are companies who will build fiber optic cables to meet your requirements, and can often ship them to you within a day or two after you place the order.

Fiber optic horizontal cables are sometimes installed as part of a structured cabling system. However, in the vast majority of structured cabling systems today, Category 5 or 5e twisted-pair horizontal cables are used to deliver Ethernet signals to the desktop. Fiber optic backbone cables are commonly found in structured cabling systems. These backbone cables typically contain 12 or 24 fibers, but they may also contain dozens of fibers. For large backbone cable installations, fiber optic cable manufacturers will build cables to order depending on your requirements.

The TIA/EIA 568-A structured cabling standard provides specifications for installing both backbone and horizontal segment fiber optic cables in a building. The TIA/EIA standard is described in Chapter 14, *Structured Cabling*.

Fiber optic Ethernet transceivers for use on multimode fiber are based on LED transmitters which emit a form of light that is not dangerous to the eye. However, Ethernet single-mode fiber optic equipment and other network devices based on single-mode fiber typically use laser light.

Sufficiently powerful laser light can damage the retina in your eye without causing any feeling of pain. Treat all fiber optic cables with caution. Beware of looking directly into any fiber optic cable, and observe safety precautions when working around fiber optic cable systems.

Fiber Optic Core Diameters

The thickness of the core optical fiber used in fiber optic cables is very small, and is measured in millionths of a meter, called micrometers (μm) or microns. One frequently used type of multimode fiber optic cable consists of a *graded-index* cable, in which the individual pieces of fiber have a 62.5 μm fiber optic core and 125 μm outer cladding (62.5/125). Multimode cable is also available with a 50 μm core and 125 μm cladding.

Single-mode fiber has a much smaller core with the same 125 μm outer cladding. Commercial single-mode fibers have core diameters that can vary over the range of approximately 8–10 μm. They are collectively referred to as 10 μm fiber in the standard. By way of comparison, a human hair has a diameter of about 100 μm.

Fiber Optic Modes

A fiber optic "mode" is a path that light can follow in traveling down a fiber. As the name implies, multimode cable has a larger core designed to support multiple modes, or paths, of light propagation. When an incoherent light source such as an LED is coupled to multimode fiber, then multiple paths of light from the LED are transmitted over the cable as shown in Figure 16-1.

An advantage of the larger core is easier coupling of the light source to the cable. A disadvantage is that the wider corridor for light transmission allows the multiple paths of LED light to bounce off the sides of the fiber. When this happens, these

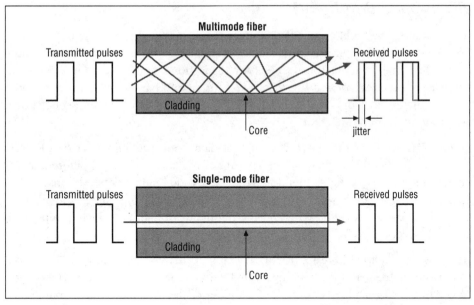

Figure 16-1. Modes of light

light paths arrive at the far end slightly out of phase, causing the light pulse to become dispersed or spread out. This modal dispersion, or *jitter*, of the signal can cause problems with signal recovery at the far end. The longer the distance, the more signal dispersion there will be at a given signaling rate.

Single-mode fiber has a smaller core optimized to propagate a single mode, or path. When long wavelength light (e.g., 1300 nanometers[*]) is injected into this fiber, then only one mode will be active and the rays of light will travel down the middle of the fiber. When a coherent light source (e.g., a laser) is coupled to a single-mode fiber, then the single beam of laser light is transmitted over the cable.

With single-mode fiber, the signals don't bounce against the cladding of the fiber, meaning there is no modal signal dispersion. Therefore, the light can travel a much longer distance without signal problems. The smaller core requires more precision to couple the light source to the cable, which is one reason why single-mode equipment is more expensive.

It is possible to couple a coherent laser light source to a multimode fiber. However, when this was done for Gigabit Ethernet, it was discovered that there can sometimes be a problem with signal propagation over the cable. This potential problem is called Differential Mode Delay (DMD), and is further described later in this chapter.

---

[*] A nanometer (nm) is one billionth of a meter.

Fiber Optic Bandwidth

The distance over which an Ethernet signal will travel down a multimode fiber segment is primarily affected by signal strength and signal jitter, or dispersion. Multimode fiber manufacturers specify a dispersion rating based on a figure of merit called the *bandwidth-length product,* or simply bandwidth. The bandwidth for multimode fiber optic cable is variously listed as megahertz-kilometers, shown as either MHz-km or MHz*km.

A 200 MHz-km fiber can move 200 MHz of data up to one kilometer or 100 MHz of data as far as two kilometers. The amount of modal dispersion is different at different frequencies of light; therefore, the bandwidth rating depends on the frequency of light being sent over the cable. When using this spec, you need to know both the bandwidth rating and the frequency of light for which it applies on a given cable.

There is no way to field test a fiber optic cable to derive a bandwidth-length product. Instead, the bandwidth ratings can be found in vendor spec sheets if you know the vendor and part number of the fiber cable. Multimode fiber optic media is manufactured in a range of bandwidths, although one of the most common is 62.5/125 μm cable with a 160 MHz-km modal bandwidth at a wavelength of 850 nm.

Single mode cable does not have the modal dispersion characteristics of multimode fiber, and therefore is not provided with a bandwidth rating.

Fiber Optic Loss Budget

The power losses on an optical link must be small enough to allow the signal to be received accurately. The optical loss budget is the total optical power loss allowed through all fiber cables and patch cords and all associated connectors on the segment. Optical power loss, or attenuation, is expressed in dB/km (decibels per kilometer) at a specified wavelength. The "km" portion is typically assumed, and you will often see fiber optic loss measurements expressed using only the "dB" portion.

Optical loss is measured with fiber optic test instruments that can tell you exactly how much optical loss there may be on a given segment at a given wavelength of light. The more connectors you have and the longer your fiber link cable is, the higher the optical loss will be. If the connectors or fiber splices are poorly made, or if there is finger oil and/or dust on the connector ends, then there will be higher optical loss on the segment. When working with fiber optic cables it is very important to keep the ends of the fiber optic cable clean. In addition, dust caps should be provided for any unused connectors to avoid the accumulation of dust and oil on the fiber optic equipment and cables. Fiber optic cleaning pads saturated with alcohol are available for cleaning the ends of fiber optic jumpers before installation.

Note that a number of fiber optic loss meters use LED light sources operating at a typical wavelength of 850 nm. There can be a problem when using such testers for Gigabit Ethernet, since they may produce an attenuation reading that would cause an otherwise acceptable Gigabit Ethernet fiber link to be rejected. Gigabit Ethernet links use laser light, which propagates more efficiently than LED light in most cases. Therefore, a loss reading performed with an LED-based tester may report a higher loss value than a tester with a laser light source.

One way to deal with this is to measure the segment length instead of the loss. Segment length is one of the most important cabling parameters for Gigabit Ethernet fiber optic links, and will often determine whether a link will function. Field testers which can measure the length of a segment can help qualify a Gigabit Ethernet segment, assuming the link attenuation is not excessive. In other words, if the total segment length is acceptable and the link connectors and splices are correctly installed, then the odds are good that the link will work.

If the link length is within the correct limits and there are still problems with the link, then you need to carefully check attenuation. To get the most accurate attenuation test you must use a laser light source that operates at the same wavelength as the Gigabit Ethernet port you intend to use.

Fiber Optic Connectors

A variety of fiber optic connectors are used, depending on the cable type and the Ethernet media system. The most commonly used fiber optic connectors as of this writing are the ST and the SC connector. The ST connector is specified for use on 10BASE-FL equipment. The SC connector is specified for use on 100BASE-FX and 1000BASE-X equipment. A new connector called the MT-RJ is showing up on many Ethernet hubs, since it is compact and allows vendors to fit more fiber optic ports on a given hub module or faceplate. Other "small form factor" fiber optic connectors have been developed, such as the 3M Volition VF45, and you may find these in use as well.

ST connector

An ST fiber optic connector, which means "straight tip," is a registered trademark of American Telephone & Telegraph Company. The formal name of the ST connector in the ISO/IEC international standards is *BFOC/2.5*. Figure 16-2 shows a pair of fiber optic cables equipped with ST plug connectors.

The ST connector is a spring-loaded bayonet connector whose outer ring locks onto the connection. The ST connector has a key on an inner sleeve along with

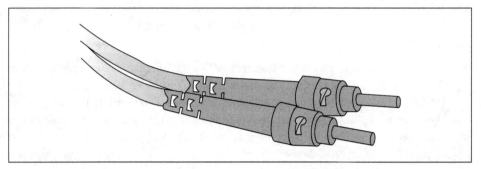

Figure 16-2. ST connectors

the outer bayonet ring. To make a connection, you line up the key on the inner sleeve of the ST plug with a corresponding slot on the ST receptacle. Then you push the connector in and lock it in place by twisting the outer bayonet ring. This provides a tight connection with precise alignment between the two pieces of fiber optic cable being joined.

SC connector

SC, meaning "subscriber connector," is a registered trademark of NTT Advanced Technology Corporation. The duplex SC connector shown in Figure 16-3 is the recommended connector in the 100BASE-FX and 1000BASE-X standards, and is the one most widely used by vendors.

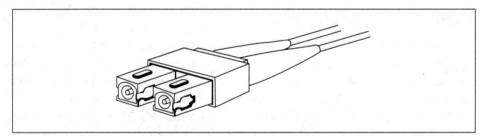

Figure 16-3. Duplex SC connector

The SC connector is designed for ease of use; the connector is pushed into place and automatically snaps into the connector housing to complete the connection. Make sure to seat the connector firmly, pushing until it has "clicked" into place. An SC connector may still work if it is not installed tightly, but you will encounter high error rates and eventually the link may completely fail.

MT-RJ connector

The standard recommends the use of the duplex SC fiber optic connector for both 1000BASE-SX and 1000BASE-LX fiber optic media segments. However, there is nothing to prevent vendors from using other fiber optic connectors. You may find vendors using the more compact MT-RJ connector on 1000BASE-SX ports. The MT-RJ connector is shown in Figure 16-4.

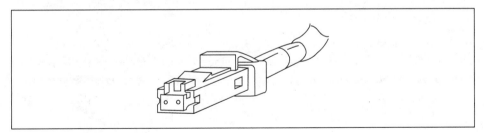

Figure 16-4. MT-RJ connector

The MT-RJ connector provides both fiber connections in a space the size of an RJ-45 connector. Since the MT-RJ connector takes up about half the space required by the SC connectors, this allows vendors to provide more 1000BASE-SX ports on a switching hub.

Building Fiber Optic Cables

Fiber optic patch cables can readily be purchased with fiber optic connectors already installed, allowing you to make relatively short-distance fiber connections quite easily. However, many fiber optic systems are installed to cover long distances between buildings or as backbone systems inside buildings. In this case, the typical installation is based on raw fiber, which is pulled into place and then terminated with fiber connectors that are installed in fiber optic patch panels. Long fiber optic segments may require the installation of several fiber optic cable segments, which are spliced together into a continuous cable.

There are a variety of fiber optic cable types and sizes designed to meet virtually any installation requirement. While it's not rocket science, terminating a fiber optic cable in a connector and splicing raw fiber ends together requires specialized equipment and skills. During installation there are a number of special techniques that may be used for fiber optic cable splicing and terminating. Testing and verifying the operation of fiber optic cables also requires special equipment and training on how to operate the equipment. That's why most sites turn to certified fiber optic installers and cable contractors for fiber optic installation and testing on segments that require cable termination and splicing.

Signal Crossover in Fiber Optic Systems

A signal crossover is required to make a connection between an Ethernet transceiver attached to a station and the transceiver located in an Ethernet hub port. To make the data flow properly, the transmit data output of one transceiver must end up at the receive data input of the other transceiver, and vice versa. When connecting two nearby devices with a fiber optic patch cable, you must ensure that the transmit data at one device is connected to the receive data at the other device, and vice versa.

In the twisted-pair Ethernet system, signal crossover is typically done inside the Ethernet hub port, and the structured cabling standard recommends wiring the twisted-pair cable segment straight-through. Unlike twisted-pair Ethernet, the structured cabling standard recommends that signal crossover for fiber optic horizontal segments be done in the cabling segment, and not at the Ethernet hub.

For horizontal fiber optic segments installed as part of a structured cabling system, the connectors on the fiber optic cable should be oriented to achieve the crossover. For example, fiber optic cables are typically terminated in a set of fiber optic connectors located at the work area and the wiring closet. For a fiber optic cable with two optical fibers in it, fiber #1 is connected to the A connector at the work area end of the segment and the B connector at the wiring closet end. Fiber #2 is connected to the B connector at the work area, and the A connector at the wiring closet. This way, the user or the network technician can connect fiber optic Ethernet ports to the fiber optic connectors on the horizontal cabling using straight-through fiber optic patch cables. They need not concern themselves about the signal crossover since it is already accomplished in the fiber optic horizontal segment.

On the other hand, backbone fiber optic cable systems that go between floors of a building, or between buildings on a campus are typically wired straight through. When making a connection between an Ethernet hub and a backbone fiber optic system you need to make sure that the signal crossover is achieved in the patch cable at one end of the link.

10BASE-FL Fiber Optic Characteristics

The 10BASE-FL media system is described in Chapter 8, *Fiber Optic Media System (10BASE-F)*. The 10BASE-FL fiber link system uses LED transmitters operating at a wavelength of 850 nm. The optical loss budget for a 10BASE-FL link segment must be no greater than 12.5 dB.

As a very rough rule of thumb, a length of standard grade 62.5/125 fiber optic cable carrying 10 Mbps signals and operating at a wavelength of 850 nm will have roughly 3–4 dB loss per 1,000 m. The loss could be higher depending on the number and quality of the splices in the cable. You can also expect anywhere from 0.5 dB to around 2.0 dB of loss per fiber optic connection point, depending on how well the connection has been made.

The older FOIRL segment standard specified the same type of 62.5/125 µm fiber optic cable, and had the same 12.5 dB optical loss budget. The 10BASE-FL specifications were designed to allow backward compatibility with existing FOIRL segments. The major difference is that the 10BASE-FL segment may be up to 2,000 m in length if 10BASE-FL equipment is used on both ends of the segment, while the FOIRL segment was limited to a maximum of 1,000 m.

Alternate 10BASE-FL Fiber Optic Cables

Over the years, a variety of fiber optic cables have been used in various proprietary networks and cabling systems. The IEEE 802.3 standard states that these cables may also be used as alternates to the standard 62.5/125 cable in a 10BASE-FL link. Cables with a 50 µm fiber optic core and 125 µm outer cladding (50/125), as well as 85/125 and 100/140 cables are considered alternate cables. The standard notes that details for the use of alternative cables are not provided, and their use may reduce the maximum achievable distance of a segment.

The difficulty here is that the use of these cables causes a mismatch between the size of the fiber optic core on the alternate cables and the standard 62.5 µm size of the receiver and transmitters on 10BASE-FL equipment. While the alternate cables can be terminated in standard ST fiber optic connectors and connected to 10BASE-FL equipment, there can be a significant loss in signal due to the mismatch in size. When using cables with a core size other than 62.5 µm, the losses due to mismatch can be as high as 5 or 6 dB or even more. In that case, the total length of the segment must be reduced to accommodate the higher losses at the connection points at each end of the segment.

100BASE-FX Fiber Optic Characteristics

This system, which is described in Chapter 10, *Fast Ethernet Fiber Optic Media System (100BASE-FX)*, typically operates over multimode fiber using LED transmitters with a wavelength of 1350 nm. There is an 11 dB optical loss budget allowed per 100BASE-FX segment. A typical performance rating for standard grade multimode fiber operating at 1,350 nm provides roughly 1 dB loss per 1,000 m of cable. You can also expect something in the neighborhood of 0.5 to 1.5 dB loss per connection point, depending on how well the connection has been made.

Alternate 100BASE-FX Fiber Optic Cables

The ANSI media standard, upon which 100BASE-FX is based, notes that alternate multimode fiber optic cables may be used. This includes cables with a 50 µm fiber optic core and 125 µm outer cladding (50/125). It also includes cables with an 85 µm core and 125 µm cladding (85/125), and cables with a 100 µm core and

125 µm cladding (100/125) may also be used. The difficulty is the same as with the 10BASE-FL system: the mismatch between the size of the fiber optic core on the alternative cables and the 62.5 µm size of the receiver and transmitters on 10BASE-FX equipment.

While the alternative cables can be terminated in standard fiber optic connectors and connected to 100BASE-FX equipment, there will be a significant loss in signal due to the mismatch in size. Optical signal losses due to mismatch can be as high as 5 or 6 dB. In that case, the total length of the segment must be reduced to allow for the higher losses at the connection points to the 100BASE-FX equipment at each end of the segment.

1000BASE-X Fiber Optic Characteristics

There are two varieties of Gigabit Ethernet fiber optic media: 1000BASE-SX and 1000BASE-LX, which are described in Chapter 12, *Gigabit Ethernet Fiber Optic Media System (1000BASE-X)*. The 1000BASE-X Gigabit Ethernet fiber optic system uses laser light that operates at frequencies invisible to the human eye, and that may be active even when a port is not connected to a cable.

 Due to the risk of retinal damage, beware of looking directly into fiber optic cables or Gigabit Ethernet ports, and always observe safety precautions when working around any fiber optic cable system.

The 1000BASE-SX short wavelength media type operates at a wavelength of approximately 850 nm (770–860 nm is the range allowed in the specification) and requires multimode fiber optic cable. The 1000BASE-LX long wavelength media type operates at a wavelength of approximately 1300 nm (1270–1355 nm is the allowed range) and can be used with either multimode or single-mode fiber optic cable. You cannot see the laser light, since visible light ranges in wavelength from 455 nm (violet) to 750 nm (red). The 850 nm and longer wavelengths are in the infrared range.

In the Gigabit Ethernet system, the fiber optic loss budget is a major determinant of segment length. Following are the worst-case optical loss budgets for the 1000BASE-SX and 1000BASE-LX segments, as well as the 1000BASE-LX/LH "long haul" segment. The 1000BASE-SX and 1000BASE-LX numbers are taken directly from the Gigabit Ethernet standard, and provide the typical maximum distance for the segments. According to the standard, the *minimum* distance between two stations for all segment types is 2.0 m (6.56 feet). Therefore, the shortest fiber optic cable you can use on any Gigabit Ethernet fiber link is 2 m.

In Tables 16-1 through 16-3, "Channel insertion loss" accounts for the static power losses in the fiber optic cable, fiber optic jumper cables and all connectors. The maximum distances in the tables are estimates based on the assumption that the total loss from connectors and splices will be 1.5 dB on a multimode link and 2.0 dB on a single-mode link.

The "Link power penalties" are not part of the static power losses and cannot be measured with link loss testers. Instead, link power penalties are used in the standard to account for various issues including modal noise, relative intensity noise and intersymbol interference. The combined set of cable and connector losses and link power penalties makes up the total power budget for the link.

1000BASE-SX Loss Budget

The 1000BASE-SX short wavelength media type can only be used with multimode fiber. The distances achieved over multimode fiber vary according to the fiber specs. One major fiber optic cable vendor estimates that approximately 80 percent of the U.S. installed base of 62.5 µm MMF cable has a bandwidth specification of 160 MHz-km at 850 nm. The widely used TIA-568-A structured cabling standard also specifies 160 MHz-km bandwidth for 62.5 µm cable at 850 nm, and 500 MHz-km at 1300 nm. Therefore, in the U.S., the odds are good that 62.5 µm MMF cabling installed prior to 1999 will have these ratings. Newer installations may choose to use the new versions of multimode fiber with optimized bandwidth and light transmission characteristics being offered by vendors.

Table 16-1. Worst-Case 1000BASE-SX Loss Budget and Penalties

Parameter	62.5 µm MMF		50 µm MMF		Unit
Bandwidth measured at 850 nm wavelength	160	200	400	500	MHz-km
Link power budget	7.5	7.5	7.5	7.5	dB
Operating distance	220 721.78	275 902.23	500 1,640.42	550 1,804.46	meters feet
Channel insertion loss[a]	2.38	2.60	3.37	3.56	dB
Link power penalties[b]	4.27	4.29	4.07	3.57	dB
Unallocated margin	0.84	0.60	0.05	0.37	dB

[a] Operating distances used to calculate channel insertion loss are the maximum values.
[b] Link penalties are used for link budget calculations. They are not requirements and are not meant to be tested.

As you can see from Table 16-1, the widely used 62.5 µm multimode fiber with 160 MHz-km bandwidth only supports a 220 m maximum link distance. This distance is considerably shorter than the 2 km that can be achieved on a Fast Ethernet fiber segment. However, vendor ingenuity is being brought to bear on the issue of increasing Gigabit Ethernet distances over multimode fiber. For example, new versions of multimode fiber optimized for laser light are being produced which make it possible to reach longer distances.

Some vendors are developing proprietary Gigabit Ethernet fiber optic transceivers that can increase multimode fiber distances. The new transceivers use multiple wavelengths of light to split the Gigabit Ethernet signal into several signals, each operating at a lower frequency. This makes it possible to reach up to 2 km over multimode fiber. This approach would require that you use the same vendor's transceivers at each end of the link, since this equipment will not be part of the standard when initially deployed. It's possible that some version of these new transceivers will later become adopted by the standard. At that point, the technology would become vendor neutral and you could expect interoperability between vendors.

1000BASE-LX Loss Budget

The 1000BASE-LX media type may be coupled to either multimode or single-mode fiber. When used with single-mode fiber, there is no modal dispersion or differential mode delay effects and the channel losses are quite a bit lower. For that reason, the distance achievable on single-mode fiber is much longer than with multimode fiber. When used with multimode fiber, DMD effects require that a mode conditioning patch cable be installed for links over 300 m in length. This patch cable is described in more detail later in this chapter.

Table 16-2. Worst-Case 1000BASE-LX Loss Budget and Penalties

Parameter	62.5 μm MMF	50 μm MMF		10 μm SMF	Unit
Bandwidth measured at 1300 nm wavelength	500	400	500	N/A	MHz*km
Link power budget	7.5	7.5	7.5	8.0	dB
Operating distance	550 1,804.46	550 1,804.46	550 1,804.46	5,000 16,404.2	meters feet
Channel insertion loss[a]	2.35	2.35	2.35	4.57	dB
Link power penalties[b]	3.48	5.08	3.96	3.27	dB
Unallocated margin	1.67	0.07	1.19	0.16	dB

[a] Operating distances used to calculate channel insertion loss are the maximum values.

[b] Link penalties are used for link budget calculations. They are not requirements and are not meant to be tested.

As you can see in Table 16-2, the longer wavelength (1300 nm) used in 1000BASE-LX equipment also travels longer distances over typical multimode fibers. Given these longer distances, why not use 1000BASE-LX equipment everywhere? The answer has to do with cost. The lasers used in 1000BASE-LX equipment are typically two or three times more expensive than those used in 1000BASE-SX equipment.

1000BASE-LX/LH Long Haul Loss Budget

A widely used variant of the 1000BASE-LX media type includes a long haul (LH) transceiver that provides a more powerful laser. The higher output laser makes it possible for Gigabit Ethernet signals to travel much longer distances over single-mode fiber. The details of the link power budget for long haul transceivers may vary, depending on the power of the transceiver. Therefore, you need to check with your vendor for details.

Table 16-3 contains the long haul power budget listed by one major vendor of equipment with 1000BASE-LX/LH ports, Cisco Systems. This particular long haul port type is based on a type of Gigabit Interface Converter (GBIC) that is widely used by other vendors as well. GBICs are described in more detail in Chapter 6, *Ethernet Media Fundamentals*.

Table 16-3. 1000BASE-LX/LH Long Haul Loss Budget

Parameter	10 μm SMF	Unit
Link power budget	10.5	dB
Operating distance	10,000 32,808.4	meters feet
Channel insertion loss[a]	7.8	dB
Link power penalties[b]	2.5	dB
Unallocated margin	0.2	dB

[a] Operating distances used to calculate channel insertion loss are the maximum values.

[b] Link penalties are used for link budget calculations. They are not requirements and are not meant to be tested.

Differential Mode Delay

Differential mode delay (DMD) only occurs in multimode fiber, and only when a laser light source is connected to the multimode fiber. The DMD effect is a result of beam splitting caused by the way some multimode fiber cores are structured during manufacturing. This causes a small drop in the index of refraction, or *response curve*, of the cable. When a laser is coupled into the direct center of such a cable, two or more modes, or paths, can be excited. The multiple paths cause signals to arrive at the receiver at slightly different times resulting in signal jitter. This, in turn, can make it difficult to demodulate the signal at the far end.

DMD does not occur in all multimode fibers. Some test reports indicate that roughly 10 percent of installed multimode fibers may have this problem. Even in fibers that exhibit the problem, the amount of DMD may vary from one fiber to the next. Unfortunately, there is no reasonable way to field test multimode cables for the presence of DMD. Carefully controlling the manufacture of multimode cables can entirely avoid DMD effects, but that is no help for existing fiber installations.

For incoherent light sources (LEDs) this is a non-issue, since all modes are simultaneously being used, which swamps any DMD effect. As it happens, this is also a non-issue for 1000BASE-SX links, despite their use of lasers. Further testing by the standards group found that the *coupled power ratio* over an SX link was high enough to swamp any signaling effects caused by DMD. In short, at the SX wavelength and link distances the signal jitter caused by DMD is not a significant problem. However, DMD is still a major issue for 1000BASE-LX lasers when they are coupled to multimode fiber.

Mode-Conditioning Patch Cord

The engineers on the standards committee found that DMD can be prevented in 1000BASE-LX links connected to multimode fiber cables by slightly offsetting the coupling of laser light into the cable. This avoids the beam splitting that can occur in some MMF cables when laser light is launched into the direct center of the cable. This type of offset signal launch is called mode conditioning. An outboard mode-conditioning patch cord must be used when an LX port is connected to a MMF fiber link.

Figure 16-5 shows the construction of a mode-conditioning patch cord. The mode-conditioning patch cord contains a splice in the middle, in which the single-mode fiber is carefully connected to the multimode fiber with a slight offset from center.

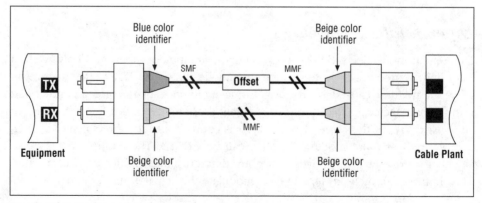

Figure 16-5. Mode conditioning patch cord

This keeps the single-mode laser light from entering the multimode cable at dead center, avoiding any DMD problems.

The standard notes that the single-mode end of the mode-conditioning patch cable should be labeled "To Equipment," and the multimode end labeled "To Cable Plant." To help with identification, the plastic covering of the single-mode fiber connector should be blue and the multimode connectors should all be beige.

A mode-conditioning patch cord should be used at each end of the link when connecting 1000BASE-LX equipment to a multimode fiber optic segment. Make sure that the TX port on the equipment is connected to the single-mode portion of the mode-conditioning patch cable. The multimode fiber used in the conditioned launch cable should match the multimode fiber plant. In other words, if your fiber plant uses 62.5/125 MMF, then that's the type of fiber that should be used in the conditioned patch cable as well.

17

Ethernet Repeater Hubs

A repeater is a device that allows you to build multi-segment half-duplex Ethernet systems. Repeaters do this by linking the segments together, making the whole system function as though it were a single large segment. Individual half-duplex media segments are of limited length to ensure acceptable signal timing and signal quality for the entire length of the segment. When linking segments together, repeaters act upon the Ethernet signals, regenerating the signal and restoring the timing. This ensures that each frame makes it through the entire Ethernet system intact, and that every station in the Ethernet system will receive the frame correctly. The configuration guidelines that apply to all types of half-duplex systems are described in Chapter 13, *Multi-Segment Configuration Guidelines*.

Repeaters have been widely used to build extended Ethernet systems for years. However, many network designs today are based on switching hubs to take advantage of the extra bandwidth and other capabilities that switching hubs can provide. The cost of switching hubs has rapidly decreased in recent years, and therefore many network designers use switching hubs instead of repeaters for all new network installations and for upgrades from older systems. Switching hubs are described in Chapter 18, *Ethernet Switching Hubs*.

A repeater is intended to provide a simple and inexpensive way to link two or more network segments. By using repeaters, you can build large half-duplex Ethernet systems that can span the maximum distance allowed in the configuration guidelines. Repeaters are not stations, and do not require an addressed Ethernet interface to operate. However, an Ethernet interface may be included to provide communication with management software on the repeater.

The earliest repeaters were simple two-port devices that operated at 10 Mbps and linked a couple of coaxial segments. Later, repeaters were built with many ports and were used at the hub of a star cabling system. That's why repeaters are often called *repeater hubs*, or just *hubs*. However, calling them hubs can be confusing, since there are also switching hubs which operate quite differently than repeaters. Therefore, when someone tells you that a certain device is a hub, you need to find out what kind of hub it is—repeater or switching.

We will look at basic repeater operation first, and then list any specific repeater issues for the 10-, 100-, and 1000 Mbps Ethernet systems. Also included are sample configurations for 10- and 100 Mbps repeaters. After seeing how repeaters work at all three speeds, we'll then look at some of the ways repeaters can be packaged and used in network designs. Finally, we describe the network management standard for repeaters, and show you how to interpret the management information provided in the standard.

Collision Domain

The collision domain is an essential concept to keep in mind when dealing with repeaters. A collision domain is formally defined as a single Carrier Sense Multiple Access with Collision Detect (CSMA/CD) network in which there will be a collision if two stations attached to the system transmit at the same time. Network segments linked with one or more repeaters function together as a single local area network (LAN) system, or collision domain.

Figure 17-1 shows two repeater hubs connecting three computers. Since only repeaters are used to make the connections between segments in this network, all of the segments and computers are in the same collision domain. The configuration guidelines provided in the standard apply to a single collision domain, in which multiple segments are linked with repeaters. The guidelines also describe how long the media segments can be and how many repeaters can be used in a given LAN.

An Ethernet switching hub, on the other hand, terminates a collision domain. Packet switches such as switching hubs and routers make it possible to link many Ethernet LANs together in a campus network system, over distances longer than is possible with repeaters alone. Even after switching hubs were developed in the late 1980s, repeaters were widely used since they were the least expensive way to build large Ethernets. These days, switching hub costs have dropped so far that they are close to repeater hubs in cost. Many Ethernet systems are now entirely based on switching hubs, since switching hubs provide a number of useful features beyond the capabilities of repeater hubs.

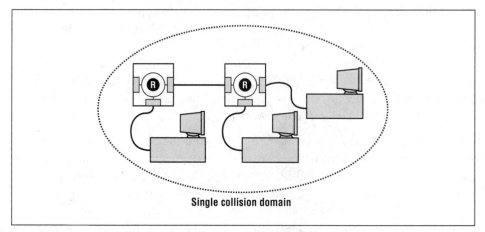

Figure 17-1. Repeater hubs create a single collision domain

Basic Repeater Operation

Repeaters come in all shapes and sizes, and there are a variety of connection methods used to link repeaters together to provide multiple repeater ports. The first repeater specified in the original Ethernet standard was designed for the 10 Mbps system. Later, repeater standards were developed for 100- and 1000 Mbps systems. Basic repeater functions are the same for all three systems:

- Enforcing collisions on all segments.
- Restoring the amplitude of the signal.
- Retiming the signal.
- Restoring the symmetry of the signal.
- Fragment extension.

The repeater is designed to extend the reach of an Ethernet system by compensating for the normal wear and tear on an electrical signal as it propagates along the segments. Each of the functions listed above is performed so that every station attached to a network composed of a set of repeated segments can function as though the network were a single segment.

Signals sent through a repeater are retimed using the repeater's own precise timing circuits. This prevents the accumulation of signal jitter as a signal travels over multiple segments. The repeater also regenerates the signal to the signal amplitude and symmetry specs in the standard, which restores the signal as it travels over the segments linked by the repeater. By restoring the timing, signal strength and symmetry of the signal, the repeater ensures that signals will make it through the entire Ethernet LAN intact.

Collision Enforcement

One of the most important services the repeater performs is that of enforcing collisions on each segment. Repeaters do this by transmitting a collision enforcement jam signal, just like stations do after a collision. Assume that we have a repeater attached to two segments, labeled A and B. Upon detecting a collision on segment A, the repeater will transmit a collision enforcement jam signal on both segments. This ensures that any station trying to transmit at that particular moment will be able to detect the collision and, in turn, make the two cable segments function as though they were one segment connecting all stations. In this way, the repeater makes sure that all stations in the same collision domain are able to hear all collisions and respond appropriately.

When a station detects a collision while it is transmitting a frame, then the station transmits 32 bits of jam signal. If the collision was detected very early in the frame, then the preamble is completely transmitted before sending the jam signal. The jam signal ensures that the collision fragment that results will persist on the channel long enough to be detected by all stations. When a repeater detects a collision and transmits a collision enforcement signal out its ports in response, it sends a 32-bit jam signal composed of alternating ones and zeroes. After the jam, the repeater *continues* sending alternating ones and zeroes, to end up with a total signal that is at least 96 bits long. This ensures that a minimum transmission is 96 bits long, providing enough bits to ensure signal detection on a cable segment that has been idle.

Fragment Extension

Another service that the repeater provides is to extend short collision fragments. If a signal being repeated is less than 96 bits in length including the preamble, the repeater will extend the signal so that the total number of bits output by the repeater equals 96. This ensures that a short collision fragment will survive a trip through a maximum-sized network, and will be properly recognized and discarded by all stations as the fragment propagates through the system.

Automatic Partitioning

Auto-partitioning is designed to protect the network from a faulty segment. Segment faults may include a cable break, a faulty connector, or a missing terminator on a coaxial segment. The auto-partitioning algorithm allows a repeater to stop reacting to collisions on the failing segment. This prevents a faulty segment from affecting all segments to which the repeater is attached. The repeater will shut off signals received from the failing segment after more than 30 consecutive frame transmission failures have occurred. This is called *partitioning the segment*. A repeater will also partition the segment when a collision signal persists for an excessive period of time. Excessive collisions can occur due to a twisted-pair patch cable with excessive signal crosstalk that causes a *phantom collision* to be detected during every frame transmission. Incorrect or missing terminating resistors on coaxial cable segments can also cause excessive collisions.

Partitioning means that signals from the failing segment are not repeated onto any other ports of the repeater, and that collisions on the failing segment are ignored. When a repeater detects excessive collisions on segment B and partitions the segment, it will stop sending jam signals onto segment A. This protects segment A from possible hardware failures on segment B. Even while partitioning the segment, the repeater continues trying to send frames onto the failing segment. This is done to make sure the repeater can respond when the segment is working correctly again. If a large enough portion of a frame makes it onto a partitioned segment without problem (from 450 to 560 bit times), then the repeater will assume that normal operations can immediately resume, and the partitioned segment will be put back into full communication.

This scheme works very well for solid failures, such as a missing terminator on a coax segment. On the other hand, there are situations where this doesn't always work as well as you'd like. If the problem on the failing segment is marginal or intermittent, then the auto-partitioning mechanism may not provide much protection for segment A. That's because the auto-partitioning mechanism is quite fast about restoring operations. It only takes one good frame being transmitted onto the failing segment to restore full operation. There will then be at least 30 consecutive collisions enforced onto the good segment before the repeater partitions the failing segment again. Therefore, an intermittent failure can still cause many collisions on the good segment, due to the auto-partitioning circuit repeatedly re-enabling communications with the failing segment.

The Limit on Repeaters

Since repeaters improve the signals on an Ethernet, you may be wondering why the configuration guidelines place a maximum limit on the number of repeaters in the path between any two stations. A primary reason for the limit on the number of repeaters is to control the maximum signal propagation delay in a collision domain. Another reason for this limitation is related to the minimum interframe gap. The 10 Mbps Ethernet standard defines an interframe gap of 9.6 microseconds (0.0000096 seconds), which means that stations may not transmit frames on the network more closely spaced than 9.6 µs. The interframe gap is 0.96 µs in Fast Ethernet and .096 µs in the Gigabit Ethernet system. The presence of an interframe gap helps establish the recovery time for an Ethernet interface, after which it must be ready to accept a new frame.

However, the story is complicated by something called interframe gap (IFG) shrinkage. Two successive frames may experience a different level of bit loss along the same path. As each frame passes through a 10 Mbps repeater, the repeater will regenerate the lost preamble bits. If the first frame has experienced more bit loss than the second one has, then the IFG between them will shrink as they leave the repeater.

Consequently, back-to-back frames can end up separated by less than the 9.6 μs IFG as seen at a receiving station. Gap shrinkage is expected behavior, and some amount of IFG shrinkage is allowed in the standard. However, if the IFG between successive frames gets too small due to travelling through several repeaters, then the interface may not be able to recover in time to read the next frame. The result could be a source of lost frames as interfaces find they can't keep up. To prevent this potential loss of frames, the configuration guidelines in the standard limit the total number of repeaters that may be in the frame transmission path.

Repeater Buying Guide

The standard defines the way in which the repeater must operate, and all vendors should conform to those specifications. However, repeater packaging and added features vary a great deal. There are many repeaters available on the market, and they come in all shapes and sizes. The very first 10 Mbps Ethernet repeaters had two ports equipped with 15-pin AUI connectors. These AUI ports provided a connection for thick coaxial segments and fiber optic link segments.

When the thin Ethernet system was developed, multiple thin Ethernet ports were built into the repeaters. The ports were equipped with transceivers, and thin Ethernet coax segments could be attached directly to them. Unlike the coaxial media systems, the 10BASE-T twisted-pair link segment requires the use of repeaters to build networks that can support more than two stations. Repeater hubs with 10BASE-T ports are available in all manner of configurations, including 4-, 8-, 24-port, and more.

Repeater hubs with 10BASE-T ports are widely used. When Fast Ethernet was developed in the mid-1990s, repeater hubs were built to operate at 100 Mbps. However, large repeater-based Fast Ethernet systems are not common. At the same time that Fast Ethernet was developed, switching hub costs were dropping very rapidly. As a result, many Fast Ethernet systems are based on switching hubs instead of repeaters. The drop in switching hub costs is also a major reason that no vendor sells Gigabit Ethernet repeater hubs. Gigabit Ethernet is most often used in backbone systems, and these days the vast majority of backbone network designs are based on high performance switching hubs.

Chassis Hubs

A chassis hub is a modular chassis that supports a set of individual boards, or modules, which are installed in the chassis. Each board may provide some number of repeater ports for a given media type. By accommodating multiple boards, chassis hubs make it possible to support many ports in a relatively small space. The individual boards communicate with each other over one or more signal buses provided inside the chassis hub.

Chassis hubs were developed to help conserve limited space in wiring closets. For example, a structured cabling system provides many twisted-pair segments in a building. Since each connection to a twisted-pair station takes up a single port on a twisted-pair repeater, connecting lots of stations on a floor means you have to provide a lot of ports in the wiring closet. One way to accommodate those connections is to purchase a twisted-pair multiport repeater in the form of a modular board that gets inserted into one of the slots of a chassis hub. That way, when you use up all the ports on your original board and need to attach more stations, you can add more boards to the hub.

From this simple idea, a new market for repeaters grew. Instead of using individual standalone repeaters, with each standalone repeater supporting a particular type of network connection, you can use a single chassis hub to support many different network connections in the same amount of space. The convenience, flexibility and new capabilities provided by chassis hubs led to a rapid expansion of products in the repeater hub market. There are many chassis hubs available, and they support a bewildering array of options. Chassis hubs are also available with a combination of backplanes in them to support both repeating and switching operations.

Figure 17-2 shows a chassis hub with three modular boards, providing eight ports each. A fourth slot is empty, and can be equipped with a module when needed. The power supply and control module can be found on the right-hand side of the hub.

One thing to be aware of is that you cannot swap boards between the chassis hubs from different vendors. Each vendor's hub uses a different size of board and a different kind of backplane setup to link the boards together. Therefore, when you buy hub equipment, you are making an investment in a particular vendor as well, since you will only be able to expand your chassis hub by buying equipment from the original vendor.

Another concern is that providing a lot of Ethernet ports in a single chassis hub can be too much of a good thing. A single power supply failure in the hub will cause all of the ports to stop functioning. That's why some vendors provide redundant power supplies for their hubs; in case one supply fails, the other can quickly

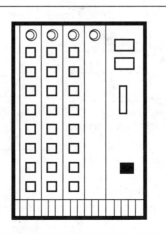

Figure 17-2. Chassis hub

take over. It's also why network designers may prefer to use standalone repeater hubs equipped with a smaller number of ports, instead of chassis hubs. The standalone repeater hubs can be linked together to add more ports when required.

Stackable Repeaters

Another way of packaging repeaters that became very popular is the use of stackable repeater hubs. Stacking makes it possible to link repeater hubs equipped with a special expansion connector together so they can function as one large *logical repeater*. This is equivalent to a single repeater, also known as a single *repeater hop*, for the purpose of counting repeaters as in the configuration guidelines provided in Chapter 13.

In Figure 17-3, stackable repeaters are shown operating in two modes: independently, and connected with an expansion cable. When operating independently, the special expansion connector is not used, and each repeater counts as a single repeater. However, the ports on both repeaters are combined when the special expansion connector is used to link stackable repeaters together. The expansion connector links the internal repeater electronics of each box, so that the combined set of repeater ports now function as a single repeater.

Stackable repeaters make it possible for you to add repeater devices at any point in your network and link them together so they function as a single logical repeater. A stackable repeater is typically a lot less expensive than a chassis hub, making it possible to start a network inexpensively, allowing you to add more stackable repeaters as needed. If you later decide to separate your network into multiple segments connected to ports on a switching hub, stackable repeaters can easily be reconfigured to accommodate the new design. In addition, stackable

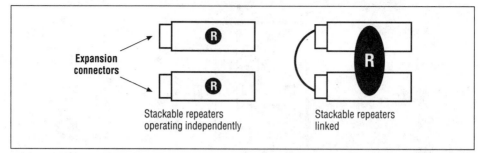

Figure 17-3. Stackable repeaters

repeaters have a variety of management options, from no management for the least expensive repeaters, up to repeater stacks that provide redundant management capabilities in case one of the repeater hubs fails.

Note that each vendor uses a different scheme for the expansion cable and connection system, so you cannot link stackable repeaters from different vendors. Further, the expansion cable is typically quite short, usually only a foot or so in length. This means that stackable repeaters must be close together, preferably stacked directly on top of one another as the name implies. Also note that the design of a stackable repeater and expansion bus is different for each vendor. You need to pay careful attention to each vendor's guidelines and instructions on how to link their stackable repeaters together, and to the maximum number of repeaters and ports that may be linked.

Be aware that some vendors label their repeaters stackable, but only mean that their repeaters can be piled on top of one another and linked with a normal external Ethernet segment. This does not provide the special advantage of combining the ports in two or more repeaters so that they function as a single repeater hop. You can usually tell if a repeater is stackable by the presence of a special stacking cable port. These are often labeled "link port," or "expansion port." If in doubt, ask the vendor whether all repeater ports on separate devices can be linked to function as a single repeater hop.

Figure 17-4 shows two configurations using repeater hubs. In the first configuration, two stations are linked with two separate repeaters. The two separate repeaters are connected together using a normal Ethernet segment of some kind (e.g., a twisted-pair cable). This configuration counts as two repeaters in the path between the two stations. In the second configuration, two stations are linked together using repeater ports on two stackable repeaters. The stackable repeaters are connected together using the special expansion port on each repeater, and all ports are functioning as a single repeater. This configuration counts as a single repeater in the signal path between the two stations.

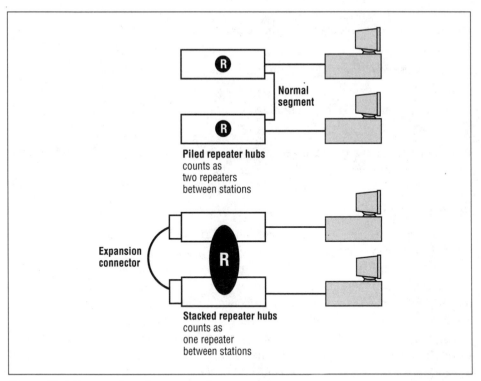

Figure 17-4. Repeater hops between stations

Repeater Signal Lights

Repeater troubleshooting lights can be very useful for keeping an eye on the operation of the network. However, troubleshooting lights can only provide a very rough indication of network activity. That's because the duration of the lights is artificially stretched so that the light will stay on long enough for the human eye to see it. For that reason, a steadily glowing activity or collision light does not mean that the network is saturated with traffic. Far from it. The amount of time the lights are stretched is quite large compared to the speed of events on the network. For example, a single 64-byte frame will take 51.2 μs to transmit on a 10 Mbps Ethernet system. This event is typically stretched to about 50 milliseconds (ms) to make it visible to the eye, which makes the duration of the light last approximately 1,000 times longer than the actual frame transmission.

A repeater may have a set of lights for each segment to which it is attached. Useful lights for each segment might include:

Transmit
    Indicates traffic transmitted onto the segment.

Receive

> Indicates traffic received from the segment.

Collision

> Indicates a collision detected on the segment.

Partition

> Indicates that the auto-partitioning circuit has detected a fault and has isolated the segment.

Along with the lights for each segment, you may also find lights that indicate the status of the entire repeater and its power supply.

Managed Hubs

Repeaters may also be equipped with an optional management interface to support network management capabilities, resulting in a *managed hub*. In some chassis hubs, you provide network management by using one of the hub slots for a supervisor board equipped with network management software. Stackable repeater hubs may come with management capability built in, or may be unmanaged. Management typically adds to the cost of the hub. On the other hand, a managed hub can be very useful when troubleshooting problems on your network. Information on errors and other statistics provided by management software in repeater hubs is described later in this chapter.

Secure hubs

As part of a management package, some vendors optionally provide some type of network security in their repeater hubs. The typical offering includes intruder protection, address authorization and eavesdrop protection. All such security features are proprietary. There is no standard for the operation of a secure repeater hub, and each vendor may implement the security options differently.

Intruder protection

Intruder protection can be configured to disable a port or to warn the network administrator when an unauthorized 48-bit media access control (MAC) address shows up as a source address on a given port. Some vendors also provide notification when any new MAC address is seen. For systems to detect unauthorized MAC addresses, the network manager must create a list of authorized addresses for that port.

Some hubs will automatically build a list of MAC addresses heard on a port, which you can then use as a basis for configuring the addresses you wish to allow on the port. Oftentimes, the list of MAC addresses that may be configured is small, typically anywhere from one to four addresses.

Eavesdrop protection

Eavesdrop protection is based on hiding the data in frames that go out a given port of a repeater hub. This can help prevent one common form of network attack, which is based on using packet "sniffer" software on a computer to read in all frames seen on a network segment and extract passwords or other information. Packet sniffing can be done by setting the computer's Ethernet interface to "promiscuous" reception mode in which it reads in all frames, not just those frames addressed to it.

The eavesdrop protection scheme is configured with one or more MAC addresses of approved stations connected to a given port on the secure hub. The set of MAC addresses that can be configured for a given port is quite often very small. As in the intruder protection scheme, some hubs may require that you do this by hand. Other hubs will automatically acquire the addresses of the stations seen on a given port. You can then instruct the management software on the hub to regard a number or all of those addresses as being authorized for that port. Once the hub learns the address(es) authorized for a given port, it can then "scramble" the data in all frames except the ones sent to the authorized address.

Actually, the frame data is most often not scrambled in any cryptographic sense. Instead, the data in the frame is typically overwritten with some standard pattern, although different vendors may use different patterns or even allow you to select whether to overwrite the frame data using all zeroes or all ones. This prevents anyone from being able to use a program to unscramble the data. The secure hub also does not scramble the addresses of the frame, nor does it change the data in packets sent to the multicast or broadcast address. This ensures that normal network operations, such as dynamic address discovery using multicast or broadcast, are not affected.

The secure hub approach can help prevent a variety of common network attacks based on reading the contents of all frames on a network segment. It is important to understand that this approach provides only a weak form of security, and does not prevent other forms of security attacks on a network. There are many such attacks, including those based on using broadcast-based protocols to discover the addresses of other stations on the network and then attacking those stations directly.

You need to be aware of the limitations of this approach. For example, a secure hub is typically designed to keep track of only one, or at most a few, MAC addresses on a given port. Therefore, you need to make sure that the number of stations behind a secure port does not exceed the limit supported by the hub. Otherwise, the hub will garble the data for stations beyond the limit, which can appear to be a mysterious network failure. Some stations on that port will work, and others won't. In addition, if another repeater hub is connected to the port of a secure hub by some mistake, it will count all garbled frames as Cyclic Redundancy Check (CRC) errors.

For some network designs based on repeaters, eavesdrop protection can be significantly better than nothing. For example, secure repeater hubs have been popular in dormitory network designs which frequently use stacks of repeater hubs to support many ports in a building. In that case, secure hubs can be used to make it difficult for someone to run a sniffer program in the privacy of their dorm room and overhear other user's data. If you are willing to pay the premium for this optional capability, and are careful to design and configure the system correctly, secure hubs can be useful in such circumstances.

10 Mbps Repeaters

In this section, we look at issues specific to 10 Mbps repeaters. We also show some sample 10 Mbps repeater configurations.

Preamble Restoration

Each frame starts life with a complete preamble that totals 64 bits. The preamble bits are there to give the components in a 10 Mbps network system time to detect the presence of a signal, and to begin reading the signal in before the important frame data shows up. A certain amount of signal loss may occur in a 10 Mbps system due to the inevitable small delays caused by startup time in the electronics and by signal propagation time as the Ethernet frame moves through the various devices on the network.[*]

A repeater reads in every frame transmitted on the network. As the frame is sent, the repeater begins by transmitting 64 bits in the preamble format so that the frame being repeated always has a complete preamble.

SQE Test Signal and 10 Mbps Repeaters

The SQE Test signal is used on the 10 Mbps AUI interface to verify the operation of the collision detect circuits. It does this by sending a test signal from the transceiver to the Ethernet interface after each frame transmission. While this works well for an ordinary Ethernet station, the SQE Test signal can cause problems for

---

[*] The preamble is maintained in Fast Ethernet and Gigabit Ethernet systems to provide compatibility with the original Ethernet frame. However, both Fast Ethernet and Gigabit Ethernet systems use more complex mechanisms for encoding the signals that avoid any signal start-up losses. As a result, these two systems don't need preamble restoration.

repeaters. The operation and configuration of the SQE Test signal is described in Appendix C, *AUI Equipment: Installation and Configuration.*

To make all repeated segments function like one big segment (which is the repeater's role in life), it's important for a repeater to react to events on the network segments as fast as possible. Due to the interframe gap, a normal Ethernet interface in a station has no need to react to anything immediately after a frame has been sent. A repeater, on the other hand, is required to monitor the signals on a network segment at all times, and does not have any "dead time" during which it can receive a SQE Test signal.

According to the 802.3 standard, the SQE Test signal should be enabled on all 10 Mbps external transceivers with one major exception: SQE Test *must be shut off* if the external transceiver is connected to an IEEE 802.3 repeater. This whole issue of whether to enable or disable SQE Test affects only external 10 Mbps transceivers with a 15-pin AUI interface.

Repeaters with built-in 10 Mbps thin Ethernet and twisted-pair Ethernet transceivers have their transceiver chips built-in and are wired with the SQE Test signal disabled. Only external 10 Mbps transceivers attached to 15-pin AUI connectors can be configured incorrectly for a repeater.

It's important to note that many 10 Mbps twisted-pair Ethernet hubs are repeaters. The reason for disabling the SQE Test signal for 802.3 repeaters has to do with signal timing in interaction with the SQE Test signals.

If you leave the SQE Test signal enabled on an external 10 Mbps AUI transceiver that is connected to a repeater, your network will probably continue to function. However, you can end up with some signal interactions that may result in slower network performance. It is not unusual to see this problem in 10 Mbps systems. That's because it's easy for an unsuspecting user or network manager to connect a repeater hub to an existing transceiver cable without checking to see if the transceiver has SQE Test enabled.

SQE Test and slow network performance

Due to the interaction between the repeater and the SQE Test signal, it's possible to experience very slow network performance when an external transceiver with SQE Test enabled is connected to a repeater. If you leave the SQE Test signal enabled on an external transceiver connected to a twisted-pair repeater hub, the electronics in the hub will misinterpret each burst of the SQE Test signal as news of a real collision.

With SQE Test enabled on the external transceiver, the repeater sees what it thinks is a collision signal after every frame it transmits. One task of a repeater is to make sure all segments hear all collisions. Therefore, the repeater sends a *collision enforcement jam* signal of 96 bits out to all other ports of the repeater for each collision it thinks it hears. This type of jam signal is part of the normal operation of the repeater. However, the more frames are sent through a repeater connected to an external transceiver with SQE Test incorrectly enabled, the more jam signals are generated.

Effects of False Jam Signals

A flood of falsely generated jam signals occupies time on the network and can collide with normal frame transmission attempts, unnecessarily increasing the collision rate. These falsely generated jam signals will not be seen by most monitoring devices, as they usually count full-sized frames as traffic and ignore short signal events like a jam sequence.

Depending on such things as the traffic rate and transmitted frame sizes, an Ethernet channel has a given amount of idle time available for frame transmission. A flood of unnecessary jam sequences can unnecessarily occupy this idle time, which makes it more difficult for the computers attached to the network to find an idle instant in which to transmit a frame. The result is that users may report a "slow network." Since the jam fragments are not visible to network monitoring devices, the monitoring equipment you use might report a reasonable traffic rate while the network is acting as though it is heavily loaded. That's why you want to be absolutely certain that the SQE Test signal is turned off when attaching a 10 Mbps repeater to an external transceiver with a 15-pin AUI interface.

It's hard to detect this problem, since a repeater connected to an incorrectly configured external transceiver will continue to function more or less adequately. However, higher traffic rates will generate more and more jams leading to slower network response. Note that if two or more external transceivers connected to a given repeater hub are misconfigured, it's possible to get into a self-sustaining loop and generate so many jam sequences that the network essentially screeches to a halt.

Sample 10 Mbps Repeater Configurations

Next, we will look at several network configurations based on 10 Mbps repeaters. These configurations are not provided as examples of the best possible design, since it's impossible to provide a single design or even a set of designs that is optimal for all network situations. Instead, these basic configuration examples are intended to show you how network segments can be connected together with 10 Mbps repeaters. We'll start with an Ethernet topology based on a coaxial cable backbone, which was often used in the earliest Ethernet systems.

Figure 17-5 shows five repeaters connected to a common backbone segment based on thin coax. The repeaters, in turn, are connected to various segment types which support five stations.

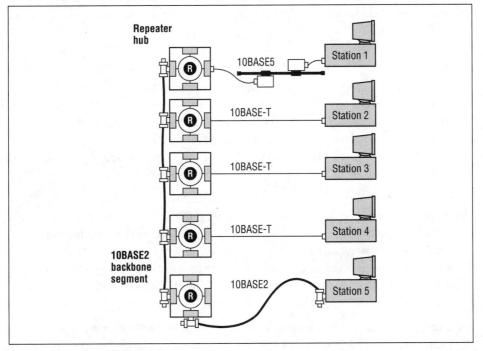

Figure 17-5. Coax backbone

Note that this is one way to configure a 10 Mbps Ethernet system that uses more than four repeaters. Although there is a total of five repeaters in this design, there are no more than two repeaters in the signal path between any two stations, which easily meets the 10 Mbps configuration guidelines. That's because all repeaters are connected together over a single coaxial backbone segment. A network design based on this configuration might locate all of the repeaters in the same equipment closet, linking them together with short 10BASE2 cables. The backbone segment could also be used to link multiple closets.

There are significant limits to the configuration shown in Figure 17-5. For one thing, the 10BASE2 segment that links the repeaters only provides a single 10 Mbps network channel. Another limitation of this type of configuration is that this media system cannot be upgraded to a higher speed operation in the future because coax-based Ethernet is limited to a maximum speed of 10 Mbps. Many sites prefer to use backbone media segments that can handle higher speeds, such as fiber optic media or at least Category 5 twisted-pair cable. This makes it possible to upgrade the network to support faster Ethernet systems in the future.

Another limit to this design is that any failure on the single coaxial backbone segment will disrupt communication between all repeater hubs. If one of the 10BASE2 backbone cable segments comes loose, the entire coaxial segment will stop working, making it impossible for any of the repeaters to send data to one another over the backbone cable.

Stackable repeaters reduce hop count

If you want to use media segments capable of running at higher speeds, then your network design must be based on a star topology with point-to-point link segments. A star topology is required since Fast Ethernet and Gigabit Ethernet only use point-to-point link segments. An advantage of this approach is that there are only two devices at each end of a given link segment, which limits the effect that any segment failure may have on your total network system.

In Figure 17-6, we show five separate repeater hubs. In this case, they are stackable repeaters, with the top two repeaters linked together over an expansion bus. This assumes that the top two repeaters are located close to one another, since the expansion bus for stackable repeaters is typically a very short cable. Stations 1 and 2 are effectively connected to the same repeater as a result of being linked to ports on two stackable repeaters that are, in turn, linked together with an expansion cable.

All other repeaters in this configuration are connected to one another with standard Ethernet point-to-point link segments. In this design, there are a total of four repeater hops between Station 1 and Station 5. If the top two repeaters had not been stackable, there would have been five repeaters in the longest path between two stations on this network.

This design does not provide any expansion capability for future network growth, since it is already at the maximum number of repeater hops allowed in the configuration guidelines. One way to reduce the number of repeaters used would be to reconfigure the system as shown in Figure 17-7.

Fiber optic 10 Mbps repeater hub

A design based on a fiber optic repeater hub is shown in Figure 17-7. The fiber optic hub is used to provide a set of connections to other hubs in a building. In this design, the fiber optic hub becomes the backbone for the network.

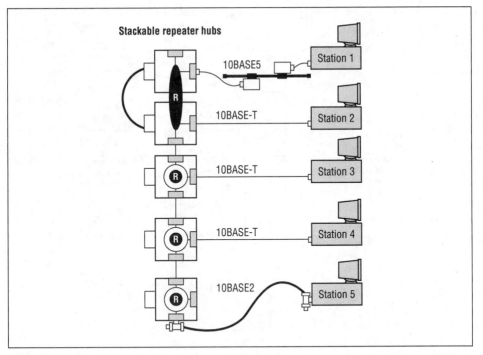

Figure 17-6. Stackable repeaters

The fiber optic hub may link to a single hub on each floor, or several hubs on a floor may be stacked or linked together. A standard point-to-point segment from the stack of hubs could then be connected back to the fiber optic hub. This is another way that stackable hubs can hold down the total number of repeater hops in a collision domain. As your network system grows, you can also upgrade the hubs to faster technology as required. The use of fiber optic media for your backbone segments provides greater flexibility for future upgrades, since fiber optic media can support Fast and Gigabit Ethernet speeds.

100 Mbps Repeaters

Repeaters are required in 100 Mbps collision domains that link more than two stations, since all stations in a Fast Ethernet system are supported on link segments. The 100 Mbps repeater is much like the 10 Mbps repeater and performs many of the same basic functions, including:

- Enforcing collisions on all segments.

- Restoring the amplitude of the signal.

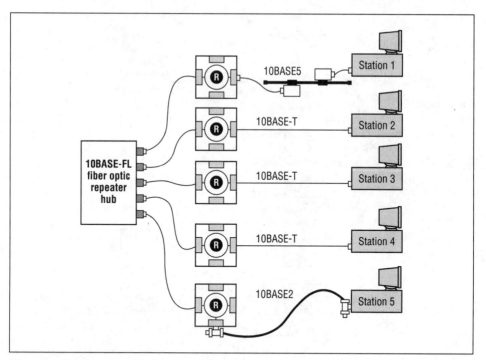

Figure 17-7. Fiber optic backbone

- Retiming the signal.

- Restoring the symmetry of the signal.

Note that the 100 Mbps repeater does not perform preamble restoration or fragment extension. The signaling systems and media segments used for 100 Mbps Ethernet are not susceptible to the same bit loss and frame fragment transmission issues that occurred in the original 10 Mbps system. Therefore, these services do not have to be performed by the 100 Mbps repeater. The configuration guidelines that apply to 100 Mbps repeaters are described in Chapter 13.

100 Mbps Repeater Types

The Fast Ethernet standard defines two types of repeater: Class I and Class II. The standard recommends that these repeaters be labeled with the Roman numeral "I" or "II" centered within a circle. Only one Class I repeater may be in the path between any two stations in a collision domain, and two Class II repeaters may be in the path between any two stations. The link between the two Class II repeaters is typically limited to 5 meters (m).

A Class I repeater can be used to link different Fast Ethernet media systems. It has larger timing delays than a Class II repeater, since it must translate the signal encoding from one media system to another. The decoding and encoding process in Class I repeaters uses up a number of bit times, limiting the system to only one Class I repeater in a given collision domain. A Class I repeater uses up so many bit times that there are no bit times left over for a Class II repeater in the timing budget of a collision domain. Therefore, you cannot mix Class I and Class II repeaters. The Class I repeater operates by decoding line signals on an incoming port, and then re-encoding them when sending them out on other ports. This makes it possible to repeat signals between media segments that use different signal encoding techniques, such as 100BASE-TX/FX segments and 100BASE-T4 segments, allowing these segment types to be mixed within a single repeater hub.

Unlike Class I repeaters, a Class II repeater does not perform signal code translation. Instead, all ports of a Class II repeater are required to use the same signal encoding system, and the Class II repeater simply repeats the encoded signal to all other ports. This provides a smaller timing delay, with the limitation that Class II repeaters can be used to link only segment types that use the same signal encoding technique.

Segment types with different signal encoding techniques (e.g., 100BASE-TX/FX and 100BASE-T4) cannot be mixed together in a Class II repeater. However, since 100BASE-TX twisted-pair and 100BASE-FX fiber optic segments use the same signal encoding system, a 100BASE-T Class II repeater can be used to link them. The only difference between these two media systems is that they send the encoded signals over different kinds of cable. A maximum of two Class II repeaters can be used within a given collision domain.

Automatic partitioning

Auto-partitioning in 100 Mbps repeaters is required for all ports. In a 100 Mbps repeater a port will be partitioned when over 60 consecutive collisions occur for a given frame transmission attempt, whereas in a 10 Mbps repeater it takes over 30 consecutive collisions to partition a port.

100 Mbps repeater buying guide

Repeater packaging is much the same for both 10 Mbps and 100 Mbps repeaters, and everything that applies to buying 10 Mbps repeaters also applies to the 100 Mbps variety. Like 10 Mbps repeaters, Fast Ethernet repeater boards may be installed in chassis hubs. Fast Ethernet repeaters are also sold in standalone packages and as stackable repeater hubs, and may be optionally equipped with management capabilities as well.

Sample 100 Mbps Repeater Configurations

Next, we provide several Fast Ethernet configuration examples. As in the case of the 10 Mbps configuration examples, there is no attempt to provide an ideal configuration. Instead, these are simply examples of how things can be hooked up.

As shown in Figure 17-8, a Class I repeater allows you to connect segment types with different signaling systems to the same repeater hub. Both the TX and FX segment types use the same signal encoding system, which is based on the ANSI FDDI standard. However, the T4 system uses a different signal encoding system to provide Ethernet signals over four pairs of Category 3 cable. Figure 17-8 shows a Class I repeater linking a T4 segment with a TX segments. The maximum collision domain diameter (i.e., the maximum distance between any two stations) in a system using a Class I repeater and twisted-pair cables is 200 m.

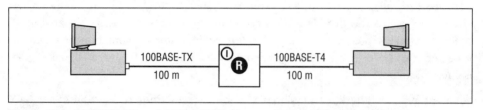

Figure 17-8. 100BASE-TX and 100BASE-T4 segments linked with a Class I repeater

Figure 17-9 shows two Class II repeaters linking two stations with 100BASE-TX segments. The maximum diameter of a system with two Class II repeaters and twisted-pair segments is 205 m. If both station segments are 100 m long, then that leaves 5 m for the inter-repeater link. According to the configuration guidelines, if the segments are shorter than 100 m, then the inter-repeater link may be longer, provided that the maximum station-to-station diameter of the system does not exceed 205 m.

While a longer inter-repeater link might appear to be useful, you should carefully consider the drawbacks of doing this. Once the inter-repeater link has been made longer than 5 m, you have placed a requirement on your system that the segments connected to stations must always be shorter than 100 m. This requirement may not be obvious or well understood by other installers who may install a 100 m link at some later date, in which case the network might not function correctly. The safest and most reliable approach is to keep the inter-repeater link short to avoid these problems. Stackable Class II repeaters can be purchased, which makes it possible to link the repeater ports together into one large logical repeater, and dispense with an inter-repeater link entirely.

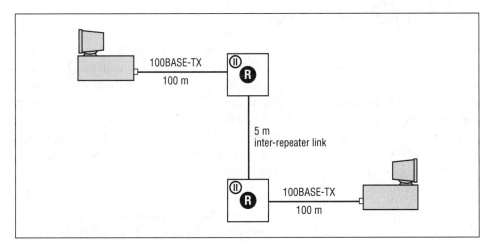

Figure 17-9. Class II repeaters with an inter-repeater link

1000 Mbps Gigabit Ethernet Repeater

The Gigabit Ethernet repeater functions much like a Fast Ethernet repeater, restoring signal timing and amplitude. It, too, possesses the ability to partition ports with excessive collisions, and can detect and interrupt abnormally long transmissions (*jabber*).

Like all other Ethernet repeaters, the Gigabit repeater makes it possible to extend the reach of a half-duplex shared Ethernet system. However, because of the timing restrictions on a half-duplex Gigabit Ethernet system, only a single Gigabit Ethernet repeater is allowed. The half-duplex segment configuration guidelines for Gigabit Ethernet are described in Chapter 13.

Given that the configuration rules are extremely simple, there is no need for any Gigabit Ethernet repeater configuration examples. Because of the limits on Gigabit Ethernet half-duplex configuration, an example could only show a single repeater with stations connected to it. Further, all Gigabit Ethernet equipment sold today only supports full-duplex mode. Gigabit Ethernet repeaters are not being sold by vendors, and there are no half-duplex Gigabit Ethernet systems. Instead, all vendors are providing Gigabit Ethernet ports on switching hubs, which are described in Chapter 18.

Note that there exists a device called a buffered distributor that has also been given the confusing name of Gigabit "full-duplex repeater." This device has been sold by a few vendors, and you may see references to it in buyer's guides or other literature. This device is actually a very simple type of switching hub, as described in Chapter 18 in the section entitled "Buffered Distributor."

Repeater Management

Normal repeater operations do not require human intervention and don't need a management interface in order to function. However, repeater management makes it possible to monitor the operation of the repeater ports, and allows the network manager to shut off repeater ports if necessary. Without the optional management capabilities, you would have no way of finding out what errors the repeater hub may be seeing, which can be extremely valuable when it comes to troubleshooting your network. Although managed hubs are somewhat more expensive than unmanaged ones, you should seriously consider the advantages of optional management capabilities when purchasing a repeater hub.

The Ethernet standard describes a set of management specifications for repeaters. These specifications describe the organization of management information, and mandatory and optional sets of statistics that are supported when a repeater is equipped with management capabilities. The mandatory functions are part of any managed Ethernet repeater, and provide a minimal set of capabilities and information. Most vendors also implement some or all of the optional statistics and actions to provide more information of use to network managers. While the formal structure of management information is defined in the Ethernet standard, the actual specification that most vendors use for management objects is an RFC, called *Definitions of Managed Objects for IEEE 802.3 Repeater Devices.* *

Repeater Management Interface

The vendor typically equips the repeater with an Ethernet interface to provide access to the management functions. Packets can be sent to this interface via any port on the repeater, making it possible to interact with the management system using a management application that runs on a PC or other computer located anywhere in the network system. Vendors often supply the required management application software for a relatively low cost. Communication with the management software in a repeater hub also requires the use of a high-level network protocol to carry the information over the network between the hub and the management application running on a computer.

The IEEE 802.3 standard does not specify which network protocol may be used, leaving it to the marketplace to make this decision. The most widely used network protocol for communicating with management software on repeaters (and most other network devices) is the Simple Network Management Protocol (SNMP),

---

* RFC stands for *Request For Comments*, which is a standards document created by the Internet Engineering Task Force (IETF). As of this writing, the most recent version of the repeater management RFC is RFC 2108, published in February 1997. URLs for the RFCs can be found in Appendix A, *Resources*.

which typically uses Internet Protocol (IP) packets to communicate with the hub. Network management software packages that use SNMP protocols are widely available.

Managed repeater hubs frequently provide a console port that allows you to connect a terminal directly to the hub and interact with the management interface. This allows you to initially configure the hub and provide it with a network address. In many cases, you can also use the console port interface to look at some of the management information without having to buy separate management software.

Some vendors supply a management interface on the repeater that is also equipped with telnet server software, making it accessible over the network using the standard telnet application in the TCP/IP suite. This provides a *virtual terminal* connection between the telnet application running on your computer, and the management interface in the repeater hub. This, in turn, makes it possible to connect to the repeater hub using any TCP/IP-equipped computer and the telnet application. When you run the telnet application, what you see is much like connecting a terminal directly to the ASCII terminal port on the hub. The difference is that you can connect to the hub remotely via telnet from anywhere on the Internet.

An advantage of this approach is that many computers come equipped with TCP/IP and telnet software, which means that you do not have to buy special management software to interact with the management interface on the hub. Telnet also works well over modem links, making it possible for the network manager to make a dial-up connection to the network and look at the hub management information in response to trouble calls. A disadvantage of the telnet interface is that it frequently doesn't supply all of the information or management controls that are provided with a graphical user interface.

Repeater Management Information

The information provided by a managed repeater is organized as a set of several different *objects*, which include counters that hold statistics and other status information reported by the hub. Also included are objects that allow the management software to enable or disable a port, reset the repeater, and so on. Objects are grouped into three packages, known as the Basic Control Package, the Performance Monitoring Package, and the Address Tracking Package.

Repeater management objects are further organized into one of three main classes:

Repeater object class
    Contains those objects necessary for overall repeater management.

Group object class

> Contains objects used to manage collections of ports, making it possible to cluster ports into groups, or modules, and providing visibility of the entire group. A group could be a 12 or 16 port repeater card that fits into a modular chassis hub.

Port object class

> Contains objects used to manage or monitor the operation of individual ports in the repeater group.

When a vendor equips a repeater hub with optional management capabilities, the standard requires that the basic control package be provided, which is primarily concerned with repeater configuration information and repeater status. The performance monitoring package is optional, and provides additional statistics for each port. The address tracking package is also optional, and provides information related to the MAC address of frames received on each port.

The optional performance monitoring port counters are reported by most managed hubs. In general, the fewer errors the better. However, when looking at these counters on a repeater hub, you will often see a small number of errors. As long as the error rate is low, you should not be concerned. Acceptable error rates for these counters are not defined in the standard, since the rates will vary depending on the amount of traffic, quality of the cabling system, amount of electrical noise at a given site, and so on.

Framing Function

In operation, a repeater is not concerned with counting the total number of bits in a frame or detecting errors in frames. Instead, it is designed to serially repeat bits coming in one port out onto all other ports. Therefore, the specification for managed objects in a repeater also includes some basic functions which are needed to collect the management information. Data can flow *through* a repeater port in both directions. Thus, when you are collecting management information on a port, you need to know in which direction the management system is viewing the information, in order to make sense of what the management information is telling you. A variety of management statistics can be collected and reported by the management interface on a repeater, both for the repeater as a whole and for each port on the repeater.

For each repeater port, the management system can detect when carrier (activity) has been sensed on that port. It can also provide a timing function for the activity to detect overlong events. The management system can also report when the transceiver located in the repeater port has detected a collision. The rest of the statistics deal with the content of a frame, and are generated by looking at the frame coming *into* a repeater port from the network segment. Remember, a repeater doesn't know anything about the frame fields beyond the preamble. However, the management interface needs to know about the frame fields in order to count data, detect the occurrence of a CRC error, etc.

To detect frame errors, the management interface also provides a *framing function*. The framing function is used to recognize the boundaries of an incoming frame on a repeater port by monitoring the occurrence of carrier and the decoded data stream. The framing function then detects the preamble, and the remaining bits of the frame are aligned on octet boundaries. If there are not an integral number of octets, a framing error is detected. The framing function is only provided for the management interface, and is not part of normal repeater operation. With the framing function in place, the management interface can inspect the incoming frame on a port, and determine how many octets it contains, what the source address is, whether there has been a CRC error, and so on.

The management interface is only eavesdropping on the bits going through a repeater, and does not slow down repeater operations. Given that only a single packet can be on the channel at any given time in a half-duplex system, the management interface does not have to be extremely high performance in order to monitor the frame traffic. Instead, all the management function has to do is watch the single stream of bits going through a repeater for each frame transmission and analyze the frame errors.

Repeater Port Statistics

Next, we will take a detailed look at the port statistics that can often be found on a managed hub. We will also mention which errors may be indications of serious problems. Following the definitions of the individual port statistics, we will then see what an actual hub management interface looks like and show you how to read the statistics.

The following definitions are taken from the RFC on managed objects, and from vendor manuals. Although most vendors use the RFC definitions, there is nothing to prevent them from creating their own definitions for one or more of the managed objects. To be absolutely certain as to the definition and contents of a counter on a given device, you need to check the vendor documentation for that device.

Readable Frames

This counter may be displayed in a vendor's management interface as "Good Frames" or the equivalent. The standard defines this as a count of the total number of valid frames detected on a port. Valid frames are from 64 to 1,518 bytes in length, have a valid frame CRC, and are received without a collision.

Readable Octets

This counter contains the number of total octets, or bytes, received on a port. This number is determined by adding the total frame length to this counter at the completion of every valid frame. This provides a rough indication of the total data transferred.

Frame Check Sequence Errors

The Frame Check Sequence (FCS) field of the frame is used to carry a 4-byte CRC polynomial. The CRC checks the validity of the received frame, and can indicate when any bit errors have occurred during frame transmission and reception. This counter is incremented once for every frame received with an invalid frame check sequence (CRC error). The frame must also be of valid length (64 to 1,518 bytes), and be received without a framing error or a collision.

CRC errors can be caused by electrical noise that has been coupled into the cabling system, by bad cabling and connectors, or perhaps by errors in the electronics of a transmitting interface. Ideally, the number of CRC frames seen on a segment should be zero. However, you will typically encounter a small number of CRC errors over time in a normal network.

The maximum bit error rate objective defined in the standard for 10 Mbps media systems is around 1 error in 10^9 bits.* This is the worst-case bit error rate, which means that a properly built and operating media system should not have more than one bit error in every 10^9 bits transmitted. Most media systems will operate considerably better than this. Given that a maximum size normal frame consists of 12,144 bits (1,518 bytes), then you could expect approximately one error in every 82,345 maximum-sized frames at the worst-case bit error rate. Frame rates and frame sizes vary widely on Ethernet systems, so it is impossible to provide any hard limit on the number of CRCs seen per day that would be useful in all cases.

You should be very concerned if this counter is continually incrementing, or if the CRC rate exceeds something on the order of one in about 80,000 large frames on a 10 Mbps system. Many LANs have a preponderance of smaller frames of about 256 bytes. At that size, it's possible to have one CRC error every 500,000 or so frames given the bit error rate above. Most media systems operate considerably

---

* Higher speed Ethernet systems have more stringent objectives. For example, the 1000BASE-X system has a worst-case bit error rate objective of 1 error in 10^{12} bits.

better than the bit error rate objective in the standard, and may not see a CRC error in millions of frames.

Alignment Error

Alignment error counts the number of frames detected on a port with both an FCS error and a framing error. A framing error is caused by a frame that does not contain an integral number of octets. Such a frame does not end on an octet boundary, but is some odd number of bits in length. To be counted as an alignment error, a frame must also be received without a collision, and must be within the range of a valid frame size (64 to 1,518 bytes). If the frame is counted as an alignment error, then it is not also counted as an FCS error.

If an Ethernet controller fails to properly detect the end of the preamble and the beginning of the frame fields, it can read in a frame such that the frame fields are not correctly aligned on octet boundaries. Such a frame will not pass the FCS check, and would normally be counted as an FCS error. However, this form of FCS error does not indicate a bit error problem on the channel. Instead, it occurs when the interface does not properly read in the frame for whatever reason. Therefore, the alignment error counter was provided for frames that have both a framing error and an FCS error. A small number of alignment errors may occur over time in a network. As long as the rate is low, and as long as this counter is not continually incrementing, these errors would not be an indication of a serious problem.

Frames Too Long

An overlong frame is one that is received with an octet count greater than the maximum frame size of 1,518 bytes. An overlong frame can occasionally be emitted when a computer is powered on or reboots and then performs a test of its network interface. In this case, the test may consist of filling the interface buffer memory with ones or zeroes, and then sending the entire contents of buffer memory out as an overlong frame. For this reason, an occasional overlong frame may be expected in a normal network. As long as the rate is not too high, and as long as the counter is not continually incrementing, there should be no problem.

Short Events

A short event counts the number of times activity was detected on the port for less than the short event maximum time. The short event maximum time is a range of from 74 to 84 bit times.

A short event may indicate an externally generated noise pulse that was coupled into the network media system and received by the repeater. Noise pulses like this could result in damaged frames, or false or late collision detect. A short event could also be due to software on some station that starts to transmit a frame and then aborts the process very early in its transmission. A 10 Mbps repeater will perform fragment extension of a short event, causing it to be counted as a *runt* on the interconnect ports of other repeaters. A 100 Mbps repeater does not perform fragment extension.

Runts

Most runts are the result of a collision, and as such, are a completely normal and expected event on an Ethernet. A runt could also be caused by an interface that aborts a frame transmission for some reason. Runts are automatically discarded by all station interfaces, and have no impact on the performance of an interface. Since a valid collision must occur sometime in the first 512 bits of the frame transmission, a runt is defined as being smaller than 512 bits, but larger than a short event. This counter provides a look at normal network operations, and does not indicate an error.

Collisions

This counter does nothing more than count the number of times that a collision has been detected on the port.

Late Events

A late event counts the number of times a collision is detected after the late event threshold. Essentially, a late event, or late collision, is a collision that occurs after the 512-bit collision window has passed when a frame is being transmitted. A late collision is counted in both the collision and late event counters.

A late collision indicates a serious problem in the network, since all valid collisions must occur in the first 512 bits of the frame transmission. Late collisions cause lost frames and can result in greatly reduced performance for applications. Networks that exceed the configuration guidelines may result in late collisions. Another possible cause of late collisions in a twisted-pair network may be excessive signal crosstalk causing phantom collision detections that occur late in the frame. Such crosstalk can be caused by the use of incorrect cabling, or by cables being incorrectly wired.

Late events can also be caused if a station connected to a repeater port is mistakenly set in full-duplex mode. Repeaters are by definition half-duplex devices, and all stations connected to them must operate in half-duplex mode. A full-duplex station connected to a repeater port will send data whenever it pleases, without obeying the CSMA/CD channel arbitration rules. This can result in late collisions being detected on ports with half-duplex stations whose transmissions were collided with by the full-duplex station.

Very Long Events

Very long events count the number of times the transmitter is active for greater than the jabber protection timer allows. The jabber timer is set to a range of from 40,000 to 75,000 bit times.

Very long events can be caused when some station goes berserk and begins transmitting constantly, indicating either a failure of the Ethernet interface in that station, or a problem with the devices used to connect that station to the network. This counter can help locate the port that is receiving the jabbers. You may need to shut off stations one at a time to find which machine is jabbering.

Data Rate Mismatches

This counts the number of times where the signal frequency or data rate of the incoming signal is detectably different from the signal frequency used by the repeater. A data rate mismatch can occur if a station has an interface with a timing clock that is out of specification and is sending signals at a data rate that is slower or faster than the specifications. This counter can help locate the port that is receiving the incorrect signals. You may need to shut off stations one at a time to find which machine is sending frames with incorrect signal timing.

Auto Partitions

This counter is incremented each time the port has been partitioned from the network.

Last Source Address

This counter is in the optional address tracking package. It saves the value of the source address field in the last frame received on the port.

Source Address Changes

This counter is also in the optional address tracking package. It counts the number of times the source address field of received frames changes. This can indicate whether a port is connected to a single station, or to a multi-user network channel.

Using the Management Interface

Management information can be used to generate all manner of displays for network managers to look at. Various SNMP-based management applications can store the data, draw color graphs showing the statistics for a hub or port, and even present the data as automatically generated graphs on a web page.

The following examples show a bare bones ASCII display of the actual counters taken from a managed hub. This hub is equipped with an ASCII terminal port. It can also use SNMP protocols to interact with management software running on another computer to provide much prettier and more useful graphs. This hub also provides access to the counters via telnet. Our examples were taken while using the telnet program to access the character-oriented terminal display in the hub. While this display is extremely simple, it can also be very handy since it allows a network manager to log into the hub and take a quick look at operations without having to run a full-blown SNMP management application.

Figure 17-10 shows overall hub statistics. This display provides the sum of all individual port counters. The management software allows you to give names to the entire hub and to each port. This hub has been named "RSC 10BASE-FL Hub," indicating in this case that it is a 10 Mbps fiber optic hub located in the Recreational Sports Center building on a major campus. Not all of the statistics listed above are provided. Each vendor can decide which of the performance statistics they may want to show.

```
                          RSC 10BASE-FL Hub

      Good Frames:          3477883250  |###################################
      CRC Errors:                    0  |
      Alignment Errors:              0  |
      Runt Frames:                2122  |
      Long Frames:                   1  |
      Bad Frames:                  132  |
      Total Frames:         3477883383  |###################################
      Transmit Collisions:           0  |
      Port Collisions:        24732454  |
      Late Collisions:               0  |
      Short Events:                131  |
      Jabber Lockups:                0  |
      Port Partitions:               8  |
      Data Rate Mismatches:          0  |
                                        -----------------------------------
```

Figure 17-10. Repeater hub statistics

This hub shows 131 short events and 1 long frame, for a total of 132 bad frames seen by all ports in the hub. Given that this hub has been running for a long time without a reset of the statistics displays, this low level of errors is quite acceptable. Let's look at an individual port next.

Figure 17-11 shows the statistics for port 6 of module 1 in this repeater. This is a stackable repeater, with two modules connected together using an expansion interface. The management software allows you to view each of the modules separately, and to look at any port on either module. The port name indicates that this port of the repeater hub is connected to a router located in the Performing Arts Center (PAC) on the campus.

```
                         RSC 10BASE-FL Hub
                             Module 1
                        Port 6 - PAC hubrouter

    Good Frames:        363955696   |###################################
    CRC Errors:                 0   |
    Alignment Errors:           0   |
    Runt Frames:                3   |
    Long Frames:                1   |
    Bad Frames:                 1   |
    Total Frames:       363955697   |###################################
    Port Collisions:     10844808   |#
    Late Collisions:            0   |
    Short Events:               0   |
    Jabber Lockups:             0   |
    Port Partitions:            1   |
    Data Rate Mismatches:       0   |
                                     -------------------------------------
```

Figure 17-11. Repeater port statistics

Things look pretty good, with no large error counts. This is a fiber optic repeater hub, and fiber optic media systems tend to run very clean, given that the media is immune to electromagnetic interference. On metallic media systems you may see a small number of CRC errors reported, but as long as the CRC rate is very low and is not incrementing rapidly, it is nothing to worry about. Bit errors can occur no matter how good your cabling system is, and when you're moving a lot of data through a system there are eventually some errors. You know you have a problem when the error rate is very high, or the errors are continually incrementing.

The number of collisions shown on this port is nearly 30 percent of the number of good frames shown, which might lead you to think that the long-term average collision rate for this port is around 30 percent. However, you must remember that the counters in a management agent, such as the repeater hub, can wrap around and start over from zero when they hit their maximum. A 32-bit counter is typically used for 10 Mbps Ethernet, and a counter of that length will roll over after holding a little over 4 billion events (4,294,967,300 to be precise). The standard notes that a counter should be large enough to continue counting at the maximum rate for a given statistic for at least 58 minutes without rolling over. Therefore, 64-bit counters may be used in faster Ethernet systems.

Note that this port has counted over 3.4 billion total frames, and there's nothing to say that this is only the first time around for this counter. A management application that is receiving data from this hub over a period of time can be equipped with longer counters, and would be able to note when the counters in the management agent have wrapped.

However, when telnetting into the hub to take a quick snapshot of hub counters, you will probably find that there is no indication of counter wrap in the display you get. In other words, the counter we are looking at here may have already counted over 4 billion frames, wrapped to zero, and then counted another 3.4 billion. Meanwhile, the collision counter still has a long way to go before wrapping back to zero. Therefore, you cannot assume that the collision rate is around 30 percent for this port. Instead, you can use the management interface to clear the counter displays and then wait five or ten minutes to see what the actual rate is. Before you clear the displays, you should make a note of any other counters of interest.

Figure 17-12 shows what port 6 looks like after the counter displays were reset to zero. We've waited for about five minutes and then taken another snapshot of the statistics. Now the collision rate is less than 3 percent of the total frames. This is a much more realistic picture of the current statistics on this port.

```
                         RSC 10BASE-FL Hub
                             Module 1
                      Port 6 - PAC hubrouter

  Good Frames:             2416   |###################################
  CRC Errors:                 0   |
  Alignment Errors:           0   |
  Runt Frames:                0   |
  Long Frames:                0   |
  Bad Frames:                 0   |
  Total Frames:            2416   |###################################
  Port Collisions:           67   |#
  Late Collisions:            0   |
  Short Events:               0   |
  Jabber Lockups:             0   |
  Port Partitions:            0   |
  Data Rate Mismatches:       0   |
                                   -------------------------------------
```

Figure 17-12. Repeater port statistics after reset

This survey of the most commonly displayed port statistics provides you with enough background to read and understand the important counters in a managed repeater. You should also read the manual that came with your managed repeater to find out which features are supported and what set of statistics are available. Vendors often have their own names for the standard management objects they provide, so reading the manual can be essential when it comes to figuring out what the management information actually means.

The SNMP network protocol has defined a further set of management functions in an SNMP management information base (MIB) called the Remote Monitoring (RMON) MIB. RMON makes it possible to provide much more information about the traffic on a given port, and some vendors support some or all of the RMON capabilities in their hubs. The RMON MIB, and what it can do for you, is described in more detail in Chapter 20, *Troubleshooting*.

18

Ethernet Switching Hubs

Ethernet switching hubs allow you to build large Ethernet systems that extend beyond the limits of a single collision domain. They also link Ethernet segments that operate at different speeds and control the flow of traffic through a system. Switching hubs improve the reliability of Ethernet systems, and can vastly increase the amount of Ethernet bandwidth available for use. In recent years, the cost of switching hubs has plummeted while the performance and set of features has increased. As a result, Ethernet switching hubs are widely used today.

The operation of a switching hub is based on Ethernet bridging. Bridges are packet switches that operate at the level of Ethernet frames. The earliest Ethernet bridges were two-port devices that could link two Ethernet segments together. Later, it became possible to design and sell bridges with many ports, which were used in the hub of a cabling system, which is how they came to be known as a switching hub. In this chapter we use the word "bridge" and "switch" interchangeably when describing how these devices function.

This chapter describes how switching hubs function, and how they can be used to extend the reach and capability of an Ethernet system. The use of switching hubs in network designs is a big topic, and one that cannot be fully explained here. Instead, we provide a basic introduction to the technology and a quick look at the many features of switching hubs. This makes it possible for you to see some of the ways that these devices can be used to improve the operation of your network. We will start with the basic concepts of bridge and switch operation, and then show how they can be used in actual network designs.

Brief Tutorial on Ethernet Bridging

Ethernet bridging technology was first delivered in the mid-1980s, typically in the form of two-port devices that could help segment a large Ethernet into separate Ethernet LANs, as shown in Figure 18-1. The devices linked two LANs, forming a *bridge* between them, hence the name. As the cost of bridge electronics dropped and the performance of bridging chips improved, it became possible to build bridges with many more ports and more powerful capabilities inside the box. A device with more than two ports of bridging became known as a *switching hub*. Nowadays, even two-port bridges are often called switches.

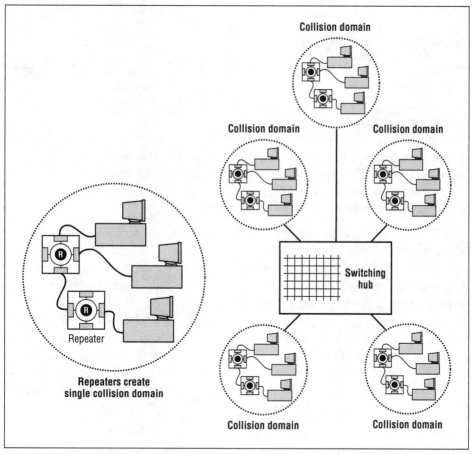

Figure 18-1. Switches interrupt the collision domain

At their most basic level of moving frames from one LAN to another, bridges and switching hubs operate identically. The major difference is in the increased number of ports and the enhanced capabilities of switching hubs, which led to a change in the marketing of these devices. Vendors wanted some way to differentiate a low-end bridge that just does basic bridging from the more expensive and flexible switching hub products that provide many more ports and more capabilities than basic bridges.

Note that the operation of bridges and switching hubs is not specified in the 802.3 Ethernet standard. Instead, these devices are based on the 802.1D standard, which provides rules for forwarding (switching) an Ethernet frame from one port to another, based on the destination address of the frame. While the 802.1D standard provides rules for moving frames between ports of a bridge and for a few other aspects of bridge operation, the standard does not specify bridge performance or packaging.

Transparent Bridging

Ethernet bridging is based on the 48-bit media access control (MAC) addresses found in Ethernet frames. Frames are defined at Layer 2, the Data Link layer of the OSI seven layer network architecture. That's why you will sometimes hear bridges and switches called link layer devices, as well as Layer 2 devices or Layer 2 switches. Bridges are designed so that their operation is transparent to the stations on the network, which explains why this approach to linking network segments and LANs is also called *transparent bridging.* Transparent means that you can connect a bridge to an Ethernet and it will automatically begin working, without requiring any changes on the part of the stations.

Installing a bridge makes a major change in the round-trip timing guidelines for an Ethernet, since the bridge terminates a collision domain. The definition of a collision domain is a single Ethernet system in which two or more stations transmitting simultaneously will encounter a collision. That's because all stations in a given collision domain share a single Ethernet channel. A single collision domain has significant restrictions. For one thing, all of the segments in a single collision domain are linked with repeaters. Therefore, all of the segments are required to operate at a single bit rate, which may be 10-, 100-, or 1000 Mbps. Another restriction is that Ethernet systems linked with repeaters are limited in size, due to the maximum segment lengths and the maximum number of repeaters that may be allowed in a given collision domain.

Replacing a repeater with a switch in an Ethernet composed of several segments creates separate Ethernet LANs, or separate collision domains. Each segment or LAN linked with a bridge operates as a separate collision domain. This makes it possible to connect Ethernet segments that operate at different speeds, and to create larger Ethernet systems by linking multiple collision domains together.

Switches also limit the effects of signal and frame errors in a network system. A single misbehaving station can cause problems for all stations in a given collision domain. A switch limits the scope of signal and frame errors by creating multiple collision domains, each of which supports a smaller number of stations. In 802.1D switches, signal errors caused by failing segments or stations will not be propagated between the collision domains. When a switch transmits a frame, it does so by re-sending the frame using the Ethernet interface located in each port of the switch. The frame signals and frame fields are completely regenerated, preventing any accumulation of frame or timing errors as a frame travels through the network. This can provide a major improvement in the reliability of your network.

Address Learning

A bridge controls the flow of traffic between Ethernet segments with the automatic traffic forwarding mechanism described in the IEEE 802.1D bridging standard. Traffic forwarding is based on address learning, and bridges make traffic forwarding decisions based on the addresses of the Ethernet frames. To do this, the bridge learns which stations are on which segments of the network by looking at the source addresses in all of the frames the bridge receives. If you recall, when a station sends a frame it puts two addresses in the frame. These two addresses are the destination address of the station it is sending the frame to and the source address of the station sending the frame.

The way this works is fairly simple. Unlike a normal station that only reads in frames directly addressed to it, the Ethernet interface on each port of a bridge runs in "promiscuous" mode. In this mode, the interface reads in all frames it sees on the connected LAN, not just the frames that are being sent to the bridge's own MAC address. As each frame is read in on each bridge port, the bridge software looks at the source address of the frame and adds the source address to a table of addresses that the bridge maintains. This is how the bridge figures out which stations are reachable on which ports. Figure 18-2 shows a bridge linking two LANs with three stations on each LAN.

For convenience in the figure, we use short numbers for station addresses, instead of actual 6-byte MAC addresses. As stations send traffic, the bridge receives every frame sent and builds a table, or *forwarding database*, that shows which stations can be reached on which ports. After every station has transmitted at least one frame, the bridge will end up with a forwarding database such as that shown in Table 18-1.

This database is then used by the bridge to make a packet forwarding decision. This process is called *adaptive filtering*. You will also see this type of bridge called a *learning bridge*, because it has the ability to dynamically acquire new addresses. The ability to learn makes it possible for you to add new stations to your network

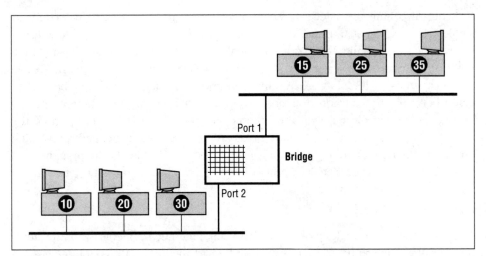

Figure 18-2. Address learning in a bridge

Table 18-1. Forwarding Database Maintained by Bridge

Station	Port
15	1
25	1
35	1
10	2
20	2
30	2

without having to manually configure the bridge. If the bridge receives a frame that is destined for a station address that it hasn't yet seen, the bridge will send the frame out all ports other than the port on which it arrived. This process is called *flooding*, and is explained in more detail later.

Learning bridges can also unlearn. The bridge keeps track of the age of each address entry in the address database and deletes the entry after a period of time (typically five minutes) if no frames are received with that source address. This allows you to move stations around from one segment to another without worrying about the bridge permanently maintaining address tables that do not reflect reality.

Traffic Filtering

Once the bridge has built up a database of forwarding addresses, it has the information it needs to filter traffic selectively. While the bridge is learning addresses, it is also checking each frame to make a packet forwarding decision based on the destination address in the frame. Let's look at how the forwarding decision works in a bridge equipped with two ports, Port 1 and Port 2, as shown in Figure 18-2. In our first example, we'll show how a bridge decides to forward a frame from one port to another.

Let's assume that a frame is sent from Station 15 to Station 20. Since the frame is sent by Station 15, the bridge reads the frame in on Port 1 and uses its address database to determine which of its ports is associated with the destination address in this frame. In this case, the destination address of the frame corresponds to Station 20, and the address database shows that to reach Station 20 the frame must be sent out Port 2 in order for it to arrive at its destination.

The bridge places the frame on the queue for transmission on Port 2, and the frame is ultimately transmitted on Port 2 and reaches its destination. The bridge is provided with short term buffer memory for each port, in case the output segment is busy when the frame arrives for transmission. Frames are placed in this buffer memory before transmission onto the segment. During this process, a bridge transmitting an Ethernet frame makes no changes in the data, address, or type fields of the frame. Using our example, the frame is transmitted intact on Port 2, exactly as it was received on Port 1. Therefore, as far as a station can tell, the frame could have gone through a repeater, or a bridge, or nothing at all. As far as frame delivery is concerned, the operation of the bridge is transparent to all stations on the network.

In our next example, let's assume that the bridge receives a frame on Port 1 that is sent from Station 15 to Station 35. The bridge goes through the same process of comparing the destination address of the frame (Station 35) to the list of addresses it has stored in its forwarding database. However, since the destination address of the frame received on Port 1 matches one of the station addresses reachable on Port 1, the bridge knows that the frame does not have to leave the LAN to get to its destination. Since the frame is already on the correct LAN, it will be correctly received, and the bridge can filter the frame by simply discarding it instead of forwarding it out another port.

This is how a bridge keeps local traffic isolated, preventing the flow of unnecessary traffic on a network system. This is a major advantage of a traffic filtering bridge, and is very different from the operation of a repeater, which is required to repeat a received frame out onto all other ports. Every segment connected with a repeater will hear all of the traffic on the LAN. However, segments or LANs connected with a bridge only hear the traffic that is destined for them. Bridge filtering reduces the total traffic load seen on a LAN, thereby making more bandwidth available for use.

Frame flooding

In a process called flooding, a bridge may forward a frame out *all* ports other than the one it was received on. If there is no match in the bridge's address database for a frame's destination address, then the bridge will forward the frame to all ports, thereby "flooding" the frame. Transmitting a frame out all ports guarantees that a frame with an unknown destination address will reach all segments and LANs linked by bridges, and be heard by the correct destination host. This keeps things working when an address has aged out of the bridge filter table, whether because the station hasn't transmitted anything for a while, or because the station was moved. All 802.1D bridges are required to flood unknown frames.

Some vendors provide lower cost "workgroup" bridges or "half bridges" which do not adhere to the 802.1D standard. These bridges are often built with limited address memory and address filtering capabilities to hold down cost. They typically have a designated "backbone" port, and they do not learn addresses on the backbone port or flood unknown traffic from the backbone port onto the other *workgroup* ports of the bridge. Only devices that transmit on the workgroup side of the bridge are learned by the forwarding database, at which point the bridge will forward frames sent to the learned address from the backbone port.

If the workgroup station does not transmit for a while and its address ages out of the database, communication from the backbone to the workgroup station will cease, because this type of bridge does not flood frames received on the backbone port with unknown addresses. This can lead to weird network problems that may be very difficult to troubleshoot. To avoid this, you need to ensure that the bridge you buy is compliant with the 802.1D standard, and is designed to filter and flood frames on all ports.

Broadcast and Multicast Domains

A multicast address is a group address that multiple interfaces can be configured to receive. Therefore, a single frame with a multicast destination address can be received by a set of stations listening to that multicast address. Broadcast is a special case of multicast, and is the group of all stations. Therefore, a packet sent to the broadcast address (the address of all ones) is received by every station on the LAN. Bridges are designed to link segments into a given LAN, so all bridges flood broadcast packets out all ports belonging to a LAN—except the port the broadcast was received on. This way the broadcast packets can reach all stations in the LAN.*

---

* Most bridges have no way of discovering where stations listening to a given multicast address may be located. Therefore, they will also flood all multicast packets out all ports other than the ports the multicasts were received on. More sophisticated high-end bridges can use multicast group discovery protocols to limit the propagation of multicast packets.

The concept of a broadcast domain is an important one to understand. By default, bridges do not filter broadcasts. That's because bridges are designed to make all Ethernets linked with bridges operate as though they were one large Ethernet. Therefore, a bridge must behave like a repeater in the case of broadcast packets, and send them out all ports.

Referring back to Figure 18-1, the image on the left-hand side is a set of segments linked with two repeaters. Segments linked with repeaters create a single collision domain, and a single broadcast domain. A broadcast or multicast frame sent by any station in a network linked with repeaters will be seen on all segments, just like any other frame sent through repeaters. The right-hand side of Figure 18-1 shows a bridge or switch linking several Ethernet LANs, each operating as a separate collision domain. However, the entire set of LANs linked with the bridge functions as a single broadcast domain.*

Stations send broadcast and multicast packets for a number of reasons. Some high-level network protocols use broadcast or multicast frames as part of their address discovery process. Broadcasts and multicasts are also used for dynamic address assignment, which typically happens when a station is first powered on and needs to find a high-level network address to begin communications. Multicasts may be used by certain multimedia applications, which send audio and video data in multicast frames for reception by groups of stations. Multicasts may also be used by multi-user games as a way of sending data to the group of game players.

Therefore, a typical network will always have some level of broadcast and multicast frames. Broadcast and multicast flooding by bridges means that you need to limit the total number of stations linked by bridges so that the broadcast and multicast rate does not get so high as to be a problem. A Layer 3 switch, also called a router, can be used to create separate broadcast domains, since a router does not automatically forward broadcasts and multicasts. Router operation is discussed in more detail later in this chapter.

Spanning Tree Algorithm

A difficulty with the bridge packet forwarding mechanism we've just described is that it's possible to end up with two segments, both connected to two bridges, so that the bridges are in parallel. Without some way to stop the traffic, parallel bridges linking the same segments will get into a forwarding loop. In such a loop, broadcast and multicast traffic circulates endlessly and continues to grow as new traffic is transmitted, until the traffic rate gets so high that the network is saturated.

---

* To be accurate, we should call this a *multicast domain*, since the broadcast address is simply an example of a multicast address. However, this is commonly called a *broadcast domain* in the industry, so we will use the more commonly known term, even if inaccurate.

Loops like this are fairly easy to achieve, since in a sufficiently complex network system it can be difficult to know whether or not the bridges are positioned in such a way as to create loop paths. To prevent forwarding loops, the IEEE 802.1D bridging standard provides a spanning tree algorithm.

The purpose of the spanning tree algorithm is to allow bridges and switches in a given Ethernet system to dynamically create a loop-free set of paths. A bridged system must never have a loop path in it, or traffic could cycle endlessly around the loop. The spanning tree algorithm makes sure that bridges create a loop-free system, even in a complex network with lots of potential paths through bridges and switching hubs. Operation of the spanning tree algorithm is based on configuration messages sent by each bridge, using a multicast address that has been reserved for spanning tree operation. All IEEE 802.1D compliant bridges listen to frames sent to this address, so that every bridge can send and receive spanning tree configuration messages.

The configuration messages contain information that allows any set of bridges to automatically elect a *root bridge*. The election is based on the numeric value of Ethernet addresses used in the interfaces of each bridge, among other items. All other things being equal, the bridge with the lowest numerical value Ethernet address is elected the root bridge. The root bridge then proceeds to send out configuration messages. Each bridge uses the information in the configuration messages it receives to calculate the best path from itself to the root bridge. The configuration information is designed to make it possible for each bridge to select the ports that will be included in the spanning tree and to automatically shut off the ports that could cause a loop path to occur. This ability to shut off ports is the mechanism that insures that a set of Ethernet bridges can automatically configure themselves to produce loop-free paths in a complex network system.[*]

Advantages of Switching Hubs

At its most basic, a switching hub performs the same traffic filtering and spanning tree functions as an original two-port bridge. Along with these abilities, switching hubs also support many more ports. Therefore, switching hubs have a more complex architecture inside them to allow multiple conversations to simultaneously occur between ports of the hub. This ability to support multiple simultaneous conversations between the ports is a chief feature of switching hubs. There is a wide

---

[*] Work is currently underway on an 802.1w supplement to the standard, describing an enhanced spanning tree protocol that reduces the amount of time it takes for the spanning tree protocol to complete its work. A URL listing the status of this supplement may be found in the section on "Standards Documents and Standards Organizations" in Appendix A, *Resources.*

range of switching hubs available today, and many hubs have sophisticated added features which are briefly described later in this chapter.

There are a lot of ways to use bridges and switching hubs in network designs, and it is impossible to provide a complete description of all applications in the space of a single chapter. However, we can show some of the basic ways in which bridges and switching hubs can be used to improve the operation of an Ethernet system. Following these examples, we will look at some of the advanced capabilities provided by switching hubs.

Improved Network Performance

One major way in which any bridge or switching hub can improve the operation of a network system is by controlling the flow of traffic. The ability to control traffic makes the switching hub a useful tool for the Ethernet designer faced with continually growing station populations and increasing traffic loads. With careful attention to the location of switching hubs in your network system, you can often keep network traffic localized to a smaller set of network segments. This allows the total network system at your site to grow larger without sending traffic to all network segments.

For example, switching hubs can help isolate the local traffic generated by a cluster of high performance servers and client workstations, and keep that traffic from swamping a larger network system.

Figure 18-3 shows a set of clients and two servers linked with repeater hubs. A switching hub is used for their connection to the building network, isolating their traffic from the rest of the network segments in the building. Due to the traffic filtering capabilities of the switching hub, all of the local traffic between the clients and the servers stays local and is not sent over the rest of the network in the building.

When using switching hubs, you need to think carefully about the flow of traffic in your system. Simply removing a repeater and replacing it with a switching hub is not guaranteed to automatically provide a major improvement in network bandwidth. You need to make sure that the clients and servers that are exchanging the major amount of traffic are located appropriately with respect to the switching hub. Consider what would happen if the majority of the clients for the servers shown in Figure 18-3 were on the other side of the switch, with the rest of the building segments. In that case, most of the server traffic would still have to go through the switching hub and into the building network, negating the traffic isolating advantage of the hub.

When installing a switching hub, you need to do what you can to make sure that the traffic local to a cluster of servers and clients stays local. We accomplished this

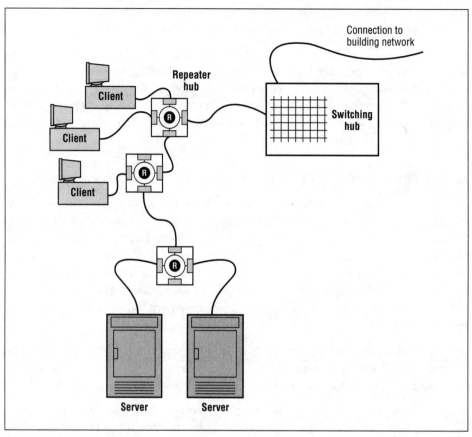

Figure 18-3. Isolating client-server traffic

in Figure 18-3 by locating the hub at the edge of the server-client cluster where the connection to the rest of the building network is made.

Linking Segments at Different Speeds

Another major advantage of bridges or switching hubs is that they can link LAN segments that run at different speeds. This is possible because a switching hub is essentially a special-purpose computer equipped with multiple Ethernet interfaces that can operate at different speeds. A switching hub can read in a frame on a port operating at 10 Mbps, store the frame in local memory, and then send the frame out on a port that operates at 100 Mbps. This cannot be done with repeaters, since all segments linked with a given repeater hub must operate at the same speed. Figure 18-4 shows a multi-speed switching hub being used to provide high-speed access to a server.

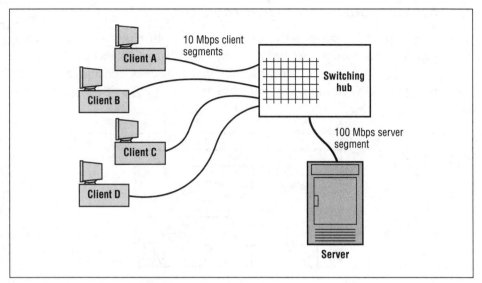

Figure 18-4. Switching hub linking different speed segments

In this network design, the server is connected to a 100 Mbps Fast Ethernet segment attached to the multi-speed switching hub. The client machines each connect to 10 Mbps switching ports on the hub. Access to the server is by way of the 100 Mbps link, which helps make sure that the client traffic cannot overwhelm the port that feeds the server segment.

This last point is important and deserves to be emphasized. In this network design, it's likely that several of the clients will be simultaneously trying to retrieve data from the server, and the connection to the server could be overwhelmed. If the server port only operated at 10 Mbps and all clients sent a frame to the server at the same instant, this could easily lead to situations where the buffers for the 10 Mbps server port would be oversubscribed. This, in turn, would cause the switch to drop frames destined for that port. Linking the server to the switching hub with a Fast Ethernet segment that moves data ten times faster than any of the client segments helps avoid this problem.

The connection method shown here for the clients illustrates a special advantage of switching hubs: the ability to provide large amounts of bandwidth inside the switching hub and to support multiple simultaneous connections. Since every port on the switching hub in our example is a switched port, each client gets its own 10 Mbps Ethernet channel directly into the switching hub. Clients connected to their own ports on a switching hub don't have to contend with other stations for the use of that bandwidth, effectively providing the clients with their own private 10 Mbps network channel.

Hybrid Switching and Repeating Hubs

Vendors also provide hybrid hubs that incorporate both repeating and switching functions, and that include support for multi-speed LAN segments as well. As an example of the hybrid approach, the hub in Figure 18-5 contains a four-port 10 Mbps repeater hub, a four-port 100 Mbps repeater hub, and several switched ports.

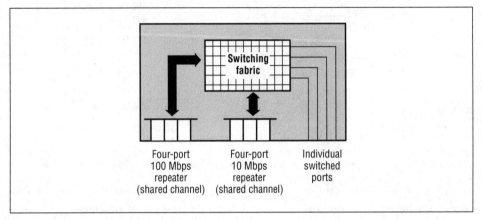

Figure 18-5. Hybrid switching and repeating hub

This hub allows you to link four clients using a single 10 Mbps Ethernet channel by way of the repeater hub. The repeater is then linked to a 10 Mbps port of the switch inside the hub. A server or client with a Fast Ethernet interface could be attached to the ports of the 100 Mbps repeater hub. The other switching ports of the hub can provide any number of things: Fast Ethernet connections to servers, 10 Mbps connections to other clients, or connections to other hubs and Ethernet LANs.

Buffered Distributor

Buffered distributor is the name given to a special Gigabit Ethernet device offered by a few vendors which operates like a minimal switching hub. This device, also called a full-duplex repeater or buffered repeater, uses some basic switching hub technology to link two or more Gigabit Ethernet segments. It does not filter addresses like a normal bridge or switch, and instead forwards all incoming traffic to all connected links (except the originating link). Its packet forwarding behavior is somewhat like that of a repeater, hence the confusing "full-duplex repeater" name. However, a true Ethernet repeater operates as a half-duplex device on all ports, since it only functions with half-duplex shared channels on which the

CSMA/CD media access control (MAC) protocol is used to arbitrate access to the channel. Therefore, the term "full-duplex repeater" doesn't make much sense.

The buffered distributor is constructed internally like a switching hub. It has buffer memory on each of its ports and every port is operated in full-duplex mode. Stations at the other end of the links must also operate their interfaces in full-duplex mode to avoid the need for carrier extension and the overhead that it adds to the transmission of short frames. Internally, the distributor minimizes costs by using a single shared bus channel to connect all ports together.

Port buffers can hold one or more incoming frames on each link before forwarding the frames out all other ports. To help avoid buffer congestion, all ports must operate at the same speed. The buffered distributor also requires 802.3x flow control to help control port buffer overflow. This is done by managing traffic flow from the stations by sending and receiving flow control frames with stations connected to the ports. However, this requires that the station interfaces must also support the optional 802.3x flow control standard, so that they can respond to flow control commands from the buffered distributor. The flow control is asymmetric; the stations respond to commands from the buffered distributor but cannot send flow control commands to the distributor.

Essentially, you can think of the buffered distributor as a very minimal and very simple switching hub. It has no address filtering, no switching fabric speed beyond 1 Gbps, and no ability to provide multi-speed support (10 Mbps, 100 Mbps) on its ports. Ports with incoming traffic go through arbitration inside the box for the opportunity to send data out all other ports. Once having done that, traffic from the port that wins arbitration is simply forwarded out of the other ports; flow control is provided to help manage port congestion. A buffered distributor may also be equipped with a single standard bridging port operating at 10 or 100 Mbps for connection to an existing Ethernet system.

The buffered distributor approach makes it possible to provide a lower cost Gigabit Ethernet switching device than a full-fledged switching hub. That's because a full-fledged Gigabit Ethernet hub must have a high-bandwidth switching fabric and also provide address filtering and many other features. As it happened, the cost of fully equipped Gigabit Ethernet switching hub ports has dropped so quickly that there hasn't been much of a market opportunity for the buffered distributor. Therefore, they have not been widely deployed.

Switching Hub Performance Issues

A single Ethernet LAN (collision domain) is a system designed to move Ethernet frames between stations. It operates at a known bit rate and a known maximum frame rate.* All Ethernet segments of a given speed will have the same maximum bit rate and frame rate characteristics. However, when you add a switching hub to your network system, you are creating a more complex system. Now the performance limits of your network become a combination of the performance of the Ethernet LANs and the performance of the switch. It's up to you to make sure that the switch you buy has enough performance to do the job.

Switches are equipped with multiple Ethernet interfaces, each of which can send bits over the Ethernet channel at the speed of the Ethernet media system to which it is attached. However, the performance of the switch itself may not be able to sustain the full frame rate coming in from all ports. In other words, should all ports simultaneously present high traffic loads to the switch, the switch may not be able to handle the full traffic rate and may begin dropping frames. This is known as *blocking*, which is the condition when a switching system has no further resources available to provide for the flow of data through the switch. A *non-blocking switch* is one that provides enough internal switching capability to handle the load even when all ports are simultaneously active.

Typical switch hardware has special support circuits that are designed to help improve the speed with which the switch can handle a frame and look up frame addresses in the address filtering database. The support circuits and high-speed buffer memory are more expensive components. The total performance of a switch is a trade-off between the cost of high-speed memory and other high performance components, and the price most customers are willing to pay. Therefore, you will find that not all switches perform alike.

Some less expensive devices may have lower packet forwarding performance, smaller address filtering tables, smaller port buffers, etc. Larger switches with more ports will typically have higher performance components as well as a higher price tag. Switches capable of handling the maximum frame rate on all of their ports are sometimes described as non-blocking switches, capable of operating at *full wire speed* or *full media speed*. Fully non-blocking switches that can handle the maximum bit rate simultaneously on all ports are quite common these days.

Network Design with Switching Hubs

Switching hubs are designed to provide multiple simultaneous conversations. Referring back to Figure 18-4, this means that while Client A and the server are communicating, Client B and Client C can be communicating at the same time as well. In this configuration, the total network bandwidth available to stations becomes a function of the individual segments to which each station is connected,

---

* For example, a 10 Mbps Ethernet LAN can send a maximum of 14,880 frames per second when using the minimum frame size of 64 bytes.

and of the total capacity of your switching hub. Modern switching hubs are equipped with switching fabrics inside the hub that can provide several gigabits per second of switching capacity, or even considerably more.

However, the speed of the switching fabric in the hub is only one of several important considerations when it comes to moving frames through a switching hub. High traffic rate coming into the switching hub from multiple ports, all destined for a single server port on the switch, is a problem. When that occurs, it's easy to overrun the ability of the output port, no matter how much total switching capacity the hub may have. The switching hub will start dropping frames when it runs out of places to temporarily store them. A dropped frame requires the client software running on the computer to retransmit the data. Lots of data retransmission caused by a congested output port leads to a slow response for the application that is losing frames while trying to talk to the server.

Traffic bottlenecks such as these are a problem in all large network designs. When linking switching hubs together, you may encounter situations where multiple hubs send traffic over single backbone links between backbone switching hubs. Even if there are multiple parallel segments linking the backbone switches, the spanning tree algorithm will ensure that only one path is active to prevent loops in the network. Therefore, the ports of the hubs that feed the single backbone link could be facing the same situation as the oversubscribed server port just described, causing the backbone ports to drop frames. In sufficiently large network systems, a single inter-switch link may not provide enough bandwidth, leading to congestion.

There are a number of approaches that can be taken to avoid these problems in large network systems. Several vendors provide proprietary mechanisms in their switches that allow multiple parallel Ethernet links to be grouped together and used as a large "virtual" channel between backbone switches. For example, multiple Gigabit Ethernet links can be aggregated into channels operating at two, four and even eight gigabits per second. This makes it possible to increase bandwidth between busy backbone switching hubs. This approach can even be used between a switching hub and special Ethernet interface cards in high performance servers. Since these mechanisms are proprietary, you would have to use the same vendor's switches for all such backbone links.

A new 802.3ad link aggregation standard is being developed to provide a vendor-neutral way to operate Ethernet links in parallel. This standard is expected to be formally adopted early in 2000. Another approach is to use Layer 3 routers instead of Layer 2 switches, since routers don't have to rely on a spanning tree algorithm. This makes it possible for routers to provide more sophisticated traffic moving mechanisms that allow multiple channels to be used as backbone links.

Network design issues such as these require a good deal of knowledge about the mechanisms used to direct the flow of traffic through various devices such as switching hubs and routers. This is also an area that is undergoing rapid evolution, and new mechanisms for moving traffic around large networks are continually being invented and tried out in the marketplace.

Switch Performance Measurement

Switch performance is typically rated in terms of the maximum switching capacity of the switch fabric inside the hub, and in terms of the maximum number of packets per second that the bridge can filter and forward on all ports. This gives you a rough idea of how good the performance of the bridge may be in your system. However, the rates of switching and of filtering and forwarding are only a few measures of switch performance.

All switches contain some high-speed buffer memory in which a frame is stored, however briefly, before being forwarded onto another port or ports of the switching hub. This mechanism is known as *store-and-forward switching.** A larger amount of buffer memory allows a bridge to handle longer streams of back-to-back frames. This gives the switch improved performance in the presence of bursts of traffic on the LAN. Some vendors provide a pool of high-speed buffer memory that can be dynamically allocated to switch ports as needed.

As you can see, the subject of packet switch performance can get complex rather quickly. When using switches, you need to keep your network load requirements in mind. For example, if your network includes high-performance clients that place demands on a single server or set of servers, then whatever switching hub you use must have high enough performance and sufficient port buffers to handle the task.

Advanced Features of Switching Hubs

Next, we'll provide a quick listing of some of the advanced features that you might encounter in the switching hub marketplace. The market for switching hubs is evolving rapidly as vendors compete to add value to their hubs with a variety of extra features and capabilities.

---

* Some switches support a mode of operation called *cut-through switching*, in which the frame forwarding process begins before the entire packet is read into buffer memory. This is done in an attempt to reduce the time required to forward a frame, called *forwarding latency*. All IEEE 802.1D compliant switches operate in store-and-forward mode, in which the packet is fully received into high-speed port buffer memory (stored) before being forwarded.

Switch Management

Just like repeater hubs, switches can be provided with management software that collects and displays statistics on network activity and errors. Most switches include some level of management capability, and vendors frequently provide inexpensive management application software that runs on PCs. This software is used to extract the management information from the switch and display it to the network manager. The vast majority of management packages these days use the Simple Network Management Protocol (SNMP) to provide a vendor-neutral way to deliver management data. Some network management packages based on SNMP protocols can also extract management information from a wide range of equipment, and not just switching hubs.

Another very useful feature for monitoring and troubleshooting switching hubs is a *snoop port*, also called a *span port*. This feature allows you to direct a copy of the traffic from one or more ports on the switch to the span port. A network analyzer can then be placed on the span port to provide more information about network traffic. Vendors have adopted a wide range of approaches to span ports, with different capabilities and limitations depending on the particular implementation. Since a switch filters traffic, you cannot simply install a network monitor on any port of the switching hub and monitor all traffic the way you can with a repeater hub. Therefore, a span port is a very useful feature that can make it possible for you to track down a network problem on a segment connected to a switching hub.

Many vendors also provide support for the SNMP Remote Network Monitoring (RMON) standard. RMON support on each port of a switch allows the network manager to extract useful network statistics on a port-by-port basis. RMON is described in more detail in Chapter 20, *Troubleshooting*.

Switching hub vendors may also provide support for the Switch Monitoring (SMON) standard. This standard is described in RFC 2613, "Remote Network Monitoring MIB Extensions for Switched Networks, Version 1.0," which was published in June 1999.* The SMON standard provides extended facilities for monitoring traffic that flows through switching hubs, beyond those provided by the RMON standard. This includes the monitoring of virtual LANs (VLANs) and tracking priority traffic flows. Both VLANs and priority traffic are described later in this chapter.

Custom Filters

Custom filters make it possible for a network manager to specify frame filtering based on a number of parameters. The range of custom filters supported by

---

* Access to RFCs is provided in Appendix A.

switching hubs varies widely among vendors. Lower cost devices typically won't have custom filtering capability, while higher cost and higher performance devices may offer a complete set of filters that the network manager can set. By using these filters, a network manager can configure switching hubs to control network traffic based on the addresses of Ethernet frames, the type field of the Ethernet frame, etc. Some switching hubs will also let you set filters to look into the data field of the frame and control filtering of frames based on the high-level protocol data carried in the frame. While all of this may sound quite useful, the use of custom filters extracts a certain price in added complexity, the possibility of hard-to-debug network failures, and reduced performance.

For one thing, it can be quite a complex undertaking to set up filters correctly, as well as to maintain the filters that you have in place. As your network grows, you will need to keep track of which switches have which filters in them, and make sure that you can remember how the filters you have set up affect the operation of the network system. It can often be difficult to predict what the total effect of a custom filter may be. The most dangerous filters are ones that are set to look for a certain value in the data field of the frame.

This kind of filter is typically an attempt to control the flow of a certain high-level protocol, by identifying some part of the protocol in the data field of the frame and filtering it. Unfortunately, it's hard to predict what kind of data a frame may be carrying. A filter set up to check for some specific value can end up stopping frames that you didn't want to limit, just because those frames happen to have the same pattern in their data field. A filter set up to trap one set of hex digits at a given location in the data field of a frame may work fine for the network protocol you are trying to control. However, the same filter could be blocking a network protocol you didn't even know existed.

Debugging a failure caused by a wayward filter can be quite difficult. It's usually not very obvious why an otherwise normally functioning Ethernet isn't working for a specific protocol or a certain set of stations. Therefore, you should regard the use of custom filters as something to be done with extreme care. By using custom filters you are effectively placing "magic numbers" in the data link layer of your network, and you may find that they can cause as many problems as you are trying to resolve.

Further, custom filters may cause a performance penalty in a switch, because of the amount of time required for the switch to check each frame against the filters that have been set. Quite often, the use of custom filters is an attempt at greater control over some network interaction at the high-level network protocol layer of operations. In that case, you should consider using Layer 3 routers that operate at the network layer to automatically provide this level of control without having to write special filters.

Congestion Management

A number of proprietary mechanisms have been developed in an attempt to deal with congestion in switch ports.* One approach is called *backpressure congestion management*, in which the switch causes the stations on a congested port to defer their transmissions by asserting carrier on that port. The switch may do this by sending a signal pattern onto the congested ports, perhaps made up of alternating ones and zeroes like a preamble, thereby asserting carrier on those LANs and inhibiting transmission attempts by other stations. This can be done for a period as long as 20 milliseconds (ms) on a 10 Mbps network. This provides a breathing space during which the switch can continue to drain the transmit queue by sending frames on the backbone port.

A vendor-neutral mechanism for use in congestion management on full-duplex links has been developed as part of the IEEE 802.3x standard described in Chapter 4, *Full-Duplex Ethernet*. The 802.3x system is based on Ethernet flow control using PAUSE frames. Although most low-end and small switches sold today operate without any congestion management mechanisms, higher performance backbone switches will typically provide support for the full-duplex flow control standard.

Traffic Management

Managing the priority of traffic flow to direct traffic intelligently through a switch or to favor certain categories of traffic is another special capability of switching hubs. The IEEE 802.1p standard provides support for traffic-class expediting and dynamic multicast filtering.† The 802.1p standard also provides a Generic Attribute Registration Protocol (GARP) that can be used by switches and stations to exchange information about various capabilities or attributes that may apply to a station or switch port. The traffic-class expediting portion of the 802.1p standard provides traffic prioritization in a switching hub, so that certain traffic may be favored for transmission when congestion occurs on a port.

The dynamic multicast filtering portion of the standard provides mechanisms that switches and stations can use to identify which ports to use when forwarding multicast packets. For example, a station can use the GARP Multicast Registration Protocol (GMRP) to signal a switch that the station is interested in receiving traffic destined for a specific multicast group address. In this instance, a multicast-based

---

* A comparison of two congestion management approaches used in switches may be found in *The Use of Carrier Sense for Congestion Control in Half-Duplex Switched LANs*, by Rich Seifert, August 1996. A copy of this paper is located at: *http://www.bellereti.com/ethernet/papers.html.*

† The 802.1p standard is part of the latest revision of the 802.1D standard, published in 1998.

application on the station would use GMRP to interact with the switch port, and indicate which multicast traffic that the station was interested in receiving.

Virtual LANs

Another optional feature of switching hubs is the ability to group traffic flow in a switch into virtual LANs, or VLANs. At its simplest, a VLAN is a group of switch ports that behave as though they are an independent switching hub. This is done by manipulating the frame forwarding software in the switching hub. Consider that, at the most basic level, a switching hub is a special-purpose computer equipped with multiple Ethernet ports. The switching hub software is designed to forward frames to various ports based on a set of rules and a forwarding database. By manipulating those rules, a vendor can change the behavior of the switching hub, to provide such things as VLANs.

If the vendor supports VLANs on a switching hub, then they typically provide a management interface so that the network manager can set which ports belong to which VLANs. For example, we could set up an 8-port switching hub so that ports 1 through 4 are in one VLAN (call it the Green VLAN), and ports 5 through 8 in another VLAN (call it the Red VLAN). These VLANs act as separate broadcast domains, and a broadcast or multicast sent on the Green VLAN will not be transmitted on any ports belonging to the Red VLAN. Therefore, the VLANs behave as though you had split the 8-port switching hub into two independent 4-port switching hubs.

In recent years, vendors have provided many other VLAN capabilities. For example, VLANs can now be based on the contents of frames instead of just ports on the hub. In this mode of operation, frames are passed through a set of filters as they are received on a switching hub port. Filters are set up to match some criteria, such as the source address in the frame or the contents of the type field. VLANs are defined that correspond to these filters, and depending on which set of criteria the frames match, the frames are automatically placed into the corresponding VLAN. In this case, a VLAN is used to create a virtual network based on the frame traffic that meets a given filter criteria.

However, vendors didn't stop there. There are also mechanisms that allow VLANs to span multiple switching hubs. Special proprietary frame tagging mechanisms have been widely used to identify, or tag frames in terms of which VLAN they belong to. Switching hubs that understand these proprietary frame tagging mechanisms can then support VLANs that span multiple switching hubs and their ports.

802.1Q VLAN standard

The IEEE 802.1Q VLAN standard was published in 1998. This standard provides a vendor-independent way of implementing VLANs. The VLAN tagging scheme used

in 802.1Q results in four new bytes of information being added to the frame following the source address and preceding the type/length field. This increases the
maximum frame size in Ethernet to 1522 bytes.

Figure 18-6 shows what happens when the 4-byte VLAN tag header is added to an
Ethernet frame. The original fields of the frame are unchanged, and the 4 bytes of
the tag header are added prior to the Length/Type field. This shifts the original
Length/Type, Data and FCS fields to the right by 4 bytes.

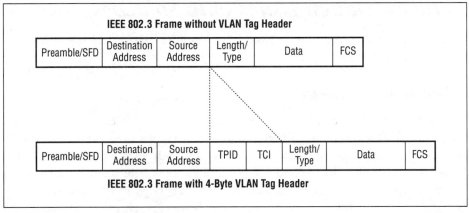

Figure 18-6. 802.1Q VLAN Tag Header

An Ethernet frame carrying an 802.1Q VLAN tag will be 1522 bytes in length if the
frame is also carrying a full 1500 bytes of data in the data field. After extensive
analysis, the standards engineers determined that all Ethernet interfaces they tested
could accommodate the extra 4 bytes of information without any problems. The
change in maximum frame size was specified in the IEEE 802.3ac supplement, and
adopted as part of the Ethernet standard in 1998.

The *Tag Protocol Identifier* (TPID) is a 2-byte field that identifies the frame as a
tagged frame. For Ethernet, the value in this frame is 0x8100 hex, which is a valid
Ethernet type identifier. The next 2 bytes contain the *Tag Control Information*
(TCI). Three bits of this field are used to carry priority information based on the
values defined in the 802.1p standard. Therefore, the 802.1Q standard extends the
priority handling aspects of the 802.1p standard by providing space in the VLAN
tag to indicate traffic priorities. This allows traffic priority information to be sent
between switches using the VLAN protocol. The TCI also carries the *VLAN Identifier* (VID), which is a 12-bit field that uniquely identifies the VLAN to which the
frame belongs.

As you can see, the VLAN approach to manipulating traffic flows through switching hubs can get very complex. VLANs based on arbitrary frame information and

that span multiple switching hubs make it possible for a network manager to link a given station with a given VLAN. This, in turn, allows the manager to "move" stations to different VLANs by using a network management application to interact with the VLAN software on the switching hub. At this point things can become complex enough that the network manager is forced to use a network management application, since there is no easy way of keeping track of which station belongs to which VLAN in which switching hub.

Network Design Issues with Switches

Next, we will look at some other issues that can affect network designs based on switching hubs.

Seven Hop Maximum

The 802.1D bridging standard recommends that there be no more than seven bridges or switches in the path between any two stations in a given LAN consisting of switching hubs. The concern here is that each switch takes a small, but finite, amount of time to forward a frame from one port to another. With seven switches in the path, there are a total of 14 switch hops in the total round trip between sending a frame to a station at the farthest reach of the network, and receiving a reply.

The *seven hop maximum* is an attempt to limit the total delay that can be experienced by an application, based on simulations of application performance and worst-case switch delays. This maximum applies only to single LANs built using switches, and was developed at a time when switches were slower in operation than they are today. The concern was that some time-critical LAN-based applications might experience excessive delays if the round-trip time through a set of bridges grew too large. These days, applications that use Internet Protocols (IP) are designed to tolerate significant delays if necessary, and they can transit large numbers of routers and switches without problems. However, it's still a good idea to design your LAN to limit the total number of switches in the path between any two stations.

Bridging Between Different LANs

Given that a bridge is essentially a special-purpose computer with multiple Ethernet interfaces, it might seem like a simple enough matter to replace one or more of the Ethernet interfaces with other LAN technologies. Then you could use the bridge to link completely different LAN technologies together, such as Ethernet and 802.5 Token Ring. All modern LANs use 48-bit addresses assigned by the IEEE. Therefore, it would seem possible that a switch could be developed that read in a frame from one LAN, and then translated that frame into a different kind of frame for transmission on a different kind of LAN.

However, the task of switching between different kinds of LANs is more complex than it may seem at first glance. One problem is that each LAN system has its own frame format, and each type of frame carries different amounts of data. Ethernet frames may contain a maximum of 1500 bytes of data, while 802.5 Token Ring and FDDI frames may be sent with, say, 4500 bytes of data in them.

In practice, this difference between LAN systems can make it quite difficult for a switch to make everything work transparently at the data link level of network operation. What would happen, for example, if a station equipped with a FDDI interface tries to send a frame with 4500 bytes of data through the switch to a station on the Ethernet? The switch cannot stuff 4500 bytes of data in an Ethernet frame, so it's not a simple matter of translating a FDDI frame into an Ethernet frame. One way to make this work is to set all of your stations on the FDDI ring to transmit smaller frames, thereby losing the advantage of using larger frames on FDDI. Another way to make it work would be to use a router to make the link between FDDI and Ethernet. A router operates at the network protocol layer, and the TCP/IP protocols provide a mechanism for fragmenting and reassembling packets when necessary.

Just to make things more confusing, some vendors provide Layer 2 switches that can do fragmentation for certain high-level Layer 3 protocols (typically TCP/IP). However, these same switches do not support the rest of the network layer services found at Layer 3 of the network specifications. At this point, it's not clear what kind of device this is, since the Layer 2 switch is performing one basic Layer 3 function, but is leaving out the other useful functions that occur at the network layer of operation.

Multiple systems for identifying data

Another issue is the problem of dealing with different methods of identifying which high-level protocols are being carried in the frame. A number of such protocols, including TCP/IP, use the type field when sending frames between Ethernet-equipped stations. The type field identifies which type of high-level protocol is being carried in the frame. However, high-level protocols operating on other LAN systems may use the IEEE Logical Link Control (LLC) system for identifying the protocol type being carried in a frame. Linking an Ethernet station using the DIX frame format with a station on a different LAN system using the LLC format is difficult. You need to translate the type field identifier into something that can be carried by the IEEE LLC fields, and vice versa.

Vendors have managed to build Layer 2 switches that do this in certain circumstances. However, translating between frame formats is a difficult task and may not work for all high-level protocols, due to the odd way that some high-level protocols have dealt with the LLC fields. The point is that translation bridging is complex. A translation bridge must deal with the task of making a large network out of dissimilar network systems by somehow translating between various frame formats and protocol encapsulation schemes.

On the other hand, network layer routers were specifically designed for the task of building larger networks using dissimilar network technologies. Routers operate at the network layer by unpacking each frame, looking at the protocol packet carried in the data field of the frame, and moving the protocol packet onto its destination by transmitting it onto another network. Because of the way they operate, routers are not attempting to make a system of dissimilar LANs operate like one large LAN. Therefore, routers do not have to deal with the complexities of transparent frame translation that a translating bridge is faced with.

Routers

A router is a device that operates at the network layer, or Layer 3 of the OSI model (see Chapter 1, *The Evolution of Ethernet*). Routers are designed to link many network technologies, and are frequently used in large campus and enterprise networks. At the network layer of operation, you can find a wider range of mechanisms that are designed to deal with the issues that can arise when building large network systems. By operating at the network layer, routers can easily deal with computers attached to everything from slow serial links to high-speed LAN systems.

In sufficiently large and complex networks, and especially networks with multiple network technologies, you may wish to use a router for the advantages that it can bring. Many vendors provide routers with multi-protocol capabilities, making it possible to deal with a variety of high level protocols in a single device. While routers are more complex to configure than switches, the advantages they can provide tend to offset the added complexity of their operation for many network managers.

In operation, a router unpacks the Ethernet frames it receives, and deals with the high-level protocol data carried in the frame. When a router hears an Ethernet broadcast, it does the same thing all other stations on the channel must do: it reads the frame in and tries to figure out what to do with it. Broadcasts from a client station attempting to discover a service on a server station on that network are simply dropped by the router, since it has nothing to do with them.

Therefore, unlike a switching hub, a router does not automatically forward broadcast and multicast frames. Because of this, routers limit the flow of broadcasts and multicasts to the local LAN. This creates separate broadcast domains and protects a large network system from the high multicast and broadcast traffic rates that can occur when you link a large number of stations together with Layer 2 switches. This is a major advantage, both for the reduced traffic levels, and for the reduction in performance problems that can be caused by excessive levels of broadcast packets.

Routers or Switching Hubs?

Although they can both be used to extend Ethernets by building larger network systems, routers and switching hubs operate in very different ways. It's up to you to decide which device is best suited to your needs, and which set of capabilities is most important for your network design.

Both switching hubs and routers have advantages and disadvantages. Some advantages of switching hubs are:

- Switching hubs typically provide larger amounts of switching bandwidth and more ports for lower cost than a router.
- Switching hubs are simpler to install and operate.
- Switching hubs are transparent to the operation of an Ethernet.
- Switching hubs can provide automatic network traffic isolation.

Some disadvantages of switching hubs are:

- Switching hubs do not automatically block broadcast frames. This allows broadcasts to propagate throughout your network and makes all of your stations vulnerable to network software bugs or poorly designed software that generate high levels of broadcasts.
- Switching hubs typically cannot load-share across multiple network paths. However, the various link aggregation protocols can provide some basic load-sharing capabilities on aggregated links.
- When linking dissimilar LANs, switching hubs may drop packets that are too large to forward without special fragmentation software.

Some advantages of routers are:

- Routers block the flow of broadcasts. Routers also have the ability to structure the flow of traffic through a system based on Layer 3 network protocol addresses. This allows you to design more complex network topologies, while still retaining high stability for network operations as your network system grows and evolves.
- Routers provide the ability to link multiple IP networks without packet fragmentation problems.

- Routers use routing protocols that can provide information about paths such as the bandwidth of the path. Using that information, routers can provide best-path routing, and can use multiple paths to provide load sharing.

Some disadvantages of routers are:

- Routers are more complex to configure, and require routing software for each high-level protocol suite that you need to route.

- Routers cannot provide support for non-routable protocols that were designed to work on a single LAN and that do not provide the information required for routing.

These advantages and disadvantages need to be considered when deciding on the appropriate technology for extending your Ethernet system. As always, the network world is in rapid evolution, and things are changing all the time. For example, as fast switching circuits continue to drop in price, vendors are making routers available at lower costs.

Also, the world of switching hubs is rapidly evolving, and switches are being given capabilities that are more router-like. Switches that can base their forwarding decisions on network layer protocol addresses are sometimes called "L3 switching hubs." This is shorthand for Layer 3, or the Network Layer of the OSI reference model that was introduced in Chapter 1. Multilayer switches are now available which combine Layer 2 switching and Layer 3 routing capabilities in the same box. An L3 switching hub can be configured to provide both Layer 2 switching hub services and Layer 3 routing services on a per-port basis. You need to carefully evaluate these approaches to extending networks and decide how well they will fit into your network system, given the requirements at your site.

IV

Performance and Troubleshooting

Part IV describes the important topics of Ethernet performance and troubleshooting. The Ethernet performance chapter describes both the performance of a given Ethernet channel, and the performance of the network system as a whole. The troubleshooting chapter includes a tutorial on troubleshooting techniques and describes the kinds of problems you are likely to encounter with twisted-pair and fiber optic systems.

Part IV contains these chapters:

- Chapter 19, *Ethernet Performance*
- Chapter 20, *Troubleshooting*

19

Ethernet Performance

Performance is an umbrella term that means different things to different people. To a network designer, the performance of Ethernet equipment means the ability of that equipment to operate at the full bit and frame rate of the Ethernet channel. On the other hand, for the user of a network, performance often refers to how quickly the network-based application they are using responds to their commands. In this case, the performance of the Ethernet channel that the user's computer is connected to is only one component in a whole set of entities that must work together to deliver network applications.

Since this is a book about Ethernet local area networks (LANs), we will focus on the performance of the Ethernet channel. Along the way, we will also show how the performance of the network is affected by the whole set of elements that provide application services between computers.

Network performance includes a range of components and concepts. The first part of this chapter discusses the performance of the Ethernet channel itself. We will examine some of the theoretical and experimental analysis that has been used to determine the performance of an Ethernet channel. Later, we discuss what reasonable traffic levels on a real-world Ethernet can look like. We also describe what kind of traffic measurements you can make, and how to make them.

In the last part of the chapter, we show that various kinds of traffic have different response time requirements. We also show that response time performance for the user is the complex sum of the entire set of elements used to deliver application services between computers. Finally, we provide some guidelines for designing a network to achieve the best performance given the type of applications being used, the size of the network, and other considerations.

Performance of an Ethernet Channel

When calculating the performance of an Ethernet channel, researchers often use simulations and analytic models based on a deliberately overloaded system. This is done to see what the limits of the channel are, and how well the channel holds up to extreme loads. Over the years there have been many studies made of an Ethernet channel. The simulations and analytic models used in these studies have become increasingly sophisticated in their ability to model actual Ethernet behavior. Early simulations frequently made a variety of simplifying assumptions to make the analysis easier, and ended up analyzing systems whose behavior had nothing much to do with the way a real Ethernet functions. This produced some odd results, and led some people to deduce that Ethernets would saturate at low utilization levels.

Persistent Myths About Ethernet Performance

Due to the incorrect results coming from simplified models, there arose some persistent myths about Ethernet performance, chief of which was that the Ethernet system saturated at 37 percent utilization. We'll begin with a look at where this figure comes from, and why it has nothing to do with real-world Ethernets.

The 37 percent number was first reported by Bob Metcalfe and David Boggs in their 1976 paper that described the development and operation of the very first Ethernet.* This was known as the "experimental Ethernet," which operated at about 3 Mbps. The experimental Ethernet frame had eight-bit address fields, a 1-bit preamble, and a 16-bit CRC field.

In this paper, Metcalfe and Boggs presented a "simple model" of performance. Their model used the smallest frame size and assumed a constantly transmitting set of 256 stations, which was the maximum supported on experimental Ethernet. Using this simple model, the system reached saturation at about 36.8 percent channel utilization. The authors warned that this was a simplified model of a constantly overloaded channel, and did not bear any relationship to normally functioning networks. However, this and other studies based on the simplified model as applied to 10 Mbps Ethernet appear to have led to a persistent myth that "Ethernet saturates at 37 percent load."

This myth about Ethernet performance persisted for years, probably because no one understood that it was merely a rough measure of what could happen if one used a very simplified model of Ethernet operation and total worst-case traffic load assumptions. Another possible reason for the persistence of this myth was that this

---

* Robert M. Metcalfe and David R. Boggs, "Ethernet: Distributed Packet Switching for Local Computer Networks," *Communications of the ACM*, Vol. 19, No. 5 (July 1976) pp. 395–404.

low figure of performance was used by salespeople to convince customers to buy competing brands of network technology and not Ethernet.

In any event, after years of hearing people repeat the 37 percent figure, David Boggs and two other researchers published a paper in 1988, entitled "Measured Capacity of an Ethernet: Myths and Reality."* The objective of this paper was to provide measurements of a real Ethernet system that was being pushed very hard, which would serve as a corrective for the data generated by theoretical analysis that had been published in the past. The three authors of the paper, Boggs, Mogul and Kent, noted that these experiments did not demonstrate how an Ethernet normally functions. Ethernet, in common with many other LAN technologies, was designed to support "bursty" traffic instead of a constant high traffic load. In normal operation, many Ethernets operate at fairly low loads, averaged over a five minute period during the business day, interrupted by peak traffic bursts as stations happen to send traffic at approximately the same time.

In the Boggs, Mogul, and Kent paper, a population of 24 workstations were programmed to constantly flood a 10 Mbps Ethernet channel in several experimental trials, each using a different frame size, and some using mixed frame sizes. The results showed that the Ethernet system was capable of delivering data at very high rates of channel utilization even when 24 stations were constantly contending for access to the channel. For small frames sent between a few stations, channel utilization was as high as 9.5 Mbps, and for large frames utilization was close to the maximum of 10 Mbps (100 percent utilization). With 24 stations running full blast, there was no arbitrary saturation point of 37 percent utilization, which is something that LAN managers who had been using Ethernet for years already knew, nor did the system collapse with a number of stations offering a high constant load, which had been another popular myth. Instead, the experiments demonstrated that an Ethernet could transport very high loads of traffic among this set of stations in a stable fashion and without major problems.

Figure 19-1 shows a graph of Ethernet utilization from the Boggs, Mogul, and Kent paper.† This graph shows the maximum channel utilization achieved when up to 24 stations were sending frames continuously. The frame sizes range from 64 bytes on up to 4,000 bytes. Any frame larger than 1,518 bytes exceeds the maximum then allowed in the Ethernet specification, but the larger frame sizes were included in this test to see what would happen when the channel was stress-tested in this

---

* David R. Boggs, Jeffrey C. Mogul, Christopher A. Kent, "Measured Capacity of an Ethernet: Myths and Reality," *Proceedings of the SIGCOMM '88 Symposium on Communications Architectures and Protocols*, ACM SIGCOMM, August 1988. Also available as a research paper from Digital Western Research Laboratory, Research Report 88/4.

† Boggs, Mogul, and Kent, "Measured Capacity of an Ethernet," Figure I-1, p. 24, used by permission.

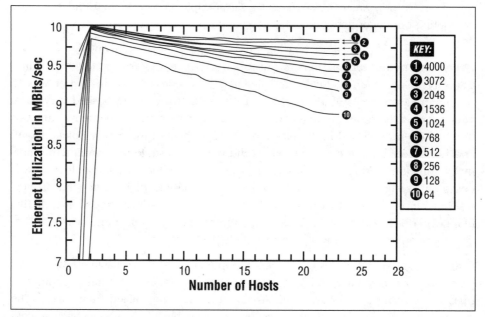

Figure 19-1. Ethernet utilization graph

way.* The graph shows that even when 24 stations were constantly contending for access to the channel, and all stations were sending small (64-byte) frames, channel utilization stayed quite high at around 9 Mbps.

The Boggs, Mogul, and Kent paper also provides some guidelines for network design based on their analysis. Two points they made are worth restating here:

*   Don't put too many stations in a single collision domain. For best performance, use switching hubs and routers to segment the network into multiple collision domains.

*   Avoid mixing heavy use of real-time applications with bulk-data applications. High traffic loads on the network caused by bulk-data applications produce higher transmission delays, which will negatively affect the performance of real-time applications. (We will discuss this issue in more detail later in this chapter.)

Ethernet Channel Analysis

The Boggs, Mogul, and Kent paper noted that some of the theoretical studies had been made of Ethernet performance were based on simulations that did not

---

* The current maximum frame size is 1522 bytes. The change in maximum frame size was made in 1998 to accommodate VLAN information. This is described in Chapter 18, *Ethernet Switching Hubs.*

appear to accurately model Ethernet behavior. Building an accurate simulator of Ethernet behavior is difficult, because transmissions on an Ethernet are not centrally controlled in any way; instead, they happen more or less randomly, as do collisions. In 1992, Speros Armyros published a paper showing the results of a new simulator for Ethernet that could accurately duplicate the real-world results reported in the Boggs, Mogul, and Kent paper.* This simulator made it possible to try out some more stress tests of the Ethernet system.

These new tests replicated the results of the Boggs, Mogul and Kent paper for 24 stations. The new tests also showed that under worst-case overload conditions, a single Ethernet channel with over 200 stations continually sending data would behave rather poorly, and access times would rapidly increase. *Access time* is the time it takes for a station to transmit a packet onto the channel, including any delays caused by collisions and by multiple packets backing up in the station's buffers due to congestion of the channel.

Further analysis of an Ethernet channel using the improved simulator was published by Mart Molle in 1994.† Molle's analysis showed that the Ethernet *binary exponential backoff* (BEB) algorithm was stable under conditions of constant overload on Ethernet channels with station populations under 200. However, once the set of stations increased much beyond 200, the BEB algorithm begins to respond poorly. In this situation, the access time delays encountered when sending packets can become extremely unpredictable, with some packets encountering rather large delays.

Molle also notes that the capture effect described in Chapter 3, *The Media Access Control Protocol*, can actually improve the performance of an Ethernet channel for short bursts of small packets. However, the capture effect also leads to widely varying response times when trains of long packets briefly capture the channel. Finally, Molle's paper describes a new backoff algorithm that he created to resolve these and other problems, called the *Binary Logarithmic Arbitration Method* (BLAM). BLAM was never formally adopted by the Ethernet standard, for the reasons explained in Chapter 3.

Molle notes that constantly overloaded channels are not a realistic model of real-world usage. What users of the network are interested in is response time, which includes the typical delay encountered when transmitting packets. Highly congested channels exhibit very poor response times, which users find unacceptable.

---

* Speros Armyros, *On the Behavior of Ethernet: Are Existing Analytic Models Accurate?*, Technical Report CSRI-259, February 1992, Computer Systems Research Institute, University of Toronto, Toronto, Canada.

† Mart M. Molle, *A New Binary Logarithmic Arbitration Method for Ethernet*, Technical Report CSRI-298, April 1994 (Revised July 1994), Computer Systems Research Institute, University of Toronto, Toronto, Canada.

Figure 19-2 shows a graph from the Molle paper, displaying the effects that channel load and the number of stations (hosts) have on response time.* The chart shows that the average channel response time is good until the channel is seeing a constant load of more than about 50 percent. The region from 50 percent constant load to about 80 percent constant load shows increased delays, and above 80 percent constant load the delays increase rapidly.

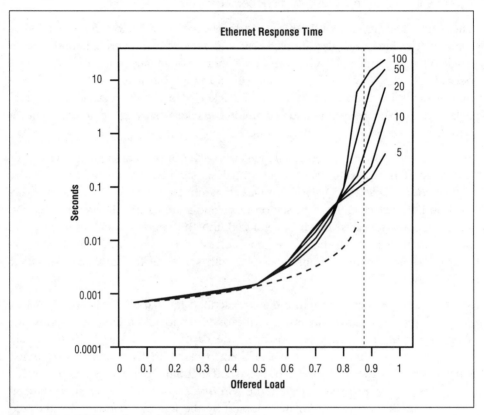

Figure 19-2. Ethernet channel access time

Another element is the variation in channel access times, known as *jitter*. For example, real-time traffic carrying audio information in packets will work best on an uncongested channel that provides rapid response times. Heavily loaded channels can result in excessive delay and jitter, making the audio bursty and difficult to understand. Therefore, excessive jitter will be unacceptable to the user of real-time applications.

---

* Molle, *A New Binary Logarithmic Arbitration Method for Ethernet,* Figure 5, p. 13, used by permission.

The Molle study shows that there are three major operating regimes for an Ethernet channel:

Lightly loaded

From 0 to 50 percent average utilization, measured over a one second sample time. At this level of utilization, the network responds rapidly. Stations can send packets with very low access delays of about 0.001 second or less on a 10 Mbps channel. The response of real-time applications will be acceptable.

Moderate to heavy load

From 50 to 80 percent average utilization measured over a one second sample period. At this point, the channel begins to show larger delays in the range of 0.01 to 0.1 second on a 10 Mbps channel.

This kind of transmission delay will not be noticeable to applications like the Web, telnet, bulk file transfers, or when accessing file servers or databases. However, transmission delays may be large enough for some packets that real-time applications could experience negative effects from variable delay. Short-term traffic bursts into this region should not be a problem, but longer-term load averages at this rate of utilization are not recommended for best performance.

Very high load

From 80 to 100 percent average utilization measured over a one second sample period. At this rate, the transmission delays can get quite high, and the amount of jitter can get very large. Access delays of up to a second are possible on 10 Mbps channels, while even longer delays have been predicted in simulations. Short-term traffic bursts into this region should not be a problem, but long-term average loads at this rate would indicate a seriously overloaded channel.

The lessons learned in these studies make it clear that users trying to get work done on a constantly overloaded LAN system will perceive unacceptable delays in their network service. Although constant high network loads may feel like a network "collapse" to the users, the network system itself is in fact still working as designed; it's just that the load is too high to rapidly accommodate all of the people who wish to use the network. The delays caused by congestion in shared communication channels are somewhat like the delays caused by congested highways during commute times. Despite the fact that you are forced to endure long delays due to a traffic overload of commuters, the highway system isn't broken; it's just too busy. An overloaded Ethernet channel has the same problem.

Measuring Ethernet Performance

Now that we've seen how an Ethernet channel behaves under extreme load, let's look more closely at how to monitor a normally operating channel. Monitoring the total amount of traffic on an Ethernet requires a device that operates in *promiscuous receive mode*, reading in every frame seen on the LAN. Looking at every frame with a general-purpose computer requires a network interface and computer system that can keep up with high frame rates.

Several years ago, most general-purpose computers had a hard time keeping up with traffic on an Ethernet segment. That's one reason why some of the first monitoring devices used on Ethernet segments were designed as special-purpose standalone "probes," dedicated to the task of reading in frames. A network monitoring probe runs continuously in promiscuous reception mode and provides a set of statistics on the performance of the segment. Since the probe has nothing to do but read in packets, it can be optimized for this task. In addition, monitoring probes are less expensive than dedicating a general-purpose computer to monitor each Ethernet system you have.

These days it's considerably harder to monitor an Ethernet system, since many Ethernets are built using segments connected to a switching hub. In the past, it was easy enough to hook a monitoring probe to a coaxial cable media segment to see all frames from all stations on the segment. Also, for systems based on repeater hubs, you can hook a probe to a port on the repeater and view the traffic. However, you can't hook a standalone probe to a port on a switching hub to monitor network traffic. That's because a switching hub uses address filtering to isolate traffic, as described in Chapter 18. Instead, you need to monitor the switching hub itself, or use a monitoring device connected to a "snoop" port on the switching hub. Both repeater and switching hubs are sold with built-in management, which allows you to monitor the utilization and other statistics on each port as well as for the entire device.

One useful method for collecting utilization and other statistics is provided by the Remote Network Monitoring (RMON) and Switch Monitoring (SMON) standards. The RMON standard defines a set of statistics groups, such as the History Group, to provide periodic statistical sampling of performance data. The SMON standard builds on RMON's capabilities by adding a set of capabilities specifically designed for monitoring traffic flows through switching hubs. A repeater or switching hub equipped with RMON and SMON makes it possible for management software running on another computer to extract utilization statistics from the hub over various time scales. Standalone probes equipped with RMON can also be installed on a repeater or switching hub port to collect and report utilization and other data.

Using these monitoring standards, you can extract utilization averages over 5-, 15-, and 30-minute time scales, or any other period you specify to the management software. This makes it possible to produce a set of reports on utilization, to see whether the network is overloaded, and to see how long periods of congestion may last. The RMON and SMON standards are based on the Simple Network Management Protocol (SNMP). Using SNMP-based management software is discussed in more detail in Chapter 20, *Troubleshooting*.

Measurement Time Scale

Before you set out to measure the network load on a real network, you need to determine what time scale to use. Many network analyzers are set by default to look at the load on an Ethernet averaged over a period of one second. One second may not sound like a long period of time, but a 10 Mbps Ethernet channel operating flat out can theoretically transmit 14,880 frames in that one second. A 100 Mbps Ethernet could send ten times that amount, and a Gigabit Ethernet can send one hundred times that amount, or 1,488,000 frames per second. By looking at the load on a network in one-second increments, you can generate a set of data points that can be used to draw a graph of the one-second average loads over time. This graph will rise and fall, depending on the average network traffic seen during the one-second sample period.

The one-second sample time is handy when looking at the performance of a network in real time. However, most network systems consist of more than one network channel, and most network managers have better things to do than spend all day watching the traffic load on Ethernet channels. Management software exists that will automatically create reports of network utilization, and store them in a database. These reports are used to create charts that show traffic over the busy hours of a work day, or the entire day, week, or month.

Since the traffic rate on a LAN can vary significantly over time, you really need to look at the average utilization over several time periods to get an idea of the general loads seen on the network. The traffic on most LANs that support a number of stations tends to be bursty, with large short-lived peaks. Peak network loads can easily go to 80, 90, or 100 percent measured over a one second interval without causing any problems for a typical mix of computers and applications. The frequency of the peak loads will increase as the network traffic increases, but as long as the peaks do not last too long, the people using the LAN will not notice. The longer the period of time over which you average the traffic, the more the peaks and valleys will flatten out to provide a more general figure of load.

Collecting Statistics

Whether you use SNMP statistics from a hub, probe, network analyzer, or a general-purpose computer to look at network load, you need to determine which numbers you want to track. For an Ethernet system, the minimal set of things you might consider keeping track of include:

- The utilization rate of the network over a series of time scales.

- The rate of broadcasts and multicasts. Excessive rates of broadcasts can affect station performance, since every station must read in every broadcast frame and decide what to do with it.

- Basic error statistics, including Cyclic Redundancy Check (CRC) errors, late collisions, jabbers, oversize frames, alignment errors, etc. These error counters are described in Chapter 17, *Ethernet Repeater Hubs*.

- The rate of collisions as a percentage of the packets sent. On a channel that is functioning correctly, the percentage of collisions is of no particular interest, since they occur normally as part of traffic flow on an Ethernet. On a typical channel, the more traffic there is, the more collisions you will see.

   However, very high collision rates on lightly loaded networks could be an indication of trouble. For example, very high collision rates (e.g., greater than 100 percent) as a percentage of traffic sent could be an indication of a failure in the media system, causing excessive collisions or false collision detect.

The time scales you choose for generating utilization figures are a matter of debate, since no two networks are alike and every site has a different mix of applications and users. Depending on how well the application mix tolerates those loads, some sites may be willing to tolerate a much higher load average than others.

Network managers often choose to create baselines of traffic that extend over several time scales. With the baselines stored, they can then compare new daily reports against previous reports to make sure that the channel is not staying at high loads during the times that are important to the users. Very high loads during the work day that last longer than a few seconds, or tens of seconds, will cause unacceptable delays for most users. For example, system backups can take a fair amount of time to perform and place a heavy demand on your network. To ensure that your users have priority access to the network, it's recommended that you perform backups at night, when the likelihood of user traffic on the network being high is minimal.

Constant monitoring also provides evidence of overload that can be useful when responding to complaints about network performance. Given the wide variability in application mix, number of users, and so on, it is quite difficult to provide any rules of thumb when it comes to network load. Some network managers report that they regard network traffic as approaching excessive load levels when:

- Utilization averaged over the eight-hour workday exceeds 20 percent.
- Average utilization during the busiest hour of the day exceeds 30 percent.
- Fifteen-minute averages exceed 50 percent at any time during the workday.

Notice that these recommendations are not based on the three operating regimes derived from Molle's paper. The three operating regimes that Molle studied are based on one second average loads.

An eight-hour average utilization that reaches 20 percent is a heavily smoothed graph, which does not show the short-term peaks. During the business day, we can assume that transient peaks went much higher than 20 percent. More importantly, we can assume that when the long-term average gets that high, the peak traffic loads may have been lasting for long periods, producing unacceptable response times for the users.

There are many ways to generate graphs and reports of network utilization. Table 19-1 displays some raw RMON data collected with an SNMP-based management program. RMON samples are being collected every 30 minutes for the total number of packets, octets, broadcasts and multicasts seen by the probe.

Table 19-1. RMON Data Output

Time Stamp	Packets	Octets	Broadcast	Multicast	Utilization
09:42:10	138243	41326186	882	383	2
10:12:10	161295	51701901	828	397	2
10:42:10	168389	58580988	868	391	3
11:12:10	2775468	559286267	1283	280	25
11:42:10	604774	111504337	1231	275	5
12:12:10	836423	126693664	1218	415	6
12:42:10	164848	59062247	1117	500	3
13:12:10	221535	94692849	1343	980	4

The average utilization on the channel over the 30-minute period is also collected. Notice that during the 30-minute period from 11:12 to the next sample at 11:42, the average utilization was 25 percent. This average is high for such a long period of time in the middle of the workday, and users of the network will probably complain about poor response time during this period.

A shorter sample time would very likely have shown much higher peak loads lasting for significant periods of time, which were causing the poor response times that generated the complaints. The RMON standard also provides a way to look at the "top senders" of data during a given period of time. Now that we know there have been some very high loads seen on this network, we could use the RMON top senders data to locate the source of the overload.

When collecting utilization information, it's up to you to determine what load levels are acceptable to your users, given the application mix at your site. Note that short-term averages may reach 100 percent load for a few seconds without generating many complaints. Short-term peaks such as this can happen when large file transfers load the channel for a brief period. For many applications, the users may never notice the short-term high loads. However, if the network is being used for sensitive real-time applications, then even relatively short-term loads like this could cause problems.

When the reports for an Ethernet begin to show a number of high utilization periods, a LAN manager might decide to keep a closer eye on the network. You want to see whether the traffic rates are stable, or to see if the loads are increasing to the point where they may affect the operation of the network applications being used. The network load can be adjusted by limiting the number of stations supported by a given Ethernet. This can be done by breaking a large Ethernet into smaller pieces with switching hubs or routers. Heavy-duty users or servers may be connected to single ports of a switching hub, moving the congestion to the inside of the hub. In this case, you need a high performance hub capable of handling the load.

Users with very delay-sensitive applications that may also be placing a heavy load on the channel could benefit from full-duplex Ethernet links directly to a port in the switching hub. The full-duplex mode of operation shuts off the Ethernet media access control (MAC) protocol, eliminating any jitter and delay that might result from the use of the Ethernet MAC protocol on a heavily loaded channel. Heavy-duty servers may also benefit from a full-duplex link, since this increases the available bandwidth by allowing the server to send and receive data simultaneously.

Network Performance and the User

The studies we described in the first part of this chapter provide a look at the outer limits of Ethernet channel performance using the original 10 Mbps Ethernet system. Given that single computers can heavily load 10 Mbps channels, most people these days do not try to share a single 10 Mbps channel with 200 stations. Instead, a single collision domain is used to support at most a few dozen machines.

Even the occasional collision domain supporting a larger number of stations is not expected to operate at constant 100 percent loads. The analytical studies and experiments show that an Ethernet channel with a reasonable number of stations will be stable even at high average loads. However, we've also seen that network users may be quite unhappy with the response times they get when a high load is placed on the network for too long a time. Therefore, when designing an Ethernet we need to be concerned about maintaining good response time. The best way to maintain good response is to provide enough Ethernet channels and bandwidth to avoid congestion.

Data Throughput Versus Bandwidth

The analytical studies we saw were interested in measuring total channel utilization, which includes all application data being sent as well as the framing bits and other overhead it takes to send the data. This is useful if you're looking at the theoretical bandwidth of an Ethernet channel. On the other hand, most users want to know how much data they can get through the system. This is sometimes referred to as *throughput*. Note that bandwidth and throughput mean different things.

Bandwidth is a measure of the capacity of a link, typically provided in bits per second (bps). The bandwidth of Ethernet channels is rated at 10 million bits per second, 100 million bits per second, and one billion bits per second. *Throughput* is the rate at which usable data can be sent over the channel. While an Ethernet channel may operate at 10 Mbps, the throughput in terms of usable data will be less due to the number of bits required for framing and other channel overhead.

The numbers we come up with for a 10 Mbps channel can simply be multiplied by 10 for a 100 Mbps Fast Ethernet, and by 100 for Gigabit Ethernet. On an Ethernet channel, it takes a certain number of bits, organized as an Ethernet frame, to carry data from one computer to the other. The Ethernet system also requires an interframe gap between frames, and a frame preamble at the front of each frame. The framing bits, interframe gap and the preamble constitute some necessary overhead required to move data over an Ethernet channel. As you might expect, the smaller the amount of data carried in the frame, the higher the percentage of overhead. Another way of saying this is that frames carrying large amounts of data are the most efficient way to transport data over the Ethernet.

Maximum data rates on Ethernet

We can determine the maximum data rate that a single station can achieve by using the size of the smallest and largest frames to compute the maximum throughput of the system. Our frame examples include the widely used type field, since frames with a type field are easiest to describe. The IEEE 802.3 frame format with 802.2 logical link control (LLC) fields will have slightly lower performance, due to the use of a few bytes of data in the data field that are required to carry the LLC information.

Table 19-2 shows the data size being carried in each frame as well as the *system overhead* required to transmit the data. This overhead includes both the non-data framing fields and the bit times used for the preamble and interframe gap. The non-data fields of the frame include 64 bits of preamble, 96 bits of source and destination address, 16 bits of type field, and 32 bits for the frame check sequence field which carries the CRC. The interframe gap on a 10 Mbps system is 9.6 microseconds, which is equivalent to 96 bit times. Total it all up, and we get 304 bit times of overhead required for each frame transmission. With that in mind, we can now calculate, theoretically, the number of frames that could be sent for a range of data field sizes—beginning with the minimum data size of 46 bytes, and ending with the maximum of 1,500 bytes.

The calculations provided in Table 19-2 are made using some simplifying assumptions, as they say in the simulation and analysis trade. These assumptions are that one station sends back-to-back frames endlessly at these data sizes, and that another station receives them. Another assumption is that there are never any collisions. This is obviously not a real-world situation, but it helps us provide the theoretical maximum data throughput that can be expected of a single 10 Mbps Ethernet channel.

At 14,880 frames per second, the Ethernet channel is at 100 percent load. However, Table 19-2 shows that, while operating at 100 percent load, a 10 Mbps channel moving frames with only 46 bytes of data in them can deliver a maximum of 5,475,840 bits per second of data throughput.

Table 19-2. Maximum Frame and Data Rate for 10 Mbps Ethernet

Data Field Size (Frame Size)	Maximum Frames/sec	Maximum Data Field Bits/sec
46 (64)	14,880	5,475,840
64 (82)	12,254	6,274,084
128 (146)	7,530	7,710,720
256 (274)	4,251	8,706,048
512 (530)	2,272	9,306,112
1,024 (1,042)	1,177	9,641,984
1,500 (1,518)	812	9,744,000

This is only about 54.7 percent efficiency in terms of data delivery per channel utilization. If 1,500 bytes of data are sent in each frame, then an Ethernet channel operating at 100 percent constant load could deliver 9,744,000 bits per second of usable data for applications. This is over 97 percent efficiency in channel utilization. These figures demonstrate that, while the bandwidth of an Ethernet channel may be 10 Mbps, the throughput in terms of usable data sent over that channel can vary quite a bit. It all depends on the size of the data field in the frames, and the number of frames per second.

Network performance for the user

Of course, frame size and data throughput are not the entire picture either. As far as the user is concerned, network throughput and response time includes the whole set of elements in the path between computers that communicate with one another. That set of elements includes:

- The performance of the high-level network protocol software running on the user's computer. Some network software stacks may operate faster than others.

- Overhead required by the fields in high-level protocol packets.

- The performance of the application software being used. For example, some file-sharing applications use less sophisticated network protocols that require the application to keep track of any lost packets and re-transmit data as required. File-sharing performance in the face of occasional dropped packets can fall drastically, depending on the amount of time required by application-level timeouts and re-transmissions.

- Performance of the user's computer, in terms of CPU speed, amount of random access memory (RAM), backplane bus, and disk I/O speed. The performance of a bulk-data transfer program such as file transfer is often limited by the speed of the user's disk drive. Another limit is the speed at which the computer can move data from the network interface onto the disk drive.

- Performance of the network interface installed in the user's computer. This includes the amount of buffer memory that the interface may be equipped with, as well as how fast the interface driver software may be.

As you can see, there are many elements in the total path that delivers results to the user's screen. The question most network managers want answered is: "What traffic levels can the network operate at and still provide adequate performance for the users?" However, it becomes quite clear that this is not an easy question to answer. Some applications require very rapid response times, while others are not that delay-sensitive. The size of packets sent by the applications makes a big difference in the throughput that the applications can achieve over the network channel. Further, mixing delay-sensitive and bulk-data applications may or may not work, depending on how heavily loaded the channel is.

So how does the network manager decide what to do? There's still no substitute for common sense, a familiarity with your network system, and some basic monitoring tools. There's not much point in waiting for someone to develop a magic program that understands all possible variables of network behavior. Such a program would have to know what kind of computers you are using, and how well they perform. Perhaps it would also automatically analyze your application mix and load profile and call you on the telephone to report problems. Until the magic program arrives, you can do some basic monitoring yourself. For example, you could develop some baselines for your daily traffic so that you know how things are running today. Then you can compare future reports to the baselines to see how well things are working on a day-to-day basis.

Of course, Ethernets can run without being watched very closely, and small Ethernets may not justify monitoring at all. On a small home network supporting a few stations, you probably don't care what the load is as long as things are working. The same is probably true for many small office networks. Even large Ethernet systems—spanning an entire building or set of buildings—may have to run without analysis. If you have no budget or staff for monitoring, then you may have very little choice except to wait for user complaints and then wade in with some analysis equipment to try to figure out what is going on. Of course, this has a severe impact on the reliability and performance of your network, but you get what you pay for.

The amount of time, money and effort you spend on monitoring your network is entirely up to you. Small networks won't require much monitoring, beyond keeping an eye on the error stats or load lights of your hub equipment. Some hubs can provide management information by way of a telnet interface, as described in Chapter 17. This makes it easier to monitor the error counts on the hub without investing very much money in management software. Larger sites that depend on their networks for their business operations could reasonably justify the expenditure of a fair amount of resources on monitoring. There are also companies that will monitor your hubs, network devices and RMON probes for you, for a fee.

Network Design for Best Performance

Many network designers would like to know ahead of time exactly how much bandwidth they will need to provide, but as we've shown in this chapter, it's not that easy. Network performance is a complex subject with many variables, and it's a distinctly non-trivial task to model a network system sufficiently well that you can predict what the traffic loads will be like.

Instead, most network managers take the same approach that highway designers take, which is to provide excess capacity for use during peak times and to accommodate some amount of future growth in the number of stations being supported. The cost of Ethernet equipment is low enough that this is fairly easy to do. Providing extra bandwidth helps to ensure that a user can move a bulk file quickly when they need to. Extra bandwidth also helps ensure that delay-sensitive applications will work acceptably well. In addition, once a network is installed, it attracts more computers and applications like ants to a picnic, so extra bandwidth always comes in handy.

Switching Hubs and Network Bandwidth

The most cost-effective way to provide more aggregate bandwidth is to install switching hubs. This provides you with multiple Ethernet channels, and makes it possible to upgrade channels to higher speed operation. Each port on a switch can operate at different speeds, as needed. Each channel connected to a switch is capable of delivering the full bandwidth of the channel to the set of stations on that channel. You can link stacks of repeater hubs to a switch, for example, or single computers can be connected to their own port on a switching hub. Examples of switching hub configurations are provided in Chapter 18.

Growth of Network Bandwidth

Network-based computing is now taken for granted, and virtually all computers in the workplace are connected to networks. More and more people are acquiring computers, and those computers are all being connected to networks. This provides constantly increasing demands for more bandwidth. As sites install more computers, they also tend to install more network-based applications, increasing the demand for bandwidth yet again. Huge amounts of electronic mail are now flowing over the nets. Local sites have come to depend on network-based database applications, file servers, and automated backups of file systems. These and many other applications are leading to a constantly increasing appetite for more bandwidth.

The incredibly rapid growth of the Internet over the last several years has also had a major impact on the traffic flow through local networks. In the past, many computing resources were local to a given site. When major resources were local to a workgroup or to a building, network managers could depend on the 80-20 rule of thumb.*

With the growth of Internet-based applications, network designers are discovering that the 80-20 rule has been inverted. As a result of the Internet and the development of corporate intranets, a large amount of traffic is being exchanged with remote resources. This causes severe strain on backbone network systems, as traffic that used to stay local is now being sent over the backbone system to reach the intranet servers and Internet resources.

---

* This rule stated that 80 percent of traffic on a given network system would stay local, and 20 percent would leave the local area for access to remote resources.

Change in Application Requirements

Not only does the traffic continue to increase, but multimedia applications that deliver streaming audio and video to the desktop are becoming even more popular as access speeds to the Internet increase. These applications can take up a lot of bandwidth, and they place new demands on network response time. Excessive delay and jitter can cause problems with real-time multimedia applications, leading to breakups in the audio, and to jerky response on video displays. It is difficult to tell in advance what the performance of a multimedia application is going to be like. Network managers should plan to test such applications before their use is widely adopted on the network, to see what impact the application makes on the network, and what kind of performance can be achieved under typical network loads.

Multimedia applications are currently undergoing rapid evolution, and it's not clear how heavily these applications will affect the operation of your network. Fortunately, many multimedia applications are designed for delivery over the Web. These applications typically expect to encounter low speed modem connections or other serial connections. Therefore, these applications use sophisticated data compression and buffering techniques and other approaches to greatly reduce the amount of bandwidth they require, and to continue working in the presence of low response times and high rates of jitter. Because of this design, these types of multimedia applications will very likely perform quite well even on heavily loaded campus Ethernets.

Design for the Future

About the best advice anyone can give to a network designer is to assume that you will need more bandwidth, and probably sooner than you expected. Network designers should:

Plan for future growth and upgrades

> The computer business in general, and networking in particular, is undergoing rapid evolution. Assume that you are going to need more bandwidth when you buy equipment, and buy the best performance that you can afford today. Expect to upgrade your equipment in the future. While no one likes spending money on upgrades, it is a necessity when technology is evolving rapidly.

Buy equipment with an eye to the future

> Hardware evolution has become quite rapid, and hardware life cycles are becoming shorter. Beware of products that are at the end of their product life cycle. Try to buy products that are modular and expandable. Investigate a vendor's track record when it comes to upgrades and replacing equipment.

Look for "investment protection" plans that provide a trade-in discount when upgrading.

Be proactive

Keep an eye on your network utilization, and regularly store data samples to provide the information you need for trend analysis and planning. Upgrade your network equipment before the network reaches saturation. A business plan, complete with utilization graphs showing the upward trend in traffic, will go a long way toward convincing management at your site of the need for new equipment.

20

Troubleshooting

The best kind of troubleshooting you can do is no troubleshooting at all, and the best way to minimize troubleshooting is to insist on reliable network designs based on conservative practices. On the other hand, there are a lot of components and devices in a network system, and something is bound to eventually go wrong, even in the best of networks. For those times when your network develops a problem requiring troubleshooting, you need to know how to go about the task of tracking down the failure. There are many ways for things to go wrong in a complex network system. However, the basic approaches to troubleshooting described in this chapter can help you find any problem, no matter how complex the network system may be.

Since reliable network design is the best way to avoid network downtime in the first place, we'll begin this chapter with some guidelines for building a reliable network. We will describe two important pieces of information you will need when troubleshooting: network documentation, and baselines of network activity so that you have some idea of normal traffic behavior on your network. Knowing how to organize the troubleshooting task can help speed the process. Therefore, we will look at the troubleshooting model, including fault detection and fault isolation. These concepts make it possible for you to isolate a problem in any network, big or small.

After looking at the basic troubleshooting concepts, we'll take a tour of the common problems that can be found in the two most widely used cabling systems:

twisted-pair and fiber optic. The information in this chapter is based on years of experience in the field, and on real-world reports from network managers at sites all over the globe. Finally, we look at network operation above the level of cables, and describe troubleshooting based on Ethernet frames and high-level network protocols.

Reliable Network Design

One of the best ways to avoid unnecessary network downtime is to make a special effort to design for reliability. Probably the single most important way to improve reliability is to make sure that your network cabling and signaling system meets all standards, and is correctly built using quality components. Over the years, a number of surveys have found that roughly 70 to 80 percent of all network failures are related to the network medium. The network medium includes the cables, connectors and hardware components that make up the signal-carrying portion of an Ethernet system. Many problems with media systems are due to:

- Improperly installed hardware.
- The use of incorrect components.
- Network designs that violate the official guidelines.
- The result of some combination of the above.

Ethernet is a mature technology with years of proven multi-vendor interoperability. In practice, what this means is that you can buy Ethernet equipment from a wide range of vendors, mix it all together, and expect your system to work well. Ethernet equipment is designed to be reliable, and the network devices you buy from vendors will rarely fail. However, none of this will help you keep your network running if the media system used to link the equipment together is not built correctly. Therefore, the best way to avoid network problems, long troubleshooting sessions, and network downtime is to make sure that your media system is designed and built to be as reliable as possible.

To create the most reliable network, you should:

Design for reliability from the start

Installation of cables and other hardware represents a major part of the expense and effort in any network installation. Once things are installed, they tend to stay the way they were originally built. Therefore, you really only have one opportunity to do things right: at the beginning, when the network is first being designed and installed.

Network reliability is a goal that should always be kept in mind when designing and building a network. Reliability is the result of choosing the network topology that provides the most manageable network system, given your resources.

Don't stretch the rules

Reliability is also improved by choosing quality network components and installing them carefully and correctly, and by resisting the urge to stretch the rules. The specifications contain sufficient engineering margins to allow for some variation between components purchased from different vendors and used together on the same network. However, a maximum-sized Ethernet system is carefully engineered right out to the last nanosecond of signal delay and jitter budget. Nonstandard equipment, overlong cables, and other such kludges can and will cause problems.

Keep your network designs within the official guidelines and you will have many fewer problems with your network as time passes and the system grows and expands. To help you accomplish this task, the official guidelines for the various media systems are described in Part II of this book.

Design for future growth

It's a truism that networks never shrink—they only grow. It can be quite surprising how fast they grow, too. That's why the prudent network designer always tries to accommodate network growth in every network design. You should do this even if present-day users are only thinking about today's needs, and haven't yet thought about how many stations they'll need to support tomorrow. One way to make sure that your network design can be safely expanded in the future is to use only standard equipment in your network, and to carefully follow the configuration guidelines.

Avoid "temporary" networks that can become a permanent embarrassment

It is sometimes tempting to build a temporary lash-up just to get something going until resources can be found to build a "real" network. While this may sound reasonable, it can lead to problems. For one thing, temporary networks have a habit of becoming permanent once users start depending on them to get their work done. Additionally, lash-up networks are usually designed with no thought of future network expansion, making network reliability a real challenge.

Network Documentation

When the network is down, you want to focus your time on troubleshooting the problem, not documenting the network system. Therefore, one of the most important troubleshooting tools that you can provide for your network is an accurate and up-to-date network map and cable database. Network systems are always growing and changing, so network maps and cable databases require constant updating. Even if you don't always update your documentation, having something on hand is much better than nothing when the network is failing and you have to find out where the problem is located.

There are several drawing packages and database systems sold for network and cable documentation tasks. The high-end packages are expensive, since they are typically based on computer-aided design (CAD) software and include a database for handling large numbers of network devices and cable segments. The mid-range drawing packages are designed for smaller networks and are easier to use and less expensive to buy. An easier way to get started is to use the software provided by some hub vendors. These are typically low-end packages that include a limited-capability drawing system for small network maps, and a way to store information about devices and network segments.

Without documentation, you must begin your troubleshooting with the time-consuming task of finding out how the system is laid out, where the equipment is located and where the cables go. To speed troubleshooting, your cables should be labeled to make it easier to track the cables down using the information in a cabling database. Without any labeling on the cables, and without a cable database to list the cables and show how they are laid out, you can spend quite a lot of time hunting for cables and tracing their paths.

Equipment Manuals

Another important set of documents are the equipment manuals. It is often said that the first rule of intelligent tinkering is "Save all the parts." For intelligent networking we can restate this as "Save all the manuals." You should set up a storage place for manuals, and put every manual you receive into it. Even the single-sheet instructions that sometimes come with small devices like transceivers should be saved. Having a complete collection of manuals can save a lot of time when it comes to verifying the correct configuration of a device. It can also save time when it comes to figuring out what the lights on a given device may mean. When troubleshooting, you often need to know the exact meaning of the troubleshooting lights on equipment; this can sometimes be hard to tell without a manual as the labels used for some lights may be very cryptic. Further, some vendors use their troubleshooting lights to indicate multiple things, depending on the color of the light, or whether the light is constantly lit or flashing.

You should always remember that troubleshooting lights that indicate activity such as receive, transmit, or collision detect are artificially stretched in length to make them visible to the human eye. The amount of time the lights are stretched is quite large compared to the speed of events on the network. For example, a single 64-byte frame will take 51.2 microseconds (μs) to transmit on a 10 Mbps Ethernet system. This event is typically stretched to about 50 milliseconds (ms) to make it visible to the eye, which makes the duration of the light approximately 1,000 times longer than the duration of the actual frame transmission. Therefore, you can only use these lights as a very rough measure of activity. If the network is busy, these lights may be continually lit, which might appear to be an indication of overload or excessive collisions. However, there is no way to accurately determine such problems from these lights simply because the lights are designed to be on for an artificially long time to make them visible.

System Monitoring and Baselines

When you are trying to find a problem on a network, it can be very useful to know what the normal traffic patterns and error rates look like on that network. By equipping your network with managed hubs and Simple Network Management Protocol–based (SNMP) probes, and by regularly polling this equipment to determine traffic levels and error levels, you can create a set of reports that can be stored for future use. When troubleshooting a problem, these reports can be consulted to determine what the normal error rates and traffic rates may be.

Network monitoring packages are available that provide regular polling and report creation for networks. Some of these packages can automatically generate reports and provide them over the Web. This makes it very easy to access the information when you need to find out what the traffic and error profiles have been for a given Ethernet system. A few examples of network monitoring packages are provided in Appendix A, *Resources*.

The Troubleshooting Model

When troubleshooting a network, it helps to have a plan of attack. An effective way to go about troubleshooting a network uses a combination of the scientific method and the technique of divide and conquer.

The scientific method of troubleshooting is based on forming hypotheses and testing them. Using your knowledge of the symptoms and of how networks operate, you form one or more hypotheses to explain the behavior you are seeing, and then perform tests to see if those hypotheses hold up.

The troubleshooting model in Figure 20-1 outlines the steps in a scientific troubleshooting process.

1. *Discover the problem.* This is the fault detection stage, in which you are notified of a problem. Notification may be done by automatic fault detection software, or users may call you with a problem report.

2. *Gather facts.* This is a process of acquiring information about the problem. This is rather like the game of "Twenty Questions," in which you ask leading questions to gather information.

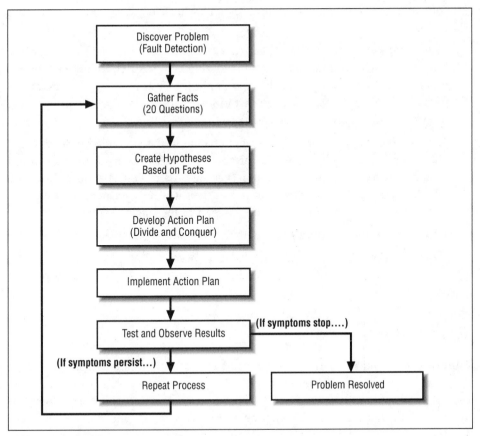

Figure 20-1. Troubleshooting model

3. *Create hypotheses.* Based on the facts you have gathered and your knowledge of how the network functions, you should be able to create one or more hypotheses about the source of the problem. When doing this, you want to make sure that you do not overlook the obvious. Indeed, you want to test the obvious hypothesis first, before spending time on more complex theories. Try to avoid jumping to conclusions, and do not make unnecessary assumptions about the cause of the problem. Make sure that the hypothesis you create can adequately account for the symptoms and other information you have collected.

4. *Develop an action plan.* At this stage, you may have enough information to begin tests of a given device in the network. A test might be as simple as replacing the device with a spare, and then checking to see if the problem was resolved. On the other hand, at this stage you may need to further isolate the problem, in which case your action plan may include some variety of

"divide and conquer," or binary search, which is described later in this chapter.

5. *Implement your action plan.* When troubleshooting a problem, try to make only one change at a time. The goal is to eliminate suspected problems one at a time, to limit the number of things you are trying to test and evaluate at any given moment. This way, you can avoid losing track of the problem by trying to evaluate too many things at once.

6. *Test and observe results.* After making a change in the system, you need to test and observe the results, to make sure that you have resolved the problem. If your action plan was based on a binary search, then the test should show you whether the problem is still active. If not, then it is now located in the portion of the network that you have isolated as part of the binary search.

7. *Repeat the troubleshooting process.* If the symptoms still persist, you need to repeat the process until you have resolved the problem.

To resolve a network problem, you need to know how to go about detecting and isolating the problem.

Fault Detection

Fault detection and isolation are at the core of the troubleshooting process. Once you have detected a problem and tracked it down, then you can resolve it. However, the task of fault detection and isolation can be quite complex. The complexity arises from the number of components in the network, the number of users, and the wide range of applications and high-level protocols that may be used over the network.

Fault detection can cover a wide range of activities. There are some fault detection systems that will send periodic probe packets to your network equipment to test the reliability of your system. If the equipment doesn't respond after a certain number of tries, it is marked as being down and you are notified. This sort of fault detection is often done with large network management applications based on SNMP. It can also be done more informally using locally developed programs and scripts, or public domain software.

For an IP-based network, a fault detection system may use an application called *ping* to send echo request packets to network devices.* When an IP device

---

* The name of the *ping* program comes from the "ping" sound a sonar locator makes when sending sound waves out and detecting objects by their reflection. The *ping* process is much like the sonar system, in that it sends an echo request packet out to a device on the network and receives a "reflection" (echo reply) in response. The story of the origin of the *ping* program can be found at *http://ftp.arl.mil/~mike/ping.html*.

receives an echo request packet, it will send an echo reply, thereby providing a basic reachability test. Many devices equipped with SNMP management software are also equipped with IP networking software and will respond to echo request packets sent by *ping*. A *ping*-based fault detection system can be designed to send a set of *ping* packets to each IP-equipped device on the network. By sending a series of *ping* packets and keeping track of how many are received, the fault detection system can monitor your network and provide notification when a device fails to respond.

The fault detection stage is often performed by a user who calls up to report that they are unhappy with the way an application is working. These calls can be more difficult to sort out, since there are a wide range of elements involved. These include whether or not the user's computer has a properly functioning network connection. They also include whether or not the application is configured or is being used correctly, and whether the user's computer is functioning properly.

The process of determining if there is a fault, and if so, where the fault is located, is somewhat like the game of Twenty Questions. This is a game in which your opponent thinks of something, and you are allowed to ask twenty questions to discover what it is that they are thinking of. In the actual game your opponent must answer truthfully, and supplies simple "yes" and "no" answers. In the network troubleshooting version of Twenty Questions, you are trying to find out what kind of network problem is being reported, and where the problem may be located. Unlike the game, the person reporting the problem is usually not trying to hide the information from you, and is not limited to *yes* or *no* answers.

Still, for many users the network is a mysterious entity full of unknown devices, and their answers may sound very much like the replies to a real game of Twenty Questions. The challenge for the network manager is to come up with a series of questions that can elicit the information required to define the problem and locate the failing component.

Gather Information

Symptoms and complaints can help indicate what the problem is and where it is located. You need to collect as much information as you can, asking the following questions:

- Exactly who is experiencing the problem? Which set of machines are involved, and which network segments?

- Does the problem occur at a certain time?

- How frequently does the problem occur?

- When did the problem first appear?

- When was the exact time of the last occurrence of the problem?

- Has anyone made a change or addition to the network system recently? If so, what was the change and when did it occur?

- Is an error message being generated, and if so, exactly what does it say?

- Is it possible to provide an example of a specific workstation that is having the problem, and a detailed description of what the workstation is doing when the problem occurs? What application is being run? Is there a server involved, and if so which one?

- Can the problem be reliably reproduced?

Fault Isolation

The next stage is to isolate the failure to some portion of the network. When you are involved in isolating a fault on a network, there are several basic approaches you can take. These include determining the network path, duplicating the symptom, and using a binary search to home in on the problem.

Determining the Network Path

There are many components in a network system, and the next task is to figure out which components are in the path of the fault that you are trying to locate. This is where a complete set of network maps and a cable database can save a great deal of time.

If you are on the trail of a problem in connectivity between a set of workstations, or between a client and a server, then you need to know what the network path between those elements looks like. This includes the cable segments, and any repeater hubs, switches, routers, etc., that might be involved. Consider a set of three workstations on a given network channel that cannot communicate with the rest of the world, while three other workstations on that same channel are still able to talk to one another. In this case, you need to find out exactly what the channel consists of. In doing so, you may discover that there are two repeater hubs involved. If so, the repeater hub supporting the three workstations that can no longer communicate probably has a faulty connection to the rest of the network. Here, your solution is easy: simply fix the faulty repeater connection. If the workstations in that channel are then able to communicate, your problem has been resolved.

At one level, a problem such as the one we've just described can look very mysterious. Echo packets can be sent to and received from three workstations on that network channel with no problems, while three other stations on the same channel do not respond. Meanwhile, if you log into the console of one of the "failing" workstations, you will find that it is operational and can communicate with the other two workstations that are also out of contact with the rest of the network. All of this can seem quite odd at first, since all six workstations are on the "same" network segment. Unless you happen to know that the three failing workstations are on their own repeater hub, this sort of thing can lead to a fair amount of head scratching. Only when you know that there are multiple repeater hubs involved does it become clear that there must be some problem with connectivity between one of the hubs and the rest of the network system.

Duplicating the Symptom

If the symptom can be easily duplicated, such as the solid lack of connectivity for the three workstations mentioned above, then troubleshooting the problem can proceed rapidly. However, if the problem is intermittent, it can be much more difficult to figure out what may be going wrong. Solid failures at least give you something to work with, so that you can alter various conditions in the network and then retest the system to see if the failure has gone away.

With an intermittent failure, you are faced with a very difficult troubleshooting situation. In this case, you may need to bring some more sophisticated tools to bear. You may wish to install a Remote Network Monitoring (RMON)–equipped network probe to monitor the loads and error statistics on the network segment. The RMON probe may be able to collect enough information to determine the location of the problem. Some problems only seem to occur when the network is heavily loaded. In that case, you may want to use a network analyzer to inject an artificially high load on the network segment to see if you can replicate the reported failure. This is probably best done during off-hours when people are not trying to use the network to get their work done.

Binary Search Isolation

A major troubleshooting tool is the "divide and conquer" approach, which is more formally known as the *binary search*. A binary search isolates the problem through a process of repeatedly cutting the problem area in half, then testing to see if the remaining network is functioning normally. You start the binary search by disconnecting, or otherwise isolating, one-half of the network and then testing the remaining half to see if the problem still exists. This locates the problem on one particular half of the network. Once located, you split the malfunctioning portion of the network in half again, and so on in an effort to reduce the number of possible network sections that could contain the fault.

Depending on how it is done, a binary search can be disruptive, which may limit its usefulness. If a network is solidly down, you may have very little choice but to perform a binary search to isolate the failing portion of the network. For networks that are still functioning but exhibiting some problem, you may want to come in during off-hours to perform a binary search, reducing the impact on the users.

The goal of a binary search is to quickly isolate the failing portion of the network so that you can do more intensive tests to find the failing component. The value of a binary search is that it is the quickest way to find a failing component in a large system. Mathematics tells us that a binary search can find a single component in a system of 1,048,576 components using only 20 tests. However, in the real world, things aren't this simple. For one thing, the speed with which you can perform a binary search depends on how much information you have about the network. Again, a well-documented network is much easier to troubleshoot than one that has little or no documentation at all.

For best results with a binary search, you need to be looking for a solid failure. Each time you split the network system in half you need to test the remaining half to see whether the problem still exists. If the problem is intermittent, it can be very difficult to tell if you are making any progress in the binary search. Even with a solid failure, you cannot resolve the problem if you lose track of where it is. Each time you divide the network in half, you need to thoroughly test each half to make sure that the problem still exists, or is gone and presumably is on the isolated portion of the network.

Dividing network systems

How you divide the network depends on the media system in question, and the network components involved. Sometimes you can effectively "divide" a network system by installing a bridge or switching hub. This can help isolate cabling and signal errors to the collision domain on one side of the hub or the other.

Twisted-pair and fiber optic media systems based on repeater and switching hubs can be easy to divide into sections. A binary search can often be performed simply by reconfiguring hubs. To do this, you need to investigate the layout of the equipment before conducting a binary search. Then, by shutting off certain hubs and/or changing the connection points of cables in the system, you can perform a binary search to isolate a problem.

Long coaxial cable systems present a much more difficult problem. To do a binary search, you often must divide these systems by segmenting the cable. You can start at the middle of the cable, break the cable at that point, and install terminators on the two ends of the cable that are exposed. This is much easier to do on a thick coax system if you have already installed a barrel connector in the middle of the cable. The barrel connector allows you to simply unscrew the coax cable connections and install a terminator on the two cable ends.

If barrel connectors don't already exist, then you have to cut the cable and install new connectors on the cut ends. As you can imagine, this process can take a fair amount of time, during which the network will be completely down. Therefore, you do not want to use this approach until every other means of testing the cable and network system has been exhausted. In any event, once you have segmented the cable, one-half of the system will be isolated allowing you to perform tests to see which half is causing the problem.

Troubleshooting Twisted-Pair Systems

This section will describe tools and techniques used to troubleshoot twisted-pair cabling systems, including a quick tour of the common problems found in those systems.

Twisted-Pair Troubleshooting Tools

The most commonly used tool for troubleshooting a twisted-pair cabling system is the hand-held cable tester. Also called *cable meters* or *pair scanners*, these portable devices come in a wide range of capabilities and prices. A good quality cable tester can provide a great deal of information about your cable system, and can save a great deal of time when troubleshooting a cable problem.

The currents and voltages used to carry Ethernet signals over twisted-pair wires are small and pose no threat to the user of Ethernet equipment. However, the twisted-pair wires used for telephone services may carry large currents and voltages used for ringing circuits or to power circuit repeaters used in high-speed data lines.

Before handling any wire in a cabling system, you should make sure that the wire is not carrying dangerous voltages or currents. Always observe standard safety practices when working on any type of wire, and take all necessary precautions to avoid electrical shock.

Cable testers can be very low-end tools that may only be able to check for the presence of wires on the correct pins of an RJ-45–style connector. While these testers can be handy for a quick "go, no go" check of a cable segment, they often don't provide enough information for thorough troubleshooting.

Cable testers can also be much more sophisticated tools that can provide all the basic wiring checks and can analyze the signal carrying characteristics of the wire pairs in your cabling system. High-end cable testers can also test for electrical noise impulses on the cable, as well as testing the cable for length, to make sure that a twisted-pair segment does not exceed the 100 meter (m) length recommendation. A high-end cable tester may also come with software that enables the tester to download cable test reports to a PC, allowing you to keep an entire database of cable tests and to print reports when needed.

A high-end cable tester can ensure that a cable segment actually meets the Category 5 (or 5e) signal specifications from one end of the segment to the other. If you are using 1000BASE-T twisted-pair Gigabit Ethernet over Category 5/5e cabling, then you need to ensure that your tester complies with the latest testing standards. The testing standards and the Category 5/5e cable standards are described in Chapter 14, *Structured Cabling*.

Testing for compliance with the Category 5/5e signal specifications is a complex task, requiring a number of sophisticated tests to be performed at various signal frequencies. Tests must be made for total signal attenuation at various frequencies, the amount of Near End Signal Crosstalk (NEXT) that occurs at various frequencies, and so on. Accurate testing requires a high quality tester. While low-cost testers may provide a series of basic attenuation and crosstalk tests, for example, they may not be able to accurately determine whether a twisted-pair segment meets all of the Category 5/5e signal specifications.

Common Twisted-Pair Problems

This list of common problems is based on years of networking experience, including information on network failures reported by network managers at many sites around the globe.

Twisted-pair patch cables

Quite a number of problems on a twisted-pair segment can be traced to patch cables. People often attempt to reduce costs by making their own patch cables, leading to a number of different failure modes. The most reliable patch cables are those which have been built by a reputable manufacturer under controlled conditions using high-quality materials. Even when purchasing ready-made cables, you should beware of very low-cost patch cables, since they may not meet the cable specifications, or they may be made from inexpensive materials that can result in a loss of signal quality. Problems to look for with patch cables include:

Incorrect wire type

Patch cords should be built using stranded conductor wire. Using solid conductor wire in a patch cable is a serious mistake, since it cannot withstand bending or twisting. Eventually a solid conductor will crack, usually right at the RJ-45–style connector on the end of the cable. This leads to intermittent connections, or to open connections on one or more wires that can cause several kinds of problems, including increased bit error rates (Cyclic Redundancy

Check, or CRC, errors) and slow network performance. Worse yet, many RJ-45 plugs were designed for stranded conductor wire. If used incorrectly on solid conductor cable, these plugs will cut through the solid conductor, virtually guaranteeing an intermittent connection.

Patch cables for 1000BASE-T Gigabit Ethernet require high quality stranded cable (and high quality connectors) for best performance. Gigabit Ethernet sends signals on all four pairs at high rates, and this intense signaling requires high quality cable to avoid signal errors. Make sure to use the best quality patch cables you can find for Gigabit Ethernet links.

Incorrect cable type

A common mistake in 10BASE-T systems is to use a telephone-grade patch, or "silver satin," cable to make the connection between an RJ-45 socket in the wall and an Ethernet interface in a computer. Although these cables have stranded wires in them, the stranded wires are typically very thin and are not twisted together, leading to high signal loss and large amounts of signal crosstalk.

While a silver satin patch cable may seem to work in a 10BASE-T system, the twisted-pair segment will be experiencing signal errors, causing the network applications to retransmit lost packets, which eventually leads to complaints about slow network performance. Silver satin cables should never be used to make a connection to a standard 10BASE-T transceiver. Silver satin cables will typically fail to work at all for Fast Ethernet systems.

Incorrectly wired patch cable

Homemade cables may be incorrectly wired, which is something that can be tested with a cable tester. A cable tester can provide a "wire map" of a cable, showing which wires are connected to which pins. This can detect whether the cable has a split pair problem, in which the correct pairing of the wires in the cable is not maintained.

Another problem is homemade patch cords made using a four-pair cable, but with only two pairs (four wires) crimped into place on the connectors at each end. This is sometimes done since several Ethernet media types only need connections on pins 1, 2, 3, and 6. The other four wires are then cut off flush with the end of the cable before the RJ-45–style connector is installed. This sort of cable can cause high bit error rates on Fast Ethernet segments. Even if you are not using the other four wires in a cable, all four pairs (eight wires) should be properly terminated in the RJ-45–style connector for best results.

50-pin connectors and hydra cables

A number of 10BASE-T hubs come with 50-pin connectors to conserve space on the hub. This requires the use of 25-pair cables, to make a connection between the hub and the wire termination equipment in a wiring closet. Sometimes a building cabling system will use 50-pin connectors, but the hub equipment will have individual RJ-45–style connectors on it. In this case, a *hydra*, or *octopus*, cable may be used. A hydra cable has a 50-pin connector on one end connected to a short length of 25-pair cable, which is then broken out as a set of 12 smaller cables each equipped with an RJ-45 connector. Things to look for with hydra cables and 50-pin connectors include:

Loose 50-pin connectors

The 50-pin connector is not standardized, and connection methods vary. Some vendors use locking clips or Velcro straps, some equip their connectors with screws, and some have a combination of clips and screws. If not solidly locked down, the 50-pin connector can come loose, often at one end, while still remaining on the hub. A quick glance might indicate the connector is in place, but might not reveal that the connector is slightly loose at one end, causing an interruption in service or intermittent service to some ports. Always make sure these connectors are firmly in place and locked down.

Multiple disturber crosstalk in hydra cables and 25-pair cables

For 10BASE-T systems, Near End Crosstalk (NEXT) causes the most problems. NEXT occurs when a signal is coupled from a transmitting wire pair into a receive wire pair at the end nearest the transmitter, since that's where the signal is strongest. A typical four-pair twisted-pair cable will support one, or at most two, 10BASE-T connections. However, 25-pair cables and hydra cables are typically used to support multiple 10BASE-T connections. When all of these connections are simultaneously active, it is possible for the multiple signals on the transmit pairs (multiple disturbers) to couple into receive pairs of the cable, causing increased crosstalk and bit errors. This can be difficult to troubleshoot, since it may only occur when most of the wire pairs are active. Testing this is also difficult, since it requires test equipment that can activate all transmit pairs while testing for crosstalk on the receive pairs.

Twisted-pair segment cabling

Twisted-pair patch cables and 50-pin connectors are found on the ends of a twisted-pair segment. However, most of the twisted-pair cable in a given segment is in the 90 m of cable that travels between the telecommunications closet and the work area in a structured cabling system. This is the cable that gets routed through ceilings and walls, and is terminated at each end with an RJ-45–style jack. Things to look for in a twisted-pair segment include:

Excessive amount of untwisting at the wire termination points

For a segment to meet Category 5 signal specifications, it must have low levels of signal crosstalk. Crosstalk is reduced when the wires in each pair are tightly twisted together. If the two wires in each wire pair are untwisted too far when the wires are installed in a wire termination point, then excessive crosstalk can result, leading to signal errors on the segment. A high quality cable tester can determine if a segment meets the crosstalk requirements.

Too many wire terminations

An excessive number of patch panels or punch-down blocks on a given segment can lead to problems with signal reflections on the wire pairs of that segment. Each connection point in a cable represents some level of impedance mismatch to the flow of signals, and too many connection points can reduce signal strength and cause signal errors. A high quality cable tester can determine if there is a problem with excessive signal loss or signal reflections.

Incorrect cross-connect wire

In a Category 3 system with punch-down blocks used in the segment, a connection may be made between punch-down blocks using a length of telephone-grade cross-connect wire. If this wire is not twisted and rated for Category 3 operation, then the performance of the entire segment will be reduced. Incorrect cross-connect wires should not be a problem in Category 5 system, since a Category 5 system must use only patch panels and patch cords rated for Category 5 performance in the horizontal link to meet the signal specifications.

Stub cables

An Ethernet system based on existing Category 3 or voice-grade telephone wiring may encounter *stub cables* (also known as *bridge taps*), leading to increased signal reflections and noise on the segment. A stub cable is an abandoned telephone cable leading from a punch-down block to some other point in the building. It may have been installed to support a telephone in an office, and then later the telephone was disconnected. With telephone systems, stub cables aren't a major problem. However, if the telephone cabling is also used to support 10BASE-T operation, then old stub cables may cause signal reflections and increased bit errors. Again, a high-quality cable tester can indicate whether a segment meets the signal requirements for carrying Ethernet signals.

Troubleshooting Fiber Optic Systems

This section will describe tools and techniques used in troubleshooting fiber optic cabling systems, including a quick tour of the common problems found in this type of system.

Fiber Optic Troubleshooting Tools

A fiber optic media segment is based on sending pulses of light over a cable containing glass fibers. Consequently, it does not use electrical signaling and is immune to electromagnetic interference, greatly reducing the number of things that can go wrong. The tools required for splicing and terminating fiber optic cables are expensive, and are typically used only during the installation of a cabling system. Given this, most sites have their fiber optic systems professionally installed, which also helps ensure that the cable installation will be done properly, minimizing the chance of cabling problems in the fiber optic system.

One of the simplest and safest tests of a fiber optic link is to connect a fiber optic Ethernet port or outboard fiber optic transceiver to each end of the cable. If the link light comes on, you can assume the segment works okay. Another simple test is to use an inexpensive fiber optic cable tester based on a light source and light meter to test the segment.

A riskier method is to shine some light into one end of the cable and check to see that it comes out the other end. Shining light down a cable requires nothing more exotic than a flashlight, although there are some flashlights specially made for the task that have a fiber optic connector on them and come equipped with a bright LED source. This makes it easy to connect the flashlight to a fiber optic jumper and inject light into one end of the cable. Since you don't need to hold the flashlight in place, you are free to go to the other end of the cable and check for light.

It can be difficult to predict how the cables are connected together in a large and complex cable system. Therefore, a safer way to look at the end of the fiber in this test is to put a piece of thin tissue paper over the end of the fiber and look for the red dot of light on the tissue. Of course, the light has to be in the visual range for you to see it. Also, you may need to darken the room to see any light through the tissue paper.

Typical FOIRL, 10BASE-FL, and 100BASE-FX transceivers for use on multimode fiber are based on fiber optic LEDs that emit a form of light that is not dangerous to the eye. However, Gigabit Ethernet and other single-mode Ethernet fiber equipment or other network services use laser light sources.

Laser light can damage the retina in your eye without causing any feeling of pain. Beware of looking directly into fiber optic cables, and observe safety precautions when working around fiber optic cable systems.

You should treat all fiber cables with caution, and never look into cables that may be carrying laser light. If you are unsure about what kind of light a fiber optic cable may be carrying, then do not look into it with your eye. Use fiber optic test equipment instead.

More sophisticated analysis can be done with equipment that sends a calibrated amount of light over the link, and measures the exact amount of light loss found from one end of the fiber optic segment to another. This method can help reveal marginal links where the optical loss is high. For best results, you want to keep the loss as low as possible, so that there is some room for the inevitable small loss of light output and receiver sensitivity that occurs with component aging.

Much more sophisticated analysis can be done with an Optical Time Domain Reflectometer (OTDR). An OTDR is an expensive tool that can measure the amount of light reflected by any discontinuities in the cable. This results in a screen display that can provide a good deal of information to an expert user. The information includes a measure of total attenuation on the link, as well as pinpointing the exact location of signal loss. An OTDR can also determine whether the loss is at a cable splice, a connector, or an excessively tight bend in the cable. A professional cable installer will typically own an OTDR, which they can use to evaluate the performance of a newly installed system.

Common Fiber Optic Problems

The following is a list of common troubleshooting problems, based on years of networking experience, and on information on network failures reported by network managers around the globe:

Connectors incorrectly installed

Odd as it may sound, it is possible to operate a fiber optic link with connectors that are not firmly in place, as long as enough light can get across the link. There are a variety of fiber optic connectors in use; some use a bayonet connector, while others screw or snap into place. No matter which connection method is used, if the connector is not firmly seated, it could cause problems.

Fiber optic links may work even though a connector is loose. At some point the connector ends may vibrate far enough apart, or may get dirt or dust on them. When that happens, the light levels will be too low and the link will come to a stop. Therefore, it is important to make sure that each fiber optic connector is correctly installed and firmly seated.

Dirty cable ends

Fiber optic connectors come with dust caps, which must be kept in place until the connectors are used. If the dust caps are left off, the ends of the fiber optic cable inside the connector can accumulate dust, dirt, and oil. This will reduce the amount of light that can get through the cable. Finger oils from touching the ends of the cables are also a cause for reduced performance in a fiber optic segment. Keep all dust caps in place until a connector is used. Before installing a cable, use a fiber optic cleaning pad to remove dirt and oils from the end of the cable.

Component aging

As fiber optic components age, the amount of light a transmitter can send, and the optical sensitivity of receivers is reduced. On very long or marginal links with high loss, this can lead to intermittent failures. One way to troubleshoot this problem is to try new fiber optic transceivers at each end of the link. You can also test the link with a fiber optic power meter to see what the total amount of optical loss may be. This will help determine whether the amount of light carried over this link is marginal.

Data Link Troubleshooting

The next step up from cable troubleshooting is Ethernet frame troubleshooting at the data link layer. Layer 2 of the OSI reference model is the data link layer, which describes how the Ethernet frame operates. Data link troubleshooting involves the statistics that hubs, interfaces and management probes can provide about Ethernet frame activity and errors. Frame error reports can be very useful when tracking down a problem, since they can help you figure out what kind of problem it might be and where it might be located.

Troubleshooting based on frame statistics has two major components, the first of which is collecting the data. This can be done by using a management station to extract frame statistics from devices on your network. The second component is interpreting the data. It is one thing to collect a bunch of frame statistics, but is another thing to make sense of the statistics you have collected.

The task of collecting and interpreting frame statistics varies depending on the number of devices from which you are collecting the data. A given troubleshooting session may include looking at the frame statistics on a single repeater hub, in which case the pattern of frame errors can tell you a number of things about the segments connected to that repeater. Repeater statistics and what they mean are described in more detail in Chapter 17, *Ethernet Repeater Hubs*.

You can also collect frame statistics at regular intervals from a large number of devices on your network. In this case you will most likely drown in data if you try to look at all the individual statistics you collect. Some vendors provide network management packages, which can generate network *health reports*. Health reports only list those devices and segments on which a sufficient number of serious errors have been detected. This can save a great deal of time when it comes to interpreting frame statistics retrieved from a large network.

Collecting Data Link Information

Repeater hubs and Ethernet interfaces located in both switching hubs and workstations can provide statistics and error reports useful for troubleshooting. Ethernet management is not required for normal operations, and management capabilities may be optional equipment on these devices. The management information collected from Ethernet devices is described in a set of Internet Request For Comments (RFC) documents. RFCs are available online, and access information for the management RFCs is listed in Appendix A.

The RFCs on Ethernet management include a set of Management Information Base (MIB) documents. A MIB is used to provide a formal description of the information that can be acquired with SNMP. While the MIBs described in the RFCs are formal documents and are not exactly easy to read, they do provide capsule descriptions of each item of management information that can be provided by a given device. A workstation equipped with SNMP-based network management software can extract management information from repeater hubs, switching hubs, and even Ethernet interfaces in user workstations.

Collecting Information with Probes

A network monitoring probe can be installed on a segment, operating continuously in promiscuous reception mode to provide a set of statistics on the performance of the segment. In the past, a monitoring probe could be directly connected to coaxial cable media segments, but without special hardware you can't easily connect a standalone probe to the middle of a twisted-pair or fiber optic point-to-point link.

To deal with this problem, you can either purchase optional management capability with your hubs, or install a probe on a port of the hub. A probe on a repeater port will automatically see all traffic on the Ethernet channel. To use a probe on a switching hub, you will need snoop port capability on the hub. A snoop port is programmed to copy traffic from other ports on the hub to the snoop port for monitoring or analysis.

Collecting Information with RMON and SMON

The Remote Network Monitoring (RMON) and Switch Monitoring (SMON) standards define a set of information groups that provide management information about the operation of a network. These standards are provided as additional sets of SNMP MIBs. This means that the RMON and SMON standards are simply different ways to structure management information for acquisition with an SNMP-based management tool. A repeater, switching hub, or standalone probe equipped with one or both of these standards makes it possible for a management application to extract all manner of useful statistics over various time scales. The SMON standard was recently developed as a way of extending RMON capabilities when it comes to monitoring traffic flows through switching hubs. As this newer standard is adopted by vendors you will see it become more widely used. Currently, RMON is the most widely used monitoring standard, and that's what we will discuss in detail here.

Standalone probes equipped with RMON can also be installed on a repeater port or switching hub snoop port and used to collect and report a wide range of information. There are currently two RMON standards, RMON Version 1 and RMON Version 2.

RMON Version 1

The first RMON standard is the most widely deployed, and includes a set of nine groups that provide a wide range of capabilities, including:

Statistics
> The statistics group provides roughly the same sort of error information found in the repeater and hub management standards. The statistics group includes the number of packets, including broadcasts, multicasts, and collisions. Errors include CRC/alignment, undersize, oversize, fragments (including runts and short events), and jabber.

History
> This group defines the ability for an RMON agent to collect data over several lengths of time, to provide trend analysis. Data are collected in samples, referred to as "buckets." A typical sampling setup might include filling 50 buckets of 30 second sample information, making it possible to provide a trend analysis of 25 minutes. Another setup could include 50 buckets of 30-minute sample information, providing a trend analysis over the last 25 hours. The sample information can include the number of packets, number of octets, number of errors, etc.

Host
> This group contains statistics associated with each host discovered on the network. A list of source and destination Media Access Control (MAC) addresses seen on the network is built, and statistics are kept for all the frames sent and received on those addresses.

Host top n
> This group provides a list of hosts ordered by one of their statistics. The list can show the top senders of traffic, top receivers, top errored frames, etc.

Traffic matrix

This group stores statistics for conversations between pairs of addresses. It provides a count of packets, octets, and error packets sent between pairs of hosts.

Alarm

This group allows a management station to set a series of alarm thresholds. Traffic and error rates are compared to preset thresholds, and a message is sent to the management station when the thresholds are exceeded.

Filter

This group allows a management station to set up filters against which packets are matched. Packets that match the filter can then be used to trigger events, alarms, or packet capture.

Packet capture

The packet capture group allows the packets that match a filter to be captured by the RMON probe to be stored in local memory. These packets can then be displayed by the management station at a later time.

Event

The event group allows a management station to set a threshold for some event, and then a log entry is made on the management station when an event threshold is crossed. An event can be created for any time a packet matches a packet filter, for example, and the event logged with the management station.

All nine groups of RMON Version 1 provide an extensive set of management capabilities. A number of these groups, such as packet capture and storage, and packet filtering, can be resource-intensive. These groups require significant local processing and storage capabilities on the device supporting the collection of information into RMON groups. That's why vendors may only implement a subset of RMON groups on their switching hubs and other devices. Some RMON is better than none, given that the primary purpose of a switching hub is to switch frames, not to monitor the network. Therefore, you may need to purchase a standalone probe with enough memory and CPU power to handle all nine levels of RMON if you want to use the full set of RMON capabilities.

Sample of RMON statistics

Table 20-1 is a sample of RMON statistics acquired from an RMON probe. This probe was placed on a network segment in response to complaints about network performance on that segment. The probe uses the RMON history group to collect statistics every 30 minutes, producing the following display.

Table 20-1. RMON Error Statistics

Time Stamp	CRC	Fragments	Jabbers	Undersize	Oversize	Collisions
10:42:10	0	2	0	0	0	184
11:12:10	2599927	15575	0	0	0	13943
11:42:10	380312	11239	2	0	0	11685
12:12:10	661786	4533	0	6	0	2881
12:42:10	0	2	0	0	0	90

Notice that the rate of CRC errors suddenly jumps very high in the half-hour periods from 10:42 to 11:12, from 11:12 to 11:42, and from 11:42 to 12:12, after which everything returns to normal. Network performance during that period was unacceptable to the users. Now that we've discovered that there are high error rates, we need to further isolate the problem to see if we can find a single port or device that is generating the errors.

There are several things we can do to further isolate the problem. For example, if the repeater or switching hubs at this site provide statistics, we could look at the ports of the hubs for high error rates. This way we can narrow down the location of the device (or devices) causing the problem. Another approach might be to use our network management software to set some alarms or event thresholds in the RMON probe. We could set the RMON probe to trigger an alarm when CRC errors increase, and to provide a list of top 10 Ethernet traffic generators at that time. This would help us narrow the search for the problem device.

RMON Version 2

The RMON Version 2 standard adds a set of more sophisticated analysis capabilities to the base set of RMON groups. These analysis capabilities include the ability to analyze high-level protocol data to see traffic rates and distribution at the network layer of operations, or Layer 3 of the OSI reference model. The added RMON Version 2 groups include address mapping between Ethernet MAC addresses on stations and their high-level network protocol addresses. They also include traffic statistics by application layer protocol for each network layer address, traffic statistics for network layer addresses, and so on. These extended RMON capabilities make it possible for network management applications to provide information on web traffic distribution, database accesses, email traffic, and many other applications.

Network Layer Troubleshooting

Network layer troubleshooting refers to Layer 3 of the OSI reference model, which describes the operations of high-level network protocols. Network layer troubleshooting includes statistics on high-level network protocol operations, network applications like email, etc.

Network layer analysis can be done using RMON Version 2 probes in conjunction with network analysis software. Another network layer tool is the *protocol analyzer*, which is a device that can capture packets and display the network layer protocols carried in those packets. A protocol analyzer provides a way to look at network operation above the data link layer.

Network layer analysis requires a knowledge of network layer protocols and how they operate, as well as high-level applications and how they function. Since there are a number of network layer protocols, there is quite a lot of information to cover at this layer of network operations. There are also a very wide range of applications that use those protocols to send data to one another over various network links, including Ethernet.

A description of network layer operations and analysis is beyond the scope of this book. You should be aware, however, that there are a number of network layer analyzers. These analyzers can provide information about the operation of the data link layer as well. Depending on the complexity of your network, you may want to invest in a network layer analysis tool to help troubleshoot problems that may be occurring between applications that run over the network.

It is not uncommon to encounter complaints about poor network performance even though the Ethernet data link channel is running fine and is not exhibiting any overloads. Applications such as client/server databases may be functioning slowly because the server is overloaded, improperly configured, or for any number of other reasons that have nothing to do with the operation of the Ethernet channel. Some high-level analyzers provide an expert analysis mode that can find and flag problems at the network and application layers, such as excessive network protocol retransmissions causing reduced performance.

V

Appendixes

The final part of this book includes a list of resources for further information and a description of the thick and thin coaxial media systems. Also included is a guide to AUI equipment installation and configuration.

Part V contains these appendixes:

- Appendix A, *Resources*
- Appendix B, *Thick and Thin Coaxial Media Systems*
- Appendix C, *AUI Equipment: Installation and Configuration*

A

Resources

The following resources may be consulted for further information. Resources are listed here as examples only, and no endorsement is implied of any particular company or software package. Many of the items listed here are online references available on the World Wide Web.

AUI Slide Latch Retainer

The 15-pin AUI slide latch retainer mentioned in Appendix C, *AUI Equipment: Installation and Configuration*, is a small plastic locking device that can help keep an AUI connector slide latch in place.

- AUI slide latch retainers are available as a product called ET-Lock, provided by the A 'n D Cable Products company. They are available from the manufacturer at *http://www.andcable.com/*.

Buyer's Guides

When it comes to finding Ethernet products, a useful source of information is the buyer's guide. Several of the major computer magazines and networking trade journals listed below publish short buyer's guides based on a specific product that they are evaluating. Annual buyer's guides are also published by several networking magazines, which list hundreds of vendors and thousands of products. The following are a few of the magazines which publish buyer's guides:

Data Communications
Publishes an annual networking directory (*http://www.data.com/directory/*).

Network Magazine

> Publishes a magazine dedicated to networking (*http://www.networkmagazine.com/*).

PC Magazine

> Publishes equipment review articles and buyer's guides (*http://www.zdnet.com/pcmag/*).

The Silicon Valley Networking Lab

> Provides access to some of their test reports on Ethernet equipment (*http://www.svnl.com/*).

Cable and Connector Suppliers

There are many cable and connector suppliers. This list provides a sample of a few major companies. These web sites can provide a considerable amount of information about structured cabling and connectors.

AMP

> A major supplier of connectors (*http://www.amp.com/*).

Anixter

> Cable and connector distributor *(http://www.anixter.com/)*.

Belden Cable

> A major supplier of coaxial cable built to Ethernet standards, twisted-pair cables, and many other kinds of cables (*http://www.belden.com/*).

Hubbell Premise Wiring

> A supplier of structured cabling components (*http://www.hubbell-premise.com/*).

Molex Premises Network (formerly Mod-Tap)

> A supplier of structured cabling components (*http://www.mod-tap.com/*).

Panduit

> A supplier of structured cabling components (*http://www.panduit.com/*).

Siecor

> A supplier of fiber optic cabling and components (*http://www.siecor.com/*).

Siemon

> A supplier of structured cabling components (*http://www.siemon.com/*).

Cable Testers

Hand-held cable testers are widely used for testing twisted-pair and fiber optic cabling systems. The following list provides access to several vendors of hand-held cable testers. This list should be considered incomplete, and no endorsement of any tester is implied by inclusion in this list.

Fluke
> *http://www.fluke.com/nettools/*

Hewlett Packard/Scope
> *http://www.scope.com/*

Microtest
> *http://www.microtest.com/*

Wavetek Wandel Goltermann
> *http://www.wwgsolutions.com/*

Cabling Information

These web sites provide information on cable testing issues and cabling systems. The web sites for hand-held cable testers are also a good source for cable testing and cabling standards information.

Cabling Design
> This site provides tutorials and other cabling information (*http://www.cabling-design.com/*).

Cabletesting.com
> This site, which provides cable testing information, is associated with the Microtest company (*http://www.cabletesting.com/*).

Ethernet Jumbo Frames

One Gigabit Ethernet vendor has developed a proprietary system of sending over-sized Ethernet frames, called *jumbo frames*, to increase throughput on high-speed Ethernet links. While the use of jumbo frames has been adopted by some other vendors, there is no official IEEE standard for jumbo frames and therefore no way to guarantee interoperability. The following URLs provide access to some documentation on jumbo frames, and to an IETF draft document on jumbo frame encapsulation:

- The Alteon products listing page, which provides a link to jumbo frame information, available at *http://www.alteon.com/products/.*

- An IETF draft document on jumbo frame encapsulation, available on the Web at *http://search.ietf.org/internet-drafts/draft-kaplan-isis-ext-eth-ip-clns-2-00.txt.*

Ethernet Media Converters

As their name implies, media converters are used to convert from one Ethernet media type to another. These devices can come in handy when you need to connect equipment that operates at the same Ethernet speed, but supports different Ethernet media types. They can also be used to provide an extended-distance link. A number of vendors provide media converters. The following brief list is necessarily incomplete, and no endorsement is implied by inclusion in the list.

Allied Telesyn
> Provides a full line of Ethernet equipment as well as media converters (*http://www.alliedtelesyn.com/*).

Canary Communications
> Provides a wide range of media converters (*http://www.canarycom.com/*).

IMC Networks
> Provides media converter products, some of which include SNMP management (*http://www.imcnetworks.com/*).

Transition Networks
> Provides a range of products to convert copper media to fiber optic (*http://www.transition.com/*).

Ethernet Vendor Codes

The first 24 bits of the MAC address contains the *organizationally unique identifier* (OUI), which is assigned to a vendor by the IEEE. That information, in turn, can be useful when it comes to tracking down misbehaving stations. Each manufacturer of Ethernet interfaces acquires a unique OUI from the IEEE, which is then used to create a unique 48-bit address that gets assigned to each interface the manufacturer builds.

If you know the manufacturer's OUI number (vendor code), you can use that number to identify which computer may be causing network problems. This is not a foolproof mechanism, however, since some vendors may buy their boards from other manufacturers. Networking vendors may also acquire other vendors, at which point the OUI belongs to the new owner.

List of OUIs Maintained by the IEEE

The IEEE maintains a public list of vendor OUIs. The only OUIs listed by the IEEE are ones that vendors give them permission to publish. A vendor may regard the number of OUIs it has requested as competitive information that they would prefer not to have revealed, in which case you will not find that vendor's OUI on the

IEEE list. The IEEE also provides instructions for acquiring an OUI. This information can be found at *http://standards.ieee.org/regauth/oui/index.html/*.

List of OUIs Compiled by Volunteers

A more complete online list of OUIs has been compiled by Michael Patton with the help of volunteers from all over the world. This list also contains Ethernet type field identifiers and other information. The list can be found at *http://www.cavebear.com/CaveBear/Ethernet/*.

Ethernet Web Site

In my abundant free time, I maintain a web site for Ethernet information. A wide range of Ethernet resources may be found on this site, including an online reference guide to Ethernet media systems. The Ethernet web site also includes technical papers on Ethernet and pointers to other web pages with Ethernet information, and is available at *http://www.bellereti.com/ethernet/ethernet.html*.

FAQs on Cabling and Ethernet

Frequently Asked Questions (FAQ) lists can be useful repositories of much needed information. A FAQ typically consists of a set of questions and answers posted on network and mailing list forums and accumulated into a FAQ by one or more volunteers. The Internet FAQ Archive provides access to a variety of FAQs. The archive may be found at *http://www.faqs.org/faqs/*.

Since FAQs are a volunteer effort, the quality can vary considerably. FAQs may contain much that is useful; they may also contain out-of-date, inaccurate, or incorrect information.

- A FAQ for LAN cabling issues may be found at *http://www.faqs.org/faqs/LANs/cabling-faq/*.

- A FAQ for Ethernet issues is available. Be aware that a number of items in this FAQ are incorrect. The Ethernet FAQ may be found at *http://www.faqs.org/faqs/LANs/ethernet-faq/*.

Network Analyzers

There are many network analyzer products available, and it is impossible to list them all, or even to list a representative sample. The following references are provided as an example of what a couple of widely used network analyzer products look like and what they include.

- The Network Associates Sniffer can be found at *http://www.nai.com/asp_set/ products/tnv/intro.asp*.

- The Shomiti Systems Surveyor can be found at *http://www.shomiti.com/*.

Networking Magazines and Trade Journals

There are a number of magazines and trade journals that cover networking issues and that provide a guide to the networking marketplace. Several of these magazines and journals provide tutorials and technical articles that are a useful source of information on a wide range of networking topics.

A few of the more LAN-oriented magazines and trade journals are listed here. Most of the trade journals are not for sale. Instead, you can request a free qualification form, and if you are employed in the field or otherwise involved in networking, you may qualify for a free subscription.

InfoWorld
Weekly tabloid, available free to qualified subscribers (*http://www.infoworld. com/*).

InternetWeek
Weekly tabloid, available free to qualified subscribers (*http://internetwk.com/*).

Network Magazine
Monthly magazine, available by subscription (*http://www.networkmagazine. com/*).

Network World
Weekly tabloid, available free to qualified subscribers (*http://www.nwfusion. com/*).

Network Management Information

The following resources can be consulted for further information on network management issues.

The Cooperative Association for Internet Data Analysis (CAIDA)
This site provides access to a wide range of tools used for network management (*http://www.caida.org/Tools/taxonomy.html*).

MRTG
MRTG is a widely used public domain software package that uses SNMP to monitor network equipment. MRTG data is used to generate a set of graphs which can be viewed with a web browser. You can find the MRTG homepage at *http://ee-staff.ethz.ch/~oetiker/webtools/mrtg/mrtg.html*.

Netperf

Netperf is a public domain application that can stress-test a network with high data rates as well as provide network performance information. Netperf runs on Unix and Windows computers. A copy may be found at *http://www.netperf.org/netperf/NetperfPage.html.*

The Network Operation Center On-Line (NOCOL)

The NOCOL public domain software package runs on Unix systems and provides fault detection of network devices based on IP *ping* and many other protocols. A copy may be found at *http://www.netplex-tech.com/software/nocol/.*

Simple Network Management Protocol (SNMP)

SNMP software and information can be found at *http://www.snmp.cs.utwente.nl/.*

Requests for Comments (RFCs)

When an official standard is developed for the Internet Protocol (IP), it is published in a numbered document called a Request for Comments (RFC). RFCs can be found at *http://www.rfc-editor.org/.*

There are several RFCs that define SNMP MIBs which describe Ethernet devices. You can find the formal description of the frame errors and other statistics being collected in these documents. Some Ethernet RFCs of interest include:

- RFC 1650, *Definitions of Managed Objects for the Ethernet-like Interface Types using SMIv2.*

- RFC 1757, *Remote Network Monitoring Management Information Base.* This is the RMON Version 1 MIB.

- RFC 2021, *Remote Network Monitoring Management Information Base Version 2.*

- RFC 2108, *Definitions of Managed Objects for IEEE 802.3 Repeater Devices using SMIv2.*

- RFC 2613, *Remote Network Monitoring MIB Extensions for Switched Networks Version 1.0.* This is the SMON MIB.

Standards Documents and Standards Organizations

This book is primarily based on the 802.3 IEEE Ethernet standard. However, there are a number of other standards groups and industry organizations involved in networking.

BICSI

The Building Industry Consultants Service International (BICSI) offers a set of informational publications for cabling professionals. The BICSI web site may be found at *http://www.bicsi.org/*.

BICSI offers a course on cabling systems and working with cabling contractors. More information can be found at *http://www.bicsi.org/dd100.htm*.

Fibre Channel Standards

The Fibre Channel standards, including the GBIC standards, can be found at *http://www.fibrechannel.com/technology/tech_frame.htm*.

IEEE Organizationally Unique Identifier (OUI)

An OUI is a 24-bit globally unique assigned number used in the family of IEEE 802 LAN standards: Ethernet, Token Ring, etc. The IEEE Standards Association (IEEE-SA) assigns and manages OUIs. The IEEE-SA web page for listing and requesting an OUI may be found at *http://standards.ieee.org/regauth/oui/*.

IEEE 802.1 Rapid Reconfiguration of Spanning Tree

The 802.1w supplement to the 802.1 standard is being developed to provide faster operation for the spanning tree protocol. The goal is for the spanning tree protocol to complete its dynamic configuration in less time than the 30–50 seconds that are now required. This improves network uptime when changes are made to a network based on switching hubs. The status of the new spanning tree work can be found at *http://grouper.ieee.org/groups/802/1/*.

IEEE 802.3 (Ethernet) Standard

The formal IEEE Ethernet standards are a moving target, since old versions of the standards are continually being updated, and new standards are continually being created. The IEEE standards catalog for Ethernet may be found at *http://standards. ieee.org/catalog/IEEE802.3.html*.

The latest IEEE standard for Ethernet is 1,268 pages long, and is listed in the IEEE catalog as follows:

> 802.3, 1998 Edition Information technology—Telecommunications and information exchange between systems—Local and metropolitan area networks—Specific requirements—Part 3: Carrier sense multiple access with collision detection (CSMA/CD) access method and physical layer specifications.

This edition includes all contents of the 8802-3:1996 Edition, plus IEEE Std 802. 3aa-1998, IEEE Std 802.3r-1996, IEEE Std 802.3u-1995, IEEE Std 802.3x&y-1997, and IEEE802.3z-1998.

Price U.S. $387.00
ISBN 0-7381-0330-6
Product Code: **SH94652-NYF**

Copies of the latest IEEE Ethernet standard may be ordered from the IEEE:

IEEE Customer Service
445 Hoes Lane
PO Box 1331
Piscataway, NJ 08855-1331
(800) 678-IEEE (in the US and Canada)
(732) 981-0060 (outside of the US and Canada)

IEEE Higher Speed Study Group

Now that the Gigabit Ethernet standard is complete, a new higher speed Ethernet standard is in the early stages of development. Details about the speed of this system and the technology to be used in the next generation of Ethernet are being decided in an IEEE higher-speed study group. The presentations and meeting notes for this group may be found at *http://grouper.ieee.org/groups/802/3/10G_study/public/index.html*.

Telecommunications Cabling Standards

The Telecommunications Industry Association (TIA) provides a set of widely used structured cabling standards. This set includes the *Commercial Building Telecommunications Cabling Standard, ANSI/TIA/EIA-568-A-95*. The TIA and access to the standards can be found at *http://www.tiaonline.org/*.

The International Organization for Standardization (ISO) publishes a cabling standard called *ISO/IEC 11801:1995, Generic cabling for customer premises*. The ISO can be found at *http://www.iso.ch/*.

The TIA/EIA 568A cabling standards and the ISO/IEC 11801 cabling standard can also be purchased from Global Engineering. The Global Engineering web site can be found at *http://global.ihs.com/*.

Global Engineering Documents
15 Inverness Way East
Englewood, CO 80112
(800) 854-7179 (U.S. and Canada)
(303) 397-7956 (outside the U.S.)
(303) 397-2740 (Fax)

Other Standards Organizations

Web sites for standards organizations and vendor consortiums include:

American National Standards Institute (ANSI)
  http://www.ansi.org/

Institute of Electrical and Electronics Engineers (IEEE)
  http://www.ieee.org/

Internet Engineering Task Force (IETF)
  The IETF creates engineering standards for the TCP/IP protocol suite, including SNMP management standards for Ethernet. The IETF may be found at *http://www.ietf.org/*.

Electronics Industries Association (EIA)
  http://www.eia.org/

Wireless Ethernet

The IEEE 802.11 wireless LAN standard describes several approaches for sending LAN signals via radio waves. The following web sites provide access to more information on wireless LANs and wireless Ethernet.

- The IEEE 802.11 wireless LAN working group page can be found at *http://grouper.ieee.org/groups/802/11/index.html*.

- The IEEE standard for 802.11 wireless LANs can be found at *http://standards. ieee.org/catalog/IEEE802.11.html*.

- The Telecom Research site provides information on a wide range of wireless technologies, at *http://www.telecomresearch.com/*.

- The Wireless Ethernet Compatibility Alliance (WECA) provides information on wireless equipment interoperability, and can be found online at *http://www. wirelessethernet.org/*.

B

Thick and Thin Coaxial Media Systems

This appendix describes the coaxial Ethernet media systems. These were the first media systems used for Ethernet, and were standardized in the early 1980s. Today, the vast majority of Ethernets are based on twisted-pair and fiber optic media, and coax media is considered obsolete for most uses. However, many coaxial systems were built and a number of them are still in use.

We'll use the same format to describe the coax media systems and cables as do the media and cabling chapters earlier in the book. The first two sections of this appendix describe the 10BASE5 and 10BASE2 media systems. The next section describes how to build and install coaxial cables, connectors, and transceiver taps. The last section describes how to troubleshoot both thick and thin coaxial cable systems.

Thick Coaxial Media System

The thick coaxial media system (10BASE5) was the first Ethernet media system specified in the original DIX standard of 1980. The 10BASE5 media system is limited to 10 Mbps signals, which severely restricts its usefulness as a backbone network, due to incompatibility with higher speed systems. If later you needed to link things together at higher speeds, you would be forced to replace your 10BASE5 media system with twisted-pair or fiber optic cables, depending on the distance you needed to cover.

Rather than go to the trouble of installing a thick coax system only to have to replace it later, virtually all new network installations are based on twisted-pair cabling and fiber optic backbone cables. Nonetheless, thick coaxial cable was the only game in town for a number of years in the 1980s, and older thick coaxial systems may still lurk in ceilings or under machine room floors at your site.

10BASE5 Signaling Components

The following set of signaling components may be used in the 10BASE5 system to send and receive signals over the media system:

- Ethernet interface equipped with a 15-pin AUI connector.

- Attachment Unit Interface (AUI) transceiver cable.

- External 10BASE5 transceiver, also called a medium attachment unit (MAU).

Ethernet Interface

A 10BASE5 interface is typically equipped with a female 15-pin AUI connector to provide a connection to an external transceiver. Figure B-1 shows a Network Interface Card (NIC) designed for installation in a computer.

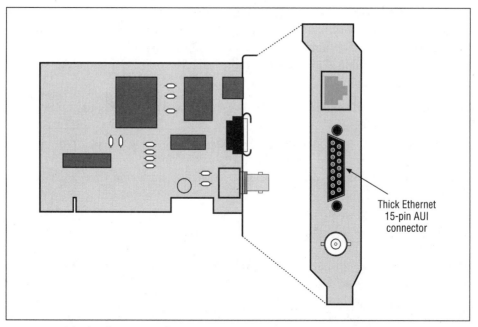

Figure B-1. Thick Ethernet interface

This particular card is equipped with three connectors that allow an attachment to a variety of 10 Mbps Ethernet media systems. The 10BASE5 support is based on the 15-pin AUI connector, which allows a connection to an external 10BASE5 transceiver.

Transceiver Cable

In the 10BASE5 system, the transceiver cable is required to make a connection between the interface and the external transceiver attached to the thick coax cable.

10BASE5 Transceiver

An external transceiver is required to attach a 10BASE5 interface to a thick coaxial cable. Figure B-2 shows a 10BASE5 transceiver equipped with the most widely used cable attachment mechanism, sold by AMP Corporation.

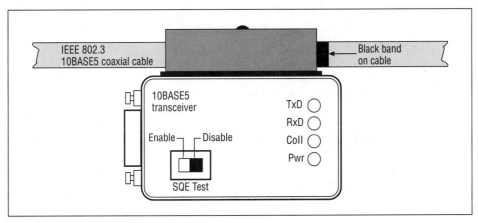

Figure B-2. 10BASE5 transceiver

This attachment consists of a metal and plastic clamp that makes a direct physical and electrical connection to the coaxial cable. This clamp is also called a *transceiver tap*. To install the clamp, you must drill a hole into the thick coaxial cable in a process known as tapping the cable. Instructions for installing a tap can be found in the "Installing Transceiver Taps on Thick Coax" section later in this appendix. Since this clamp may be installed while the network is active, it is also called a *non-intrusive tap*.

10BASE5 Signal Encoding

Signals sent over the 10BASE5 media system use a system called Manchester encoding, which is described in Chapter 6, *Ethernet Media Fundamentals*. 10BASE5 transceivers send and receive signals over a media segment that consists of a coax cable with two conductors: an inner conductor and an outer shield. This pair of conductors is used to send and receive signals. Since a thick coax segment provides a single pair of conductors for the signal path between stations, it can only be operated in half-duplex mode.

Physical line signaling

A 10BASE5 transceiver sends Manchester-encoded signals over thick coax cables by transmitting electrical currents. The transceiver sends two currents: a steady DC offset current and a signaling current that changes in amplitude to represent ones and zeroes. The offset current is −41 milliamperes, providing a baseline around which the signals are sent. The current used to send the actual signals travels through a range of from zero to −90 milliamperes peak-to-peak on the coaxial cable.

The coax cable segment appears to the transceiver as an electrical circuit consisting of the two conductors. The two coax conductors are connected together with two 50 ohm terminating resistors, one at each end of the cable. Two resistors connected in parallel in this fashion result in a circuit with a total resistance of approximately 25 ohms. According to Ohm's Law, the currents sent into this circuit by the transceiver will develop a steady DC voltage offset of about −1 volt, with a signal voltage that ranges from zero to −2 volts.

10BASE5 Media Components

The following set of four media components are used to build a thick coaxial cable segment:

- Thick coaxial cable.
- N-type coaxial connector.
- N-type barrel connector.
- N-type 50 ohm terminator.

Details on thick coaxial cable and N-type coaxial connectors and terminator can be found in the "Coaxial Cables and Connectors" section later in this appendix.

Connecting a Station to 10BASE5 Ethernet

Figure B-3 shows a station, in this case a desktop computer, with a thick Ethernet NIC, which has a 15-pin female AUI connector equipped with a sliding latch. The matching 15-pin male AUI plug on the transceiver cable is equipped with a pair of locking posts that fit into the sliding latch on the female AUI connector located on the interface.

The other end of the transceiver cable is equipped with a 15-pin female connector and sliding latch. This end is connected to the male connector and locking

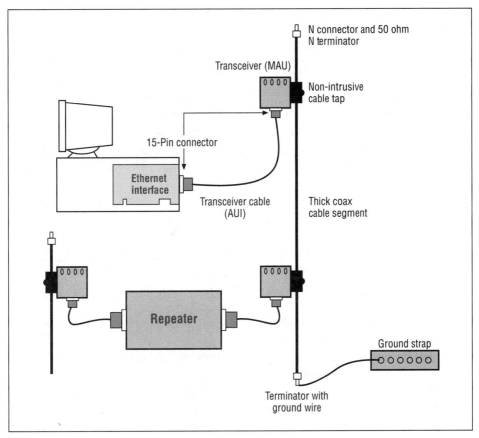

Figure B-3. Connecting a station to a 10BASE5 Ethernet system

posts provided on the transceiver. Once again, the sliding latch is used to hold the two connectors together.

Also shown is a two-port repeater, used to link the two thick coax cable segments together. The same kind of transceivers and transceiver cables used for a computer connection to the coax are used to connect the repeater to the coax segments. Please note that the SQE Test signal must be disabled on the transceivers connected to the repeater. Operation and configuration of the SQE Test signal is described in Appendix C, *AUI Equipment: Installation and Configuration.*

One of the thick Ethernet coax segments is shown with a grounding connection. The grounding connection is made between an N terminator equipped with a grounding connection, and a grounding strap connected to the building ground system. Proper grounding technique at *one and only one* point on the coax cable segment is necessary to provide a sufficient ground for electrical safety. Grounding techniques and coax electrical safety are described in the "Coaxial Cables and Connectors" section, later in this appendix.

10BASE5 Configuration Guidelines

The Ethernet standard contains guidelines for building a single 10BASE5 thick coax segment, as well as guidelines for linking multiple segments into a larger half-duplex system. Table B-1 lists the single segment guidelines for a 10BASE5 segment. The configuration rules for linking multiple 10 Mbps segment types with repeater hubs are described in Chapter 13, *Multi-Segment Configuration Guidelines*.

Table B-1. 10BASE5 Single Segment Guidelines

Media Type	Maximum Cable Length	Maximum Number of Transceivers (per segment)
Thick coax 10BASE5	500 m (1640 feet)	100
Transceiver Cable	50 m (164 feet)	N/A

A thick coaxial segment is formally known as a *mixing segment* in the multi-segment configuration guidelines. A mixing segment is defined as one that may have more than two transceiver connections. The guidelines in Table B-1 show that a given segment of thick coaxial cable can support up to 100 such connections. This distinguishes a thick coax segment from a link segment, since a link segment built according to the standard can have only two connections, one at each end.

Thin Coaxial Media System

The specifications for the thin coax (10BASE2) Ethernet media system were published in 1985. The thin coax system is based on a thinner, more flexible variety of coaxial cable than the one used in thick Ethernet systems. This system also eliminates the need for an externally attached transceiver and transceiver cable, thereby lowering the cost of a station attachment to the network earning it the nickname "Cheapernet."

As with the 10BASE5 thick coax system, the 10BASE2 media system can only carry 10 Mbps signals. However, thin Ethernet can still come in handy for networking small groups of computers, or building quick lash-ups in a computer lab. Thin coaxial Ethernet is also used in home networks and small workgroup local area networks (LANs) where cost is a major concern and a single 10 Mbps channel may provide sufficient bandwidth. For that reason, there are still a number of thin Ethernet systems in use.

10BASE2 Signaling Components

The following signaling components may be used in the 10BASE2 system to send and receive signals over the media system:

- Ethernet interface with a built-in 10BASE2 transceiver.

- AUI transceiver cable.

- External 10BASE2 transceiver (MAU), used if the NIC does not provide a built-in 10BASE2 transceiver.

10BASE2 Ethernet Interface

Figure B-4 shows a 10BASE2 network interface card designed for installation in a computer.

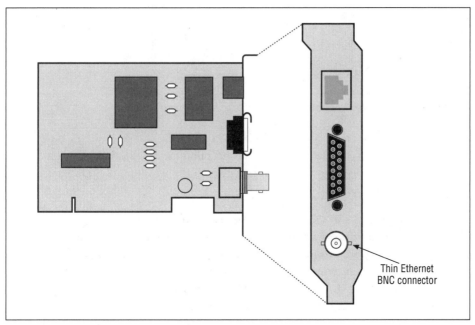

Figure B-4. 10BASE2 Ethernet interface

This particular interface is equipped with three connectors that allow an attachment to a variety of Ethernet media systems. The thin Ethernet connector is the female BNC coaxial connector shown at the bottom of the interface card.

Transceiver Cable

In the 10BASE2 system, a transceiver cable may be used to make a connection between the Ethernet interface and an external 10BASE2 transceiver. However, the transceiver cable is not needed if there is a built-in transceiver in the 10BASE2 interface. The transceiver cable can be dispensed with entirely if the external 10BASE2 transceiver is small enough to fit directly onto the 15-pin AUI connector on the Ethernet interface.

External 10BASE2 Transceiver

Stations equipped with Ethernet interfaces that only have a 15-pin AUI connector can also be connected to a thin Ethernet coax segment using an external thin Ethernet transceiver, as shown in Figure B-5.

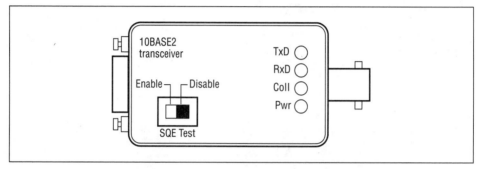

Figure B-5. External 10BASE2 transceiver

An Ethernet interface equipped with a built-in 10BASE2 transceiver can be directly attached to a thin coaxial segment and has no need for an external transceiver.

10BASE2 Signal Encoding

Signals sent over the 10BASE2 media system use Manchester encoding. The signal encoding, physical line signaling, and collision detection mechanisms for the 10BASE2 media system are identical to those used for 10BASE5. This explains why you can buy modular transceivers with interchangeable coaxial connectors that can be used on either 10BASE5 or 10BASE2 systems. Since the signaling is identical, the only thing that needs to be changed on the transceiver is the medium dependent interface (MDI) which provides a direct connection to the coaxial cable.

10BASE2 Media Components

The following set of media components are used to build a thin coaxial segment:

* Thin coaxial cable.
* BNC coaxial connector.

- BNC T and barrel connector.

- BNC 50 ohm terminator.

Details on thin coaxial cable and BNC coaxial connectors and terminator can be found in the "Coaxial Cables and Connectors" section, later in this appendix.

Connecting a Station to 10BASE2 Ethernet

Figure B-6 shows two desktop computers connected to a 10BASE2 thin coaxial cable segment. The computer on the bottom has a thin Ethernet network interface card installed. This interface card comes with a female BNC connector to which the BNC T-connector is directly attached.

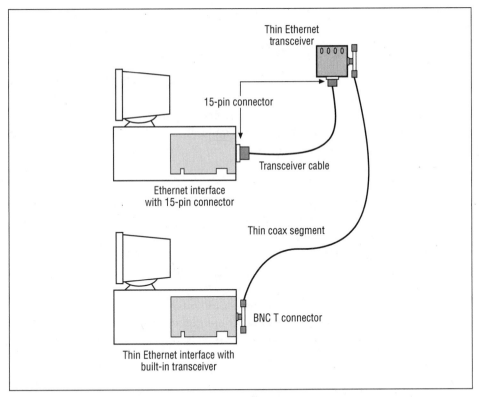

Figure B-6. Connecting stations to a 10BASE2 Ethernet system

The computer on the top has an interface with an AUI connector. This computer is attached to the thin Ethernet coax using a transceiver cable to complete the connection between the computer and the external transceiver. You can also find small external transceivers that may be attached directly to the 15-pin AUI connector on a station. This eliminates the need for a transceiver cable and makes it even easier for a station with a 15-pin AUI connector to be attached to a thin Ethernet segment.

The computer on the bottom has a thin Ethernet interface with built-in transceiver electronics, eliminating the need for an external transceiver or transceiver cable. The interface board is provided with a female BNC connector, which provides a direct connection between the transceiver on the interface and the thin coax cable segment by way of the BNC T connector.

The least expensive connection to a thin Ethernet segment is achieved by using thin Ethernet interfaces with a built-in transceiver so that you don't need to purchase an external transceiver and transceiver cable. However, as this figure shows, you can also accommodate stations with 15-pin AUI connectors by using an external coaxial transceiver equipped with a BNC tap.

10BASE2 Configuration Guidelines

The Ethernet standard contains guidelines for building a single 10BASE2 thin coax segment, as well as guidelines for linking multiple segments into a larger half-duplex system. Table B-2 lists the single segment guidelines for a 10BASE2 segment. The configuration rules for linking multiple 10 Mbps segment types with repeater hubs are described in Chapter 13.

Table B-2. 10BASE2 Single Segment Guidelines

Media Type	Maximum Segment Length	Maximum Number of Transceivers (per segment)
Thin coax 10BASE2	185 m (606.9 feet)[a]	30

[a] Minimum coax cable section length is 0.5 m (1.6 feet), which means that the minimum transceiver spacing is also set to 0.5 m.

A thin coaxial segment is formally known as a *mixing segment* in the multi-segment configuration guidelines. A mixing segment is defined as one that may have more than two transceiver connections; a thin coax segment can support up to 30 such connections.

Coaxial Cables and Connectors

This section describes how to build and install coaxial cables and connectors for the 10BASE5 and 10BASE2 media systems. We begin with a description of several items that apply to both thick and thin coaxial systems. These include coax cable safety issues, coax cable grounding, and the coax cable impedance rating.

Coax Cable Safety Rules

When working on a coax cable you should always be aware of the potential for danger, and make sure that you never place your body in the electrical path between any heavy-duty cable and ground. The 10BASE5 standard has a section, entitled *Installation and Maintenance Guidelines*, which states:

> a) When exposing the shield of the trunk cable for any reasons, care shall be exercised to ensure that the shield does not make electrical contact with any unintended conductors or grounds. Personnel performing the operation should not do so if dissipation of a high energy transient by the cabling system is likely during the time the shield is to be exposed. Personnel should not contact both the shield and any grounded conductor at any time.

> b) Before breaking the trunk coaxial cable for any reason, a strap with ampacity equal to that of the shield of the coaxial cable shall be affixed to the cable shield in such a manner as to join the two pieces and to maintain continuity when the shield of the trunk is severed. This strap shall not be removed until after normal shield continuity has been restored.

> c) At no time should the shield of any portion of the coaxial trunk cable to which an MAU or MAUs are attached be permitted to float without an effective ground connection. If a section of floating cable is to be added to an existing cable system, the installer should take care not to complete the circuit between the shield of the floating cable section and the grounded cable section through body contact.*

Before disconnecting the cable or even touching the metal connectors on a cable, you should always perform checks, such as measuring from the cable to a nearby ground, to look for large voltages and dangerous currents. It's up to you to make sure that you handle coax cable with a healthy respect for its current-carrying capabilities. You should always be alert to the possibility that the cable could be touching an exposed electrical conductor somewhere along its length and therefore carrying a dangerous charge.

Coaxial Cable Grounding

While the Ethernet signals that travel over coaxial cables are small, the coax cables themselves are capable of carrying large electrical currents. Further, Ethernet coax cables may also be quite long and travel through ceilings and under machine room floors. This can expose the cable to a number of potential electrical hazards. There's a possibility that a bare wire in a lighting fixture might touch the cable, or that some other electrical accident could occur that would cause the coax to carry a dangerous electrical current.

---

* From IEEE Std 802.3, 1996 Edition, p. 123. Copyright 1996 IEEE. All rights reserved.

The currents and voltages used to carry Ethernet signals are small and pose no threat to the typical user of Ethernet equipment. However, an improperly grounded coaxial cable installation can present an electrical hazard to anyone working with, or operating equipment connected to, the cable.

If an ungrounded coaxial cable is touching an electrically "hot" circuit somewhere in its path, it can conduct that electricity along its entire length, presenting a risk to anyone handling the cable. Before handling any cable, you should make sure that the cable is not carrying any dangerous voltages or currents. Always observe standard safety practices when working on any type of cable to avoid the risk of electrical shock.

To help prevent this occurrence, the Ethernet standard specifies that a thick or thin coax cable segment should be connected to earth ground at one point for electrical safety reasons. By making a single grounding connection to the cable, you can be assured that the accidental current will be led off to ground and blow a fuse or trip a circuit breaker. This automatically interrupts the current and protects anyone who may come in contact with the coax cable. The standard notes that either the terminator or a barrel connector on the cable segment provides a handy connection point for a single grounding connection. The grounding connection should have a minimum current rating "of at least 1,500 ampacity."

It is important to ground only one point on the coax cable, to ensure that *ground currents* will not occur. Ground current through a coaxial cable can alter the average voltage levels of the cable and disrupt the ability of a transceiver to detect data or collisions. Therefore, it is essential that only one point on the cable be grounded to ensure correct operation of the Ethernet system. To avoid ground currents you need to make sure that all connectors on the coax are properly insulated. You should also route the coax away from such objects as metal pipes and light fixtures, and tie-wrap the coax into place so that it can't be moved around.

Connector insulators

Connector insulators, called *insulating boots,* can be installed on coaxial connectors to help avoid accidental grounds and the ground currents that they can cause. The boots come in several forms. One type is split in half, and the two halves are placed around a connector and held in place with plastic cable ties. Vendors also supply fabric insulators that are held in place with Velcro, or plastic insulators that snap into place around coaxial connectors to insulate them.

Because of the danger of large currents being carried by the cable, you should never install coax cables that go outside to link Ethernets located in separate buildings. Instead, you should use fiber optic media to link networks in separate buildings, since fiber can provide complete electrical isolation. Fiber optic cable provides complete isolation from typical outdoor hazards such as lightning strikes, which can generate huge transient currents in metallic cables. These transient currents present a hazard to service personnel and can damage equipment attached to the cable.

50 ohm Impedance Rating

One of the most important cable specifications for both thick and thin coaxial cables is the characteristic impedance rating, which must be 50 ohms. Although the impedance rating is expressed in ohms, it has nothing to do with the steady state, or direct current (DC), resistance that you can measure with a garden variety volt-ohmmeter (VOM).

The DC resistance of a piece of Ethernet coax as measured by a VOM is small. For example, DC loop resistance is a measurement made by connecting the shield and center conductor together at one end of the cable, and then measuring the DC resistance between the center conductor and shield at the other end. This measures the total loop resistance of the cable consisting of the center conductor, shield and connectors. The specifications state that the total loop resistance measurement should result in a reading that is 5 ohms or less for a full-length segment of thick coax cable. The loop resistance for thin coax is 10 ohms or less for a full-length segment.

The characteristic impedance rating, on the other hand, refers to what happens when rapidly moving signals propagate down the cable. During this activity, the average impedance to the flow of signals must be 50 ohms for correct operation. There is no easy way to measure impedance, and you must rely on the vendor ratings to tell you which cable is rated at 50 ohms impedance.

Using cable with the correct impedance is essential to the health of any coax-based Ethernet system. If the wrong impedance cable is used, signals will not propagate correctly over the system. If a higher impedance piece of coax is spliced into the middle of a system that otherwise uses correct impedance cables, for example, the Ethernet signals can reflect off the higher impedance section causing frame errors.

Incorrect video cable

Thin coax systems are especially vulnerable to the use of coax cable with an incorrect impedance rating. That's because of the widespread availability of coax cable used for video signals. Coax cables used for connecting a television to a cable TV system are 75 ohm impedance cables that look a lot like thin Ethernet coax cable from the outside.

The problem is that the video cables are widely available in many hardware stores. This sometimes leads to video cable being pressed into service for thin Ethernet when no other cable can be found and a network connection is required right away. Video cables aren't the only culprits, either. Other widely used cables such as IBM 3270-style cables can look a lot like thin Ethernet coax. However, none of these cables has the correct impedance rating, and the use of any of these cables in a thin Ethernet system can cause problems.

A video technician may tell you that the impedance difference between the two cables is no big deal, and that video signals are not much affected by using cables with impedance ratings. However, when it comes to thin Ethernet operation, the impedance difference can cause major problems for the network signals.

Incorrect cable sections

Short sections of incorrect coax cable spliced into an otherwise correct thin Ethernet segment will result in an impedance mismatch that can cause signal reflections. The signal reflections can cause an increased bit error rate and increased frame errors that show up as slow network performance. The thin Ethernet system will usually continue operating, and despite the frames lost due to higher error rates the show will go on, at least for a while. However, increased traffic levels will bring increased error rates and eventually you may be forced to find the incorrect cable segments and remove them.

Due to the truly weird effects that can occur with signals carried over mismatched coax cables, you may experience mysterious failures with this kind of cable mix-up. Stations on the system may appear and then disappear like wandering ghosts, as the signal levels and rates of frame loss vary according to traffic level and the number of stations on the network.

Troubleshooting this sort of problem can be very difficult and time consuming. That's why you would be well advised to decline the favor when someone offers to splice in a piece of video or other non-Ethernet cable while claiming that "just a small piece won't hurt."

10BASE5 Coaxial Cable and Connectors

The thick Ethernet segment is based on a fairly thick (approximately 1 cm or 0.4 inch diameter) and inflexible coaxial cable. For best results, you must use thick coaxial cable that is designed specifically for use in Ethernet systems. The specifications include a 50 ohm characteristic impedance rating, and a solid center conductor and heavy shielding.

The 802.3 specifications state that the thick coax cable must be sufficiently flexible to support a bending radius of 254 mm (10 inches). Your cable vendor can provide the minimum bend radius specification of the thick coax cable you purchase. Note that if the cable is bent any tighter than the minimum bend radius, then damage may result, which could affect the quality of the signal on the cable.

Figure B-7 illustrates the construction of a thick coax cable. The outer jacket insulation of thick coax cable may be plain PVC or Teflon. A bright color is recommended for the jacket. Teflon is used for *plenum-rated* cable, which is frequently required for installation in air handling spaces (also called plenums) to meet fire regulations. Cables with PVC insulation are typically a bright yellow, while Teflon cables are often an orange shade.

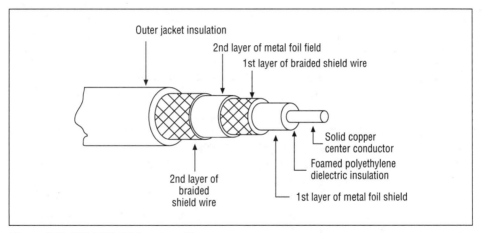

Figure B-7. 10BASE5 thick coax cable

The unusual colors help identify the Ethernet coax in the tangle of cables found in cable trays, above false ceilings, and under raised machine room floors. After all, up in the ceiling or under floors one black cable looks very much like another, but the yellow or orange Ethernet cable stands out. This is more than just a convenience, since Ethernet transceivers are physically attached to a thick coax cable by drilling holes into the cable. Before you go drilling into some thick cable you find under a machine room floor you want to make very sure it's an Ethernet cable and not a power cable.

The Ethernet standard also notes that the thick coax cable should be marked with a contrasting color located every 2.5 m (8.2 feet) to establish the correct minimum spacing for transceiver taps to the cable. This mark is typically a black band on the yellow PVC cable.

The 2.5 m marks on the coaxial cable are for transceiver spacing only. You can join sections of coaxial cable together anywhere along their length without regard to the marks. Nor do you have to worry too much about maintaining the exact spacing of the 2.5 m marks when joining two cable sections together. The transceiver spacing interval is a guideline that helps you avoid signal reflections that can occur from clumping transceiver taps too close together. If you happen to shorten the spacing between a couple of transceivers when joining two cable sections together, it won't be a big deal. As long as the majority of transceiver taps on the cable obey the correct spacing, things should work just fine.

Building 10BASE5 Segments with Multiple Cable Sections

Thick Ethernet coax is such a high fidelity cable that any slight change in the characteristic impedance between cable sections used in a given segment can have an effect on the signals sent over the coax. If the impedance mismatch is too large, then it can cause excessive signal reflections which, in turn, can result in bit errors and dropped frames.

The best way to minimize the effects of impedance mismatch is to build the whole segment from the same spool of cable. The reason is that the cable on that spool will have been made at one time on the same cable-forming machine. This ensures that all of the signal carrying aspects of the cable will be uniform; reducing the risk of impedance mismatches. However, if you build the segment out of cable sections that are not from the same lot or spool, then the possibility of an impedance mismatch exists. The standard notes that the worst-case impedance variation allowed as a result of joining two cable sections from different cable lots can be plus or minus 2 ohms, providing a 4 percent variance from the impedance specification of 50 ohms.

The severity of an impedance mismatch is related to the signal frequencies carried by the cable and to the lengths of the cable sections. To help reduce the total amount of impedance mismatch that may occur, the standard specifies the lengths of slightly dissimilar cables that would be least likely to combine into an impedance mismatch of any concern. If cable from different lots is used to build a thick coax segment, then the standard provides measurements for the sections of cable used. The cable sections should be 23.4 m (76.7 feet), 70.2 m (230.3 feet) or 117 m (383.8 feet) in length. All lengths may be ±0.5 m (1.6 feet). Vendors provide complete thick Ethernet cable sections in these standard lengths with connectors already installed.

The portion of the IEEE 802.3 standard that covers this issue reads as follows:

> If uncontrolled cable sections must be used in building up a longer segment, the lengths should be chosen so that reflections, when they occur, do not have a high probability of adding in phase. This can be accomplished by using lengths that are odd integral multiples of a half wavelength in the cable at 5MHz; this corresponds to using lengths of 23.4 m, 70.2 m, and 117 m (±0.5 m) for all sections. These are considered to be the standard lengths for all cable sections. Using these lengths exclusively, any mix or match of cable sections may be used to build up a 500 m segment without incurring excessive reflections.[*]

N-type Coaxial Connector

The standard states that each thick Ethernet coaxial cable segment must have a male N-type coaxial cable connector attached to each end. Along with the quality of the cable itself, the quality of the N-type coax connector and its installation can have a major effect on the operation of a coaxial segment. Figure B-8 shows an N-type coaxial connector.

Figure B-8. N-type coaxial connector

Installing the coaxial connectors onto the cable requires special stripping and crimping tools and must be done carefully or signal problems may result. For this reason, the correct operation of thick coaxial segments depends very much on the correct installation of the coaxial connectors. Coaxial cable connector installation procedures are described later in this appendix.

N-type Barrel

An N-type barrel connector is used to join sections of thick coax cable together. The barrel is a short female-to-female connector that allows you to connect two cable ends together. A thick coax segment that travels over an entire floor of a building, or between several floors, should have at least one barrel connection halfway along the cable. This allows you to troubleshoot any future problems with

---

[*] From IEEE Std 802.3, Fifth Edition 1996-07-29, p. 120. Copyright 1996 IEEE. All rights reserved.

the cable system by opening the cable at the barrel and splitting the cable into two segments.

Installing a barrel allows you to isolate the problem to one of the two cable segments and thereby help discover the location of the failure. A large coaxial cable system supporting multiple floors of a building could benefit from several barrels, one for every floor for example, which could save a lot of time when it comes to troubleshooting a failure on the cable system. Figure B-9 shows an N-type barrel between two male N connectors that are attached to the ends of two sections of coax cable.

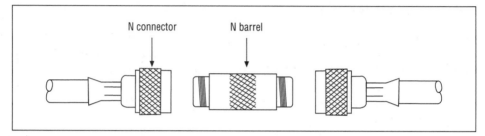

Figure B-9. N-type barrel connector

N-type Terminator

There must be an N-type 50 ohm terminator installed at each end of a thick coaxial cable segment. The terminator does not cause any signal reflections and therefore does not have to obey the 2.5 m spacing requirements used for transceiver connections. Instead, a transceiver tap can be installed next to the terminator at the end of the cable.

The terminator, shown in Figure B-10, acts to prevent signal reflections on the cable by behaving like a sponge for electrical signals. The terminator soaks up the signals when they reach the end of the cable, instead of letting them bounce back and interfere with other signals. The 50 ohm resistance of a terminator is a DC resistance that can be tested with a volt-ohmmeter. When testing a terminator, a VOM should give a reading of 50 ohms ±1 percent (1/2 ohm) according to the standard. The terminator for a thick coaxial segment must also be capable of handling at least 1 watt of power.

There are two terminators shown in Figure B-10. The top terminator is a standard female N-type that screws into the male N-type connector on the end of a thick coax segment. The bottom terminator is also a female N-type, but it includes a threaded bolt on the end of the terminator, equipped with nuts and washers. This allows a ground lead to be connected to the terminator, to provide the coax cable with a safety ground.

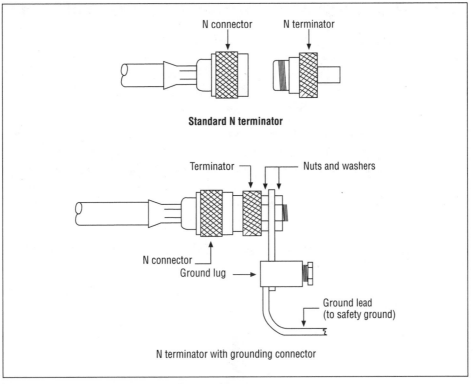

Figure B-10. N-type terminator and grounding connector

Thick Coax Cable Topology

Thick coaxial segments can only be connected in the bus physical topology. All stations in a bus topology are attached to transceivers connected to a single coaxial cable. The cable provides an electrical signal bus that is common to all stations and carries signals between all stations. That, in turn, means that the coaxial cable must be routed to within the maximum 50 m (164 feet) transceiver cable distance of each station that needs to be connected.

A major problem with the bus cabling topology is that a failure anywhere on the thick coaxial cable disrupts the electrical signal bus and therefore disrupts the operation of all computers attached to the cable. Troubleshooting a failure on a thick coax system can be a difficult and time-consuming process of segmenting the cable into smaller chunks in an attempt to find the failing cable section.

10BASE2 Coaxial Cable and Connectors

The thin Ethernet system is based on thinner (approximately 0.5 cm or 3/16th of an inch) coaxial cable that is more flexible and much easier to deal with than the thick Ethernet variety. According to the standard, the cable must have a 50 ohm characteristic impedance rating, a stranded center conductor, and must be able to support a maximum bend radius of 5 cm (2 inches).

The coax cables used in thin Ethernet systems usually have a black outer jacket, although one major vendor provides a cable specifically designed to meet the thin Ethernet specifications that has a light gray outer jacket. Since the coaxial cable is the heart of a thin coax network, you should use the best quality cable you can find, and make sure that the cable is installed correctly.

Figure B-11 shows an example of the male BNC connector that is connected to each end of a thin coax cable section. The male BNC connector is described in more detail later in this chapter.

Figure B-11. Thin coaxial cable and the male BNC connector

Multiple Cable Sections for 10BASE2 Segments

The standard states that the minimum thin Ethernet segment length is 0.5 m (1.64 feet). Therefore, the minimum distance for transceiver connections on thin Ethernet is also set to 0.5 m. This spacing acts to minimize the signal reflections caused by transceiver tap connections to the cable. Cable segments can be as long as needed, up to the maximum of 185 m.

The combined higher signal attenuation of thin coax and the shorter total segment lengths make a thin Ethernet coax segment less sensitive to the small impedance mismatches that are found in different cable lots. This makes it unnecessary to follow the strict thick coax guidelines having to do with cable lots and special cable section lengths. Therefore, unlike thick Ethernet, there are no other rules that apply to combining thin coax cable sections.

Which Cable Type?

The 10BASE2 thin Ethernet standard notes that cable types RG58A/U and RG58C/U can meet the cable specifications in the standard. The "RG" designation stands for "Radio, Government," which is a rating used for a number of coaxial cables. The "U" stands for "general utility," and the "A" and "C" refer to different versions of the cable specifications. These designators are not precise, and one vendor's set of RG58 cables may vary in specifications from one vendor to another. You can't predict much from the cable designation; the only way to tell exactly what you're getting is to look up the specifications for the cable in the vendor's catalog.

A vendor may have several cables that are rated as being RG58A/U or RG58C/U, but the construction of the cables may be different and they may have slightly different impedance ratings. When building a thin Ethernet segment, the cable that you use must have a stranded center conductor using tinned copper wires. The cable must also have characteristic impedance rating of 50 ohms and a minimum velocity of propagation that is 65 percent of the speed of light, among other parameters. The standard says that the dielectric material may be of any type, but that a solid dielectric is preferred. To make sure that you're getting the right cable, you can request cable from the vendor that is guaranteed to meet the IEEE 10BASE2 thin Ethernet specifications.

Belden is one vendor that sells a thin coax cable specifically designed to meet the IEEE standard. The Belden cable numbers for this cable are 9907 for a cable with standard PVC jacket insulation, and 89907 for the plenum version which resists high temperatures and is used where safety regulations require a more stable jacket material. Note that the Belden cable has a slightly smaller outside diameter than many other RG58-type cables, so you need to make sure that the coaxial connectors you buy will fit it correctly.

Male BNC Coaxial Connector

The standard specifies that the ends of each section of thin coax cable must be equipped with male BNC connectors. The connectors should also be provided with a non-conductive shell or other insulating arrangement to avoid accidental contact with other metal conductors in the building. The male BNC connector is smaller and easier to install than the N-type connector used on thick Ethernet coax, which is one of the major advantages of the thin Ethernet system.

The standard also recommends using high quality BNC connectors with a low DC resistance. The lower resistance is an important issue, since the resistance of each BNC connector contributes to the total loop resistance of a thin Ethernet segment.

Maintaining a low total loop resistance is essential, since the correct operation of the collision detect mechanism depends on the correct loop resistance.

The most common method for installing BNC connectors is the crimp-on method, which results in strong and reliable connections when properly done. While there are screw-on BNC connectors available, they can be impossible to install solidly on thin coax equipped with a stranded center conductor as specified in the 10BASE2 standard. Even if you manage to get them installed, screw-on connectors frequently work their way loose, causing intermittent connections that can be very difficult and time-consuming to troubleshoot. For that reason, you should definitely avoid the use of screw-on connectors.

BNC Crimp-on Connector

When installing a crimp-on BNC connector, both the center conductor and the outer shell of the connector are tightly crimped into place, making a solid mechanical and electrical connection to the cable. For correct operation, it's essential that you purchase a BNC connector that was designed to fit onto your cable. The critical cable specifications for finding the right BNC connector are the diameter of the center pin used in the connector, and the outside cable diameter of the coaxial cable.

A single type of crimp-on BNC connector will often fit a number of commonly found RG58 cables, since many of these cables have the same impedance rating and outside diameter. However, some RG58 cables, and especially some cables that are specifically designed for thin Ethernet, have outside diameters that are slightly different, requiring different BNC connectors.

You can also buy thin Ethernet coaxial cable with the male BNC connectors pre-installed. The ready-made cables supplied by some companies also come with built-in insulating covers that the thin Ethernet standard recommends for covering the exposed metal portions of the connectors. While these cables are higher cost than making your own, they can eliminate the problem of buying and learning how to use crimp tools.

Since a poorly installed BNC connector can cause all sorts of headaches on a thin Ethernet system, it's well worth the expense to make sure it's done right. Ready-made cables with insulating covers on the BNC connectors also make it much easier to keep your thin Ethernet segment isolated from accidental contact with metal portions of the building or other equipment, as the standard recommends.

BNC Ts and Barrels

The thin Ethernet system uses BNC connectors both for the coaxial cable and for attachment to the station interface. The BNC T connector, so called because of its T-like shape, is used to attach the coaxial cable to the female BNC transceiver connector located on the Ethernet interface.

As shown in Figure B-12, the horizontal part of the T connector has female connectors to which the BNC male connectors on the ends of the coaxial cable are connected. The female connectors on the T are equipped with small metal protrusions that are part of the mechanical gripping mechanism. The male connector is slid over the protrusions and then given a half turn to lock the male connector in place.

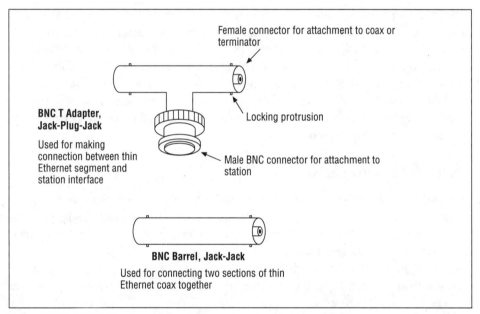

Female connector for attachment to coax or terminator

BNC T Adapter, Jack-Plug-Jack

Used for making connection between thin Ethernet segment and station interface

Locking protrusion

Male BNC connector for attachment to station

BNC Barrel, Jack-Jack

Used for connecting two sections of thin Ethernet coax together

Figure B-12. BNC T (top) and barrel (bottom) connectors.

The vertical part, or descender, of the T has a male BNC connector on its end, which is attached to the female BNC connector located on the Ethernet interface in the computer.

Vendor catalogs often use "socket" or "receptacle" for "female" and "plug" for "male" when describing connector types.

The BNC T is a passive component, and you might expect that it would never fail. Nonetheless, some installers have reported an occasional problem with thin Ethernet segments that were traced to a failing BNC T connector. Apparently, the internal components of the T may sometimes come loose and short out, causing the segment to stop working. For this reason, buying high-quality BNC Ts and keeping a couple of spares around is a good idea. High-quality BNC Ts with a gold-plated center conductor can help reduce the loop resistance on your segment.

Another connector that you may find useful for building thin Ethernet segments is the BNC barrel, shown on the bottom of Figure B-12. The BNC barrel is a short tube that has female BNC connectors on each end. Barrels can be used to connect cable sections together when you need to just join the cable ends without connecting them to a BNC T attached to a station interface.

Although it is possible to use a BNC T that is not connected to a station to act as a barrel connector, it isn't a good idea. For one thing, this leaves the unconnected end of the T exposed, making it possible for small bits of metal to touch the exposed end and short out the coax segment, which will cause all network operations to cease. In addition, each unconnected end of a T connector looks to the Ethernet signals as a short section of unterminated coax, which causes a small amount of extra signal reflection. This doesn't do the signals on your cable segment any good, and should be avoided.

Thin Coax Stub Cables

The BNC T should be connected directly to the female BNC on the interface with no intervening piece of thin coaxial cable. The standard notes that the length of a "stub" connection between the BNC connector on the interface and the coaxial cable should be no longer than 4 cm (1.57 inches). This helps prevent the occurrence of signal reflections which can cause frame errors. The 4 cm limit includes both the length of the BNC T connector and the internal wiring that leads to the transceiver chip. There is no allowance made for external cables between the interface and the BNC T connector. Figure B-13 shows that a stub cable is incorrectly located between the BNC T and the station connector.

If stub cables are used between the BNC T and the Ethernet interface, the system may seem to work, but signal reflections caused by the stub cables will cause electrical noise and result in frame errors. Frames lost due to occasional frame errors are often detected and retransmitted by the application software. This makes the system appear to work when longer stubs are used, since a small level of frame loss is not usually noticed right away. However, a large frame error rate can eventually lead to a high number of retransmissions, making the network appear to be slow. As electrical noise and frame loss get worse when network traffic increases,

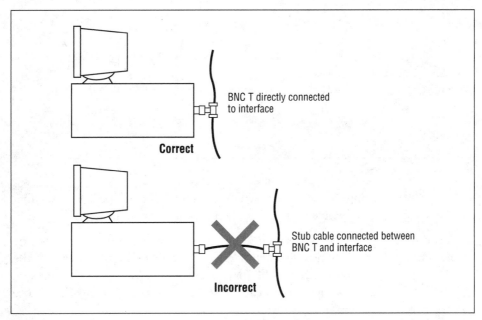

Figure B-13. Correct and incorrect BNC T connections.

the response time of applications over the network will plummet just when demand is highest.

Another odd failure that can result from the use of overlong stubs is that some stations may seem to operate like "ghosts." A station with a stub cable may seem to be available to some stations but not others. This depends on the location of the stub, the length of the stub cable, the number of stations that are turned on, and other such imponderables. You can avoid these problems by making sure that there are no stub cables in your thin Ethernet system.

BNC Terminator

Each thin coax segment must be equipped with 50 ohm terminators attached to each end of the segment. The 50 ohm resistance of a terminator is a DC resistance that can be tested with a VOM. When testing a terminator, a VOM should give a reading of 50 ohms ±1 percent (1/2 ohm) according to the standard. According to the standard, the thin coax terminator must also be capable of handling at least 0.5 watt of power. Figure B-14 shows a BNC terminator equipped with a ground connector. This terminator may be connected to one side of a BNC T, with the thin coax connected to the other side, as shown in the figure.

Note that some thin Ethernet repeaters also provide an internal 50 ohm terminated connection for a thin Ethernet segment. In some repeaters this termination

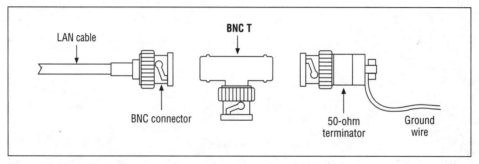

Figure B-14. BNC terminator and ground, connected to BNC T and coax

may be fixed, requiring that the coax segment must end at the repeater port. Other repeaters allow you to enable and disable the internal port termination.

It's important to make sure that there are only two terminators on a segment—one at each end. If a connection is also made to a self-terminated repeater port in the middle of a segment, then there will be three terminators attached to the segment, and the terminating resistance on the cable will be incorrect. This can cause false triggering of the collision detect signal.

10BASE2 Cable Topology

A major difficulty when wiring an office with thin coax is finding some way to install the coax and make it available for use when needed. Ideally, thin coax should be installed like a telephone jack. With this type of installation, the coax is pre-installed and is available via a cable connection in a wall plate. Then all the user needs to do is plug the coax Ethernet cable from their computer into the receptacle on the wall plate to gain access to the network. This type of connection is very similar to the way most twisted-pair Ethernet systems are wired today.

Point-to-point topology

Thin coax segments can be connected to a repeater port on one end and directly to the station in the office on the other end, with no other stations connected to the link. This type of connection is referred to as a *point-to-point topology*, as it only supports one station per segment.

Bus topology

A thin Ethernet segment may also be connected to several computers in a *bus topology*, also known as a *daisy chain topology*. In the daisy chain topology, several stations are connected together with thin coax cable sections. The cable sections are connected between the BNC T connectors at each station.

As shown in Figure B-15, a repeater is used to connect several thin coax segments. One of the thin coaxial segments is shown in the daisy chain topology, connected to stations one, two and three. You create the complete segment by connecting the short cable sections together using BNC T connectors. This kind of cable segment can support up to 29 stations and one repeater port, for a total of 30 transceiver connections on the cable.

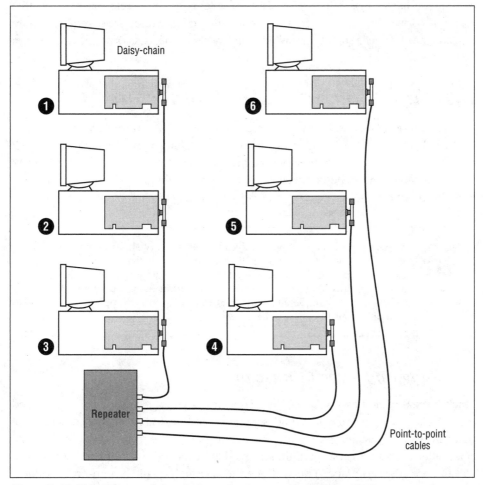

Figure B-15. Thin Ethernet daisy-chain and point-to-point cable topologies

If a section of the thin Ethernet coax is removed from the BNC T connector on the back of a computer, the entire segment will stop working, disabling the other computers. This is one drawback of the bus-wired daisy chain topology. The proper way to disconnect a station is to remove the entire BNC T connector from the female BNC on the Ethernet interface of the station. This will not disrupt the segment, since removing the BNC T keeps the entire length of the coaxial cable intact so that it continues to function.

Also shown in Figure B-15, three individual segments are connected directly to a single computer, at which point the segment is terminated. This is called a *point-to-point topology*; each segment supports only one computer. A point-to-point topology is much more reliable than a bus topology since it limits the number of computers that can be affected by cable problems to the single machine on that segment. However, this design uses more thin coax cables, and requires more repeater ports (one per station), which can increase the cost of deploying such a system.

Installing Coaxial Cable Connectors

This section describes how to install connectors on thick and thin coaxial cable, as well as the specifications and procedures for installing transceiver taps on thick coaxial cable. Only male connectors are installed on the ends of thick or thin coax cable segments. The male connectors on the coax cable are then used to connect to female connectors provided on transceivers, barrel connectors, and BNC Ts.

Attaching cable connectors involves the use of very sharp knives for stripping cable insulation as well as crimping tools that can be dangerous to operate. Many crimping tools incorporate a ratchet mechanism that, once engaged, prevents the tool from being opened until it has closed completely. Anything caught in the crimping tool, including your fingers, will be crushed.

Installing an N-type Connector

Thick coaxial cable has a solid center conductor, a layer of inner insulation (called dielectric), two layers of wire braid separated by thin foil shields, and a layer of outer insulation. Installing a male N connector onto the end of a thick coax cable is a matter of careful cable preparation, so that all of the parts of the N connector will fit correctly into place. You will need to use high-quality crimp-on N connectors and a crimping tool to avoid problems with improper crimps. An improper crimp can result in an excessive connector resistance or intermittent cable operation.

A crimp-on N connector consists of several parts, as shown in Figure B-16. An outer crimping ferrule is placed on the thick coax cable first, before anything else is done. A center contact is crimped onto the center conductor of the thick coax cable. Following that, the connector body is installed over the center pin. The

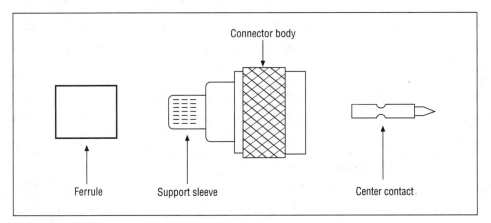

Figure B-16. N connector parts

outer crimping ferrule is then crimped into place, making an electrical and mechanical connection between the shield braids on the cable and the connector body.

Instructions are shown here for one commonly used variety of crimp-on N connector. If the vendor provides instructions for installing their connector, that should take precedence over what you read here.

1. Cut the end of the thick coaxial cable clean and square. If a rubber insulating boot is provided for the connector, slide this onto the cable. Next, slide the outer ferrule onto the cable and out of the way. Make sure the outer ferrule stays on the cable during the next sequence of steps.

2. Strip the cut end of the cable to expose the amounts of center conductor, inner insulation (dielectric) and braid shown in Figure B-17. Be careful not to cut into the solid center conductor.

3. Push the open end of the center contact into place over the solid center conductor, until it just butts against the inner dielectric as shown in Figure B-18. If the center contact does not butt against the dielectric, then trim the center conductor until the contact fits tightly. The fit of the center contact must be correct or the connector may not make the proper contact when installed.

4. The crimping tool for an N-type crimp-on connector has two dies: a small one for crimping the center contact, and a larger one for crimping the outer ferrule. Use the smaller die of the crimp tool to crimp the center contact onto the solid center conductor. Make sure that the center contact stays tightly butted against the dielectric while in the crimp tool, so that the contact is crimped into place correctly. Figure B-19 shows the center contact crimped into place on the center conductor.

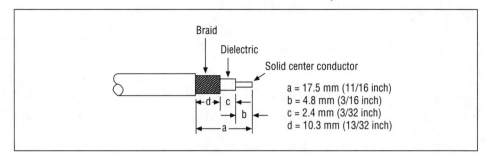

Figure B-17. Stripped thick coaxial cable

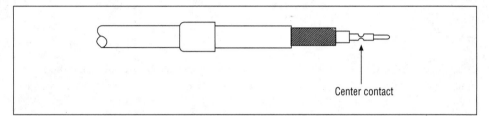

Figure B-18. Uncrimped center contact installed on a center conductor

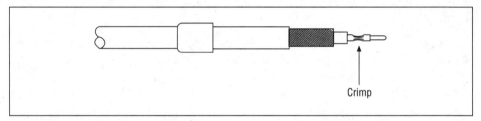

Figure B-19. Center contact crimped into position

5. Thick coaxial cable has two braided wire shields separated by foil wrap. Slightly flare both braids and foil simultaneously, to make it possible to slide the connector onto the inner dielectric of the cable. The braid and foil should slide over the support sleeve. Make sure that no pieces of braid or foil are caught inside the connector. Seat the connector firmly onto the end of the cable and check to make sure that the tip of the center contact is flush with the center pin shroud inside the N connector body. Figure B-20 shows the N connector body in place on the end of the coax cable.

6. Slide the ferrule sleeve forward until it covers the braid and support sleeve, and is in contact with the connector body, as shown in Figure B-21.

7. Place the ferrule into the large crimping die, making sure to keep the ferrule, cable and connector body together. Crimp the ferrule into place over the connector body support sleeve. The completed crimp should look like the one in Figure B-22.

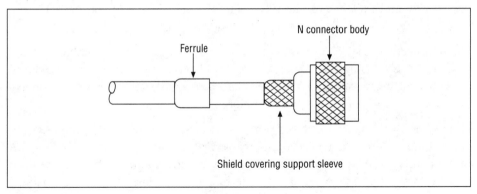

Figure B-20. N connector in place on a cable

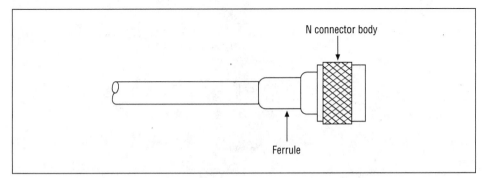

Figure B-21. Ferrule in place for crimping

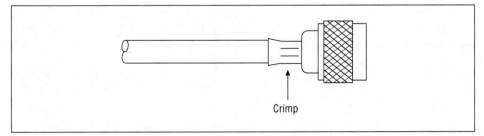

Figure B-22. Crimped N connector

This completes the task of installing a male N connector onto a thick coaxial cable.

Installing a BNC Connector

Thin coaxial cable has a stranded center conductor, a layer of inner insulation (also called the dielectric), a layer of braided wire for a shield, and a layer of outer insulation. Installing a male BNC connector onto the end of a thin coax cable is a matter of careful cable preparation to ensure that all of the parts of the BNC connector will fit correctly into place.

When installing a BNC connector, you should use a high-quality crimping tool and high-quality BNC crimp-on connectors to avoid problems with improper crimps. As with the N-type connector, an improper crimp can result in excessive connector resistance or intermittent cable operation.

A crimp-on BNC connector consists of several parts, as shown in Figure B-23. An outer crimping ferrule is placed on the cable first, before anything else is done. A center contact is then crimped onto the cable and the connector body is installed over the center pin. The outer crimping ferrule is then crimped into place, making an electrical and mechanical connection between the braid on the cable and the connector body.

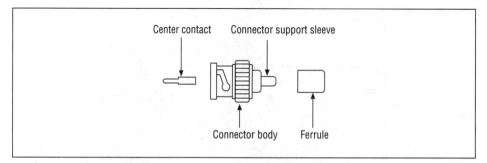

Figure B-23. BNC connector parts

Instructions are shown here for the widely available crimp-on BNC connector. If the vendor provides instructions for installing their connector, that should take precedence over what you read here.

1. Cut the end of the thin coaxial cable clean and square. Slide the outer ferrule onto the cable and out of the way. Make sure the outer ferrule stays on the cable during the next sequence of steps.

2. Strip the cut end of the cable to expose the center conductor, inner insulation (dielectric), and braid shown in Figure B-24. Be careful not to cut into the center conductor wires or braid.

3. Push the open end of the center contact into place on the center conductor, until it butts against the inner dielectric, as shown in Figure B-25. It is important that the center conductor be cut to the correct length, so that it fits inside the center contact with no bare conductor showing outside of the contact. Make sure that all strands of the center conductor are inside the center contact as well. This is a very important step, as any loose strands could cause intermittent short circuits later on when the cable is connected.

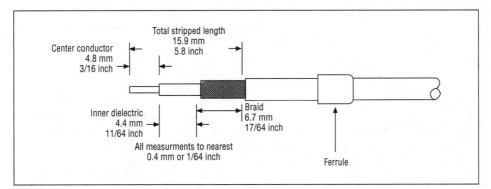

Figure B-24. Stripped thin coaxial cable

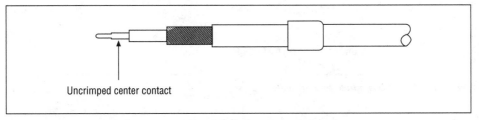

Figure B-25. Uncrimped center contact installed on a center conductor

4. The BNC crimping tool has two dies: a small one for crimping the center contact, and a larger one for crimping the outer ferrule. Use the smaller die to crimp the center contact onto the center conductor. The center contact should be crimped tightly in place on the center conductor. It's important to make sure that the center contact stays butted against the dielectric while in the crimp tool. Figure B-26 shows the center contact crimped onto the center conductor.

5. Slide the center contact through the body of the connector until the contact snaps into place and is flush with the front face of the nylon insulator of the connector. Make sure that the outer braid of the thin coax cable goes on the outside of the support sleeve of the connector body, as shown in Figure B-27.

6. Slide the ferrule sleeve forward until it covers the braid and support sleeve, and is in contact with the connector body. Figure B-28 shows the ferrule in the correct position for crimping.

7. Place the ferrule into the large crimping die, making sure to keep the ferrule, cable and connector body together. Crimp the ferrule into place over the connector body support sleeve. The completed crimp should look like the one in Figure B-29.

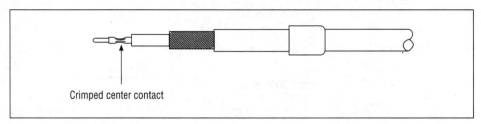

Figure B-26. Center contact crimped into position

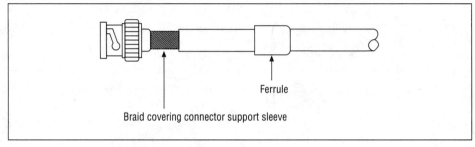

Figure B-27. Braid in place on connector sleeve

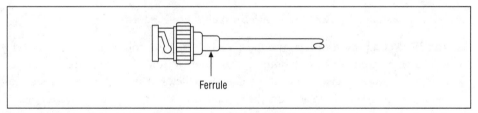

Figure B-28. Ferrule in place for crimping

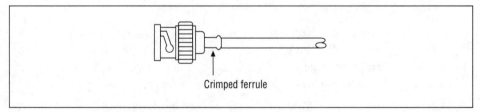

Figure B-29. Crimped BNC connector

This completes the task of installing a male BNC connector onto a thin coaxial cable.

Installing Transceiver Taps on Thick Coax

On thick coax cable, you will find black bands printed on the cable every 2.5 meters (8.2 feet). These black bands denote where a transceiver can be connected to the cable. Transceivers may be attached at any multiple of the 2.5 meter spacing. Requiring transceivers to be separated by multiples of 2.5 meters ensures that the small signal reflections caused by each transceiver connection to the coaxial cable will be sufficiently out of phase. This prevents the reflections from adding together to produce a large signal reflection that could cause signal errors. The black bands on typical PVC coax cable are printed directly on the insulation of the cable. On high-temperature plenum cable, you will find the black bands and other identification information printed on a thin strip of paper that is placed on the inside of the translucent outer layer of insulation on plenum cables. This is done since ink does not stick well when printed on the outer insulation of plenum cable.

Transceivers can be 5 meters apart or 7.5 meters apart, or anywhere on the cable as long as they are located at a black band and as long as there are no more than 100 transceivers per segment. The standard allows the spacing between the marks to vary ±5 cm, or about two inches, which means that absolute accuracy as to transceiver placement on the mark is not required.

Each transceiver absorbs a small amount of signal during the process of receiving signals. In addition, each transceiver connection to the coax system has a small effect on the electrical characteristics of the cable at the point of connection, which affects the quality of the signal on the cable. The maximum of 100 transceiver taps per segment limits the total effect on signal quality and signal level for a given coax cable segment.

The most popular way to install a transceiver on a thick coaxial cable is to use a non-intrusive tap, also known as a *vampire tap*. The name vampire tap comes from the fact that the tap has teeth that bite into the outer braid of the cable, rather like a vampire biting into someone's neck. This device, shown in Figure B-30, allows you to connect a transceiver to the cable without causing the network to come to a stop, hence the name.[*]

A non-intrusive tap assembly consists of several parts, as shown in Figure B-31. There is a clamp assembly, a tap body, two braid pins and a center probe. The clamp assembly holds the tap body tightly in place on the thick coax cable. The braid pins have sharp edges on their tops which cut through the outer insulation of the coax cable and make contact with the outer shield braid of the cable. The long part of the pins extend into the tap body. When a transceiver is installed onto

---

[*] There are also transceiver taps that are equipped with female N connectors. This requires that you cut the thick coaxial cable and install male N connectors on the cable, which are then fastened onto the female N connectors of the transceiver tap. This process brings the network to a halt, earning this tap the name of *intrusive tap*.

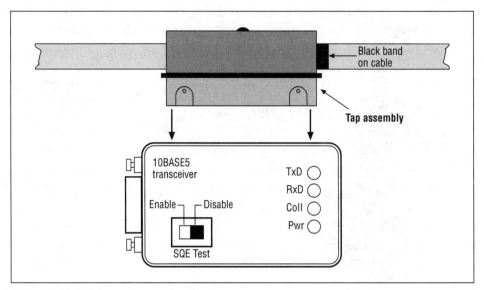

Figure B-30. Thick coax transceiver tap

the tap body, the pins make an electrical connection between the shield braid and connectors inside the transceiver.

The probe assembly fits through a hole drilled into the thick coax cable to make contact with the center conductor of the coax cable. A pin sticking out of the other side of the probe makes contact with a connector inside the transceiver, providing a connection between the transceiver and the center conductor of the cable.

1. To install the tap, first put the braid pins in place in the tap body. As stated earlier, transceiver taps must be located at a black band on the coax cable. Having found a black band, hold the tap body in place against the thick coax cable and slide the edges of the metal clamp over the plastic tap body.

2. Check for the desired placement of the tap on the black band of the cable before you tighten the clamp. Also, check for the correct orientation of the transceiver, by loosely inserting the transceiver into the tap body. This lets you make sure the transceiver is oriented correctly before tightening the clamp in place. Next, tighten the button head socket screw to hold the clamp and tap body into place on the cable, as shown in Figure B-32.

3. Once the tap is tightly secured into place on the cable, a coring tool is used to drill a hole into the cable (see Figure B-33). Insert the drill bit of the coring tool into the probe hole in the bottom of the tap body. Drill a hole into the cable by twisting the coring tool until the shoulder of the coring tool butts up against the tap body. Make sure that the hole is clean. Stray bits of braid wires

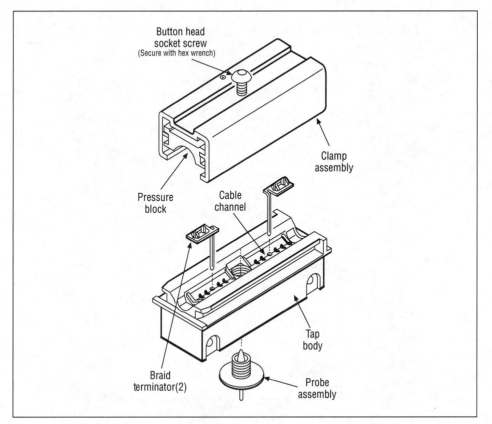

Figure B-31. Non-intrusive tap components

and shield foil can cause a short circuit and intermittent operation of the net-work.

4. The opposite end of the coring tool is a wrench, which is used to screw the center probe of the tap assembly into place. The probe makes contact with the center conductor of the cable.

5. At this point, you can use a VOM to test the resistance between one of the outer braid pins and the center probe pin. On a properly terminated cable, you should be able to measure approximately 25–27.5 ohms between the center probe and either of the braid pins. This indicates that the connectors are installed correctly, and are making contact with the center conductor and braid of the cable.

6. Once the center probe is in place, then a transceiver can be installed onto the tap body. Two screws hold the transceiver in place on the tap body, as shown in Figure B-34.

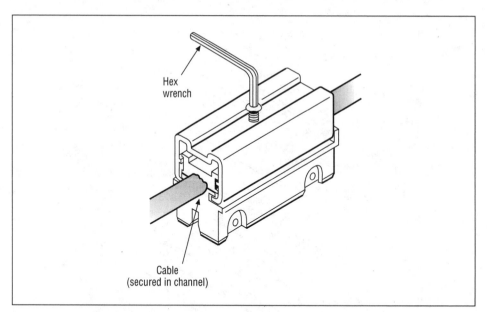

Figure B-32. Cable clamped into place

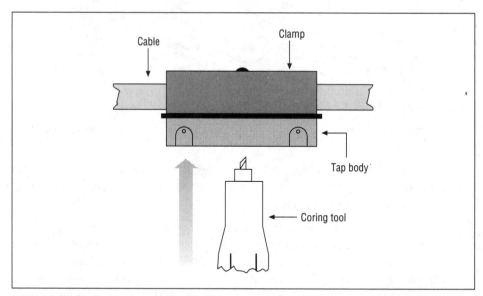

Figure B-33. Drilling a hole in the thick coax

Removing a Transceiver

If you remove the entire tap assembly from a thick Ethernet coaxial cable, you will be left with an unprotected hole that was drilled into the coax to reach the center conductor. This hole could allow moisture to enter the cable and alter the electri-

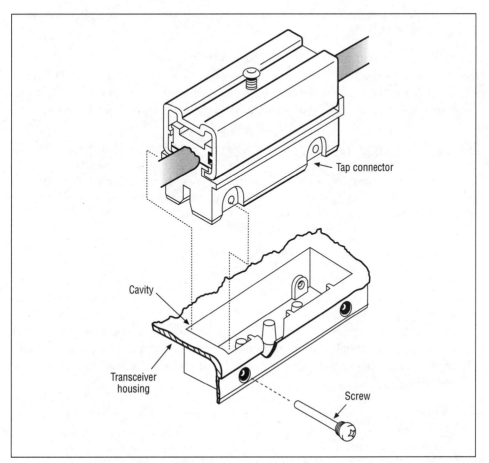

Figure B-34. Installing a transceiver onto the tap

cal characteristics of the coax. If a fragment of metal happens to fall into the hole, then the cable could short out, bringing the network to a halt.

If you must remove the tap assembly and expose the hole, then at a minimum the hole should be covered with electrical tape to keep it sealed against accidents. Some installers prefer to fill the hole with silicon caulk, also known as room temperature vulcanizing (RTV) caulk. This seals the hole and prevents any moisture from infiltrating the foam plastic insulation of the coax. Another approach is to disconnect the transceiver from the body of the tap and leave the cable tap assembly installed on the coax cable.

If you buy the tap assemblies separately from AMP, you will find that they come with a dust cover that fits over the open end of the tap. This covers up the three metal pins that are exposed there, protecting the pins from damage or electrical shorts that could bring the network to a halt. When a transceiver is removed, this cover can be re-installed on the abandoned tap and held in place with a couple of cable ties.

If you don't have a dust cover, then you can try using electrical tape to cover up the open end of the tap. The cost of a transceiver tap is relatively small. By leaving the tap on the cable and protecting the pins with a dust cover or electrical tape, you will keep the hole that was drilled in the cable from being exposed.

Troubleshooting Coaxial Cable Systems

This section will describe tools and techniques used in troubleshooting coaxial cabling systems, including a quick tour of some common problems found in both thick and thin coax cabling systems.

Coaxial Cable Troubleshooting Tools

A volt-ohmmeter is a basic test tool that can be used to check several things on coaxial media systems. With a volt-ohmmeter, you can test one end of a coax cable for the presence of the correct terminating resistor on the other end of the segment. With the terminator removed from one end of the segment, you should be able to measure roughly 50 ohms between the outer shield and center conductor of the cable. Figure B-35 shows how to test the termination resistance on a coaxial segment.

The currents and voltages used to carry Ethernet signals over coaxial cable are small and pose no threat to the typical user of Ethernet equipment. However, an improperly grounded coaxial cable installation can present an electrical hazard to anyone working with the cable or operating equipment connected to the cable.

If an ungrounded coaxial cable is touching an electrically "hot" circuit somewhere in its path, it can conduct that electricity along its entire length, presenting a risk to anyone handling the cable. Before handling any cable, you should make sure that the cable is not carrying any dangerous voltages or currents. Always observe standard safety practices when working on any type of cable, and take all necessary precautions to avoid electrical shock.

Too high or too low a terminating resistance can cause problems with signal detection on the cable. The standard notes that the terminating resistance should be 50 ohms, plus or minus 1 percent. To that value, you must add whatever cable resistance may be in the path between the point at which you are connecting the volt-ohmmeter and the terminator. For example, a thick coax system may add another 5 ohms, while a thin coax system can add up to 10 ohms. Therefore any

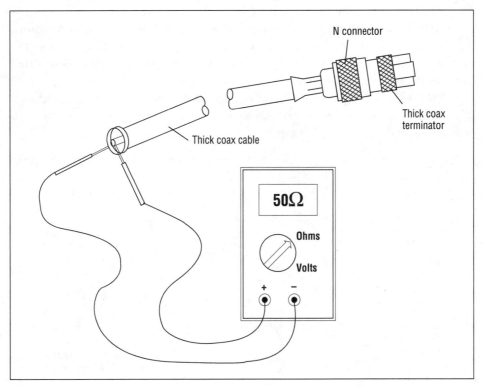

Figure B-35. Testing coaxial segment terminating resistance

value from 50 to 60 ohms is acceptable; anything beyond that would indicate a problem. Small currents that represent Ethernet signals on the cable can sometimes affect the resistance measurements of a digital volt-ohmmeter. If you get a reading that looks weird, try inverting the leads of the volt-ohmmeter when making resistance tests.

On a thick Ethernet system you can also test a newly installed transceiver tap to make sure that the conductors of the tap are making contact with the conductors of the coaxial cable. If both ends of the coax cable have terminators, then the circuit you are measuring consists of two conductors (an inner conductor and outer shield) with two 50 ohm resistors at each end. Two 50 ohm resistors wired this way places the resistors in parallel, resulting in a total resistance of 25 ohms measured between the conductors. The combination of cable resistance and the terminators should provide a measurement of around 25 to 27.5 ohms between the center conductor and outer shield of the coax cable by way of the pins in the transceiver tap. This verifies whether or not the pins are making a good connection, and that the cable is properly terminated at each end.

Another resistance check you can make is the *total loop resistance* of a coax segment to make sure that the loop resistance is not too high. The loop resistance does not include the terminating resistance. Instead, loop resistance consists of the resistance of the cable as well as all cable connectors, measured as a loop from one end of the cable to the other, and back. You check loop resistance to make sure that the cable and connectors do not add excessive resistance to the circuit; otherwise, it can cause problems with signal detection on the cable. Figure B-36 shows how to test the loop resistance.

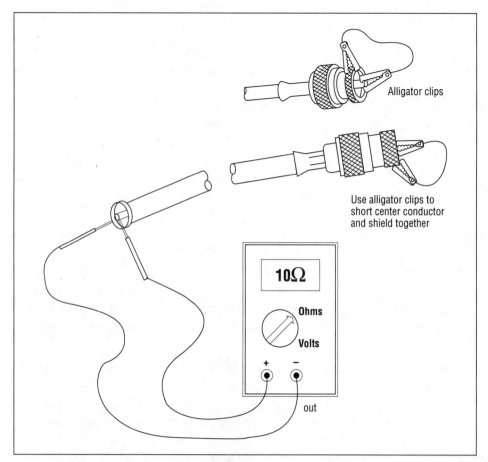

Figure B-36. Testing coaxial segment loop resistance

According to the standard, the total loop resistance of a thick coaxial cable segment should be no higher than 5 ohms. A thin coaxial cable segment should have a loop resistance no higher than 10 ohms.

A more complex and expensive device for testing coaxial segments is a Time Domain Reflectometer for metal cables, or metallic TDR. The most sophisticated form of this device is a self-contained box with a display screen on the front that looks something like an oscilloscope. This form of TDR requires some training to use, since the information provided is based on the operator's interpretation of waveforms displayed on the screen. The TDR works much like radar or sonar, sending an electrical pulse out onto the cable segment under test, then displaying the echo of the pulse. The shape of the echo, the direction of the echo pulse (whether the pulse goes upwards or downwards on the screen), and the location of the pulse on the screen can provide a good deal of information, as shown in Figure B-37.

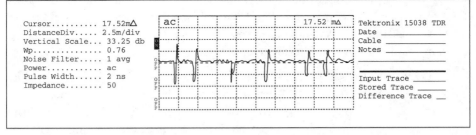

Figure B-37. Coaxial cable TDR display

When performing a TDR test of a cable, you remove the terminator from one end to make it possible to connect the TDR to the cable. A TDR that is specifically designed to work with Ethernet may include an option that allows the TDR connection to provide a 50 ohm termination, which allows the network to continue operating during the test. An experienced TDR operator can determine from the shape and location of the pulses on the screen just how long a cable segment is. They can also tell whether transceiver taps are properly installed and whether cable connectors are loose or improperly installed. TDRs will also display other problems with the cable, such as excessively tight bends.

Professional cable installers will typically own a metallic TDR, since it is worth their while to invest the time and money needed to get any benefits from a high-end TDR. Unless your site has a lot of coaxial cable, it may not be cost-effective to purchase a high-end TDR. On the other hand, a high-end TDR in the hands of an experienced operator can readily diagnose coaxial cable problems that can otherwise be quite difficult to find.

Hand-held coaxial testers

Some hand-held cable testers also include a limited form of TDR capability that automatically runs some basic TDR tests and displays the results in English on the screen of the cable tester. On such a device you might see the words "Open at 450 feet," indicating that there is an open connector on the cable, or that the cable ends 450 feet from the connection to the tester. A hand-held cable tester does not have a sophisticated display, and cannot provide the kind of information that a high-end TDR can show. However, a basic TDR function is better than none at all, and this can be a useful way to find some major faults in a coaxial cable.

A hand-held cable tester can also check for the presence of a terminator at the end of the cable, and it can be used to check the total loop resistance of the coaxial segment. If a terminator is present at the end of the cable, then a basic TDR test will not find the end of the cable. The TDR pulse will be sent out over the cable and absorbed in the terminator at the end of the cable, which may lead to a display on the cable tester such as "NEF," meaning "No End Found." This is good news if you are checking for the presence of a terminator at the end of the cable. If the terminator has been removed and you still see "NEF," then this could be an indication that there is excessive resistance on the cable somewhere, soaking up the signal before it can return to the tester.

At this point, you can set the cable tester to check for the resistance on the cable, and it can tell you what the total resistance may be. First, you must remove one of the terminators from one end of the cable in order to attach the cable tester. The total resistance measured will therefore be the 50 ohms of the remaining terminator at the other end of the cable, plus the few ohms representing the total loop resistance of the coaxial cable. This should result in a total reading in the range of 50 to 60 ohms.

Common Coaxial Cable Problems

There are two coaxial cable types used in Ethernet: thick coax and thin coax. Both coaxial cables have the same characteristic impedance (50 ohms), and transceivers send exactly the same signals over each system. However, the cables are physically different and use different connectors, which lead to different problems. We will list some common problems found on the thin coax system first, followed by the thick coax system.

Thin coax problems

Incorrect type of coaxial cable

The standard for thin coax systems requires a cable with a 50 ohm characteristic impedance rating, and a stranded center conductor, among other specifications. Incorrect cable segments in a thin Ethernet system can cause signal reflections which result in bit errors (CRC errors) and frame loss.

Loose or incorrectly installed connectors

The BNC connectors installed on the ends of thin coax segments can be a major source of problems, especially if the connectors were installed locally instead of by a manufacturer. A wrong-sized BNC connector can result in a loose crimp onto the cable that leads to intermittent and hard to find problems. It's also very easy to use an improper crimping tool, which doesn't crimp tightly enough, or to leave loose wires around the crimp-on connector, which can cause electrical problems later on.

Even worse than improperly installed crimp-on connectors are the various screw-on connectors, which are sometimes used to quickly build a thin coax segment. These connectors easily screw onto a cable end with no crimping required. They can come loose just as easily. When a connector comes loose, it can lead to intermittent connections that can be very time consuming and frustrating to track down; screw-on connectors are therefore best avoided.

Excessive number of connectors

A thin coax segment is made up of a number of cable sections connected together with BNC T and barrel connectors. It is possible to end up with so many connectors on a long segment that the loop resistance of the segment becomes too high. The total loop resistance of a thin coax segment should not exceed 10 ohms, or signal detection on the cable may not work correctly.

To check for loop resistance alone, you can remove the terminators at each end of the segment. At one end of the segment you short the shield and center conductor together, perhaps with a short jumper equipped with alligator clips (see Figure B-36). At the other end of the segment you measure the total DC loop resistance, which should be 10 ohms or less on a thin coax segment. Or, you can leave the terminator connected to the far end, and measure the combination of loop resistance and far end terminating resistance, which should result in a reading of around 50 to 60 ohms. This makes for an easier and faster test.

Overlong cable segment

As a thin coaxial network system grows to accommodate new station connections, it may also grow beyond the limits of the standard. According to the official guidelines, a thin coax segment is limited to 185 m (606.9 feet). As the cable winds in and out of each area, it can end up growing longer than this. Short of measuring the cable by hand, the only way to test for length is to remove the terminators and use a TDR to check the cable.

Stub cables

Stub cables are installed between the transceiver in the station interface and the BNC T connector on the thin Ethernet segment, as shown in Figure B-13. According to the standard, the distance between the BNC connector and the transceiver in the interface should be as short as possible, and no longer than 4 centimeters (cm). This distance is taken up by the length of the BNC T and the wires in the interface, meaning that stub cables are not allowed.

Unfortunately, stub cables often appear to work, convincing people that they can get away with using them. However, each stub cable represents some amount of signal reflection on the segment, leading to increased bit error rates and frame loss. Even if you don't notice the frame loss caused by stub cables, the signal loss will become so high at some point that you may find that some stations act like ghosts, occasionally losing connection to the network. These problems can be avoided by eliminating all stub cables.

Too many terminators

There should only be two terminators on a coaxial segment: one at each end. Sometimes a repeater will be installed in the middle of a thin coax segment, with the internal termination on the thin coax port of the repeater mistakenly left enabled. This leads to three terminators on the segment, causing problems with collision detect and network performance.

Thick coax problems

Loose or incorrectly installed connectors

The N connectors installed on the ends of thick coax segments can be a source of problems, since these connectors are often installed locally, and are very sensitive to the quality of installation. If the installation is done correctly and by the book, using the correct crimping tool and careful preparation of the cable end, then they will usually be very reliable and problem free. However, if they are installed sloppily, using an inexpensive crimping tool that does not apply enough force, and with poorly prepared cable ends, then the result can be intermittent connections that are quite difficult to track down. Screw-on N connectors have the same faults as screw-on BNC connectors: they eventually come loose and cause problems.

Dirty taps

A transceiver is installed on a thick coax cable by drilling a hole in the cable to allow the center pin of the transceiver tap to reach the center conductor of the thick coax cable. This hole must be drilled through two layers of foil insulation and two layers of braided insulation. If pieces of insulation are allowed to remain in the hole, they could cause intermittent shorts in the cable, leading to intermittent outages of the Ethernet system.

Abandoned taps

When a transceiver tap is removed from a thick coax cable it leaves behind a hole, which, if left open or uncovered, could cause problems. Any small bits of metal that fall into the hole could short out the cable, bringing the operation of the entire Ethernet system to a halt. Water could also enter the tap hole and either short out the cable or lead to intermittent operation.

Overlong cable segment

The guidelines allow a thick coax segment to be 500 m (1,640 feet) in length. However, as a network grows over time, it's possible to end up with an overlong thick coax cable segment that can lead to problems with signal strength on the cable. Short of measuring the cable by hand, the only way to test for length is to remove the terminators and use a TDR to check the cable length.

Excessive loop resistance

If a cable has too many connectors on it, or if the connectors are poorly installed and have too much resistance, it's possible to end up with excessive loop resistance on the segment. This can lead to problems with incorrect operation of the collision detect circuits in the transceivers. To check for loop resistance:

1. Remove the terminators at each end of the segment.

2. At one end of the segment, short the shield and center conductors together by using a short jumper equipped with alligator clips (see Figure B-36).

3. At the other end of the segment, measure the DC loop resistance, which should be 5 ohms or less on a thick coax segment.

Or, you can leave the terminator connected to the far end, and measure the combination of loop resistance and far-end terminating resistance, which should result in a reading of around 50 to 55 ohms. This makes for an easier and faster test.

Excessively tight cable bends

Thick coaxial cables that are bent too tight can result in signal reflections that cause increased bit errors (CRC errors) and frame loss. Excessively tight cable bends can be detected with a TDR.

C

AUI Equipment: Installation and Configuration

The 15-pin attachment unit interface (AUI) was the first equipment interface developed for Ethernet, and is used on 10 Mbps Ethernet equipment.[*] This appendix describes specific issues concerning the installation and configuration of AUI-based equipment. We begin with the AUI slide latch followed by an overview of the operation and configuration of the SQE Test signal, which applies to external AUI transceivers. Finally, we discuss the AUI port concentrator, and describe the configuration rules for this type of equipment.

The AUI Slide Latch

Rich Seifert, a member of the IEEE and one of the primary design engineers who worked on the design of the original 10 Mbps Ethernet system, has this to say about the sliding latch connectors:

> Personally, I would have saved every Ethernet user a lot of grief by not specifying the dreaded slide latch connector (used on the cable between the station and the transceiver). We really had good intentions. I was fed up with the RS-232C connectors that fell off because the tiny screwdriver necessary to tighten them down was never handy. I just didn't realize that the slide latch was so flimsy and unreliable until it was too late. Ethernet installers around the world must curse me every day.[†]

As you can probably guess from Seifert's confession, the slide latch connectors used on 15-pin AUI connectors have been a source of problems for Ethernet

---

[*] The AUI is described in detail in Chapter 6, *Ethernet Media Fundamentals*.

[†] Rich Seifert, "What Would We Change," from "Ethernet: Ten Years After," *Byte*, (January 1991), p. 319.

installers for years. In fact, the slide latch is probably the most disliked part of the entire 10 Mbps Ethernet system. That's because it is the part just about every user of AUI-based equipment has encountered. At the same time it is the part that could be voted "least likely to succeed" given the problems caused by poor design and installation.

Figure C-1 shows what a slide latch looks like in the open and closed positions before being installed on the locking posts of the mating 15-pin connector. The view is from the end of the transceiver cable, looking at the connector "end on," showing the screws that hold the sliding latch clip in place on the end of the connector. The screws are installed in the connector end, and do not move. The latch assembly fits underneath the heads of the screws with a small amount of room left to allow for movement, which lets the latch slide back and forth.

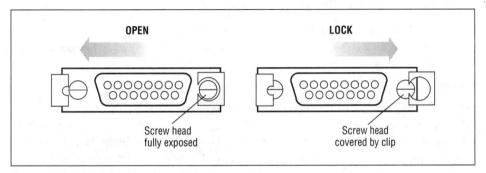

Figure C-1. Sliding latch mechanism

The clips at each end of the latch will clip onto the heads of the locking posts provided on the mating 15-pin connector—that's what holds the two connectors together. If everything about the hardware is correct, then the latch is fairly hard to move back and forth, and will "snap" into the open or closed position. If the hardware is not correct, the latch will be loose and will move easily from side-to-side.

Problems with the Sliding Latch

Despite the best efforts of the IEEE 802 committee, some vendors did not follow the specifications carefully and did not install the slide latch connectors properly on their equipment and cables. To compound the problem, there was wide variability in the quality of the slide latch, with some vendors using rather lightweight slide latch hardware, resulting in transceiver cables that fell off easily.

Although the slide latch connector may not be the world's mightiest way to connect things, it can result in a quick and secure attachment when properly installed and adequate gauge hardware is used. A good quality slide latch connection can be made solid enough to allow you to move the computer around by tugging, or more likely tripping over, a transceiver cable. Many vendors have managed to do the job right, resulting in very reliable network connections.

On the other hand, when the slide latch connector is bad, it is horrid. Slide latches that are made out of lightweight metal that bends easily can be nearly impossible to get onto the locking posts. If the vendor has also installed the 15-pin connector incorrectly, then the situation can indeed be grim. Some years ago, a few vendors mounted the 15-pin connector just behind the metal frame of the computer. This resulted in the locking pins of the 15-pin connector being located slightly too far away from the surface of the slide latch when they were connected. That, in turn, led to slide latch connectors that never made a tight fit and that fell off at the slightest provocation.

Tips for Sliding Latches

There's nothing quite as frustrating as a network problem that turns out to be equipment that has come loose due to a poorly implemented slide latch. Even worse, a transceiver cable can sometimes come half undone at the 15-pin AUI connector of the station interface.

When that happens, the power connections will be made to the transceiver, but other wires used to receive signals will not make the connection. The transceiver will show power and some signal lights will be working normally, but the station interface may not be receiving signals or may be receiving garbled signals. This condition can be quite difficult to troubleshoot, since the interface cable may look okay to a cursory glance, and it may not be immediately obvious where the failure is occurring.

Here are a couple of approaches for dealing with poorly implemented slide latches:

Use a lighter transceiver cable

> The relatively heavy and somewhat stiff standard grade transceiver cable makes the problem with lightweight slide latch connectors worse. An office grade transceiver cable, described in Chapter 6, is more flexible and lighter in weight, and presents a much smaller strain to the connector.

> While office grade cables have a limited distance due to higher signal attenuation, they are more convenient to use. They snake around furniture more easily and are less bulky and less obtrusive in an office. By using an office grade transceiver cable, you can often solve the problem of the weight of the cable pulling itself loose from the slide latch connector.

Use slide latch retainers

One way to keep the latch from sliding open is to use a special plastic retainer that was invented to deal with this problem.

The retainer looks a like a cable tie and has a wedge-shaped end with a flange that locks into place on one end of the slide latch. By occupying the space that is exposed when the latch is closed, the slide latch retainer makes it impossible for the latch to slide into the open position again. This effectively locks the slide latch into place. While these retainers are not inexpensive, many network managers decided that if they keep a single slide latch from coming open and causing a network failure then they are well worth their price. These retainers, called ET-Lock by the vendor, may be found in Appendix A, *Resources*.

Operation of SQE Test

The signal quality error (SQE) Test signal is used on AUI-based equipment to provide a test of the collision detection circuits. The SQE Test signal is also nicknamed *heartbeat*, because it occurs regularly after each frame transmission. You will sometimes find the heartbeat nickname used in documentation or on older equipment. Only 15-pin AUI-based external transceivers need to be configured for SQE Test. Ethernet ports based on the newer medium independent interface (MII) and gigabit medium independent interface (GMII) do not use the SQE Test signal.

The way the SQE Test signal works is simple. After every frame is sent the transceiver waits a few bit times and then sends a short burst (about 10 bit times) of the collision presence signal. This signal is sent over the collision signal wires of the transceiver cable back to the Ethernet interface. This tests both the collision detection electronics and signal paths. Figure C-2 shows the path that the SQE Test signal takes.

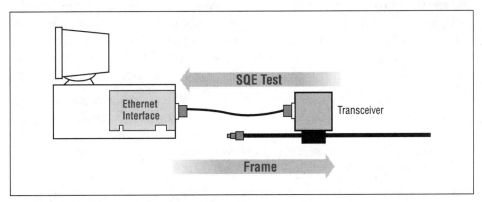

Figure C-2. SQE Test operation

The Ethernet interface in the computer receives the SQE Test signal on the collision signal wires of the transceiver cable after every frame transmission made by the interface.

Four things you should know about the SQE Test are:

- The SQE Test signal is not sent out onto the network segment. Instead, SQE Test is only sent between the transceiver and the Ethernet interface as a test of the collision detect circuits.

- The SQE Test signal does not delay frame transmissions. Since the SQE Test pulse occurs during the interframe gap, no time is lost due to SQE Test signals. An Ethernet interface can send frames as fast as possible while also receiving SQE Test signals between every frame transmission.

- Although the SQE Test signal uses a short burst of the same signals used for a collision, SQE Test signals are not interpreted as a collision by the station. The timing of the SQE Test pulse allows the station to differentiate the SQE Test signal from a real collision signal.

- The SQE Test signal *must* be disabled on an external transceiver connected to a repeater hub. The reasons for this are described in the section entitled "SQE Test Signal and 10 Mbps Repeaters," in Chapter 17, *Ethernet Repeater Hubs*.

When the SQE Test signal was first introduced in the early 1980s, transceivers could be purchased without SQE Test, or with switch-selectable SQE Test that would allow you to turn it off. Modern 10 Mbps AUI-equipped transceivers all have a jumper or a switch that allows the SQE Test signal to be disabled.

Ethernet Stations and SQE Test

For normal stations (DTEs) attached to a network segment with external AUI transceivers, the standard recommends that the SQE Test signal be enabled on the external transceiver. That's because the absence of a SQE Test signal after a frame transmission can alert the Ethernet interface that there may be a problem with the collision detection circuits. The problem could be caused by something simple, like a loose transceiver cable. On the other hand, it could be a more serious problem, like a failed collision detection circuit in the external transceiver.

Without a correctly functioning collision detect system, the Ethernet interface might ignore collisions on the network and transmit at incorrect times. While rare, this kind of failure can be difficult to debug. Ideally, network management software could alert you if it detected a problem or absence of a SQE Test signal after a frame transmission.

However, it can be difficult to derive any benefit from the SQE Test signal in the real world. Most Ethernet interface software is designed not to make a fuss if the

SQE Test signal is missing, mainly because the SQE Test is an optional signal on external transceivers and is not well understood by most users. Many vendors take the approach of silently logging the presence or absence of a SQE Test in a software counter somewhere. This avoids worried telephone calls from people asking what the error message about the SQE Test might mean.

There are other possible side effects of enabling SQE Test for external transceiver connections to normal stations. For example, the SQE Test signal can cause the collision presence light to flash on some transceivers and interfaces equipped with troubleshooting lights. That's because the SQE Test pulse is sent over the same pair of collision presence wires in the AUI cable as a real collision signal. This can cause the troubleshooting light to flash for both real collisions and SQE Test signals. Therefore, if you enable SQE Test—as recommended by the standard for all normal computers—you may need to ignore the effect that the SQE Test signal has on any collision presence lights on your network hardware.

AUI Port Concentrator

Although it isn't described in the Ethernet standard, the AUI port concentrator (shown in Figure C-3), also called a *port multiplier, transceiver multiplexor,* or *fan out unit,* is widely used in older 10 Mbps Ethernet systems.

The original port concentrator was developed by DEC and called the DELNI (for *Digital Ethernet Local Network Interconnect*). Port concentrators sold by other vendors are often referred to as DELNIs or called "DELNI-like" devices. The port concentrator was developed when thick coaxial Ethernet was the only media type available, and network designers faced a problem when it came to connecting a set of machines clustered together in a small space.

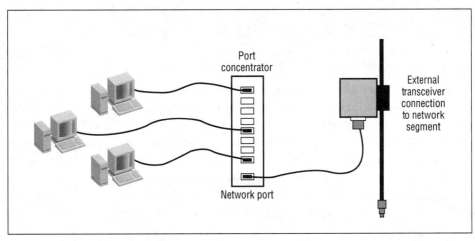

Figure C-3. Port concentrator

The problem arises because the thick Ethernet standard requires that each transceiver attachment be separated by at least 2.5 meters (m) of thick coaxial cable from the next transceiver attachment. When you needed to connect a cluster of machines to the network, you had to coil up enough thick Ethernet coax to provide sufficient cable to meet the 2.5 m transceiver spacing requirement.

By providing several (usually eight) AUI ports in a single device, vendors made it easier to connect groups of computers to an Ethernet. The eight computers are attached to the 15-pin male AUI connectors on the port concentrator. The concentrator has its own 15-pin female "network" port which provides a way to connect the concentrator to a network segment using an external transceiver. In effect, all eight computers end up sharing the single external transceiver connection to the network segment. The eight computers are not penalized for sharing a single transceiver connection, since only one computer can transmit at any given time on a half-duplex coaxial Ethernet system.

It's important to note that a port concentrator is not a repeater and does not include any signal re-timing or regeneration circuits. In terms of the timing delay budget for a standard Ethernet, the concentrator unit sits in the transceiver cable path between the Ethernet segment and the station. The added signal delay and other effects contributed by the electronics inside the concentrator are not accounted for in the official configuration guidelines provided in the IEEE standard. These effects on the signal may vary depending on which vendor built the concentrator. In addition, since the concentrator is not described in the standard, a network system using concentrators cannot be verified using the IEEE configuration guidelines.

If you use port concentrators, you should read the vendor's configuration guidelines and follow them carefully. Even then you may find that signal delays and other effects contributed by concentrators may cause problems in very large networks, or when stations are attached to the concentrator with long AUI cables.

Port Concentrator Guidelines

To account for the added delay imposed by the port concentrator's electronics, some vendors state that you must use a shorter transceiver cable for connecting a station to the port concentrator. What they are saying is that you cannot use a full-length 50 m transceiver cable because the port concentrator has internal delays of its own that need to be accounted for. One vendor notes that the electronics in their port concentrators can add a signal delay equal to about 10 m of transceiver cable. Therefore, calculation of the total length of transceiver cable from the station to the live network must also include 10 m of port concentrator cable equivalence.

An easy way to deal with all of this is to simply add the 10 m cable equivalency of the port concentrator to the length of transceiver cable used to attach the port concentrator to the Ethernet segment. This figure provides a baseline transceiver cable length for that particular port concentrator installation. When you connect a station to the port concentrator, you need to add the transceiver cable length from the station to the port concentrator to the baseline figure to get the total transceiver cable length. The total length of the station transceiver cable plus the port concentrator baseline figure must not exceed 50 meters. It would no doubt be safer to make a total of 40 m your maximum value when using a port concentrator.

Calculating Port Concentrator Cable Length

If you use office grade transceiver cables, then you need to remember that the office cable has its own cable equivalency, which is four times its length in delay compared to a standard transceiver cable.

For example, a station attached to a port concentrator with a 5 m office grade transceiver cable is equivalent to an attachment with 20 m of standard grade transceiver cable. That 20 m distance must be added to the port concentrator internal cable equivalency of 10 m. To make the correct calculation of transceiver cable length, you must also include the length of transceiver cable used to connect the port concentrator to the external transceiver on the Ethernet segment.

Port concentrators can cause signal distortion due to their placement in the frame transmission path between the stations attached to the port concentrator and the stations on the rest of the network. As a signal propagates through the Ethernet system, it is allowed to accumulate a certain amount of timing distortion, known as *jitter*. Each component in the system has a jitter budget that it must not exceed for the system to work correctly. For instance, the standard for the AUI cable includes a jitter budget of ±1 nanosecond (ns). This means that the signal traveling through an AUI cable is allowed to shift up to one nanosecond in either direction in time from its original time base.

Port concentrators have a set of electronics in them that cause a certain amount of jitter, and it's hard to design a port concentrator that will cause 1 ns or less of jitter in a signal. Therefore, you may find that a port concentrator will end up adding more jitter than the standard AUI cable is allowed to add according to the IEEE specifications. The accumulation of jitter in the signal is another reason why vendors limit the number of port concentrators you may connect together.

Problems with Concentrators

Cable equivalency in port concentrators, as well as the extra delay in office grade transceiver cables and the accumulation of jitter, can be easily overlooked, leading to problems with the network connection. If you end up with too much signal delay or too much signal jitter in the path between the station and the network connection, the operation of the network may be affected. It can be hard to predict where things will fail, since various components in your network such as transceivers and Ethernet interfaces may have slightly different performance in the presence of excessive jitter. Some interfaces may be able to pick out a signal, while others may simply fail to receive the frame.

Experience shows that problems with port concentrator connections lead to failures in which the amount of Ethernet frame loss can become quite high. Large frames seem to suffer the highest loss rate, while smaller frames may make it through a marginal port concentrator connection with a lower loss rate. Since some frames do manage to get through, the network may appear to function at first glance. However, when frames are lost, the network application must recover by re-sending them. The application software typically has a timeout based on some number of seconds of no response time, after which it will retransmit a frame. This is a slow process, and one reason why a poorly configured port concentrator connection may appear to the user as a very slow network.

Cascaded Port Concentrators

It is possible to plug the network port of one port concentrator box into a station port of another concentrator, producing a cascade of two or more port concentrators. Cascading port concentrators means that you are adding the port concentrator delays together, since the signals from the stations attached to the second port concentrator must go through the first port concentrator to reach the network segment.

The added delay and the accumulation of signal jitter can cause problems, which is why some vendors warn against this topology when the port concentrators must be attached to a "live" network. A *live network* is another way of referring to one or more normal network segments supporting stations. In other words, cascading two standalone port concentrator units together will probably work. However, connecting the cascaded concentrators to an external network may cause signal timing problems. The problems will occur due to the accumulation of timing delay and jitter in the combination of signal paths consisting of the cascaded port concentrators and the segment(s) making up the external network segment.

SQE Test and the Port Concentrator

When using port concentrators, you need to be aware of the way that the SQE Test signal is dealt with by the port concentrator. A port concentrator connected to an external transceiver with the SQE Test signal enabled will pass the SQE Test signal received from the external transceiver through every concentrator port. As such, every station attached to the port concentrator will receive SQE Test signals.

In a normal station, this is usually no problem. However, if you have a repeater attached to a port concentrator, then you need to make sure that the repeater does not receive the SQE Test signal. You can do this by turning off the SQE Test signal on the external transceiver that connects the port concentrator to the rest of the network. If you are running the port concentrator in standalone mode, you may find that the port concentrator generates its own SQE Test signal internally and sends it out on all ports. Again, this can cause problems if you have a repeater attached to one of the ports of the port concentrator.

Glossary

4B/5B

The 4B/5B code is a block encoding scheme used to send Fast Ethernet data. In this signal encoding scheme, 4 bits of data are turned into 5-bit code symbols for transmission over the media system.

4D-PAM5

Block encoding scheme used for 1000BASE-T twisted-pair Gigabit Ethernet which transmits signals over four wire pairs. This coding scheme translates an 8-bit byte of data into a simultaneous transmission of four code symbols (4D) which are sent over the media system as 5-level Pulse Amplitude Modulated (PAM5) signals.

50-pin Connector

A connector that is sometimes used on 10BASE-T hubs as an alternate twisted-pair segment connection method. The 50-pin connector is used to connect 25-pair cables used in telephone wiring systems, which are typically rated to meet Category 3 specifications. Commonly referred to as a Telco, CHAMP, or "blue ribbon" connector.

8-pin Connector

A twisted-pair connector that closely resembles the RJ-45 connector used in U.S. telephone systems, but has significantly better electrical characteristics than typical telephone-grade RJ-45 connectors.

8B6T

Block encoding scheme used in 100BASE-T4 based on translating 8-bit (binary) data patterns into six-bit code symbols which are transmitted as 3-level (ternary) signals.

8B/10B

Block encoding scheme used in 1000BASE-X Gigabit Ethernet systems, in which 8-bit bytes of data are translated into 10-bit code symbols.

10BASE-T

10 Mbps Ethernet system based on Manchester signal encoding transmitted over Category 3 or better twisted-pair cable.

10BASE2

10 Mbps Ethernet system based on Manchester signal encoding transmitted over thin coaxial cable. Also called *Thin Wire* and *Cheapernet.*

10BASE5

10 Mbps Ethernet system based on Manchester signal encoding transmitted over thick coaxial cable. Also called *Thick Net.*

10BASE-F

10 Mbps Ethernet system based on Manchester signal encoding transmitted over fiber optic cable.

100BASE-FX

100 Mbps Fast Ethernet system based on 4B/5B signal encoding transmitted over fiber optic cable.

100BASE-T

Term used for the entire 100 Mbps Fast Ethernet system, including both twisted-pair and fiber optic media types.

100BASE-T2

100 Mbps Fast Ethernet system designed to use two pairs of Category 3 twisted-pair cable.

100BASE-T4

100 Mbps Fast Ethernet system based on 8B6T signal encoding transmitted over four pairs of Category 3 twisted-pair cable.

100BASE-TX

100 Mbps Fast Ethernet system based on 4B/5B signal encoding transmitted over two pairs of Category 5 twisted-pair cable.

100BASE-X

Term used when referring to any Fast Ethernet media system based on 4B/5B block encoding. Includes 100BASE-TX and 100BASE-FX media systems.

802.1

IEEE Working Group for High-Level Interfaces, Network Management, Inter-working, and other issues common across LAN technologies.

802.2

IEEE Working Group for Logical Link Control (LLC).

802.3

IEEE Working Group for CSMA/CD LANs.

802.5

IEEE Working Group for Token Ring LANs.

1000BASE-CX

1000 Mbps Gigabit Ethernet system based on 8B/10B block encoding which is transmitted over copper cable.

1000BASE-LX

1000 Mbps Gigabit Ethernet system based on 8B/10B block encoding which is transmitted using long wavelength laser transmitters and fiber optic cable.

1000BASE-SX

1000 Mbps Gigabit Ethernet system based on 8B/10B block encoding which is transmitted using short wavelength laser transmitters and fiber optic cable.

1000BASE-T

1000 Mbps Gigabit Ethernet system based on 4D-PAM5 block encoding which is transmitted over twisted-pair cable.

1000BASE-X

Term used when referring to any 1000 Mbps Gigabit media system based on the 8B/10B encoding scheme used in Fibre Channel. Includes 1000BASE-CX, 1000BASE-LX, and 1000BASE-SX.

Address

A means of uniquely identifying a device on a network.

ANSI

American National Standards Institute. The coordinating body for many voluntary standards groups within the United States, and the U.S. representative to the International Organization for Standardization (ISO).

ARP

Address Resolution Protocol. A protocol used to discover a destination host's hardware (MAC) address when given the host's IP address.

ASIC

Application Specific Integrated Circuit. An integrated circuit chip specifically designed for a given application. ASICs allow vendors to develop high-performance network devices (such as switching hubs) with more capabilities at lower cost.

ASN.1

Abstract Syntax Notation-1. An ISO standard for machine-independent data formatting. Used as the data formatting standard for SNMP MIBs.

Attenuation

The decreasing power of a transmitted signal as it travels along a cable. The longer a cable, the greater the signal attenuation will be. This loss is expressed in decibels (dB).

AUI

Attachment Unit Interface. The 15-pin signal interface defined in the original Ethernet standard that carries signals between a station and an outboard transceiver.

AUI Cable

Also known as a transceiver cable, the AUI cable connects a station to an outboard transceiver.

AUI Connector

The 15-pin AUI connector on a station, cable or outboard transceiver that allows these devices to be interconnected.

Auto-Negotiation

A protocol defined in the Ethernet standard that allows devices at either end of a link segment to advertise and negotiate modes of operation such as the speed of the link. Other modes that can be negotiated include full or half-duplex operation and support for Ethernet flow control. If a device is equipped with Auto-Negotiation, it can determine the capabilities of the device at the other end of the link (the link partner) and select the highest common denominator of operational modes.

AWG

American Wire Gauge. This is a U.S. standard set of wire conductor sizes. "Gauge" means the diameter of the wire; the higher the gauge number, the smaller the diameter and the thinner the wire. The gauge is measured in decimal fractions of an inch. For example, a 22 AWG wire has a diameter of 0.02534 inch.

Backbone

A network used as a primary path for transporting traffic between network segments. A backbone network is often based on higher capacity technology, to provide enough bandwidth to accommodate the traffic of all segments linked to the backbone.

Bandwidth

The maximum capacity of a network channel. Usually expressed in bits per second (bps). Ethernet channels have a bandwidth of 10-, 100-, and 1000 Mbps.

Baud

A baud is a unit of signaling speed. The speed in baud is the number of discrete signal events per second. If each signal event represents a single bit, then the baud rate is the same as the bit rate per second. If more than one signal event is required to transmit a bit of data, then the baud rate will be greater than the rate of bits per second.

Bit

The smallest unit of data, either a zero or a one.

Bit Error Rate

A measure of data integrity, expressed as the ratio of received bits that are in error, relative to the amount of bits received. Often expressed as a negative power of ten. For example, the worst-case bit error rate for several 10 Mbps Ethernet media varieties is 10^{-9} (a rate of one error in every 1 billion bits transmitted).

Bit Time

The length of time required to transmit one bit of information.

Block Encoding

Block encoding is a system whereby a group of data bits are encoded into a larger set of code bits. The data stream is divided into a fixed number of bits per block. Each data block is translated into a set of code bits, also called code symbols. The expanded set of code symbols is used for control purposes, such as start-of-frame, end-of-frame, carrier extension, and error signaling.

BNC

A bayonet locking connector used on 10BASE2 thin coaxial cable segments. The BNC designation is said to stand for *Bayonet Navy Connector.* However, it is also said to stand for *Bayonet Neil-Concelman* after the names of two designers of coaxial connectors.

Bridge

A device that connects two or more networks at the data link layer.

Broadcast Address

The multicast destination address of all ones, defined as the group of all stations on a network. The standard requires that every station must receive and act upon every Ethernet frame whose destination address is all ones.

Broadcast Domain

The set of all nodes connected in a network that will receive each other's broadcast frames. A single segment or set of segments connected with repeaters (collision domain) is a broadcast domain. All Ethernet segments connected with a layer 2 switching hub are also in the same broadcast domain.

Virtual LANs (VLANs) can be use to establish multiple broadcast domains in an Ethernet system based on switching hubs.

Building Entrance

An area inside a building where cables enter and are connected to riser cables for signal distribution throughout the building.

Bus

In general: An electrical transmission path for carrying information, usually serving as a shared connection for multiple devices.

In LAN technology: A linear network topology, in which all computers are connected to a single cable.

Carrier Sense

In Ethernet, carrier sense is a method of detecting the presence of signal activity on a common channel.

Category 3

Twisted-pair cable with a Category 3 rating has electrical characteristics suitable for carrying 10BASE-T and 100BASE-T4 signals. Category 3 cable is no longer recommended for use in a building cabling system.

Category 5

Category 5 cable has electrical characteristics suitable for all twisted-pair Ethernet media systems, including 10BASE-T, 100BASE-TX and 1000BASE-T. Category 5 and Category 5e cable are the preferred cable types for structured cabling systems.

Category 5e

An enhanced version of Category 5 cable, developed to improve certain cable characteristics important to Gigabit Ethernet operation. It is recommended that all new structured cabling systems be based on Category 5e cable.

Coaxial Cable

A cable with a low susceptibility to interference. An outer conductor, also called a screen or shield, surrounds an inner conductor. The conductors are commonly separated by a solid plastic or foam plastic insulating material. Thick and thin coaxial cables are used for 10BASE5 and 10BASE2 Ethernet systems, respectively.

Collision

A normal event on a half-duplex Ethernet system that indicates simultaneous channel access by two or more stations. A collision is automatically resolved by the medium access control (MAC) protocol.

Collision Detect

A method of detecting two or more simultaneous transmissions on a common signal channel.

Conditioned Launch Cable

A special fiber optic patch cable that offsets the coupling (launch) of laser light from the center of a fiber optic cable. This avoids the phenomenon of differential mode delay, which can occur when laser light sources are coupled to multimode fiber optic cables.

CRC

Cyclic Redundancy Check. An error checking technique used to ensure the accuracy of transmitted data. The frame fields other than the preamble are used in the process of mathematically computing a checksum, which is placed in the Frame Check Sequence (FCS) field of the frame as the frame is transmitted. The receiving station uses the same process to compute a checksum and compares this checksum to the contents of the received frame FCS field. Identical checksums indicate that the frame fields were received correctly.

Crossover Cable

A twisted-pair patch cable wired in such a way as to route the transmit signals from one piece of equipment to the receive signals of another piece of equipment, and vice versa.

Crosstalk

The unwanted transfer of a signal from one circuit to another. In twisted-pair cables, the unwanted transfer of signals from transmitting wires to other wires in the cable plant. The maximum level of crosstalk is measured at the end nearest the transmitter, leading to the term Near End Crosstalk, or NEXT.

CSMA/CD

Carrier Sense Multiple Access/Collision Detect. The formal name for the medium access control (MAC) protocol used in Ethernet. The MAC protocol is described in detail in Chapter 3, *The Media Access Control Protocol.*

D Connector

A family of connectors, including the 25-pin RS232 connector, the 15-pin AUI connector, and the 9-pin connector. The outline of the connector seen end-on is roughly that of the letter "D."

Data Link Layer

Layer 2 of the OSI reference model. This layer takes data from the network layer and passes it on to the physical layer. The data link layer is responsible for transmitting and receiving Ethernet frames, 48-bit addressing, etc. It includes both the media access control (MAC) protocol and logical link control (LLC) layers.

DCE

Data Communications Equipment. Any equipment that connects to Data Terminal Equipment (DTE) to allow data transmissions between DTEs.

DIW

Direct Inside Wire. Twisted-pair wire used inside a building, which usually contains four-pairs of wires within the cable.

Drop Cable

The connection (drop) between a network device and an outlet. In the original Ethernet system the transceiver cable was sometimes called a drop cable. In twisted-pair Ethernet systems the patch cable may also be called a drop cable.

DTE

Data Terminal Equipment. Any piece of equipment at which a communications path begins or ends. The data station (computer) serving as the data source, destination, or both, for the purpose of sending or receiving data on a network.

Encoding

A means of combining clock and data information into a self-synchronizing stream of signals.

Error Detection

A method that detects errors in received data by examining cyclic redundancy checks (CRC) or using other techniques.

Ethernet

A popular local area networking (LAN) technology first standardized by DEC, Intel, and Xerox (or DIX) and subsequently standardized by the IEEE.

Fast Ethernet

A version of Ethernet that operates at 100 Mbps.

Fast Link Pulse

A link pulse that encodes information used in the Auto-Negotiation protocol. Fast link pulses consist of bursts of the normal link pulses used in 10BASE-T.

FDDI

Fiber Distributed Data Interface. An ANSI standard (ANSI X3T12) for a 100 Mbps token passing network (Token Ring) based on fiber-optic and twisted-pair cable.

Fiber Optic Cable

A cable with a glass or plastic filament which transmits digital signals in the form of light pulses.

Filter Rate

The maximum number of frames that a switching hub can continuously receive, inspect, and make a forwarding decision on.

Flow Control

The process of controlling data transmission at the sender to avoid overfilling buffers and loss of data at the receiver.

FOIRL

Fiber Optic Inter-Repeater Link. An early version of fiber optic link segment defined in the IEEE 802.3c standard.

Forwarding

The process of moving frames from one port to another in a switching hub.

Forwarding Rate

The maximum number of frames that can be forwarded by a switching hub, assuming no congestion on the network to which the output port is connected.

Frame

The fundamental unit of transmission at the data link layer of LAN operation.

Full-Duplex Media

A signal transmission path that can support simultaneous data transmission and reception.

Full-Duplex Mode

A communications method that allows a device to simultaneously send and receive data.

Gigabit Ethernet

A version of Ethernet that operates at 1 billion (1,000,000,000) bits per second.

GMII

Gigabit Medium Independent Interface. Unlike the AUI or MII, the GMII is not a physical interface. Instead, the GMII is a logical interface used in the standard to define the set of signals that flow between Gigabit Ethernet transceiver chips and controller chips inside Gigabit Ethernet ports.

Half-Duplex Mode

A communications method in which a device may either send or receive data at a given moment, but not both.

Heartbeat

See *SQE Test*.

Hub

A device at the center of a star topology network. A hub device may be a repeater, bridge, switch, router, or any combination of these.

IEEE

Institute for Electronics and Electrical Engineers. A professional organization and standards body. IEEE Project 802 is the group within the IEEE that is responsible for LAN technology standards.

IETF

Internet Engineering Task Force. The technical group that sets standards for the community of people using TCP/IP network protocols.

Impedance

A measure of opposition to the flow of a current at a particular frequency, measured in ohms.

Interframe Gap

An idle time between frames, also called the *interpacket gap.*

Internet

The Internet is the worldwide collection of networks based on the use of TCP/IP network protocols.

Intranet

An intranet is a collection of networks supporting a single site or corporate entity, and linked at the network layer of operation, using routers.

Jabber

The act of continuously sending data. A jabbering station is one whose circuitry or logic has failed, and which has locked up a network channel with its incessant transmissions.

Jabber Latch

A protective circuit in Ethernet transceivers or repeater hubs that interrupts an overlong transmission.

Jitter

Also called *phase jitter,* timing distortion, or inter-symbol interference. The slight movement of a transmission signal in time or phase that can introduce errors and loss of synchronization. The amount of jitter will increase with longer cables, cables with higher attenuation, and signals at higher data rates.

Late Collision

A failure of the network in which the collision indication arrives too late in the frame transmission to be automatically dealt with by the medium access control (MAC) protocol. The frame being transmitted will be dropped, requiring that the application detect and retransmit the lost frame, which may result in greatly reduced throughput. Late collisions may be caused by a mismatch in duplex settings at each end of a link. Another cause is excessive levels of signal crosstalk in a twisted-pair cabling system.

Link Integrity Test

On link segments, the link integrity test checks for the presence of link test pulses or link signaling activity. This test verifies that the link is connected correctly and that signals are being received correctly.

Link Layer

> See *Data Link Layer.*

Link Light

> An optional status light on a transceiver or interface card that indicates the status of the link integrity test. If this light is lit on both ends of the link, it indicates that the link is passing the link integrity test.

Link Pulse

> A test pulse sent between transceivers on a 10BASE-T link segment during periods of no traffic, to test the signal integrity of the link.

Link Segment

> Defined in the IEEE 802.3 specifications as a point-to-point segment that connects two—and only two—devices.

LLC

> Logical Link Control. A standardized protocol and service interface provided at the data link layer and independent of any specific LAN technology. Specified in the IEEE 802.2 standard.

Mbaud

> 1 million baud. See *Baud.*

MAC

> Medium Access Control. A protocol defining a set of mechanisms, operating at the data link layer of a local area network. The MAC protocol is used to manage access to the communication channel.

MAC Address

> The 48-bit address used in Ethernet to identify a station interface.

Manchester Encoding Scheme

> Signal encoding method used in all 10 Mbps Ethernet media systems, including 10BASE2, 10BASE5, 10BASE-F and 10BASE-T. Each bit of information is converted into a "bit symbol" which is divided into two halves. During the first half the signal being sent is the complement of the data bit being encoded. During the second half the signal is identical to the data symbol. This provides a signal transition in each bit symbol sent, which is used as a clock signal for synchronization by the receiving device.

MAU

> Medium Attachment Unit. The IEEE 802.3 name for the device called a transceiver in the original DIX Ethernet standard. The MAU provides the physical and electrical interface between an Ethernet device and the media system to which it is connected.

MDI

> Medium Dependent Interface. The name for the connector used to make a physical and electrical connection between a transceiver and a media segment. The 8-pin RJ-45–style connector is the MDI for the 10BASE-T, 100BASE-TX, 100BASE-T4 and 1000BASE-T media systems.

MDI-X

> An MDI port on a hub that has an internal crossover signal. This means that a "straight-through" patch cable can be used to connect a station to this port, since the signal crossover is performed inside the port.

MIB

> Management Information Base. A list of manageable objects (counters, etc.) for a given device; used by management applications.

MIC

> Media Interface Connector. Specified for use in the FDDI LAN system to make a connection to a pair of fiber optic cables. May also be used in the 100BASE-FX media system; however, the duplex SC connector is listed in the specifications as the preferred connector for 100BASE-FX.

MII

> Medium Independent Interface. Similar to the AUI, but designed to support both 10 and 100 Mbps, an MII provides a 40-pin connection to outboard transceivers (also called PHY devices). Used to attach 802.3 interfaces (MACs) to a variety of physical media systems.

Mixing Segment

> Defined in the IEEE 802.3 specifications as a segment that may have more than two MDI connections. Coaxial Ethernet segments are mixing segments.

Multicast Address

> A multicast address allows a single Ethernet frame to be received by a group of stations. If the first bit of the destination address transmitted on the Ethernet channel is a one (1), then the address is a multicast address.

N Connector

> A coaxial cable connector used for 10BASE5 thick coax segments. The connector is named after its developer, Paul Neill.

Network Layer

> Layer 3 of the OSI reference model. The layer at which routing based on high-level network protocols occurs.

NIC

> Network Interface Card. Also called an adapter or interface card. The set of electronics that provides a connection between a computer and a LAN.

Octet

Eight bits (also called a byte).

OSI

Open Systems Interconnection. A 7-layer reference model for networks, developed by the International Organization for Standardization (ISO). The OSI reference model is a formal method for describing the interlocking sets of networking hardware and software used to deliver network services.

OUI

Organizationally Unique Identifier. A 24-bit value assigned to an organization by the IEEE. Ethernet vendors use the 24-bit OUI they receive from the IEEE in the process of creating unique 48-bit Ethernet addresses. Each Ethernet device a vendor builds is provided with a unique 48-bit address, whose first 24 bits are composed of the vendor's OUI.

Packet

A unit of data exchanged at the network layer.

PAM5x5

Signal encoding scheme used in the 100BASE-T2 media system.

Patch Cable

A twisted-pair or fiber optic jumper cable used to make a connection between a network interface on a station or network port on a hub and a media segment, or to directly connect stations and hub ports together.

Phantom Collision

A false collision detect signal. In twisted-pair Ethernet systems, a phantom collision can be caused by excessive signal crosstalk. Collisions are detected on twisted-pair segments by the simultaneous presence of signal on the transmit and receive signal pairs. Excessive signal crosstalk on a twisted-pair segment can cause signals to simultaneously appear to the transmit and receive signal pairs, which triggers a false, or phantom, collision indication to the transmitting interface.

PHY

Physical Layer Device. The name used for a transceiver in the Fast Ethernet and Gigabit Ethernet systems.

Receive Collision

A collision detected on a coaxial media segment by a device that isn't actively transmitting data. Since a collision on coaxial cables is sensed by monitoring the average voltage on the cable, a device that is not actively transmitting can still detect a collision. When a receive collision is detected by an Ethernet repeater hub, it will transmit a collision enforcement jam signal on all other ports.

Phase Jitter

> See *Jitter.*

Physical Address

> The 48-bit MAC address assigned to a station interface, identifying that station on the network.

Physical Layer

> The first layer in the OSI seven layer reference model. This layer is responsible for physical signaling, including the connectors, timing, voltages, and related issues.

Plenum Cable

> A cable that is rated as having adequate fire resistance and satisfactorily low smoke-producing characteristics for use in plenums (air handling spaces). Air handling spaces are often located below machine room floors, or above suspended ceilings.

Point-to-Point Topology

> A network system composed of point-to-point links. Each point-to-point link connects two and only two devices, one at each end.

Port

> A connection point for a cable. Repeater hubs and switching hubs typically provide multiple ports for connecting Ethernet devices.

Promiscuous Mode

> A mode of operation where a device configures its network interface to receive every frame on the LAN, regardless of its destination address.

Propagation Delay

> The signal transit time through a cable, network segment, or device.

Protocol

> A set of agreed-upon rules and message formats for exchanging information among devices on a network.

Repeater

> A physical layer device used to interconnect LAN segments based on the same LAN technology and using the same data rate. An Ethernet repeater can only link Ethernet segments that are all operating in half-duplex mode and at the same speed.

RJ

> Registered Jack. A term from the telephone industry, used for jacks (connectors) registered for use with particular types of telephone services.

RJ-45

An 8-pin modular connector used on twisted-pair links. Officially, an RJ-45 connector is a telephone connector designed for voice-grade circuits. RJ-45–style connectors with improved signal handling characteristics are called 8-pin connectors in the standards documents, but most people continue to use the RJ-45 name for all 8-pin connectors.

Router

A device or process based on Layer 3 network protocols used to interconnect networks at the network layer.

SC

The initials stand for "subscriber connector." This is a type of fiber optic connector used in 100BASE-FX and 1000BASE-LX/SX fiber optic media systems. The connector is designed to be pushed into place, automatically seating itself.

Segment

An Ethernet media segment may be made up of one or more cable sections joined together to produce a continuous cable for carrying Ethernet signals.

Signal Crossover

On a twisted-pair or fiber optic link segment, the transmit signals at one end of the segment must be connected to the receiver at the other end of the segment, and vice versa.

Silver Satin

The name for the silver-gray voice-grade patch cable used to connect a telephone to a wall jack. Typical silver satin patch cables do not have twisted pair wires, which makes them unsuitable for use in an Ethernet system. The lack of twisted pairs will result in high levels of crosstalk, which can lead to slow performance on a 10BASE-T link, and complete link failures on faster links.

Slot Time

A unit of time used in the medium access control (MAC) protocol for Ethernets.

SNMP

Simple Network Management Protocol. A protocol specified by the Internet Engineering Task Force (IETF) for exchanging network management information between network devices and network management stations.

SQE

Signal Quality Error. This signal indicates the detection of a collision on the medium by the transceiver. The original DIX Ethernet standard referred to this signal as Collision Presence, however, the name was changed to SQE in the IEEE 802.3 specifications.

SQE Test

This signal tests the SQE detection and signaling circuits. The original DIX Ethernet standard referred to this signal as Collision Presence Test, also known as "heartbeat." The name was changed to SQE Test in the IEEE 802.3 specifications.

ST

Developed by AT&T, the name stands for "straight tip." This is a type of fiber optic connector used in 10BASE-FL and FOIRL links. The male end of this connector has an inner sleeve with a slot cut into it, and an outer ring with a bayonet latch. The inner sleeve is aligned with a mating key in the socket, and the outer ring is turned to complete the bayonet latch.

Star Topology

A network topology in which each node on the network is connected directly to a central hub.

Switching Hub

A switching hub is another name for a bridge, which is a device that interconnects network segments at the data link layer of network operations. Switching hubs are typically located in the center of a star topology, and provide multiple ports for connections to network nodes.

Tap

A tap is a method of connecting a transceiver to a thick coaxial cable by drilling a hole in the cable and installing a transceiver tap connection.

Telco Connector

See *50-pin Connector.*

Throughput

The rate at which usable data can be sent over the channel. While an Ethernet channel may operate at 10 Mbps, the throughput in terms of usable data will be less due to the number of bits required for framing and other channel overhead.

TIA/EIA

The Telecommunications Industry Association/Electronics Industry Association (TIA/EIA) is an organization that specifies commercial building telecommunications cable standards, including the cable category specifications.

Topology

The physical or logical layout of a network.

Station

A unique, addressable device on a network.

Terminator

A resistor used at the end of metallic baseband LAN cables to minimize reflections.

Transceiver

A combination of the words *trans*mitter and re*ceiver*. A transceiver is the set of electronics that sends and receives signals on an Ethernet media system. Transceivers may be small outboard devices, or may be built into an Ethernet port.

Transceiver Cable

See *AUI Cable*.

Twisted-Pair Cable

A multiple-conductor cable whose component wires are paired together, twisted, and enclosed in a single jacket. A typical Category 5 twisted-pair segment is composed of a cable with four twisted pairs contained in a single jacket. Each pair consists of two insulated copper wires that are twisted together.

USOC

Universal Service Order Code (pronounced "U-Sock"). An old Bell System term used to identify a particular service or device offered under tariff. Often used to refer to an old cable color code scheme that was current when USOC codes were in use.

Voice-Grade

A term for twisted-pair cable used in telephone systems to carry voice signals.

VLAN

Virtual LAN. A method in which a port or set of ports in a switching hub are grouped together and function as a single "virtual" network. All ports within a given VLAN are members of the same broadcast domain.

Wiring Closet

Also called a telecommunications closet. A room that contains one or more wire distribution racks and panels used to connect various cables together (via patch cables) to form physical networks.

Index

About the Author

Charles E. Spurgeon is the senior network architect at the University of Texas at Austin, overseeing a network that supports more than 30,000 computers. He has worked on large campus networks for 20 years, beginning in 1979 when he used to "test" network equipment by using it to read the *Science Fiction Lover's Digest* over the ARPANET. In the 1980s he helped develop the Stanford University network, which included building a number of prototype Cisco Systems routers and linking them together with Xerox PARC's experimental Ethernet running at 3 Mbps. In 1994, he created what is widely acknowledged as the most comprehensive and popular Ethernet site.

Charles, who attended Wesleyan University, lives in Austin, Texas, with his wife, Joann Zimmerman, and their cat, Sophie. In his spare time he reads seafaring novels, science fiction, mysteries, and anything else he can find on the shelves of their 4,000 volume home library. This is his third book on Ethernet.

Colophon

Our look is the result of reader comments, our own experimentation, and feedback from distribution channels. Distinctive covers complement our distinctive approach to technical topics, breathing personality and life into potentially dry subjects.

The animal on the cover of *Ethernet: The Definitive Guide* is an octopus. The octopus is a member of the class *Cephalopoda*, which also includes squid, cuttlefish, and nautili. However, unlike other cephalopods, the octopus's shell is entirely absent. Species of octopus vary in size from under an inch (the Californian *Octopus micropyrsus*) to thirty feet in length (the North Pacific *Octopus dofleini*). Like their squid cousins, the octopus can release a noxious ink when disturbed. Octopi vary in color from pinkish to brown, but are able to change their pigment when threatened using special pigment cells called chromatophores.

Octopi catch their prey—primarily crabs, lobsters, and other smaller sea creatures—with their suckered tentacles. Many species are aided by a poison these sucker cups secrete; one Australian species' venom is so potent that it can be deadly to humans.

Octopi are considered to be the most intelligent invertebrate species. They have both short- and long-term memory, and have shown trial-and-error learning skills, retaining the problem-solving gained through experience. Their sucker cups are very sensitive; a sightless octopus can differentiate between various shapes and sizes of objects as well as a sighted one.

David Futato was the production editor and copyeditor for *Ethernet: The Definitive Guide*. Melanie Wang provided quality control; Anna Snow aided with production. Ellen Troutman-Zaig wrote the index.

Hanna Dyer designed the cover of this book, based on a series design by Edie Freedman. The cover image is a 19th-century engraving from the Dover Pictorial Archive. Kathleen Wilson produced the cover layout with QuarkXPress 3.32 using Adobe's ITC Garamond font.

Alicia Cech designed the interior layout based on a series design by Nancy Priest. Mike Sierra implemented the design in FrameMaker 5.5.6. The text and heading fonts are ITC Garamond Light and Garamond Book. The illustrations that appear in the book were produced by Robert Romano and Rhon Porter using Macromedia FreeHand 8 and Adobe Photoshop 5. This colophon was written by David Futato.

Whenever possible, our books use RepKover™, a durable and flexible lay-flat binding. If the page count exceeds RepKover's limit, perfect binding is used.